Effective Budgeting
in
Continuing Education

*A Comprehensive Guide
to Improving Program Planning
and Organizational Performance*

Gary W. Matkin

Effective Budgeting
in
Continuing Education

Jossey-Bass Publishers

San Francisco • London • 1985

EFFECTIVE BUDGETING IN CONTINUING EDUCATION
*A Comprehensive Guide to Improving Program Planning
and Organizational Effectiveness*
by Gary W. Matkin

Copyright © 1985 by: Jossey-Bass Inc., Publishers
433 California Street
San Francisco, California 94104

&

Jossey-Bass Limited
28 Banner Street
London EC1Y 8QE

Library of Congress Cataloging-in-Publication Data

Matkin, Gary W. (date)
  Effective budgeting in continuing education.

  (The Jossey-Bass higher education series)
  Includes index.
  1. Continuing education—United States—Finance.
2. Continuing education—United States—Curricula.
3. Program budgeting—United States. I. Title.
II. Series.
LC5251.M35   1985   374'.973   85-45064
ISBN 0-87589-667-7 (alk. paper)

Manufactured in the United States of America

The paper in this book meets the guidelines for
permanence and durability of the Committee on
Production Guidelines for Book Longevity of the
Council on Library Resources.

JACKET DESIGN BY WILLI BAUM

FIRST EDITION

Code 8540

The Jossey-Bass
Higher Education Series

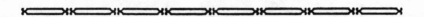

Consulting Editor
Adult and Continuing Education

Alan B. Knox
University of Wisconsin at Madison

To Milton Stern, to whom I owe this career

Preface

     Continuing education programs have been a part of our colleges, universities, public school systems, and many of our religious institutions for a long time. But with increasing frequency, community organizations and social service agencies—including museums, hospitals, professional and trade societies, and cultural, social, and alumni associations—are offering continuing education courses as well. These courses may directly serve the mission of the organization: A hospital may present a course on how to avoid or manage the stress of facing a major operation, or a museum may present a lecture series based on an exhibit. But courses may also be presented for purposes tangential to the central purpose of the organization, serving primarily to attract new members or potential donors or to gain more public exposure for the organization.

     Typically, continuing education practitioners come from fields related to the missions of the organizations they serve. As professionals, they are responsible and accountable for what they do, and no matter what their working environment, financial accountability is a measure of their professionalism. The recent growth in continuing education activity, however, has placed these men and women in positions of increasing responsibility for managing and administering educational programs—areas in which they often lack formal training. *Effective Budgeting in Continuing Education* bridges this gap. It addresses the encompassing subjects of budgeting for and financial control of continuing education courses and organizations. It is designed to be used by professionals who are involved in planning and presenting continuing education programs and to assist them in evaluating and controlling program quality as well as costs. Indeed, one of the main tenets of this book is the idea that budgeting is frequently the catalyst for program planning, and that the time when the budget is addressed is frequently also the time when central programmatic questions are uncovered and faced.

Effective Budgeting in Continuing Education is designed to be used as a reference manual as well as a comprehensive text on budgeting for continuing education (CE). It can help solve the day-to-day problems of management and control as well as provide the theoretical background on which an understanding of budgeting and control systems and procedures can be based. Although the examples presented here are taken from the large, centralized, self-supporting, university extension organization from which I draw most of my experience, they deal with details present in all CE enterprises and illustrate universals helpful in many settings. Readers will constantly be challenged to adapt the general principles outlined here to fit the organizational frameworks and specific situations they face. Whatever readers' working environments, the guidelines presented here—and the examples used to illustrate them—will help CE professionals do their jobs more effectively.

Among those who can benefit from *Effective Budgeting in Continuing Education* are programmers, who plan and organize individual programs of instruction; deans and directors, who are responsible for administering programs of continuing education; and business and financial officers of organizations involved in continuing education, whether affiliated with a university or not. This book may also prove useful to those individuals to whom the dean or director reports and to business, financial, and budget officers of the larger institutions of which the continuing education organization is a part. This category might also include board members of organizations that offer continuing education programs. Finally, this book might serve the ever-growing number of students seeking professional training in adult and continuing education practice.

Overview of the Contents

The Introduction is designed to provide an overview of budgeting and the budgetary process and covers some preliminary background and theory. Topics covered include the purposes of budgeting, the various theories of budgeting, different types of budgets, and the political and behavioral implications of budgets. The Introduction then places budgeting within the context of continuing education and notes problems common to most continuing education organizations.

Part One concerns programming and is tailored for readers who bear the responsibility for planning and organizing individual educational courses. (The *course* is the starting point of the budget process.) The chapters in Part One are designed to give programmers an understanding of the economics of the course and a theoretical model for making relevant decisions about a given course, for taking account of nonquantifiable factors such as risk and nonfinancial rewards, and for judging the financial success of a course. Chapter One defines some commonly used cost accounting terms and discusses the behavior and nature of course costs. Chapter Two presents the decision/process model for course financial planning and development, a model that includes the dynamic aspects of the job of a programmer and that recognizes the fluid and ever-changing environment that makes programming both difficult and interesting. Chapter Three applies the decision/process model to some common problems faced by programmers in developing courses: determining appropriate course fees, deciding on the level and nature of promotion expenditures, and negotiating with instructors over their compensation. It also discusses overhead costs and how their allocation may influence course development decisions. Finally, Chapter Three provides a framework that can help programmers develop an overall program strategy designed to balance rewards and risks. Part One should also be useful to deans and directors because it presents the basis on which budgeting for the larger organization depends.

Part Two is intended for deans and directors who are responsible for structuring and administering the budgeting and control systems for the continuing education organization as a whole. For programmers who are interested in understanding some of the broader aspects of their jobs and the problems faced by their directors, Part Two will provide a useful overview. Together, Parts One and Two present a vocabulary and lay the theoretical groundwork that can lead to more effective communication between programmers and their directors and can promote a more efficient operation. Chapter Four first discusses some preliminary considerations and presents the criteria for establishing an effective budgeting system within an organization. Chapter Five outlines the steps of the budget process. Using a fully developed example, this chapter presents some useful budget worksheets and computational techniques designed to produce an effective, meaningful, and comprehensive organizational budget. Chapter Six discusses some of the behavioral aspects that directors are likely to encounter in the budget process, both on the part of their subordinates and of their superiors, and offers strategies for coping with them. Chapter Seven describes the feedback and control process without which a budget system cannot work, presenting, again, a number of worksheets and reporting formats that can be useful in this process.

Part Three takes up some special problems of budgeting in continuing education. Building on material discussed earlier, Chapter Eight addresses the problems of evaluating the cost-effectiveness of promotion expenditures. Methods of allocating indirect costs and the importance of such allocations are covered in Chapter Nine. Cash and capital budgeting and the special considerations involved in dealing with inventories, independent-study programs, and publications are the topics of Chapter Ten. Chapter Eleven addresses an issue of considerable interest and importance to continuing education administrators today—the use of computers, particularly microcomputers, in budgeting and financial control and reporting. Throughout this book, reference is made to the use of computers; many of the schedules were actually produced using commercially available software and microcomputers. Several exhibits are comprehensive listings of, and can be directly translated into, data base attributes and field titles. Along with the heightened interest in computers has come a lot of misinformation and bad advice. "Quick fixes" in the form of prepackaged programs are now quite common, but, as always, the buyer, particularly the unknowledgeable buyer, had better beware. Chapter Eleven sorts through the issues involved in using computers for budgeting and control and sets forth criteria for judging the value and usefulness of computerized budgeting systems. It also provides a starting point for developing or changing a computer system.

To facilitate the use of *Effective Budgeting in Continuing Education* as a reference manual, the main headings are included in the contents. Because each term is defined only where it first appears in the text, an extensive glossary of terms is also provided. Thus, the reader who skims through the text and runs into an unfamiliar term will find the glossary helpful. Readers who are relatively unknowledgeable about management and financial matters may want to read the glossary before they begin reading the text. For readers with specific problems they wish to solve, the comprehensive index can provide quick direction to helpful sections in the text.

Assumptions About My Readers and the Institutions They Serve

My conceptions of who will read this book and how it will help them have significantly influenced both the structure and tone of this work. Because many of the professional educators who are confronted with the problems this book addresses are unfamiliar with management and financial control, some of the discussions in this book will cover territory that is new to these readers. For the book to be helpful, readers need to learn and understand the basic principles of budgeting and financial control. To help readers grasp this information, this book provides carefully detailed examples designed to illustrate complex practices and concepts clearly. Thorough study of these examples will provide readers with solid grounding in fundamentals.

The CE organization is typically part of a larger organization and is accountable to it. Being a part of a larger whole presents some special budgeting problems that I will explore in detail. For example, continuing education is often looked upon as a by-product of the mission of the parent institution. The implications of this view are significant for CE budgeting and make it an important part of the formal relationship and communication between the CE organization and the parent.

In a recent survey of directors of a wide sample of diverse organizations that offer CE programs, Anderson and Kasl (1982) found widespread ignorance about the basic financial situation of CE organizations and, in numerous cases, expressions of desire to obscure the true costs of continuing education.* Perpetuating obscurity may sometimes be politically expedient, but the budgetary process tends to clarify financial issues and may point to management decisions uncongenial to continuing educators. A book on budgeting cannot second guess all the political issues that might arise, however; it must be based on the principle that the sun should shine on every corner of the organization with equal brilliance.

Although the principles presented here are applicable to a CE organization of only one or two people presenting only a few courses (especially Part One), this book assumes an organizational setting that is large enough that problems of control and communication exist. Some of the formal and procedural forms presented in this book would be superfluous in a small, closely knit organization where everyone communicated freely and where goals were shared. Formal budgeting devices provide a means of communicating and organizing information, but when these tasks can be accomplished in other ways, budgeting may not be so important.

Effective Budgeting in Continuing Education does address some of the special problems faced by organizations that enjoy subsidies from a parent institution, the government, or other funding sources. Budgeting for a "fixed resource" organization

---

*R. E. Anderson and E. S. Kasl, *The Costs and Financing of Adult Education*, Lexington, Mass.: Lexington Books, 1982.

differs from budgeting for a "variable resource" (or self-supporting) organization, but the problems both types face are more similar than might appear at first glance.

Throughout this book I emphasize the entrepreneurial or market-oriented approach to financial control. We all seek to discover cost-efficient ways of producing desired results. In self-supporting organizations, this means that the positive difference between income and expense is maximized. In subsidized organizations, cost-efficiency is more difficult to measure; intended outcomes have to be compared to resources used. Although an explicit entrepreneurial orientation may be out of place in some institutional settings, it is hard to argue against efficiency.

Continuing educators are a practical lot, quick to adopt useful tools and quick to see through irrelevant and pompously academic guides to practice. The need to understand budgeting and to gain competence in financial management presents a challenge to many CE professionals whose educational backgrounds and work experience often leave them unprepared for the fiscal responsibility they must shoulder. The value of this book will be its usefulness in the day-to-day working lives of its readers; its purpose is to help them do their jobs more effectively.

Acknowledgments

This project could never have been completed without the help and advice of a number of people. My colleagues at the University Extension, the University of California, Berkeley, were a constant source of information and support, particularly Vivian Sutcher, assistant dean, who reviewed most of the material contained in the manuscript, providing much substantive and constructive criticism from the point of view of both programmers and departmental administration. I also relied on the advice of Don McDaniel, assistant dean; Olga Knight, director of the Extension Media Center; Mary Beth Almeda, director of Independent Study; and Rohit Patel, curriculum adviser and consultant on computers.

Helping to provide different organizational perspectives and also significant substantive criticism were a number of outside reviewers. John Buskey, associate dean of continuing studies at the

University of Nebraska-Lincoln, was particularly helpful, and I much appreciated his comments and encouragement. He was joined by Philip D. Harris, college program administrator, conferences and workshops, Brigham Young University; B. Gordon Mueller, dean of Metropolitan College, University of New Orleans; and Robert Simerly, director of conferences and institutes at the University of Illinois, Champaign-Urbana, and four other reviewers provided by Wadsworth Publishing Company who remain unknown to me. These continuing educators, in the tradition of collegiality of our profession, devoted their time and skill to reading and shaping my manuscript. I also want to acknowledge the skill of my copyeditor, Lisa Yount, who was so instrumental in tightening and providing clarity of expression to the text. If this book fulfills its intention of providing guidelines applicable to a wide variety of organizational settings, it is much to the credit of these reviewers. I would also like to thank several colleagues who helped prepare the manuscript and exhibits: Dana Daubert, Carmen Edstrom, and Stacey Kita.

Finally, and most important of all, I want to express my deepest gratitude to Milton Stern, dean of the University Extension at the University of California, Berkeley, who not only edited and reviewed the entire manuscript, providing the seasoning of many years of experience as well as a high degree of editorial skill, but also really launched me into this project and then provided me with unfailing support and encouragement over many months of preparation. My gratitude to Dean Stern extends beyond the help he gave me on this book. It was he who started me in continuing education and who, largely through his vision and personality, has kept me interested and excited in my work.

Berkeley, California   Gary W. Matkin
September 1985

Contents

Contents

Figures

The Author

Gary W. Matkin is director of administrative services for the University Extension, the University of California, Berkeley. Before assuming this position in 1978, he served as the business and budget officer for the University Extension for five years. He is a Certified Public Accountant (California) and has an M.B.A. (1970) from the University of California, Berkeley, and a B.S. (1966) from the University of San Francisco in accounting. He is completing the requirements for a Ph.D. in higher education administration at the University of California, Berkeley. Matkin has taught financial and managerial accounting at California State University, Hayward, and at the University Extension, Berkeley. He has written a number of articles and presented several papers on the financial aspects of continuing education and on research methods in adult education. Matkin has been a member of the American Institute of Certified Public Accountants since 1970 and of the National University Continuing Education Association since 1973.

Effective Budgeting
in
Continuing Education

A Comprehensive Guide
to Improving Program Planning
and Organizational Performance

Introduction:
How Budgets Work
in Continuing Education

The Importance of Budgets to the CE Professional

Budgets have been important in continuing education for a long time. Most continuing educational professionals are subject to some form of budgeting and budget restrictions. Almost every organization requires some form of accountability from its members, and the budget usually is part of that accountability. Recently, some events and trends have compelled continuing educators to use budgets even more extensively and to learn more about the budget process and the theories behind budgeting and financial control, if only to defend themselves. Some examples follow.

In California, community colleges have experienced a sharp reduction in funding, which has required them to raise "adult education" fees and to reduce staff and the number of course offerings. This funding reduction was the result of the Proposition 13 taxpayer revolt, a revolution felt in several other states with similar consequences.

A small college extension unit that had depended for more than half its income on its English as a Second Language program suddenly found that most of its students could not pay their tuition.

They were Iranian and, because of political events in Iran, could not obtain funds from their home country.

Because of mandated payroll increases and the failure of several large programs, a major self-supporting university extension operation found itself with a large operating deficit.

Facing a reduction in funding for its administrative support services, a state university began charging its self-supporting continuing education operation for accounting and other services.

Scrambling for funds to keep the operation together, the director of a community service educational program obtained donations from two private benefactors and combined them with a small, short-term grant from the state and an emergency additional allocation from the United Way Campaign. With this montage of funding, the organization continued to operate for the next six months while the director searched for a more stable funding source.

When the new dean of extension for a major university arrived, he asked to see the budget for the operation. He was given a stack of computer printouts. Three months later he still did not have any idea how much his total budget amounted to.

The increased importance of budgeting in continuing education can be categorized under several headings.

Accountability. The sharp decrease in funding for higher education has trickled down to the CE organization. Self-supporting units have been charged for services that were free to them before, and subsidized units have had their budgets cut. In this atmosphere, every financial aspect of the organization's operation comes under inspection, and the need for accurate financial information rapidly expands. Budgets become mechanisms more for control than for planning. The decline in the economy and sharply rising inflation rates in the late 1970s and early 1980s also had an effect. Units that did not watch their expenses carefully and monitor the effect of the changing economy on their student markets could find themselves in financial difficulty with startling suddenness. Realistic budget standards and effective monitoring systems became indispensable to CE management.

Other trends have also led to increased accountability. At the same time that continuing education is assuming more importance within parent institutions, CE units are coming under closer inspection by those managing the parent. Some CE organizations had previously enjoyed a form of benign neglect, but they are now too important to be ignored.

Montage Funding. Another trend contributing to an increased need for accountability is the increase in what might be called montage or multiple source funding. Few organizations today can safely rely on a single funding source. Like the community education service in our example, most organizations are funded from a number of sources, and the average number of sources is tending to increase. This usually means that parts of the budget must be kept in separate "pots" and accounted for separately so that the money dedicated to one of the organization's purposes will not be spent on another. Under these arrangements a single employee may work on projects funded from three or more sources and be required to report the number of working hours spent on each project. Montage funding also means that the whole gets harder and harder to see as the parts become more and more independent; this explains the extension dean's inability to add up his budget in the example. Budgetary techniques are necessary to keep track of the individual parts of the funding and maintain the integrity of the overall operation at the same time.

Self-Support from Tuition and Fees. As subsidies are reduced and parent institutions are placed under greater financial strain, there is a natural tendency to make the "user" pay for a greater proportion of the cost of operations. In continuing education, this means that students are asked to pay higher and higher fees to cover a larger and larger proportion of the total continuing education budget. In subsidized organizations, this can be viewed as a movement toward self-support, whereas self-supporting parent institution requirements for greater financial returns from the CE organization can be viewed as a movement toward the for-profit model of business enterprise. This movement has significant budgetary implications, as we will see later. Self-support budgeting is different from traditional institutional budgeting. Self-supporting CE units often operate more independently than subsidized units, both financially and programmatically. Funding from tuition and fees is usually "unrestricted," that is, it can be used for any purpose designated by the parent institution. The most natural use of such funding is to fund the costs of operating the CE organization. As student fee income increases as a proportion of the CE budget, the CE organization operates under fewer restrictions. This trend tends to counter the impact of montage funding.

However, the movement toward self-support by no means decreases the need for budgeting and accountability. Rather, it shifts the emphasis in budgeting from *allocation of resources* to *income generation*. In subsidized operations, control is focused on the expense budget, with preset limits on spending. Although expense control is important in self-supporting units also, the greatest attention is paid to where the money to pay expenses will come from. This usually means that the organization must become more *market oriented* and that budgets must be structured in a way that links the production of income with the costs of producing that income. This can have salutary effects, but it also often means that deserving, even the most deserving, constituencies can no longer be served. It tends to produce an unfortunate elitism in continuing education, a field that had its roots in serving the disadvantaged. However, a properly flexible budgeting system can accommodate all forms of financing.

Organization Segmentation. All these trends require that CE organizations be meaningfully divided so that financial results for each part of the organization can be measured and monitored. Increased accountability requires that the weak and the strong parts of the organization be identified. Montage funding usually carries with it a legal requirement that the individual "pots" be kept separate for accounting purposes. The market orientation of self-support requires that the organization be segmented to reflect the markets it serves so that it can more easily detect and react to changed market conditions. Segmentation forms the basis of the responsibility structure of an organization, which we will examine in detail in Chapter Four.

These factors, and many more, require that today's continuing education professional become ever more sophisticated in knowledge of the financing of continuing education and the financial aspects of presenting courses. Budgets are unavoidable tools of financial management, and a complete understanding of the theory and practice of budgeting must be a part of every CE professional's own education.

Definition and Purposes of Budgets

Budgeting is a process of planning the future operations of an organization and systematically comparing those plans with actual results. A budget is a written expression of the organization plan, expressed in dollar terms, and is used to communicate the plan to those responsible for carrying it out. It also becomes the standard against which the performance of the organization and its parts will be judged.

The notion that budgeting is a *process* and that the budget document is only one product of that process will be repeated often in this book. No one step of the process can be isolated from any other part, and the process is continuous. Once the written document is produced, it "lives" for the whole budget period, guiding and controlling actions and being compared with actual results. After this "feedback" comparison, it serves as a basis for the formation of the budget for the following period, when the cycle starts again.

Budgets and Responsibility. Properly used, budgeting is part of what is called the *responsibility structure* of an organization. When an organization reaches a certain size and complexity of operation, the responsibility for carrying out objectives must be assigned or delegated to individuals or groups of individuals within it. This is usually accomplished through *organization segmentation.* The organization is broken into manageable parts, appropriately called *responsibility centers,* and each part is given an assignment designed to serve the overall goals of the organization. The delegation of responsibility carries with it the implication of measurement and evaluation: How well has the assignment been carried out? Without an evaluation component, delegation is irresponsible. Budgets are clearly important in the responsibility structure—they communicate the extent and nature of the assigned responsibility, and they provide a measure by which performance may be evaluated. Robert Anthony, the author of several textbooks on this subject (1974, 1980), describes the process as beginning with budgeting and proceeding through the stages of operating, measuring, reporting, and finally "programming"—further planning in the light of recent events and conditions.

Purposes of Budgets. Budgets serve many purposes simultaneously. Most of these purposes are related and overlapping, although, as we will see, some may conflict. Budgets often embody *goals,* or expressions of desired future results. They may be used to develop *standards of performance* and are often part of the sanction and reward system. They can be *motivators* for employees in that the existence of a standard of performance, consistently and continuously maintained, tends to increase employee morale and bring employees more into sympathy with the goals of the organization. Budgets may also become tacitly understood *contracts* between upper and lower hierarchies of an organization, in which the lower member agrees that the budget represents an achievable goal and the upper member agrees that if the goal is achieved, rewards will be forthcoming.

As plans, budgets are also in some sense *projections of future activity.* To be effective, a plan must be realistic enough to be carried out. The idea that a budget is a projection, however, can come into conflict with the notion of the budget as a goal. Even appropriately set goals sometimes do not result in realistic projections, especially when goals are set relatively high with the knowledge that not every part of the organization will be able to live up to expectations.

Budgets also serve as a *means of communication* whereby the parts of an organization have a chance to combine their experience to produce a systematic prediction of future events. Often the annual budget hearing is the only formal contact between different levels of the organization and the only time when some really difficult problems may be exposed. The analysis of actual or potential deviations from the budget also often sparks important communication. Because they relate to the reward system, potential sources of deviation from the budget are likely to surface early, allowing management to make changes that will avoid negative effects.

Budgets help management to control an organization and are therefore part of the organization's *control structure.* Budgets allow managers to pinpoint problems and opportunities. They aid the practice of *management by exception*—the process by which the scarce and expensive organizational resource of managerial time and attention is directed to "exceptional" conditions marked by a significant degree of deviation (either positive or negative) from expectations.

Budgets also serve the planning process by *coordinating functions.* If programmers in the Business and Management Department have decided to double course offerings in the next year, they will need to inform the registration office so that it can prepare for a (hoped for) onslaught of students, the promotion department so that it can determine how to attract new students, and the person who schedules classrooms so that more space can be secured. Whenever the actions of one organizational segment have an impact on the work of another, coordination must take place. The budget can help in providing this.

Because CE organizations are often part of larger institutions, they frequently have to prepare budgets in the form demanded by those institutions. However, the primary mission of those larger institutions is usually not continuing education, and the format of the institutional budget often does not serve the functions of the CE organization. For this reason, the CE enterprise will often need to prepare a budget of its own in a format designed to meet its particular needs.

All of these purposes of budgeting should become clearer as you read through the examples and explanations in this book. Keep in mind that the book is written from the perspective of budgeting as an ideal—something rarely achieved or even desirable in reality—yet real budgets must operate in the real world, contending with practical difficulties and serving practical purposes. You will be challenged continually to translate the theoretical ideals and the illustrative examples presented in this book to your own concrete and unique situation.

Types of Budgets

In most CE organizations there is a hierarchy of budgets. Budgets are prepared for the smallest organizational subunits and then combined with budgets of successively larger units until the whole organization is included. The discussion in this book will reflect this hierarchical pattern. *Course budgets* will be the lowest order of budgeting described; they will be added together to form a budget for each programmer, which in turn will be added to budgets from the other programmers in the same department to form the department program budget. These will finally be added together (along with budgets from service departments) to form the budget for the CE organization. In most situations, this organization budget will be combined with budgets from other parts of the parent institution to arrive at the institutional budget. The highest order of budget, that is, the last and most inclusive budget, is often called the *master budget*.

Format Types. Budgets are sometimes classified by format. The two most common format types are the *program budget* and the *line item budget*. *Program budgets* (and here the word *program* is used in its broadest sense to include an organized activity of any kind) list the income and expenses projected for a particular endeavor or, more commonly, a particular responsibility center (organizational segment). A *project budget* is a special kind of program budget for the completion of a particular task that may span more than one operating period. Grants and contracts from the state and federal governments are examples of project budgets. A *line item budget* lists the categories of income and expenses (sometimes referred to as *natural classifications*) without reference to the program or purpose with which they are associated. For instance, a line item budget might have all instructional staff payroll costs for the organization listed on one line, whereas a program budget would divide instructional costs among the various departments. Line item budgets are quite common in institutional budgeting but are not particularly useful to managers of CE organizations.

Purpose Types. Budgets are also commonly designated by their primary purpose. *Operating budgets* cover the broadest range of an organization's activity and deal with income and expense related to day-to-day operations. *Balance sheet budgets,* not commonly used in CE organizations, project the value of assets, liabilities, and residual equity or fund balance of an organization.

Capital budgets are plans for the generation and expenditure of funds devoted to capital items such as real estate, equipment, and other assets that are expected to return value to the organization over an extended period, usually several budget years. Decisions about capital expenditures usually have important long-term significance to an organization and must be planned carefully. CE organizations do have occasion to acquire capital items, although often the budgeting for the expenditure is not complex enough to warrant a full budget treatment.

Cash budgets project the flow of cash into and out of an organization. They are designed to make sure that the organization does not run out of money to pay its current obligations and that excess funds are invested for maximum returns. Although many CE organizations, as part of larger organizations, are not directly concerned with cash budgeting, the CE unit will have to be aware of its impact on cash flows as cash management techniques become increasingly important to parent organizations. Cash and capital budgeting in a CE setting are discussed in Chapter Ten.

Cash budgets are one category of *financial budgets,* which are concerned with financing or sources of funding for an organization. Funding sources may be income from tuition and fees, subsidies from parent institutions, and so on. They may also include borrowing, gifts, and the recovery on accounts and notes receivable. Financial budgets may be contrasted with *expenditure budgets,* which concentrate on where and how resources will be spent, ignoring where the funds come from and not explicitly calculating the effect on cash balances. Most CE budgets are expenditure budgets; however, self-support organizations must pay attention to sources of funds.

Other Types. Budgets are sometimes categorized according to the timing of their preparation or the method underlying the evaluation of results. *Rolling* or *continuous budgets* incorporate frequent adjustments and the addition of future budgeted periods on a regular basis. Using a common form of rolling budget, one large university extension organization requires department managers to submit a budget each month covering the next twelve months of operations. In each monthly budget, the monthly budgets previously submitted may be updated and the new twelfth month is added. *Flexible* or *variable budgets* establish standards for an operating entity over a range of possible volumes of activity. This type of budget is discussed in detail in Chapter Seven. *Fund budgeting* takes place within the context of fund accounting and is designed to assure that individually established funds are used for the express purposes for which they were established. Fund accounting and, therefore, fund budgeting are pervasive and unavoidable in continuing education, and they often make life difficult for continuing educators by placing restrictions upon their options. We will discuss fund accounting in Chapter Four and describe strategies to counteract its negative effects.

Clearly there are many types of budgets and many labels for them. The vocabulary of budgeting is not precise; each organization will have its own names for budgets that will be meaningful only in its own specific institutional context. To understand what a particular budget is intended to do, you must look beyond the label to the substance.

General Theories of Budgeting

Budgeting is a practical task, but it should occur within a theoretical framework. Many theories about the budgeting process have been formulated and named, frequently with acronyms. Knowing the meaning of these acronyms and something about what each theory involves is important to an overall understanding of budgeting.

Traditional Budgeting. Most recent theories of budgeting have been developed to correct perceived defects of the traditional form of budgeting. A knowledge of the traditional form is therefore the base for understanding the later forms.

The traditional budget is a line item budget. As described earlier in the chapter, this is simply a list of income and expenditure categories (known as natural classifications) assigned to a line on a page. Budgeting under this method means the control of these line items.

The budget is usually considered in two parts, the *base* and the *increments*. Each established operating department receives funding for its basic operating functions and established programs for each budget period. Departments then vie for any additional (incremental) funding that might be available to the organization. Budget strategies thus revolve around the defense of the base from reductions and pleas or arguments for the funding of new programs from incremental funds.

Incremental funding is particularly important because such funding usually becomes a part of the base as a new program becomes established and then requires additional funding in successive years. Each department generally develops its own notion of what its "fair share" of incremental funding should be. Because of the importance of these incremental decisions, traditional budgeting became known as *incremental budgeting,* and subspecies began to be known by the manner in which incremental allocations could be requested. *Open-ended budgeting* places no restrictions on the additional amount of funding that might be requested. *Quota methods* place limits on the amount over the base that can be requested. *Alternative level budgeting* asks managers to submit budget requests assuming several levels above or below the base, say increases of 5 percent and 10 percent.

Incremental budgeting has the advantage of focusing management's attention on the important changes occurring in an organization. It also involves relatively little computational time and effort, since the bulk of the budget, represented by the base, is automatically defined and easily calculated. However, incremental budgeting has the drawback of suppressing the review of established programs, which might, by virtue of being hidden in the base, continue to be funded long after they are useful. To correct for this disadvantage, the concept of *zero-based budgeting* (ZBB) was developed. ZBB requires that the entire budget be justified every budget period and that the value of every program be reviewed.

Although laudable in its purposes, ZBB was largely a failure because of the amount of time and effort it required.

Program Budgeting. One disadvantage of traditional budgeting was that, in concentrating on line item control, with categories such as maintenance, payroll, supplies, and so on, it sometimes lost track of the underlying purposes the expenditures were supposed to serve. Program budgeting requires that the budget presentation be made in such a way that the desired end result—say, the education of 100 students in the principles of financial accounting—can be related to the costs of achieving that result. With this kind of presentation, management can more easily relate ends to means and make comparisons and judgments between programs. President Johnson required that all federal agencies submit program budgets under a system known as the *Program Planning and Budgeting System* (PPBS). This system is now considered to have failed because of two factors: It was expensive to prepare, and it increased dissension and discord between program staffs, who began to see each other as rivals for the same pot of money. This latter problem was less prominent in incremental budgeting, where every program was assured at least its base.

Although program budgeting failed, the need for a more rational approach to budgeting and planning remained clear. A number of other methods, based on the same premises as program budgeting but called by other names, therefore developed. Most currently in vogue is *management by objectives* (MBO). This is a process by which the objectives of an organization are first carefully defined and specifically stated. Next, the resources available to reach those objectives are identified. Then a plan of utilizing those resources to reach the desired objectives is worked out. Finally, results are measured by the extent to which the objectives were reached with the available resources.

The "systems approach" has also been applied to budgeting and is closely related to the program budget concept. The *management information systems* (MIS) concept, which concentrates on the kind and format of information that managers need to manage, embodies a large portion of the original program budgeting idea. So does the *program evaluation and review technique (PERT)*. All of these systems use the same order of steps in the process of managing that Strother and Klus (1982) have summarized in the following questions:

1. What do we want to do?
2. Why do we want to do it?
3. How will we do it?
4. What do we need in order to do it?
5. How will we know whether we have succeeded?

Most organizations must adopt some form of the program budgeting system; otherwise, the management task becomes too unorganized, and too many parts of the organization remain unexamined. I recommend applying a modified program budgeting approach to continuing education. This is fairly easy to do because the nature of CE is to produce programs, the most obvious example of which is the course. Program budgeting thus becomes the most natural form of budgeting for the CE organization, even if the parent institution is still enmeshed in the traditional form.

Organizational Theory and Budgeting

A general discussion of budgeting would be incomplete without some mention of organizational theory and structure, although an extensive discussion of such theory is not necessary to the purposes of this book. Perrow's *Complex Organizations* (1972) presents an excellent overview of the many theories of organization and their philosophical bases. Budgeting should serve management and should reflect the structure of the organization. The budget system therefore must be consistent with the managerial philosophy governing the organization and must be designed with a clear idea of the organizational structure.

Centralized and Decentralized Organizations. These terms have both general meanings and meanings specific to CE. In general, they refer to the location in the organization's hierarchy of the responsibility and authority to make operating decisions. (They may also refer to the geographical dispersion of the operating subunits of an organization, but in this book we will use the responsibility-related meaning.) A highly centralized organization will place most decision making in the hands of a few people at the top of the organization chart, allowing second-line management to make only the less significant, day-to-day operating decisions. Centralized organizations usually require middle and lower management to operate within a set of carefully prescribed rules and regulations and have elaborate mechanisms for monitoring compliance. In a decentralized organization, by contrast, the top level of management sets general objectives for each of its subunits and allows subunit managers broad authority in deciding how to reach those objectives.

Budgeting is useful in either type of organization, but its purposes may be different in the two types. In centralized organizations, budgeting serves primarily as a check on how well the managers are obeying the rules. It also serves an important communication function. Because upper management personnel may be relatively isolated from day-to-day operations, variations from budget are usually their earliest warning that something is going amiss and that they should review the problem area. Budgets are communication tools in decentralized organizations also, but here the communication is more of a two-way street. Budgets communicate upper management's expectations to lower management and then become a tool by which the subunit managers can monitor their own performance in attempting to achieve the established objectives. The coordinating functions of budgeting are especially important in decentralized organizations because departmentally separated units must work in concert, without direct involvement of central management.

In continuing education, the terms *centralized* and *decentralized* have special meanings that are somewhat different from those just described. In *centralized provisions,* most or all continuing education is handled by a separate operating unit or units assigned to the task by the parent. *Decentralized provisions* disperse the continuing education function throughout the institution. Thus, in some colleges and universities, a centralized extension unit provides all continuing education, whereas in others each academic department, such as the school of business, is responsible for continuing education in its own subject area. Sometimes decentralized CE provisions are served by a centralized core of service departments—registration, promotion, and so on. Again, budgeting principles will apply to both forms, but they are much more likely to be extensively utilized where the provision is centralized. In the decentralized situation, careful budgeting consistently applied to all the separate CE units often runs counter to the perceived interests of the academic schools or departments, and hidden subsidies (which we will examine shortly) obscure the true cost of presenting courses. The central administration of a decentralized provision therefore has much less knowledge and control over continuing education than the administration of a centralized provision.

Autocratic and Participative Organizations. Autocratic organizations are ruled from the top with an iron hand, with little consultation with lower members. Although autocratic organizations are usually (but not always) centralized, the term has more to do with the nature of the relationship between the top and lower management than with the locus of decision making. Participative (or collegial) organizations encourage wide participation in the functions of problem definition, decision making, and implementation; they seek to gain consensus among the members of the organization.

These two organizational styles are endpoints on a continuum of styles, and each organization will be different from others in the ways it conveys and carries out objectives. An organization's management style arises in part from the personalities of its leaders, but it also stems from the nature of the work being done. Some tasks require input from a number of people with different perspectives, and these lend themselves to participative styles. Others require that well-defined subtasks be carried out and coordinated in a precise and measured manner. Autocratic methods may be more appropriate in this situation.

Again, budgeting serves both kinds of organizations, but the form the budget takes will be a function of the style of the organization. In autocratic organizations, the budget will be primarily directed at controlling the organization, whereas in participative enterprises, the budgeting process will involve a great deal of negotiation and communication and will be part of the consensus-building process. Here, too, these descriptions are extremes, and most CE organizations will fall somewhere in between.

Budgets are tools and, like any tool, can be used in a variety of ways. Budgets can be clubs or carrots; they can be commands or requests. To be effective, budgets must be consistent with the nature and structure of the organization they serve. Otherwise they can result in confusion and discord.

Special Characteristics of CE Organizations

A number of situations characteristic of CE organizations present special problems in preparing budgets. These situations arise primarily because the CE organization is usually not entirely its own master; it exists as part of a larger institution.

Terminology

Certain terms are used in a special way in this book to further the discussion of budgeting in the continuing education context. *Course* is used to signify a single instance of organized educational activity of any kind, whether credit, noncredit, degree, nondegree, day, evening, weekend, on-campus, off-campus, conference, institute, independent study, media-based, workshop, professional, general, seminar, lecture, or lecture series. I prefer *course* to *program* for this use because *program* often carries the connotation of a series or grouping of courses and also is often used to indicate noneducational activities.

The term *programmer* is used in this book to indicate one who is responsible for planning and organizing individual courses of instruction and who is in some way responsible for the financial outcome of those courses. The programmer may be someone whose sole job is organizing courses or simply someone who is given the assignment of, say, organizing one course per year for the local museum.

A *director* is considered to be anyone who has responsibility for administering all or part of an organization that presents a number of continuing education courses each year. A CE director might also be called dean, manager, chair, head, coordinator, administrator, or, more occasionally, chancellor, vice-chancellor, vice-provost, or some similar name.

The term *continuing education organization,* often shortened to *CE organization,* is used to represent a wide variety of organizational entities that present courses of instruction. A CE organization may be part of a larger (parent) organization, or it may be a "stand-alone" organization. I will not use the term *extension* because it is more restrictive, usually being limited to colleges and universities.

In addition to terms related to continuing education, many technical terms used in budgeting, finance, and economics are employed in this book. All are defined in the text. These terms and their definitions also appear in a glossary in the back of the book.

Disassociation of Income and Expense

In many (probably most) CE organizations, the income and expense budgets are separately maintained and controlled even when it is acknowledged that they are directly related to one another. In a typical situation, the director of continuing education is expected to live within a given expense budget and is also required to produce a certain amount of income from tuition and fees or from formula-based budget allocations from governmental sources. This dual budget system fails to recognize that the production of the required income is usually dependent on the amount and nature of the resources expended. For example, the amount of money spent on promotion has a very direct effect on income produced. In fact, just about every expenditure item has some effect, direct or indirect, on income. When these natural relationships are artificially obscured, managing an organization becomes difficult. Therefore I advocate bringing together the two budgets into one master budget.

Overhead Allocations from the Parent

Many CE organizations must support some portion of the indirect costs of the parent institution. This overhead allocation can appear in many forms. It might come in the form of a direct charge for a specified service, such as $10 per student for library use during the summer. Or it might be vague and unspecified, based, for example, on a pro rata share of the costs of the registration office computed by dividing the number of CE students by the total number of students the office serves. The theory and behavioral implications of various overhead allocation strategies are discussed briefly in Chapters Three and Four and in much more detail in Chapter Nine. Although these discussions generally relate to allocations within a CE organization, the factors involved can easily be applied to allocation schemes imposed upon the entire organization.

The primary consideration in dealing with indirect cost allocations from the parent is to avoid distorted behavior, that is, behavior that is not in the best interest of the whole organization when viewed in its broadest context. For instance, charging a flat $10 per student for library services may encourage library use by CE students, since the fee remains constant regardless of actual use. This effect may or may not be in the institution's best interest. Similarly, the pro rata charge for registration costs may encourage the CE unit to concentrate on high-fee, low-enrollment courses, which again may or may not be desirable from the point of view of the overall organization. It is important that the CE director understand clearly the formula and nature of the parental charge and recognize that indirect cost allocations are essentially arbitrary ways of transferring resources from one part of an institution to another. Where serious distortions are likely to occur, the allocation scheme should either be changed or be masked from those making operating decisions. For instance, where a per-enrollment overhead fee is likely to bias programmers in favor of low-enrollment, high-fee programs, the CE director may want to offset this bias by charging overhead on some other basis in internal accounting.

Hidden Subsidies

Identifying all the resources available to a CE organization and all the costs of presenting continuing education courses is often difficult, even impossible. Anderson and Kasl (1982) report that they were unable to generate meaningful, comprehensive cost data for virtually any of the categories of adult education they studied. The reasons for this failutre included inadequate management information systems, the educators' desire to keep the information secret, and, most disturbingly, a lack of awareness of the concept of full cost and the true extent of the resources that were being devoted to the programs. One of the premises of this book is that the CE director ought to know what the organization's entire financial situation really is.

Hidden subsidies are usually items of expenditure that are devoted to continuing education but do not show up in the official continuing education budget. They are therefore "hidden" and often forgotten. These subsidies can present a significant barrier to sound management practices and informed decisions about continuing education operations. They can also, as Anderson and Kasl learned, make comparisons of the financing of programs difficult. The most common hidden subsidies include the following:

Salaries. Frequently the salaries of some people who devote part or even all of their time to continuing education activities are not included in the CE budget. This exclusion may be open and according to institutional policy, as when the salary of the dean or director and perhaps the salary of his or her clerical support is paid from other funds. On the other hand, the subsidy may be secretive and designed to subvert institutional policy, as when a secretary or clerical person in a decentralized provision actually devotes a large portion of time to continuing education but is paid out of other funds. Whenever such salaries are excluded, legally or otherwise, the costs of continuing education are understated, and the financial return is overstated.

Fringe Benefits. In some institutions, particularly those receiving financial support from state governments, the costs of fringe benefits traditionally are not included in operating budgets. The reasons for this relate to the rather rigid restrictions of fund accounting that required benefits—retirement, health, disability, and so on—which are usually not paid out in the same period in which they are earned, to be established in a separate fund. However, the disassociation of these costs from operating costs serves no valid management purpose. Furthermore, vacations, holidays, sick leave, and other fringe benefits taken by employees in the form of paid time rather than money often are not factored into cost equations. The full costs of the services of any employee are usually easy to determine, but the effective budgeting of those costs is sometimes difficult.

Office and Classroom Space. CE organizations that must rent office and classroom space are usually well aware of space costs, but when the parent institution provides such space, at least a portion of the true cost of the space is often hidden. Where the parent is a college or university and the CE organization occupies institution-owned space, CE may be charged nothing for the space or may pay only the cost of maintenance and operations. It is rare for the original cost of constructing the building or the financing costs associated with it to be charged in any way to the CE organization. This hidden subsidy can be uncovered with startling results if CE suddenly is asked to move off campus and absorb market rents. When CE uses classroom space, some parent institutions who use the classrooms for other programs during the day and view CE as a sort of by-product of their main mission will charge CE only the "incremental costs" associated with the use of the classrooms during the evening. This means that only those costs that can be identified directly with the extra use—special room setups, special cleanup tasks, and perhaps pay differentials between swing and graveyard shifts—will be charged to CE. This is justifiable because the rooms would not be used in the evening otherwise and yet they would still have to be cleaned and heated and otherwise maintained. Most of the time this form of hidden subsidy does not impair managerial decisions, but the CE director should be aware of it and of the cost of providing alternative space.

Services. Services of all kinds are likely to be provided by the parent to the CE organization free of charge or at nominal rates. These services may include purchasing, personnel, accounting, computer, storehouse, payroll and disbursement, telecommunications, registration, promotion, legal, cashiering, library, audiovisual, course approval and review, business, financial aid, printing and reprographics, transportation, and a whole host of other administrative and academic services. Part or all of these costs may be charged back to the CE organization through indirect (overhead) cost allocations or special levies. But even where the full pro rata share of the services is borne by the CE organization, the costs, by virtue of the economies of scale available to the larger parent, may be lower than the cost of the same services on the open market. The full cost of these services, which is usually difficult to estimate, may become an issue when the services are withdrawn from the CE organization or when, as is becoming more frequent, CE is asked to pay for its "fair share" of their costs. The CE director should always be aware of the existence of the costs of these services and the impact of the CE operation on the workload of service departments.

Cost of Money. By virtue of being part of a larger organization, most CE operations do not have to worry about cash flow and the day-to-day financing of their activities. After an initial capitalization, and after taking account of any subsidy that might exist, CE organizations tend to be cash flow producers rather than users because income generally flows in before the costs of presenting the courses have to be paid out. However, when the CE organization does produce a negative cash flow, the shortfall must be met by borrowing money or by using funds that otherwise could be earning interest. The cost of borrowing or of the lost opportunity to earn interest has always been all too real to the for-profit business. With the increasing sophistication of cash management techniques used in the not-for-profit sector, it is becoming an important management consideration in CE organizations, and most emphatically in parent universities, as well. Chapter Ten presents a detailed discussion of cash budgeting and cost of money.

Volunteers. Accounting and budgeting of the value of volunteered services presents a number of problems. Since volunteer services do not affect the flow of funds through an organization, they generally are not reflected anywhere in the budget. But some organizations, including CE organizations, could not exist without volunteer support, and it is just as important to budget and manage this resource well as it is to manage and budget dollar funds. Ignoring the value of contributed services can seriously distort the reporting of financial operations and lead to management errors. When and on what basis volunteer services should be recorded are two difficult questions that must be answered when volunteers are a significant factor in an organization. One museum, for instance, records the value of volunteer time only when the service performed by the volunteer would otherwise have been done by a paid employee; it is then valued at a rate of pay equivalent to what the employee would have been paid. This is a rather restrictive policy, but it does present a clear standard for accounting purposes. In general, it is good practice to record the value of volunteer services both as a source of funding and as a cost of operating in a separate line item so that adjustments for different reporting purposes can be made. However, using volunteers as substitutes for paid employees can raise collective bargaining issues. The manner of accounting for the value of volunteer services can be important when these issues are examined, so the managerial benefit of explicitly recognizing volunteer resources may be overwhelmed by negative effects.

In summary, hidden subsidies are usually hidden for a reason. From the point of view of the CE director, some of them should probably remain hidden. They are likely to come out of hiding, however, when the financial atmosphere changes for the worse. The CE director and other key members of the CE organization should be aware of their impact and, where their exclusion damages the value of budget and financial information, should take steps to include them in at least some (perhaps "for eyes only") edition of the budget.

Budgets and Human Beings

Aaron Wildavsky, in *The Politics of the Budgetary Process* (1974), defines budgeting as "the translation of financial resources into human purposes" (p. 1) and characterizes the budget as being the heart of the political process. Although Wildavsky was referring to the federal budget and national politics, his statements hold true for budgeting in any organization, including those concerned with continuing education. We will review budgeting techniques and the steps of the budget process in some detail, but the human factor must never be overlooked while the technical aspects are dwelt upon. Budgets are devised and carried out by people, and they cannot succeed in any of their purposes without the understanding and support of all those involved in the budgeting process.

Budgets are part of the formal organizational process, and their form, content, and manner and timing of preparation are usually prescribed by formal policy. The annual budget hearing is a formal interaction between management levels. At each level of budget preparation, the process of negotiation, of discussing the fairness and achievability of targets and the resources needed to reach them, is likely to take place in a more or less formal manner.

Budgets, however, also have elements of informal interaction ranging from the most cooperative and constructive to the most petty, selfish, and destructive. Budgets can be used to motivate people, control them, communicate with them, coordinate their activities, and punish or reward them. Much of the budgeting process thus is unavoidably nonscientific, subjective, and political. Although the budget is a document filled with numbers that represent a supposedly objective view of the financial target for an organization, the numbers are bound to have gotten there through a process that involved a good deal of discussion and personal opinion. When actual results are compared with budget projections, deviations will be viewed subjectively as well.

Because budgets can be used in so many ways, people's views of budgeting will depend on their experience of it. Often, alas, their views are quite negative. They see budgets as, at best, necessary evils. Programmers often resent having to prepare course budgets, and directors dread the annual budget hearing with their superiors. Careful planning is needed to diminish these negative feelings. The process by which the budget is prepared and administered should be designed to discourage distorted behavior that may impede achievement of the goals and objectives of the organization.

Excessively strict adherence to budgets is a common example of distorted behavior. Budgets are estimates, sometimes accurate and sometimes way off the mark. They are based upon assumptions about future conditions. When the estimates are inaccurate or when the assumptions prove unfounded, continued adherence to a budget may not make sense. A manager who feels he has to spend his entire expense budget even when savings are possible is probably engaging in behavior distorted by a budget system that penalizes efficiency by reducing future budget allocations on the basis of lower actual expenditures. The rules of this budget game should be altered so that efficient behavior can be rewarded.

Distorted behavior is also likely to occur when budgets are used primarily to check up on employees or control them. Employees and managers who have little say in the budget process and who know that the real purpose of the budget is to determine who is not performing properly are likely to begin "playing the budget game" primarily to avoid getting into trouble rather than to advance the organization's goals. The imposition of budgets, especially unrealistic and unachievable budgets, is also likely to produce distorted behavior in the form of hostility and frustration toward the organization and the budget process.

Used properly, however, budgets can facilitate the human interactions involved in guiding organizations. They can serve an important function in conflict resolution by providing an objective basis for evaluating alternative actions. They can help an organization focus on the issues, problems, and opportunities it faces. I believe that budgets can and should be useful to everyone associated with them. The programmer should be able to use a course budget to help decide whether to give the course in the first place, whether to continue it, and whether to repeat it next term or next year. The director should view budgeting as an integral part of planning and directing the organization. This book seeks not only to provide information about the budgeting process but to help the reader develop a positive attitude about its use.

Summary

Recent trends in continuing education make financial control and budgeting increasingly important. Issues of accountability arise more frequently now, especially as the number of funding sources multiplies, the movement toward self-support accelerates, and an increasing percentage of CE budgets is funded from student tuition and fees. The necessity of dividing or segmenting the organization into manageable parts is a natural consequence of all these factors.

Budgets are basically financial plans. They are used in organizations to plan, coordinate, control, delegate responsibility, and communicate organizational goals and objectives. Budgeting is also a continuous process, of which a budget document is only one product. The nomenclature used to describe different types of budgets derives from the purposes the budgets serve.

There are two broad categories of budgeting: traditional and program. The traditional or incremental approach is founded on the idea that each operating department needs and will receive a base of funding each budget period and that departments will vie for any additional funds. Traditional budgets are line item budgets with control focusing on the total spent in each expenditure category. Program budgets, on the other hand, relate objectives to the value of the resources needed to achieve them. They specify desired outcomes and place limits on the amount that can be spent to obtain them. Most budgets systems today use some form of program budgeting or find ways of incorporating both traditional and program budgeting into the same budget system. In this book we will use primarily the program approach to budgeting.

The structure of the organization, whether centralized or decentralized, and the managerial philosophy used by management, whether autocratic or participative, have important effects on the budget process. The forms of budgets must be consistent with the organizations they serve.

Some organizational characteristics common to CE enterprises can have important effects on the budgeting process. In many CE organizations the income and the expense budgets are dealt with separately, a technique that ignores their natural interrelationship and makes financial management difficult. Most CE organizations have to budget for some form of indirect cost allocations from their parent institutions and may have to resist distorting their own behavior because of unenlightened recharge methods. Hidden subsidies—unrecognized sources of funding support for the CE enterprise—also can distort financial reporting and therefore managerial decision making.

For good or ill, budgets affect human lives and human behavior. Behavior of people in an organization may be improved or distorted by the budgeting process, depending on the way budgets are prepared and administered. The behavior likely to result from a new or changed budget process should therefore be forecast just as carefully as any of the numbers in the budget document itself. A properly designed budget should be useful to and produce positive feelings in everyone involved with it.

Bibliography

Anderson, R. E., and Kasl, E. S. *The Costs and Financing of Adult Education and Training.* Lexington, Mass.: Lexington Books, 1982.

Anthony, R. N., and Herzlinger, R. E. *Management Control in Nonprofit Organizations.* (Rev. ed.) Homewood, Ill.: Irwin, 1980.

Anthony, R. N., and Welsch, G. A. *Fundamentals of Management Accounting.* Homewood, Ill.: Irwin, 1974.

Ingram, R. W. (ed.) *Accounting in the Public Sector: The Changing Environment.* Corvallis, Ore.: Brighton, 1980.

Louderback, J. G., III, and Dominiak, G. F. *Managerial Accounting* (3rd ed.) Boston: Kent, 1982.

McConkey, D. D. *MBO for Nonprofit Organizations.* New York: AMACOM, 1975.

Perrow, C. *Complex Organizations.* Glenview, Ill.: Scott, Foresman, 1972.

Strother, G. B., and Klus, J. P. *Administration of Continuing Education.* Belmont, Calif.: Wadsworth, 1982.

Swieringa, R. J., and Moncur, R. H. *Some Effects of Participative Budgeting on Managerial Behavior.* New York: National Association of Accountants, 1975.

Titard, P. L. *Managerial Accounting: An Introduction.* Hinsdale, Ill.: Dryden Press, 1983.

Wildavsky, A. B. *The Politics of the Budgetary Process.* (2nd ed.) Boston: Little, Brown, 1974.

⇒ *Part One* ⇐

Budgeting
for Courses
and Programs

This part of *Effective Budgeting in Continuing Education* is for everyone involved in planning individual courses of instruction. As stated in the Introduction, *courses* in this book are broadly defined to include most planned educational activities. Usually, the course is the basic entity upon which the CE budgeting system should be based.

Almost every continuing education enterprise requires that budgeting and financial planning be part of the course-planning process. Many continuing education professionals, however, find budgeting an odious task, performed primarily to satisfy institutional requirements. At least a part of this antipathy stems from lack of knowledge of the budgeting process and its potential value. This part of the book should provide you, the continuing education professional, with both the theoretical understanding and the practical skills needed to budget effectively. It should help you develop a positive attitude toward budgeting by showing you how budgeting can help you improve your courses, use your time more effectively, and evaluate and identify targets of opportunity. After reading this part, you should be able to

• understand the basic terminology and concepts of budgeting and how they relate to course budgets;

27

- prepare a comprehensive course budget, meaningfully classified and presented;
- understand when, why, and how dollar decisions regarding a course must be made; and
- establish a priori criteria for financial success and understand the several levels of financial performance.

Chapter One presents the basic terminology and concepts of course budgeting. Chapter Two relates the course-planning process to budgeting concepts, producing a dynamic decision/process model that presents a way of seeing what may happen to revenue and costs during the life of the course and highlighting natural decision points. Chapter Two also deals with the often-neglected concepts of reward/risk and opportunity costs and presents examples of course budgets. Chapter Three applies the decision/ process model to the most common problems associated with course budgeting and planning, among them:

- how to determine course fees;
- how to determine the promotion budget for a course and evaluate the cost-effectiveness of promotion;
- how to determine the effect of alternative cost mixes;
- how to determine instructor compensation rates and negotiate with instructors;
- how to determine the effect of indirect costs on the course budget;
- how to price individual services and negotiate the financial aspects of cosponsored programs; and
- how to develop an overall program plan and balanced strategy for a group of courses, based on the decision/process model.

In summary, Part One is primarily directed to programmers and presents the microeconomic aspects of budgeting in continuing education. This information is necessary for the understanding of the macroeconomic aspects presented in Part Two, which treats the second step in the hierarchy of continuing education budgeting— budgeting for the entire continuing education enterprise.

1

Understanding
the Essentials
of Course Budgeting

Course budgeting is meant to be both a planning process and a communication process. Course planning is strengthened by the preparation of a course budget because budgeting forces organized consideration and projection of the financial aspects of the course. Those who prepare course budgets need to understand the underlying phenomena they are trying to describe (namely, the possible behavior of income and expenses associated with a proposed course), and they must be able to share this understanding with others through a common vocabulary. This chapter begins with definitions and descriptions of the important concepts in the course budgeting process. These concepts are illustrated using classic textbook descriptions of the behavior of costs and income. Unfortunately, these descriptions do not include a time dimension or provide for changing variables in a flexible manner, a condition absolutely necessary for effectively dealing with the course-planning process. These "dynamic" concepts will be introduced toward the end of this chapter, thus setting the stage for Chapter Two, which describes the development of the decision/process model for continuing education budgeting.

The Budget Object

The *budget object* is the entity that is being budgeted. The term *budget object* is a technical budgeting term that may be unfamiliar and awkward to you, but it will be useful as we proceed in this explanation. In the next few chapters, the budget object is the course; in Part Two, the budget object is the entire CE organization. The specification of the budget object is an important step in the budgeting process because it helps to define clearly the questions to be answered and the level of detail necessary to answer them. In course budgeting we want to know how much we will have to charge for a course, how many enrollments will be needed to cover costs, whether or not to rent a larger room, how much we can afford to pay our instructors, and many other things. If we have used the term rather than the individual course as the budget object, we probably will not be able to answer these questions.

Let us use examples to illustrate some difficulties and considerations involved in establishing the budget object. Suppose you are planning a lecture series that will present a lecture every Wednesday night for seven weeks. It includes some well-known experts in the field and also some less popular but highly informed lecturers. You decide that the enrollment fee for the entire series should be $100 but that a significant number of people will be willing to pay $35 to hear a single lecture in the series. You therefore advertise the whole series at $100 and single lectures at $35, payable at the door.

What is the budget object here—the entire series or a single lecture? You have a choice. You could treat the entire series as a single course, calculating income as the total of series subscriptions plus single admissions and figuring all costs as belonging to the series. This would make sense if all lectures in the series were given in the same location and promoted in the same manner. However, you might decide that certain lecturers are so popular that you will need a larger auditorium (and thus have a higher room rental cost) on the nights on which they speak and that you will promote those particular lectures with radio spots. In this instance, you might want to treat each lecture as a separate course, thus defining the individual lecture as a budget object. You would then have to figure a way to allocate the overall lecture series enrollment fee ($100) to specific lectures. Although this allocation might be rather arbitrary, the control over the costs of individual lectures—important, perhaps, because of the large differences in costs that could be directly assigned to a particular lecturer—might prove valuable enough to the planning process to outweigh any distortion caused by the arbitrary allocation of income. A third way to define the budget object of this complex lecture series would be to prepare one budget for the series, including only series enrollments, and another budget for single admissions to the series. This would make sense if single admissions were looked upon as a by-product of the series or if a significant cost, say promotion, were directed at producing single admissions.

Another possible factor complicating assignment of the budget object occurs when a particular course is going to be presented a number of times and/or at a number of locations. For example, suppose you are planning a two-day course for high school seniors on skills they will need when they go to college. You will offer it in five local school districts on successive weekends. You have the choice of treating this course offering as a single budget object or as five separate budget objects. As with the lecture series, the decision will depend upon the underlying purpose of the budgeting process and the specifics of the situation. Differential costs, the possibility of charging differing fees, expectation of a significant variation in number of enrollments at different locations, and a more detailed control of financial arrangements are some circumstances that might argue for separate budgets.

It is clear that defining a budget object, a task that at first seems straightforward and simple, may be surprisingly difficult in some cases. Setting the budget object is one of the first steps in the budget process, but it requires a thorough knowledge of all the other steps and of the concepts associated with budgets and budgetary control as well as experience in the nonfinancial aspects of presenting continuing education courses. The importance of the budget object will become even more clear as we begin to define other important elements of the course budget.

Course Revenue

Course revenue is usually the easiest course budget element to calculate and the most difficult to estimate. Total revenue is commonly calculated by multiplying the fee for the course by the number of estimated enrollments. A common variation of this calculation is to determine what total income should be, estimate enrollments, and then derive the fee. But thought, intuition, and sometimes data collection are needed before this simple calculation can be made.

Estimating course income is the most important element of course budgeting. Before we examine the theory and practice of setting course fees and estimating enrollments, therefore, let us briefly examine some of the problems of defining course revenue.

Take the common instance in which the costs of presenting a course are partly subsidized by an outside agency. For example, suppose a state department of health wants to encourage radiology technicians to take a course designed to upgrade their skills. The state agrees by contract to provide $5,000 toward the estimated total cost of the course, which is $10,000. In return, the state expects that you will charge the technicians a fee considerably lower than you would normally have to charge. How should this subsidy be treated in a course budget?

The theoretical answer is that the subsidy should be treated as revenue, rather than being treated as a reduction of expense or ignored altogether. Treating it as revenue provides the truest and most comprehensive financial picture of the course and best maintains the integrity of the budget objective, since all costs associated with the presentation of a course and all sources of course revenue should be explicitly described in the course budget whenever possible. From a practical point of view, however, treating subsidies as revenue often presents problems. For those CE organizations that must follow fund accounting rules, contracts like the one just described (particularly those from government agencies) must be accounted for separately. They may not be treated in the same way as tuition and fees received from students. Often they must be established in a separate fund from which money may be disbursed only for those costs associated with the purposes designated by the sponsoring agency. The temptation is to ignore both the subsidy income and the costs to be paid from the subsidy, budgeting only for the student fees and the remaining costs.

One way out of this dilemma is to prepare a budget summarizing all course costs by funding source. Such a budget is shown in Figure 1.1.

This budget shows the two funding sources for the program and indicates how course expenses will be distributed between them. It shows the full financial picture for the course despite the fact that records of expenditures from these two funding sources will have to be kept separately on the books of the organization.

Of course there are many other, less straightforward examples of subsidies. An outside agency may guarantee a certain number of enrollments, agree to pay for particular line items in the budget, or provide a free classroom or the equipment necessary to conduct a course. Each case requires special attention to the manner in which course revenue is treated in the budget.

It should also be noted here, in preparation for a later discussion, that total revenue is often closely associated with total costs. Usually fees are set after the costs of a course have been estimated. In many contract courses—that is, courses presented in companies or agencies according to prior negotiated contracts—cost or some form of cost plus fee is the basis for determining the total contract price. This fact is important in understanding the behavior of costs and revenues in the course budgeting process: In general, revenue and costs will behave the way we want or expect them to behave. When they do not, determining the reason for deviation becomes important.

Course Costs

The first step in understanding the behavior of course costs is to understand the traditional concepts of *fixed* and *variable costs,* as well as *direct* and *indirect costs.*

Fixed and Variable Costs. Anyone who tries to estimate the costs of a particular course runs into the problem of having to determine how many people will attend. Certain costs can be estimated only by specifying the number of enrollees. These costs

Figure 1.1. Course Budget Showing Multiple Funding Sources.

	State Share	Student Fees	Total
Funds provided by:			
State Department of Health	$5,000		$5,000
Student fees (200 @ $25)		$5,000	5,000
Total fund sources	$5,000	$5,000	$10,000
Funds to be used for:			
Coordinating personnel:			
Program coordinator (5 days @ $100)	$500		$500
Clerical support (8 days @ $75)	600		600
Subtotal	$1,100		$1,100
Fringe benefits (28%):	$308		$308
Instructional staff:			
Lead instructor (15 days @ $200)	$2,000	$1,000	$3,000
Guest speakers (10 @ $50)	500		500
Subtotal	$2,500	$1,000	$3,500
Travel:			
Program coordinator to capital (300 miles RT @ $.25/mile)	$75		$75
Instructor travel (15 trips at average $100/trip)	17	$1,483	1,500
Subtotal	$92	$1,483	$1,575
Other expense:			
Course materials		$567	$567
Coffee, refreshments		450	450
Subtotal		$1,017	$1,017
Total direct costs	$4,000	$3,500	$7,500
Indirect costs:			
State negotiated overhead rate (25% of direct costs)	$1,000		$1,000
CE organization required available for indirect costs (30% of fund sources)		$1,500	1,500
Total expenses	$5,000	$5,000	$10,000

are called *variable costs* because they vary with the volume of the activity (in our case, the number of enrollments). Examples of common variable costs are meals, course materials and books, computer time, and lodging costs. The behavior of variable costs in one case is illustrated by the graph in Figure 1.2.

In this example we are planning a one-day course on small electrical power generation plants. A set of notes for the course will cost $15 to produce, hors d'oeuvres at the opening no-host cocktail

Figure 1.2. Variable Cost Graph.

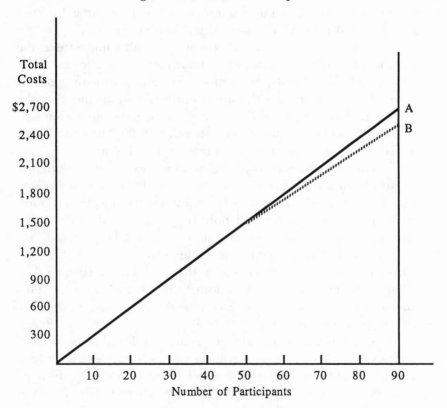

A. Variable costs = $30 per enrollee
B. Variable costs = $30 per enrollee to 50,
   $25 per enrollee after 50.

party will cost $8 per person, and coffee will cost $7 per person. Thus, every enrollee represents $30 in variable costs. If forty people enroll, our total variable cost will be $1,200 (forty enrollees times $30). In this situation, shown by line A on the graph, variable costs vary directly and proportionally with volume.

This is not always the case, however. Often the cost per enrollment can be reduced if a particular volume is reached. For example, let us suppose that the printer of the course notes agrees to charge only $10 per set for every set above fifty. This reduces the cost per enrollee, provided that fifty or more people enroll. This is shown in Figure 1.2 as a dotted line (B). We will examine this kind of variable cost behavior in more detail in Chapter Two.

Fixed costs are costs that do not vary with volume (here, the number of enrollees). Examples of fixed costs for courses are room rental, audiovisual costs, promotion costs, and instructor and staff travel costs. In our power plant example, let us assume that the room will cost $500, audiovisual costs will be $200, promotion will cost $1,500, and instructor travel costs will be $600. These fixed costs are shown by the solid line (A) on the graph in Figure 1.3.

Our total fixed costs of $2,800 do not vary with the number of enrollments. It is often the case, however, that costs remain fixed only for a particular level of volume. In our example, for instance, if the room we plan on will hold only fifty people, then when enrollment exceeds fifty we will have to rent a larger room at a higher cost. Let us say that the only alternative room available costs $1,200 instead of the $500 we had anticipated. Our fixed costs thus jump $700. This is shown as a dotted line (B) in Figure 1.3. This phenomenon is sometimes referred to as the *step function*, since the graph has a stair-step shape.

In reality, there are no truly fixed costs. Fixed costs are fixed only over a *relevant range* of volume values. The relevant range is the range of volume values over which there is no increase in fixed costs. In our example, the relevant range is zero to fifty for fixed costs of $2,800. In course budgeting it is important to recognize the relevant range for each element of fixed costs. Failure to do so can result in some rather startling deviations from the established budget.

Figure 1.3. Fixed Cost Graph.

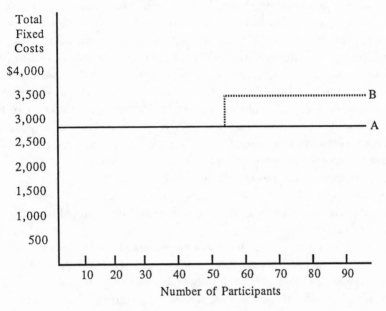

A. Fixed costs = $2,800
B. Fixed costs = $2,800 > 50 participants,
   $3,500 for < 50.

As mentioned before, true variable costs vary directly and proportionally with volume. An increase of volume of 10 percent will thus produce an increase in variable costs of 10 percent. Costs that vary in the same direction as volume but do not vary proportionally are sometimes called *semivariable* or *semifixed costs*. In these cases, an increase in volume of 10 percent will produce an increase of a smaller amount, say 8 percent, in variable costs. The volume discount on course materials shown by line B in Figure 1.2 is an example of a variable cost that does not increase proportionally with the number of enrollments. Semivariable costs are also called "semifixed" or "partly variable" because they contain elements of both fixed and variable costs. When we encounter a semivariable cost, we must break it down into its fixed and variable elements.

You may have noticed that instructor compensation was left out of our power plant example. This was done purposely, because instructor compensation can be either a fixed or a variable cost depending on circumstances. The most usual form of instructor compensation is for the instructor to be paid a specific, agreed-upon amount for teaching a course, either a specified dollar amount or a rate per hour. In either case, instructor compensation is a fixed cost and will not vary with enrollment. However, it is increasingly common to find arrangements in which an instructor is paid a certain amount per student or a certain percentage of the gross revenues received. Sometimes an instructor is guaranteed a certain amount and then paid an amount per student over a specified number of enrollments. When such arrangements apply, instructor compensation becomes a variable cost or has elements of both fixed and variable costs.

The same is true with course material costs. Rarely do we have the luxury of being able to wait until the last minute to buy or produce course notes. Such materials must often be ordered weeks in advance, which means that we have to estimate the number of enrollees. Once ordered, course materials become a fixed cost, unless unused materials may be returned for credit. If the estimate of enrollments is too low and not enough materials have been ordered, ordering additional sets on a rush basis can result in a high variable cost on those sets.

We will elaborate much more in Chapter Two on the way in which costs associated with course budgeting interact and change according to circumstances. Meanwhile, even this brief discussion shows that there are no simple formulae for developing course budgets. However, we are beginning to build a theoretical framework for understanding how the financial elements of course planning interact and how we can manipulate these elements to suit our objectives.

Direct and Indirect Costs. The first concept we considered in this chapter was the budget object. In cost accounting, there is a similar concept called the *cost object.* A cost is always a cost *of* something, and that something, the target of cost analysis, is the cost object. In this part of *Effective Budgeting in Continuing Education,* the cost object (like the budget object) is the course. In

Part Two I will be talking about budgeting for the CE organization, so the cost object will be the organization.

Direct costs are costs that can be directly and conveniently associated with a cost object. All the costs we have been talking about so far, both fixed and variable—instructor compensation, course materials, room rent, coffee, and refreshments—are direct costs of a course. *Indirect costs* are costs that cannot be directly or easily attributed to a cost object. Examples of costs usually considered indirect are administrative salaries, utilities, secretarial and receptionist salaries, rent on administrative space, and most office supplies. Indirect costs are often called *overhead costs* (or, simply, "overhead"), and these two terms will be used interchangeably throughout this text. Anderson and Kasl (1982) found that both these terms carried negative connotations of "unessential" or even "wasteful" among CE administrators and programmers. To counteract this negativity and to more clearly articulate the meaning of cost object and the hierarchical nature of costs, Anderson and Kasl defined costs in three levels: classroom costs, costs of planning and organizing educational courses, and general expenses of running the organization. However, because this definition will probably not gain universal acceptance, especially outside the CE context, I will continue to refer to direct, indirect, and overhead costs, trusting the reader to understand what the cost object is from the context of the discussion.

The distinction between direct and indirect costs arises within the context of the doctrine of *full costing*, and some of the negative associations with indirect and overhead costs have to do with a lack of understanding of this doctrine. Full costing holds that cost objects should be assigned the total cost of producing them, including those (indirect) costs that must be allocated among cost objects on some basis. I will have more to say about full costing in Chapter Nine. Indirect costs are generally accumulated (added together) in *cost pools*. The total of these pools is periodically distributed to the various cost objects in some easily calculated way.

Often indirect costs are assessed against cost objects from several levels of an organization; there is a hierarchy of pools, with one spilling costs over into another and all ultimately being allocated to the primary cost objective. This is common in continuing education because the CE organization is usually part of a larger institution. First, the institution assesses overhead to continuing education to cover the costs associated with the CE organization's use of library facilities, personnel office, accounting services, purchasing services, buildings, and so on. This assessment may be added to CE's own overhead costs—director's salary, telephone, costs, mail expenses, and so on. This entire larger pool is then assessed against individual courses.

Indirect costs cannot be clearly defined because, as noted earlier, an indirect cost in one organization may be treated as a direct cost in another. For instance, although it may be clear that the salary of the chief administrator of a continuing education enterprise cannot be directly associated with a particular course and therefore should be an indirect cost, the treatment of telephone charges may not be so clear. It is possible to count the number of calls made in behalf of a particular course, carefully keeping track of all toll calls and long distance calls and charging the course for each call. However, the cost involved in keeping track of calls this way, including the time and effort of the programmer, might not be worth the increased accuracy and accountability such measures would provide.

No course budget is comprehensive or fully useful unless it deals in some manner with indirect costs. In most cases the indirect cost rate and the allocation basis are "givens" prescribed by institutional procedures or practices. The most common methods of allocating indirect costs to individual courses are

- as a fixed percentage of total income
- as a fixed dollar figure per student
- as a fixed percentage of total expense
- as a fixed dollar figure per course or program.

Another way of assessing indirect costs against programs is to require that revenue exceed direct expenses by either a dollar amount or a fixed percentage of either income or expense. This practice "hides" the indirect cost assessment only from the budgetarily naive. The method of allocation can be an extremely important issue. Methods of allocating indirect costs will be explored further in Chapters Three and Nine.

These concepts of fixed and variable, direct and indirect costs are often confused by those who have not had to deal with cost accounting and budgeting before. Even when it has become clear that direct costs may be either fixed or variable, as previously described, it may be less clear that indirect costs may also be either fixed or variable. For instance, the first three allocation methods in our list result in indirect costs being variable costs in the course budget, while the fourth method makes indirect costs a fixed cost element.

A thorough understanding of the treatment of indirect costs is an important measure of the managerial maturity of a CE professional. As the subject is discussed further, it should become clear that there is no single correct or best method of allocating indirect costs; all methods have advantages and disadvantages. Whatever method is chosen, it will have important implications for financial decision making.

Unit Costs. Unit costs are affected by both fixed and variable costs. The *unit cost*, or cost per unit, is simply the total cost of a number of units of production divided by the number of units produced. In our context the "unit" is sometimes the course, but in this part of our discussion, the unit will be a participant. Variable costs, contrary to the suggestion of their label, remain constant *per unit*. In the example given earlier of the course on small power generation plants, the variable costs were $30 per enrollment (for now we will ignore the hypothetical cost break on materials for fifty or more). However, the fixed costs per unit decline as more and more students enroll, since each one can be assigned a pro rata share of the unchanging fixed costs. This is shown graphically in Figure 1.4. Here the variable cost per unit is depicted as a straight line (line A), parallel with the x axis at value $30, while the fixed cost per unit is shown as a curve with a negative slope (line B). Total cost per unit is the sum of these two lines (line C).

For instance, for forty enrollments the variable cost per unit is $30 (40 × $30/40), the fixed cost per unit is $70 ($2,800/40), and the total cost per unit is $100 ($30 + $70). Thus the "mix" of fixed and variable costs has a significant bearing on the behavior of unit

Figure 1.4. Unit (per Enrollment) Costs.

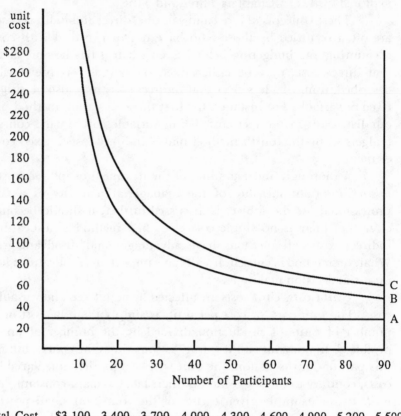

Total Cost	$3,100	3,400	3,700	4,000	4,300	4,600	4,900	5,200	5,500
Total Cost/ Participant	$310	170	123	100	86	76	70	65	61

costs. You should begin to see the implications of unit costs as we go along with this discussion.

Break-Even Analysis

We are now ready to combine the concepts we have described—revenue and fixed and variable costs—in a simple graph that begins to show how these elements interact. This graphic presentation is sometimes known as *break-even analysis* because it shows the break-even point, which is the level of volume (enrollment) required for the revenue produced to equal the total costs. However, it shows much more than this. It also has a number of limitations, which we will explore later.

Let us first recapitulate the costs in our small power generation plants course example, adding instructor compensation. Figure 1.5 summarizes these costs, ignoring the complications of fixed cost steps and variable cost changes, and adds an indirect cost allocation as a fixed cost of $200. The bottom part of the figure shows a calculation of total revenue, total costs, and the *margin*, or difference, between these two totals for various levels of enrollment.

This book will use the term *margin*, rather than the more traditional word *profit*, to indicate the difference between income and expense. For one thing, most continuing education enterprises are nonprofit, or at least are part of a larger nonprofit institution, and the word *profit* may carry a negative connotation in such settings. Furthermore, the margin on a particular course is almost always really an amount *available for overhead*—money that will be used to support other programs or cover indirect costs. "Available for overhead," used as an alternative to the term *margin*, is a useful reminder that indirect costs must be factored into the budgeting of a course. Such terminology can help a programmer in discussing a course budget with faculty members or outsiders, who often view continuing education as a "money maker."

As stated earlier, the break-even point (BEP) is the number of enrollments at which total revenue will equal total costs. This point, along with revenue and costs, is shown graphically in Figure 1.6.

The BEP is an easily understood indication of success. If enrollments exceed the BEP, we will "make money"; that is, revenue will exceed costs. If enrollments do not reach the BEP, the revenue generated will not cover all of our costs.

The BEP can be calculated algebraically, without reference to a graph, by using the following terms and equations:

Let x = the number of enrollments at the BEP
   TR = total revenue
    F = course fee

Figure 1.5. Budget Detail for "Small Power Generation Plants" Course.

```
Variable costs per student:
  Course notes                    $15
  Reception                         8
  Coffee, refreshments              7
    Total                         $30

Fixed costs:
  Promotion                     $1,500
  Room rental                      500
  Audiovisual equipment            200
  Instructor travel                600
  Instructor compensation        1,000
  Indirect costs                   200
    Total                       $4,000
```

Enroll-ment	Total Revenue	Total Costs	Margin/ (Loss)
10	$ 1,750	$4,300	$(2,550)
20	3,500	4,600	(1,100)
30	5,250	4,900	350
40	7,000	5,200	1,800
50	8,750	5,500	3,250
60	10,500	5,800	4,700
70	12,250	6,100	6,150
80	14,000	6,400	7,600
90	15,750	6,700	9,050

TC = total costs
TFC = total fixed costs
TVC = total variable costs

We know that at the BEP

$$TR = xF$$

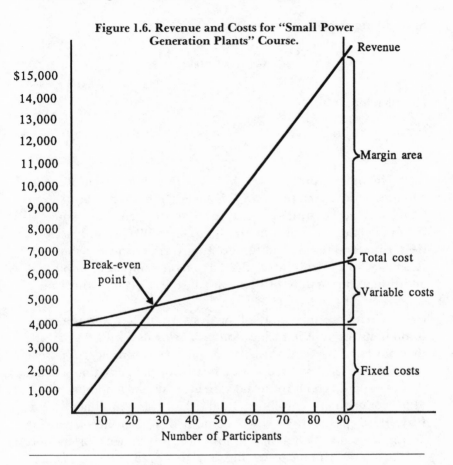

Figure 1.6. Revenue and Costs for "Small Power Generation Plants" Course.

and that:

$$TC = TFC + TVC$$

The break-even point can thus be calculated with the following formula:

$$xF = x\,(TVC) + TFC$$

Using the numbers from our example, we get:

$$\$175x = \$30x + \$4,000$$

Simplifying this equation, we get:

$$\$145x = \$4,000$$

and therefore

$$x = 27.6$$

In other words, just a bit over twenty-seven enrollments equals the break-even point for this course. This kind of break-even analysis can be quite useful in planning courses, since it incorporates many of the important variables. Where these variables (fees, costs, and the expenditures of funds) are reasonably constant, this model can yield valid results. For a more complex example and additional discussion of the use of the BEP in continuing education, refer to Noel (1982).

Useful as this kind of analysis is, it has a number of limitations. Continuing education professionals need a framework that can handle several variables at once. For example, suppose a programmer decides to propose an instructor compensation scheme that incorporates both fixed and variable costs and amounts to, say, $1,000 for up to fifty enrollments and $30 for every enrollment above fifty. This possibility, when combined with other financial decisions such as those relating to room size and cost, promotion schemes, and volume discounts on the production of course materials, creates complications that break-even analysis alone would not be able to handle easily.

Even if all the variables could be conveniently and quickly manipulated, as they might be with the aid of microcomputers and appropriate software, break-even analysis alone would not be sufficient to ensure sound course planning and budgeting. Such planning needs to incorporate certain other elements that are quite difficult to quantify and describe graphically but are nonetheless very important. Experienced programmers regularly incorporate these elements, either consciously or intuitively, when planning a course or group of courses. We call these elements "dynamic" because they represent an ever-changing process.

Dynamic Elements of Course Budgeting

Course budgets present a snapshot of expectations at a particular moment. But the world is constantly changing: New opportunities pop up, old possibilities wither, and decisions must constantly be made. Thus, dynamic theoretical concepts must be added to the static budget model to reflect the reality of the programmers' world. These dynamic elements—sunk costs, risk and reward, opportunity costs, and cost-benefit analysis—are all related and, in some cases, overlapping. A thorough understanding of them, along with an understanding of the concepts in the traditional model we just explored, is necessary for understanding the decision/process model described in the next chapter.

Sunk Costs. The term *sunk costs* may well have originated in oil exploration, where costs are almost literally "sunk" into the earth in the hope that something of value will come up. The biggest part of the cost of drilling for oil is for construction of drilling apparatus on the site of an expected oil reserve. Of course the drilling process itself is expensive, but the costs of sustaining a drilling operation—additional bit extensions, fuel, and wages—are usually small compared to the initial costs of building the drilling rig or platform. When the search is unsuccessful, the initial costs of drilling to find oil can never be recovered. The money spent on the operation is gone—"sunk," indeed.

Sunk costs have an important effect on budgeting because of a common quirk of human nature: Most of us are poor losers. To take a continuing education example, suppose you have spent weeks organizing and planning a weekend humanities conference on Hellenic Greece. You have assembled a world-renowned panel of expert lecturers on classical history, archeology, and so on, and you have tripled your normal advertising budget on such programs, spending more than $4,000 on promotion. You have set the fee at $100 and have budgeted the program to break even at 110 people. Two weeks before the program is to begin, you find that only 35 people have enrolled. What do you do?

To begin with, you will certainly view the situation with alarm. You will look at the $4,000 out-of-pocket cost in promotion and all the time and effort you have expended, and your natural impulse will be to try to salvage the program. For example, you might decide to spend $500 more on newspaper advertising, hoping to attract more people at the last minute. Because $500 seems such a small amount compared to the amount already spent, this may seem like a worthwhile gamble. But, leaving aside the educational value of your program and the loss in reputation you might face were you to cancel the lectures, it may in fact be most rational to kiss the costs sunk on this program goodbye and spend the $500 elsewhere. It might even best be spent on a program that is already an unqualified success, thus making the program even more successful and securing a higher margin on it.

Sunk costs, then, are costs that have been incurred in the past and cannot be recovered. The unpalatable truth is that these costs are not relevant to decisions that have to be made now. To allow a past error in judgment to influence a present decision often means that one simply "throws good money after bad."

Sunk costs, particularly prospective sunk costs (that is, costs that are expected to be spent prior to an indication of the eventual outcome of a project), are also known as "up-front" costs because they are put up at the beginning of a project in expectation of a return. Examples of up-front costs in continuing education are promotion costs, program development costs (including planning time and travel), and sometimes nonrefundable deposits and fees.

Understanding the notion of sunk costs is crucial to the understanding of several other dynamic elements of program planning.

Opportunity Costs. The concept of opportunity costs is largely an expansion of the truism that if you spend resources (money, time) on one thing, you cannot spend these same resources on something else. The opportunities lost by resource allocation decisions are very much a cost ascribable to those decisions, and the relative success of any enterprise can be traced largely to the quality of the decisions made about resource allocation.

To continue with our example, suppose that when you were beginning to plan the Hellenic Greece conference, you were approached by a professor of entomology who proposed to present a course on pest control for state workers and county officials. He suggested that for $4,000 he could develop the course and offer it at two locations in the state for the fall term. However, you decided that instead of spending the $4,000 on pests, you would spend it on promoting ancient Greek history. If you could have made a margin of $2,000 on the pest course, then the cost of selecting the Hellenic Greece alternative was $6,000. When that program failed, you lost not only the $4,000 spent on the Greece promotion but also the opportunity to make $2,000 on the pest control course.

A number of problems are associated with the concept of opportunity costs. For one thing, it is impossible really to know the value of the opportunities given up. The pest control course may not have generated any enrollments, in which case the value of that alternative was actually a negative $4,000, since you would have spent $4,000 on development for no return.

Another problem is that opportunities often have an indefinite gestation period. Thus there is uncertainty not only about the outcome but about the time of arrival of the outcome. For instance, the entomology professor might not have been able to deliver the course for the fall term as he promised, so it would have been pushed off to the winter or spring term. Even if we could accurately estimate the gestation period of an opportunity, it would still be difficult to compare the value of different outcomes when they will materialize at different times. For instance, should we give up an opportunity that will net us $2,000 in six months in favor of an opportunity that will net us $3,000 in ten months?

In most CE organizations, programmers rarely have the opportunity to devote any significant time to long-range planning—they are too busy planning the next term. If the short-run prospect is unhealthy, survival for the long run is in question; yet we know that long-range planning is important to the future of an organization. How then should we apportion current resources between the short run and the long run?

The logical extension of the concept of opportunity costs is to compare every proposed expenditure with every other possible expenditure. For instance, in considering the expenditure of $300 to place an ad in the newspaper, we might begin comparing this possibility with other promotional possibilities such as more brochure mailings, radio spots, or a telephone campaign. But in our efforts to maximize the return on our $300 we also might consider investing in a new copying machine, taking the president of our institution to lunch, or buying new plants to spruce up our registration office. Logically, if these alternative possibilities would yield a higher return to our organization, we should drop our plans to buy newspaper space. Practically, however, in order to reduce variables to a manageable number, we "bracket" possibilities and consider alternatives within predetermined categories. Thus, promotion cost alternatives might be compared, or two real estate programs might be compared, but rarely would potential promotion costs be compared with potential administrative costs such as rent.

Despite such practical problems, opportunity costs are constantly being estimated—consciously or not—as day-to-day decisions are made. Although they are not explicitly a part of a course budget, opportunity costs are an extremely important part of the course-planning process.

Until now, we have only hinted at one of the most important (and most ignored) of all course costs—the cost of a programmer's time. How a programmer spends time, on which projects and how efficiently, is a crucial element in the success or failure of the CE enterprise. It is ultimately an aspect of opportunity costs. If the programmer decides to spend time and energy on one program, then he or she will not be able to spend time on another (provided, of course, that the individual has enough possibilities to fill a working day). The difference in value to the organization of the programs developed and the programs not developed is the factor that determines the programmer's real worth to the organization.

Few programmers are aware of the real cost of their time to the organization that pays them, and this cost is very seldom considered explicitly in course budgeting. The *value* of programmer time is even more difficult to determine, for cost and value are not the same thing. The cost of a programmer is measured by the value of the resources (usually money) that the organization expends to engage the programmer's services, whereas the value of the programmer's time to the organization is the amount of net resources that the programmer, by dint of his or her time and effort, can generate for the organization. Let's calculate the real cost and value of a programmer's time and contrast the two measures. The total cost of a programmer to an organization begins with the obvious—the salary and benefits paid to that programmer. For example:

Annual salary	$17,000
Benefits (25%)	4,250
Total	$21,250

What does the organization get in return for this expenditure? Hours of work, of course, and (one hopes) creative, productive effort. How many hours? A typical calculation of programmer productive hours (that is, the number of hours directly spent in program development and planning) might look like this:

Total work hours per year	
(40 hrs/week × 52 weeks/year)	2,080
Less:	
Vacation (3 weeks)	120
Holidays (11 days/year)	88
Sick leave taken (estimate 1 week)	40
Professional development (2 weeks)	80
Departmental meetings (2 hours/week)	100
Other unallocated time	100
Total available productive hours	1,552

Dividing the cost by the available productive hours, we get the effective cost per productive hour of programmer time:

$$\frac{\$21,250}{\$1,552} = \$13.69$$

In other words, each hour this programmer spends in planning or presenting programs costs the organization $13.69. Of course, this cost per hour does not include a whole host of indirect charges that could logically be added. Each programmer costs the organization much more than a salary, including a nimbus of costs—telephone,

space, clerical support, administrative support, office supplies—
that cannot be allocated to specific courses. A common way of
allocating these costs is to add them to the salary and benefits of the
programmer, loading them into the cost of the programmer's time
per hour. In the interest of clarity we will leave these elements out
of our example.

The calculation of the fiscal value of a programmer to an
organization is more difficult and usually requires more
estimations. Notice that we emphasize fiscal value; there are, of
course, many values an individual might bring to an organization
that cannot be measured in direct monetary terms, and we do not
mean to diminish the importance of those values. The purpose of
this discussion is to help you, the programmer, decide how to value
your time in order to determine a standard against which to assess
opportunity costs.

Let us suppose that the programmer we used in the
preceding cost example, whom we will call Kathy, last year
produced a $25,000 margin. That is, the revenue she was responsible
for generating exceeded all direct costs of her programming effort,
including her salary and fringes, by $25,000. Her value to the
organization was thus approximately $16.10 per hour, which is the
$25,000 she produced divided by her 1,552 productive hours.

Let us suppose further that for the current fiscal year, Kathy
is budgeted to produce a $30,000 margin. Professor Laydbach of the
engineering college approaches Kathy and asks her to organize the
tenth annual conference on Rock Dropping for the Department of
Physical Manipulation. Laydbach does not want to do any of the
work for this very important and prestigious conference. He asks
Kathy to come up with a proposal on the costs of the conference,
including an amount to compensate the CE division for Kathy's
time and effort. After carefully calculating all the direct costs
associated with the conference and applying the usual indirect cost
basis to these direct costs, Kathy turns to a calculation of what she
should charge for her own effort.

Kathy estimates that over some three months she will have
to spend about 3 person-weeks (15 days, or 120 hours) on this
conference. With this information she can now calculate a price for
her services. First, she determines the cost of her time by

multiplying her hourly pay rate by the number of hours she will spend on the conference:

$$120 \times \$13.69 = \$1,643$$

Then she calculates the value of her time to the organization. Kathy realizes that if she spends three weeks on this project, she will be giving up the opportunity to plan other programs that would have their own return to the organization. In calculating the value of her time, Kathy is recognizing the opportunity cost of this project. Kathy knows that the organization expects her to produce $19.33 per productive hour this year ($30,000/1,552). Thus, the value of the anticipated opportunities that the Rock Dropping conference would not allow Kathy to realize is $2,319.60 (120 × $19.33).

The theoretical minimum, then, that Kathy should propose as a charge to Professor Laydbach is $3,962.40, the cost of her time ($1,642.80) plus the value of her time ($2,319.60). This would be a minimum offer because, first, this fee may well involve further negotiation, and it is not very good negotiation strategy to start with the acceptable minimum. Second, the calculation of cost and value in this situation represents averages over the whole year. The thoughtful programmer will aim higher than the average on course budgets, knowing that winners must offset losers. We will discuss these issues more fully in Chapter Three in the sections on pricing partial services and establishing an overall planning strategy.

These calculations can be valuable in their own right in establishing some framework for negotiating with outsiders for services. As we will see, they also help with internal calculations of the potential relative success of proposed courses.

Cost-Benefit Analysis and Return on Investment. These two closely allied terms describe a range of methods used to compare alternative courses of action. They usually attempt to quantify the opportunity costs of two or more specified alternatives. *Cost-benefit analysis* tries to compare the cost of an alternative (the total resources to be expended) with the benefit to the organization brought by the expenditure. It is usually easier to estimate the costs than the benefits, and often the benefits cannot be measured strictly in dollar terms.

For example, let us go back to the choice between the courses on Greece and pest control. In strictly dollar terms, we might analyze these two alternatives by using the following formula:

$$\frac{\text{Income} - \text{Total costs}}{\text{Sunk costs}}$$

Our sunk costs—the costs we must "sink" into either program before we have a real indication of the program's enrollment—are divided into the estimated total *net* dollar return to the organization. However, there are more than dollars involved here. What will failure to cooperate with a faculty member on a pet project "cost" in future opportunities and in reputation with other faculty members? What "benefits" would be derived from contact with the state pest control agency? How will a program on Greece enhance public image in our market? What benefit would be derived by demonstrating to the classics faculty an ability to assemble world-famous authorities on the subject? These, and many more "costs" and "benefits" not expressable in dollar terms, would undoubtedly enter into consideration of the two alternatives.

Return on investment (ROI) calculations are usually more formal expressions of cost-benefit analysis. Ideally, ROI calculations reduce the financial evaluation of alternatives to an annual percentage rate of return calculated in the same way as the rate advertised by banks and savings associations to encourage deposits. They include what is known as the *time value of money,* the idea that an amount of money can always be invested at some interest rate if the use of that money for other purposes is foregone for a specified period. A number of ROI calculation methods fall short of this goal but are easier to use. The most common ROI calculation methods are fully described in the discussion on capital budgeting in Chapter Ten. Such detailed calculations are unusual in the planning of courses at the programmer level, but a good deal of informal ROI calculations do go on in course planning and budgeting. For instance, a large and complicated program that can be presented only once may have a higher initial payoff but a lower total ROI than a program that, once developed, can be repeated many times with little additional effort. Common-sense estimates of relative rates of return and costs compared to benefits are usually sufficient for this level of decision making, especially since any quantification of projected results is based on estimate, often merely wild guesses.

Rewards and Risks. The element of risk is of great importance to the CE professional. In no other segment of higher education does the notion of financial risk play so common and important a role or risk taking so prominent a part in job performance. In fact, financial risk is so infrequent in higher education that it has become largely a pejorative term, and risk avoidance is a common behavior pattern. This attitude overlooks the fact that risk is sometimes the companion of reward. Anything new, untried, or adventuresome is also risky. For most CE operations to survive and grow, they must constantly think of something new: new programs, attempts to reach new markets.

Of course, everything we do involves some risk. Those who continually deal with financial investments understand risk more clearly than most people. They talk about the *downside risk,* the amount of resources that could be lost if everything happened for the worse, and the *upside potential,* the total amount that might realistically be gained if everything went well. Portfolio managers expect a balance in the opportunities they evaluate. If an investment has a significant downside risk, they will consider it only if it has a significant upside potential as well. Conversely, a relatively safe investment might be acceptable even if its upside potential is relatively low. Such managers seek to avoid investments with large downside and low upside potentials, and they hope to strike it rich with a low downside, high upside investment.

Continuing education professionals should probably balance their program offerings in the same way, taking a few bold steps and relying on "tried and true" programs to provide underlying stability to their offerings as a whole. When an opportunity comes along, its downside and its upside potentials should be evaluated as carefully as possible. Usually the downside risk in money terms equals the sunk (up-front) costs; if a program fails to enroll enough students, we lose all its sunk costs. Of course, we may have suffered other, unmeasurable losses as well—loss of prestige and reputation, perhaps. The upside potential for a program is usually the total income generated by the maximum number of students possible to enroll in it, less the costs of the program. There are unmeasurable rewards, too, including gaining reputation, attracting new students, and the possibility of subsequent programs that either duplicate the experimental program or are spin-offs from it.

As programmers plan programs, they should be aware of the risk factor and of their ability to influence the balance between risk and reward. For instance, the upside potential of a program can be truncated by limiting class size, which is often done to preserve educational quality or accommodate to limited classroom size. Downside risk can be minimized by keeping sunk costs low and by reducing fixed costs, perhaps in favor of increasing variable costs. For instance, instead of paying an instructor a flat fee of $500, we might agree to pay $300 plus $25 per student for every student after the twenty-fifth enrollment. This reduces our downside risk by $200 ($500 – $300) at the expense of reducing our upside potential by $25 for every student after the thirty-third enrollment ($200 \div 25 = 8$, $8 + 25 = 33$). Another way to minimize downside risk is to obtain a prior guarantee of enrollment. For instance, in the pest control course example, the state might guarantee that at least forty people from state agencies will enroll. Upside potential may be increased by such actions as lining up an alternative and larger auditorium in case enrollment exceeds initial expectations or relying on instructional methods such as film or videotape that reduce instructor compensation and do not require small class sizes.

In the continuing education setting, risk and reward factors can rarely be accurately calculated, but the relative size of the sunk costs of different programs can be calculated and measured against a rough estimate of the likelihood and consequences of the programs' success. Usually the ultimate amount of risk taking, the balancing of upside potential and downside risk, will depend on the psychology of the individual programmer, his or her relation to supervisors, and the underlying attitude toward risk that is taken by the larger institution of which the continuing education unit is a part. Usually the continuing education enterprise is looked on as experimental and innovative, and this image serves to encourage the taking of risks in return for potential rewards.

Summary

A number of concepts are basic to an understanding of budgeting, and the proper use of a budget vocabulary is important in developing a common understanding among members of an organization. Traditional textbook explanations begin with the concept of the budget object, the entity for which a budget is prepared. The textbook approach usually concentrates on the behavior of costs, describing fixed and variable costs and the methods of determining and allocating direct and indirect costs.

These are important concepts to understand, but continuing education professionals must usually go beyond these concepts to be effective in budgeting. Fully or partly self-supporting CE organizations must also project income, and often this is not easy. As the course development process proceeds, they must be aware that the meter is running—that the time and money they spend is being "sunk" into a course and cannot be recovered. In a sense, these sunk costs represent an investment in a course, and they are expected to yield a return.

Course budgeting contains some elements of investment portfolio management, including the important concepts of the break-even point, return on investment, opportunity costs, and the balancing of rewards and risks. Of course, not every programmer will make detailed calculations of the BEP, ROI, or opportunity costs, but the theoretical background presented here can add a useful dimension to the program planning process even when that process is informal. The aim of this chapter and, indeed, this book is to make programmers' decisions more self-conscious and deliberate and to provide a theoretical framework for these decisions.

We are now equipped to take the next step toward a framework for decision making in the world of continuing education, a world that is constantly changing and therefore places considerable demand on decision-making skills. The next chapter completes the conceptual/theoretical framework begun in this chapter and provides practical guides and techniques for making common decisions about courses.

Bibliography

Anderson, R. E., and Kasl, E. S. *The Costs and Financing of Adult Education and Training.* Lexington, Mass.: Lexington Books, 1982.

Anthony, R. N., and Herzlinger, R. E. *Management Control in Nonprofit Organizations.* (Rev. ed.) Homewood, Ill.: Irwin, 1980.

Anthony, R. N., and Welsch, G. A. *Fundamentals of Management Accounting.* Homewood, Ill.: Irwin, 1974.

Larimore, L. K. "Break-Even Analysis for Higher Education." In D. Borst and P. J. Montana (eds.), *Managing Nonprofit Organizations.* New York: AMACOM, 1977.

Noel, J. "Break-Even Analysis: A Practical Tool for Administrators of Continuing Education Programs." *Continuum,* 1982, *46* (1), 21–27.

Powell, R. M. *Management Procedures for Institutions.* Notre Dame, Ind.: University of Notre Dame Press, 1979.

2

Using Budgets
to Plan Courses:
A Dynamic Approach

Planning and presenting a continuing education course, as anyone who has tried it knows, is a complex process. It places considerable demands on the programmer's organizing ability. Many tasks must be performed, many details must be carefully attended to, many potential problems must be anticipated. How many courses have failed because the brochure was not mailed on time or a crucial mailing list was not received on time? How many courses have been destroyed when the lamp of the projector suddenly burned out, leaving fifty students to listen to an instructor lamely extemporizing on his subject for forty minutes?

In the midst of trying to avoid such disasters, the programmer must also continuously assess the financial and educational viability of the course. Calculation of a course budget early in the planning process is an invaluable aid in determining financial viability—at that moment. But as conditions change and new information becomes available, the financial picture can change substantially. Ideally a course budget would be revised for each new bit of information or at least would be recalculated frequently as decisions about the course have to be made. However, although microcomputers now provide the technical capability for speedy and frequent recastings of the course budget, it is usually impractical to make more than a few budgets for a course. Infinitely more useful to the programmer is a theoretical framework that makes possible the rapid understanding of the fiscal effect of changes or new information, taking into account the dynamics of the course-planning process. In this chapter we will develop this framework, building on both the traditional model of budgeting and the dynamic aspects of the process that we discussed in the last chapter.

Course Planning and Costs: An Example

Although no single, universally accepted course-planning model exists, there is a significant body of literature on the subject covering both theoretical and practical aspects. Figure 2.1 gives four examples of planning models and illustrates their diversity.

One method for organizing the course-planning process is the critical path method, whereby each element of the development of the course is plotted on a chart and its cause-and-effect relationship to each other element is shown. Another, very commonly used planning method is the checklist. A checklist merely names the tasks that must be done, usually in time sequence or at least with deadlines indicated. Here we will use the *Gantt chart* method, which has the advantage of providing a visual representation of the time dimension in the planning process.

Figure 2.2 shows a Gantt chart based on a listing of stages in the development of an imaginary course titled "Stock Market Index Futures," from the inception of the idea of the course to the review of the course's financial results. This listing is not intended to be a comprehensive expression of the steps in planning a course; it stresses steps that require decisions with financial implications. The lower part of the figure is a graph that shows the cumulative costs of the course, including the value of programmer time.

Let us go through the development of the course on Stock Market Index Futures with our fictional programmer, Cindy Entrepreneur, as she follows the steps shown in Figure 2.2. One day as she was reading the *Wall Street Journal,* Cindy ran across an article on a new investment opportunity in stock market index futures. Intrigued, she called her broker and asked him about these

Figure 2.1. Four Course-planning Models.

Houle	Nadler	Buskey	Strother
1. A possible educational activity is identified.	1. Identify learning needs.	1. Analyze planning context and client systems.	1. Set objectives and select title.
2. A decision is made to proceed.	2. Determine objectives.	2. Assess needs.	2. Determine potential clientele.
3. Objectives are identified and refined.	3. Build curriculum.	3. Develop objectives.	3. Reserve classroom.
4. A suitable format is designed.	4. Select instructional strategies.	4. Select and order content.	4. Select faculty.
5. The format is fitted into larger patterns of life.	5. Obtain instructional resources.	5. Select, design and order instructional process.	5. Print brochure.
6. The plan is put into effect.	6. Conduct training.	6. Select instructional resources.	6. Mail brochure.
7. The results are measured and appraised.		7. Formulate budget and administrative plan.	7. Order books, material.
		8. Gain assurance of participation.	8. Send out news release.
		9. Design evaluation procedure.	9. Register students.
			10. Conduct class.
			11. Evaluate.

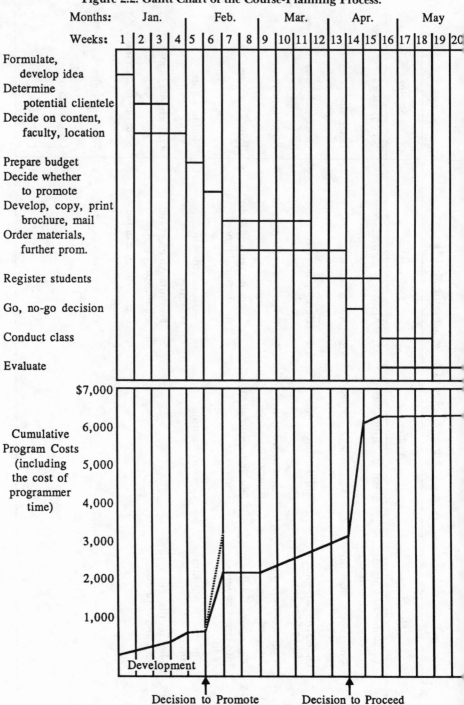

Figure 2.2. Gantt Chart of the Course-Planning Process.

futures. Her broker could add little to the information in the article. Instinctively Cindy put her own interest together with the apparent widespread lack of knowledge about this new form of investment opportunity, and she began to consider the possibility of offering a program on the subject for the upcoming spring term. Her course-planning process had begun.

Idea Inception and Development (Week 1). Theoretically, the budgetary meter began running the moment Cindy had the idea for the course, however vague it might have been. The time involved in her reading of the article and phone call to her broker represented the first costs that could be directly attributed to the course. During the next week, Cindy talked to as many people as she could about stock market futures, and, by asking her broker and representatives of other brokerage houses in her area, she identified a number of experts on this emerging investment opportunity. Cindy spent about six hours thinking about and investigating this possible course idea during that first week. Calculating the cost of Cindy's time in the same manner as we did in the last chapter, we get the following result:

Annual salary	$18,624
Fringe benefits (25%)	4,656
Total	$23,280

Productive hours
(same as calculation shown previously) 1,552

Hourly cost of productive time
($23,280/1,552) $15/hour

So, by the end of the first week, assuming that there were no costs associated with telephone calls or local travel, the total cumulative cost of course development was $90 (6 hours × $15). We will continue to trace the cumulative costs of this course as shown on the lower portion of Figure 2.2.

Determination of Potential Clientele (Weeks 2 and 3). At first Cindy thought that the course would best be directed at stockbrokers themselves, who needed quick information about this new development in order to inform their clients. Judging by her own broker's lack of knowledge, she felt there might be a real need for a highly technical course taught by high-level people and directed at stockbrokers. However, she quickly learned that most well-known brokerage houses were already doing in-house seminars and distributing literature to their employees. She therefore abandoned her first idea and turned to the users of broker services, the investors—people like herself. Examining her own attitudes toward stock index futures and comparing them with the attitudes of other investors, she began to develop a profile of her potential audience. She reasoned that those who would be interested in the course were adventurous investors, people who were willing to gamble part of their portfolios on a relatively risky investment but who wanted to know more about the market mechanics and the risks involved. Further, it seemed that this market, as well as the brokerage community, would welcome the independent, objective survey that a university continuing education course could be expected to represent. By the end of the second week, Cindy began concentrating on investors as her market.

Decisions on Content, Faculty, and Course Location (Weeks 2-4). At the same time Cindy was trying to identify her target audience, she was also making contacts with potential course instructors and learning all that she could about the subject. By the end of the third week she had formulated, with the help of several members of large brokerage firms (whom she began to refer to as her informal advisory committee), a rough outline of the course and had identified several potential instructors with whom she explored the idea of teaching it.

In the fourth week things really began coming together. Cindy had decided that the course would be conducted on three successive Tuesday nights at a well-known hotel located on the outskirts of the city, between the financial district downtown and the suburban community where she theorized that most of her potential audience lived. Each session would be two hours long, counting a twenty-minute break, and would begin at 7:30 and end at 9:30. Cindy would use three instructors, whom she would pay $500 each.

By the end of the fourth week, Cindy had spent an additional thirty hours on the course and had some other expenses, including luncheon expenses, local travel, and reference materials. The total tab for the second through the fourth weeks was $550.

Budget Preparation (Week 5). At this point Cindy knew she had better get a clear idea of the financial aspects of her potential course offering. This was an ideal time to prepare a budget. She had not yet made any major decisions about holding the course; she had not made firm commitments to instructors and could easily back out gracefully; and she had not actually signed a contract with the hotel, although she had tentatively reserved a date and a meeting room. She knew now, or could figure out with reasonable accuracy, what the course would cost to present. In the fifth week, therefore, she sat down and prepared the budget shown in Figure 2.3.

Under different circumstances, other factors might have influenced Cindy's budget timing. For example, in a course involving travel, a travel agency might require a large, nonre-

Figure 2.3. Course Budget for "Stock Market Index Futures."

```
Income   (150 @ $75)                               $11,250

Expense:
  Promotion
    Brochure                           $1,500
    Newspaper                             300    $1,800
  Teacher compensation                           1,500
  Other expenses*
    Room rental ($200 deposit advance) $1,200
    Audiovisual equipment                 100
    Coffee, refreshments ($3/person)      450
    Program support ($50/meeting)         150
    Program materials ($7/person)       1,050      2,950
      Total expense                             $6,250

Margin (income minus expense)                    $5,000
```

*Cost of programmer time of $795 not shown, to be covered by the margin.

fundable deposit by a certain date to secure accommodations; in another case, a deposit might be required to secure an auditorium or meeting place; or a binding contract might have to be executed to secure an instructor. In all these cases, budget preparation or review would probably be desirable before the decision to proceed with the course was made. Institutionally imposed deadlines and the requirements of course cosponsorship can also affect the timing of budget preparation.

Cindy really had to guess at the number of people the course might attract, but she felt that 150 was a reasonable estimate. She submitted the budget to the Director of Continuing Education, and, after discussing it with her, obtained approval. She spent four hours on the course during the fifth week (programmer time cost, $60).

Decision to Promote (Week 6). Now Cindy faced the first *natural decision point* in her planning. These points occur when a continuation of course planning, developing, or presenting means spending or committing to be spent a significant amount of money. Until now the development of this course had involved relatively little "out-of-pocket" expenditure, and the cost of Cindy's time had been the largest expense element. She could still drop the plans for the course without suffering too much, financially or otherwise. However, the moment she decided to go ahead with the course, she was committed to spending the promotion cost of the brochure, which was $1,500. The cost line on Figure 2.2 thus jumps up by $1,500 at the point when the commitment to promote is made, although the actual money transaction might not occur for weeks.

Development of Brochure Promotion (Weeks 7–11). During the next few weeks Cindy organized her brochure promotion, preparing copy, scheduling mailing, securing mailing lists, obtaining instructor biographies, and approving the brochure's design. Since all the costs of the brochure itself were anticipated at the point of the decision to promote, the only additional costs over the five-week period for brochure preparation were for Cindy's time, which was three hours ($45).

Ordering of Materials and Services; Further Promotion (Weeks 9–13). In the ninth week Cindy began to handle some of the details of the course presentation. She signed the contract for the room at the hotel and paid a $200 nonrefundable deposit. (She could still cancel her reservation on one week's notice with no further penalty.) She went ahead with her plans for newspaper advertising costing $300 and ordered ads to be run two weeks before the course was to begin. She also took steps to secure materials needed for the course. This included spending $500 for materials that had to be reproduced. She could return the softcover books for credit, but she had to commit herself to the printing of the material. She spent three hours doing these tasks. The picture, then, of cost commitments for weeks 9 through 13 looks like this:

Room deposit (nonrefundable)	$ 200
Newspaper advertising	300
Course materials (nonreturnable)	550
Cindy's time	45
Total	$1,095

Let us stop for a moment to look back at the lower part of Figure 2.2 and think about Cindy's decision-making process. We noted that the decision to promote, that is, to go forward with the course in week 6, caused cumulative costs to jump up because of promotion cost commitments. We might also add all these costs ($1,095) to that jump, since the commitment to go forward in week 6 meant that Cindy's institution had to spend that further money. In the normal course of events, Cindy would receive no new information during the later period that would cause her to reexamine her decision to proceed. The dotted line in the lower graph shows this reasoning. We thus see that the point we have called "decision to promote" is really much more than that, because there are cost elements involved besides promotion.

Registration of Students (Weeks 12–15). In the twelfth week, as a result of the promotion, students began registering for the course. Beyond answering a few questions from students and checking enrollments once in awhile, Cindy had little to do in connection with this course and incurred no direct costs in dollars or time during the registration process. Student registration was handled by the registration staff, whose time was paid for from the margins produced by the CE programs.

Go, No-Go Decision (Week 14). About a week before the class was scheduled to begin, Cindy had to make a final decision about whether or not to hold the course (go or not go with it). If she wanted to cancel, a week would give her time to notify her instructors and students of the cancellation without too great an embarrassment. It would also give her the chance to cancel the meeting room reservation and save the $1,000 additional charge. Figure 2.4 summarizes the cost situation that Cindy faced at this second natural decision point.

**Figure 2.4. Cost Summary: "Stock Market Index Futures"
Fourteenth Week.**

Item	Sunk Costs	Future Fixed Costs	Future Variable Costs
Promotion	$1,800		
Teacher compensation		$1,500	
Room rental	200	1,000	
Audio-visual equip.		100	
Coffee, refreshments			$3.00/person
Program support		150	
Program materials	550		$3.33/person
Sub-total	$2,550	$2,750	$6.33/person
Cindy's time (not budgeted)	645	150	
Total	$3,195	$2,900	$6.33/person

Note that Cindy had already "sunk" $3,195 into developing this course. If she decided to go ahead with the project, she would be committing another $2,900 plus variable costs of $6.33 per student. As explained in the last chapter's discussion on sunk costs, only these latter figures should be considered in her decision.

Cindy had been watching enrollments closely from the beginning of the enrollment period, and it was with some trepidation that she asked the registration office for an up-to-date count. Her heart sank when she learned that only forty people had enrolled. From her experience Cindy estimated that, given the rate of enrollments over the first three weeks of registration, she might expect perhaps twenty more people to enroll in the last week before the course was scheduled to begin, with another seven or eight people enrolling at the door on the first night. Her estimate of the final enrollment thus was sixty-eight, less than half the number she originally expected! Should she hold the course or cancel it?

Cindy was a veteran programmer and had had to face this kind of circumstance before. She knew that the rational way to approach this situation was to decide whether it would cost her more in net resources (not counting sunk costs) to proceed with the course or to cancel it. She now knew approximately what her income would be:

$$68 \text{ students} \times \$75.00 = \$5,100.00$$

She also knew approximately what her remaining costs would be if she proceeded. Cindy saw that proceeding with the course, even with the low enrollment, would produce an excess of income over costs:

Income	$5,100.00
Less costs	−3,330.44
Excess	$1,769.56

Cindy therefore decided to go ahead with the course, even though she was aware that it would not really "make money"; the cumulative costs, including the sunk costs, would probably exceed the estimated income of $5,100.00. When she made this decision, cumulative costs jumped by $2,900.00.

The decision Cindy faced was a common one and, given the numbers involved and the framework we have been developing, not particularly difficult to make, even though it was based upon estimates of future enrollments. In another situation, these estimates might not have led to so clear-cut a decision. Suppose only thirty people had enrolled? We will return to this set of circumstances shortly when we discuss break-even point analysis and levels of financial success.

Presentation of Course (Weeks 16–18). By the time the stock market course began, most of its costs were already expended or committed, so the graph of cost behavior in Figure 2.2 remains flat. Exceptions to this are common, however. Last-minute events and/ or enrollments outside the range predicted can change the cumulative cost picture. For instance, Cindy might have been able to talk the hotel into holding the conference in a smaller, less expensive room. If there were more enrollments than predicted, the production of more course materials, the need to acquire a larger room, and many more factors might require cost adjustments. These adjustments are important, and handling them can require alertness and even aggressive entrepreneurial action, but by and large they are not very important to the overall success of the course and do not require real decision making.

Evaluation (Weeks 16–20). Formal course evaluations can be expensive, so evaluations are usually limited to a review of student questionnaires and discussion with the instructors. The main costs of evaluation thus are usually programmer time and perhaps typist time for transcribing student comments and summarizing results. Although most evaluations concern the educational quality of the offering and students' reactions to it, it is also important to review the financial "quality" of the course and the efficacy of the decisions and decision-making process involved in it. Cindy, for instance, had to try to remember how she came up with the estimate of 150 enrollments and determine what was wrong with her enrollment-estimating process. Any major differences between actual expenses and budget projections should be analyzed to determine why and how the differences occurred. Feedback from such reviews can make the budgeting and decision-making process more useful and accurate.

Let us perform our own evaluation of Cindy's work. To begin with, study the course budget in Figure 2.5, which combines the data shown in the earlier budgets (Figures 2.3 and 2.4).

Note that in this figure we have multiplied all variable costs by our anticipated enrollment (150) to calculate margin and that we have added a variable cost—overhead—that did not appear before. A bit later we will discuss methods of allocating overhead to a single course.

**Figure 2.5. Elaborated Course Budget for
"Stock Market Index Futures" Course.**

```
Income (150 @ $75)                                        $11,250

Expenses                            Fixed    Variable

  Promotion                        $1,800
  Teacher compensation              1,500
  Other expenses:
    Room rental                     1,200
    Audiovisual equipment             100
    Coffee, refreshments ($3/person)            $450
    Program support                   150
    Program materials ($3.33/person)  550         500
         Totals                    $5,300        $950      $6,250

Margin before programmer salary
and indirect expenses                                      $5,000

Less:
  Cost of programmer time            795                     795
  Overhead ($15/person)                       2,250        2,250

      Total expenses               $6,095    $3,200        $9,295

Margin                                                     $1,955
```

Figure 2.6 is our budget graph for the course. It uses a framework similar to that in Figure 1.6 but differs from the earlier graph in important ways. Figure 1.6 showed the "traditional model," in which variable costs were positioned on top of fixed costs. In the present graph, we show fixed costs above variable. The cost of programmer time is also now shown separately from other fixed costs. Remember that even with no students, we would still theoretically be obligated to pay the fixed costs. Therefore, fixed costs begin on the graph's zero axis at their total, $6,095 (from Figure 2.5) and are added to the variable costs per student to get total direct costs. Finally we add the newly introduced overhead or indirect cost, which is here presented as a variable cost on the assumption that overhead is based on a per student rate.

Levels of Financial Success. The addition of the income line to the graph now allows us to find the several possible levels of financial success—several intersections of the income and expense lines that, in effect, represent the break-even point at different levels of cost accumulation. We are now looking at this course

Figure 2.6. Budget Graph for "Stock Market Index Futures" Course.

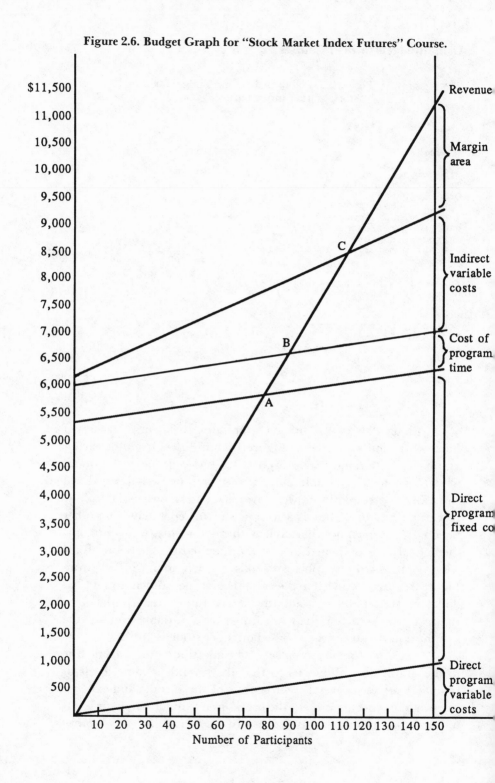

theoretically, as one that might be presented in the future, so it has no costs associated with it and the sunk cost situation described previously does not apply.

The first intersection of the income line occurs at point A. At this point, which occurs at an enrollment of about seventy-seven students, the income from the course equals (covers) the course's direct variable costs and direct fixed costs except for programmer time. At point B, which falls at about eighty-nine students, all direct costs including programmer time are covered. At point C (113 students) all costs are covered; from this point on, the course will begin to generate a true margin.

In the example we have been following, if Cindy ends up with only sixty-eight students, she will not have reached even the first level of financial success. Recall that she decided to go ahead with the course because at the time of her decision, income was expected to exceed total direct costs less those costs already paid (sunk). If Cindy continues to program at this financial level, she will end the year with a substantial deficit. If she programs at the point A level, she will cover all her direct costs but will not cover her salary. If she reaches the point B level (on the average), she will have covered all direct costs and her salary but will not have made any contribution to the organizational or institutional overhead burden. Attaining a year-end financial result equivalent to the point C level means that Cindy is pulling her weight within the organization, meeting all costs including her pro rata share of organizational overhead, but not generating any extra. Presenting courses that, on the average, exceed the point C level means that Cindy is producing a surplus for her organization.

No graph can show the dynamic elements of the budgeting process, yet these are also important. Let us consider, therefore, two dynamic elements discussed in the last chapter: reward/risk ratio and opportunity costs.

Reward/Risk Ratio. When Cindy prepared her first course budget, she took a wild guess at the number of participants expected and came up with 150. As things turned out, this was much too optimistic. However, notice that at that number she would have generated a margin of almost $2,000 and furthermore that, perhaps by renting a larger hall, she could have accommodated many more people at very little additional cost or trouble. In other words, her upside potential was open ended. Unfortunately, however, her risk was also rather high. As Figure 2.4 showed, by the time Cindy was able to get a fairly clear reading on the enrollment potential of her course (the fourteenth week), she had already "sunk" $3,195 into the planning and development of the course, including some $645 (43 hours) worth of her own time. She thus had to risk over $3,000, not including the opportunity cost of her time, to make a potential $2,000 or more on the program. In simplistic notation, the reward/risk ratio might be stated this way:

$$\frac{\$2,000}{\$3,000} = .66$$

Let us compare this program with another program Cindy was involved in: Principles of Accounting I, a small course that she presented in a local insurance company last year. The company asked her to give this course in its offices two nights a week to help its employees upgrade their skills and perhaps use as credit toward a degree. The class was limited to ten people because of the size of the classroom and the requirements of the company. Each time the course was presented, Cindy had to spend about three hours in establishing the course, dealing with the instructor, and so on before the course was held, plus another two hours at the award ceremony following completion of the course. The company guaranteed full attendance (ten enrollees). The budget for this course is shown in Figure 2.7.

Even though the success of this course is more or less assured, it could be argued that the promotion money (which is used to publicize the course in the company's in-house newsletter) and the value of Cindy's time before the course starts are "sunk" and thus "at risk." This "at risk" money amounts to $145 ($100 in promotion plus three hours of programmer time at $15). The reward/risk ratio for this course might therefore be computed in this way:

$$\frac{\$375}{\$145} = 2.59$$

Figure 2.7. Course Budget for "Principles of Accounting I."

come (10 @ $160) $1,600

	Variable		Fixed	
	Per Person	Total		
pense:				
Promotion			$100	$100
Teacher compensation			700	700
Materials	$20	$200		200
Subtotal	$20	$200	$800	$1,000

rgin before programmer time and indirect costs $600

ss:		
Cost of programmer time		$75	
Indirect costs (@ $15/person)		150	225

rgin $375

Of course we do not need this calculation to tell us that the accounting course is much less risky than the stock market course. The problem with the accounting course is that the most Cindy will ever make on it is $375, hardly anything to write home about. These two examples illustrate the typical trade-offs that programmers encounter: High risk is often coupled with potential high reward, low risk with low reward. If Cindy had a number of courses like the accounting course, she would be in good shape at the end of the year, but spending the time to develop similar courses with other companies would require the expenditure of further at-risk, up-front money and thus would decrease the courses' reward/risk ratio.

These two examples also illustrate two elements of risk measurement that are usually present in course development. The first element—the risk of losing development costs—can be measured in dollar terms. The higher the development costs, the higher the risk. The second risk, which is usually impossible to measure accurately, is the risk that not enough people will enroll. Programmers usually make some estimate of the probability of enrolling enough people to make a course financially viable. These two elements of risk are, of course, interrelated. A programmer would be willing to spend a great deal in development costs if a sufficient number of enrollments was guaranteed, as was the case with the accounting course. If development costs were very low, the programmer might be willing to try a course even if there seemed to be a relatively low probability of sufficient enrollments.

Opportunity Costs. Assuming that Cindy is brimming over with good program ideas, she must choose among those ideas and develop only a small portion of them. She spent forty-three hours on the stock market course in the hope of making $2,000 or more, while she spent a mere five hours on the accounting course in order to make $375. Again the small accounting course looks like a better opportunity, since Cindy can gain $75 per hour of her time there ($375/5) and only $45 per hour on the stock market course ($1955/43). The difference narrows a bit, however, when we add to the margin the contribution to overhead (indirect costs) of the two courses, which is higher for the stock market course because of the larger number of possible enrollments. Also, if the stock market course had proven successful, Cindy might well have been able to repeat it with less time and effort and a higher assurance of success than were possible the first time, thereby increasing the return on the investment of her forty-three hours. Assessing the relative opportunities presented by a number of alternatives is perhaps the most difficult kind of judgment that a CE programmer must make. Our "surplus per hour" calculation is merely a crude attempt at measuring opportunity costs; there are so many variables involved, including variables not measurable in dollar terms, that no single formula can be used. We will return to these concepts in the next chapter as we consider some special applications of the decision/process model in course budgeting and development.

Course Budget Format Using the Decision/Process Model

So far we have presented course budgets in simple formats. With our new understanding of the behavior of course costs and levels of financial success, however, we can now begin to use a more elaborate budget format. Figure 2.8 presents a course budget format that incorporates the elements of fixed, variable, indirect, and sunk costs. To be sure, most CE organizations use a much simpler, less comprehensive document, and they might not need some of the features included here. On the other hand, certain other features of possible importance are not included on this form. Some of those features have been incorporated in expanded option tables (Figures 2.9, 2.11, 2.12) that could be applied to budget systems that use computers. Computers allow input screens to be developed easily and recalculations to be performed rapidly. Without these machines, extremely elaborate or frequently redrawn budgets usually do not represent a cost-effective use of programmer time.

Figure 2.8 shows the budget for a course entitled "Exploring the Sierra Nevada." I have chosen an atypically large travel course for our example in order to illustrate the use of this course budget format in its broader sense. In this course, between nineteen and forty students will spend two weeks hiking in the Sierra Nevada mountains in the company of three naturalists. The naturalists will give lectures on the flora and fauna of the region and its geology. The course has been approved for five hours of credit from the Department of Biology, and a final examination will be given. For most of the distance, a mule train will carry the supplies and gear for the group. A shuttle bus will bring the group back to the starting point when the trip is over.

Let us go over this sample budget section by section, applying to it all that we have learned so far.

Description. A budget's description should include whatever information is most important for identifying the course properly. Choice of the proper description is particularly important if the budget is going to serve as an input document to some data system. For instance, if it were important to keep statistics on courses by location, say those held at a downtown center as compared to on-campus programs, the location of each course might be specified at the top of its budget. Figure 2.9 lists the number of data items, including those shown in the example, that might be important to place in the description of a course budget. (Of course, only a few items could be chosen in any given instance.) Figure 2.9 is also a comprehensive listing of course attributes that might be included in a data base.

Financial Summary. The financial summary section summarizes the financial data from the detailed income and expense

Figure 2.8. Course Budget for "Exploring the Sierra Nevada."

Description

Course name :	EXPLORING THE SIERRA NEVADA	Credit/noncredit :	CREDIT
Course I.D. :	EDP 232	Semester units :	5
Programmer :	JOE JONES	CEU'S :	0
Assistant :	BILL SMITH	Contact hours :	75
Term :	SUMMER '85	Minimum enroll :	19
Date begins :	JUNE 1, 1985	Maximum enroll :	40
Date ends :	AUGUST 31, 1985	Go, no-go :	MAY 1, 1985
Location :	SIERRA NEVADA	Budget preparer :	JONES
Department :	BIOLOGY	Budget approved :	
Teacher name :	MUIR		

Financial Summary

Item	Total			
Expected enrollment	35			
Income	$ 14,000			

Expenses		Variable	Fixed	Sunk
Promotion	$ 900	$	$ 900	$ 900
Instructional costs	2,700	1,050	1,650	
Other expenses	3,561	2,240	1,321	800
Cost of programmer	1,000		1,000	500
Indirect costs	3,150	350	2,800	
Total expenses	$ 11,311	$ 3,640	$ 7,671	$ 2,200

Margin (income - expenses) $ 2,689 (H)

Enrollment needed to cover

$$\text{Direct costs} : \frac{A}{\text{Av. fee} - E} = \frac{3,871}{400 - 94} = 12.65$$

$$\text{Direct costs} + \text{programmer} : \frac{B}{\text{Av. fee} - F} = \frac{4,871}{400 - 94} = 15.92$$

$$\text{Cost to proceed less sunk (go)} : \frac{C - D}{\text{Av. fee} - G} = \frac{7,671 - 2,200}{400 - 104} = 18.48$$

$$\text{All costs} : \frac{C}{\text{Av. fee} - G} = \frac{7,671}{400 - 104} = 25.92$$

$$\text{Reward/risk ratio} : \frac{H}{D} = \frac{2,689}{2,200} = 1.22$$

Income

Type Fee	Fee	Enrollment	Gross	Pass-Through	Total
Type 1	$ 450	20	$ 9,000	$ 1,000	$ 8,000
Type 2	400	15	6,000		6,000
Type 3					
Type 4					
Totals		35	$ 15,000	$ 1,000	$ 14,000

Figure 2.8. Course Budget for "Exploring the Sierra Nevada," Cont'd.

Item	Variable Costs — Per Person	Variable Costs — Total	Fixed Costs	Total Costs	Sunk Costs
Promotion					
Catalogue (per cost guide)	$	$	$ 250	$ 250	$ 250
Brochure printing			150	150	150
Brochure mailing			200	200	200
Paid advertising			300	300	300
Other					
Subtotal promotion	$	$	$ 900	$ 900	$ 900
Instructional costs					
Instructor compensation					
MUIR	$	$	$ 1,000	$ 1,000	$
GUEST LECT.			500	500	
GUIDE / LECT.	25	875		875	
Subtotal	$25	$ 875	$ 1,500	$ 2,375	$
Instructor travel			150	150	
Reader fee	5	175		175	
Subtotal inst. costs	$30	$ 1,050	$ 1,650	$ 2,700	$
Other Expenses					
Room rental	$	$	$	$	$
Audiovisual equipment					
Course materials	18	630	300	930	300
Meals, coffee, etc.	46	1,610		1,610	500
Staff expenses			96	96	
Other PACK TRAIN			750	750	
INSURANCE			75	75	
SHUTTLE BUS			100	100	
Subtotal other	$ 64	$ 2,240	$ 1,321	$ 3,561	$ 800
Total direct costs	$ 94 (E)	$ 3,290	$ 3,871 (A)	$ 7,161	$ 1,700
Cost of programmer time			1,000	1,000	500
Subtotal	$ 94 (F)	$ 3,290	$ 4,871 (B)	$ 8,161	$ 2,200
Indirect costs					
Registration fee	$ 10	$ 350	$	$ 350	$
Other (20% of income)			2,800	2,800	
Subtotal indirect	$ 10	$ 350	$ 2,800	$ 3,150	$
Total expenses	$104 (G)	$ 3,640	$ 7,671 (C)	$ 11,311	$2,200 (D)

Figure 2.9. Course Budget Heading Items.

Course identification number
Course name
Term
Programmer name
Course academic number
Section number
Enrollment minimum
Enrollment maximum
Go, no-go decision date
Prerequisites
Fee(s)
Schedule:
    Date course begins
    Date course ends
    Day(s) of week
    Dates
    Time of meeting
    Exceptions to schedule   (holidays, other exceptions)
Academic department   (where course approvals are required)
Credit designation   (undergraduate, graduate, non-credit professional, continuing education unit)
Number of units   (credit only, semester, quarter)
Number of continuing education units
Course contact hours
Number of meetings
Hours per meeting
Format description   (workshop, seminar, lecture series, performance, traditional course)
Subject matter name or code
Mailing list interest code
Location:
    General description   (state, city, downtown center)
    Address
    Building
    Room
    Other
Capacity of room
Is teacher compensation dependent on enrollment
Date(s) course roster required
Teacher:
    Name

Figure 2.9. Course Budget Heading Items, Cont'd.

Address
Home phone
Work phone
Social security number
Highest degree
Business affiliation
Payroll status
Title
Academic department

---

sections that follow. In addition, the financial summary shows some important calculations that are useful in judging the financial viability of the course. The most important calculation is the margin (income – expense), which in our example is $2,689. Figure 2.8 shows only five of the many other calculations that could be made. Remember that course budgets are most useful when they are compared with something. They can be used as a standard against which actual results may be judged, or they can be compared with similar programs or other opportunities for programming. If a course has been presented before, its budget can be compared with the financial statement of the previous year's course.

Figure 2.8 includes a calculation of the break-even point for each of the three success levels described earlier in the chapter, using a formula that may at first seem unfamiliar. The formula shown on the budget can be derived in the following way:

where

S = fee
E = enrollments (the unknown)
F = fixed costs
V = variable cost per person

Break-even occurs where

$$SE = F + VE$$

Rearranging terms to get the unknown on one side of the equation:

$$SE - VE = F$$
$$E(S - V) = F$$

Dividing by the quantity $(S - V)$ to isolate the unknown:

$$E = \frac{F}{S - V}$$

The break-even enrollment calculations in the Financial Summary section of the budget shown in Figure 2.8 use this formula. We could compare the results of these calculations with those for other courses or with our own ideas about the chances of achieving enrollment levels of thirteen or sixteen or twenty-six. Note that the "go" position is reached at the point where income equals fixed costs less sunk costs, or about nineteen students. That is, at an enrollment of nineteen students the remaining cost of presenting the course will equal the income generated. The meaning of the reward/risk calculation has already been discussed.

Income. Because a course will often have different fees, our budget format provides four lines for "type fee." In our example, students who need transportation to the trailhead (Type 1) are charged $50 more than those who arrange to get to and from the trailhead on their own (Type 2). The number of estimated enrollments at each fee is shown, and the "gross" amount of income (enrollments times fee) is calculated.

The next column, labeled "pass-through," is useful in limited situations. It is included mainly to make a further point about the nature of income and expense and the impact of certain types of transactions on the behavior of costs. For courses that involve significant student travel and accommodation costs that are built into the fee of the course, the multiplication of fee times enrollments can present a significant distortion of income and margin as compared with other courses. Such costs can be said to "pass through" to the vendor; that is, we collect the fee from each student and immediately pass some of it on to a vendor (airline, hotel, and so on). These costs may be necessary to the course, but they are peripheral to the instructional process and, it can be argued, do not really represent tuition or fee income. If, for instance, the students had to arrange and pay for these items themselves, as is often the case, these costs would never be recognized in the financial records of the sponsoring organization. In our example, the $50 transportation charge is treated as a "pass-through" cost, since it really has nothing to do with instruction.

Although this may seem to be a rather abstract theoretical point, it can have some very practical consequences. Consider the budgets for the two courses shown in Figure 2.10, a course (A) with no pass-through costs and an identical course (B) to which has been added $5,000 in student accommodation and other pass-through fees.

Figure 2.10. Two Course Budgets Showing Effect of Pass-Through Costs.

	Course A Amount	%	Course B Amount	%
Income	$5,000	100%	$10,000	100%
Expenses				
Promotion	$ 500	10%	$ 500	5%
Instructor compensation	2,000	40%	2,000	20%
Materials	200	4%	200	2%
Student accommodations	0	0%	5,000	50%
Total expenses	$2,700	54%	$7,700	77%
Margin	$2,300	46%	$2,300	23%

It is apparent from the figure that both income and expense are considerably overstated in Course B and that, when expenses and margin are expressed as a percentage of income, there are rather significant differences. This effect can distort the comparison of one course to another or the year-end financial results for one programmer to another. If overhead or indirect costs are allocated on the basis of a percentage of income or expense, rather than as a stated dollar amount per student as was done in our example of the stock market course, then Course B would have to bear a much greater overhead burden than would Course A. These kinds of distortions can be avoided by reducing both income and expense by an amount equal to the pass-through costs. In Figure 2.8 I have chosen to show pass-through costs as a reduction of income and have ignored them as an item of expense.

Expenses. The expense section of our example course budget (Figure 2.8) adopts the columnar arrangement used by George Talbot at Brigham Young University (1983). I believe this is the optimal arrangement for a comprehensive course budget. It shows first the variable cost per person and then the total variable costs based on the projected enrollment. Next it shows fixed costs and finally the total of both fixed and variable costs, to arrive at total course costs. The last column is reserved for sunk costs and requires that the programmer, at the time the budget is prepared, estimate the costs that will be expended or obligated before the decision on whether to hold the course is made. Most CE organizations do not require this calculation to be made in the course budget process, but, as we saw in the financial summary, estimations of sunk costs can be important in analyzing prospective courses. See Talbot for another example of a course budget in this same general format, a further explanation, and some calculation exercises.

The order in which expenses are presented is entirely a matter of custom. However, it is important to group related expenses together so that they can be subtotaled. Let us go through the expense section of our sample budget item by item.

We begin our expense section with promotion expense, both because promotion is one of the first expenditures for a course and because it involves important early decisions. Many kinds of costs may be associated with the promotion of a course; just a few are shown in our example. Figure 2.11 lists a number of other promotion costs that could be included in a budget calculation. Note that all these costs will be "sunk"; that is, they will be expended before the go, no-go date is reached.

Instructional costs in our example include not only the amounts we pay to the instructors but also the costs associated with them, such as travel costs. Reader fees are also included in instructional costs; here, we are paying a reader $5 per student to score the final examination.

The arrangement we have made with the guide/lecturer is the first variable cost in our budget. He is a graduate student who is familiar with the area and has agreed to share his knowledge with students on a one-to-one basis throughout the trip, as well as providing support for the leaders, for $25 per student. Our budget

Figure 2.11. Promotion Cost Categories.

	Notes
Media categories	
Printed	
Catalogue	Usually where course is included with many others in a large piece.
Brochure	This can be further described in terms of its size—number of panels—or degree of finish.
Flyer	
Poster	
Newsletter	
Personal letters	
Advertising	
Radio[a]	[a]Further described by station.
Television[a]	
Newspaper[b]	[b]Further described by paper name or by type of market reached—for example, trade publication, in-house bulletin, local press.
Magazine[b]	
Cost categories	
Printed materials	
Editing[c]	[c]These can be further described as either outside or in-house.
Layout[c]	
Pasteup[c]	
Illustration	
Cover design[c]	
Author fees	
Copyright fees	
Typesetting[c]	
Printing[c]	
Paper costs	
Envelopes	
Staff time	
Mailing costs:	
Postage	Shown by class of mail.
Distribution by means other than mail	
Mail house (handling) charges	
Folding	
Binding	
Stuffing	
Sorting	
Affixing labels	

Figure 2.11. Promotion Cost Categories, Cont'd.

Delivery to post office
Administrative costs
Cost of warehouse and storage
Purchase of mailing lists   This can be further categorized.
Label extraction charges
Advertising
Press releases
   Writing
   Printing
   Distribution costs
Production costs
   Actors' fees
   Audiovisual equipment
   Other   This can be extensive.
Space costs, spot costs
Other
   Displays/exhibits
   Press kits
   Hospitality, entertaining
   Telephone selling

---

shows the $25 per student multiplied by the anticipated thirty-five students to get a total of $875 for his total estimated payment.

Again, the format and choice of items in the instructor compensation section should be tailored to individual needs. For instance, we could have added descriptive cost categories besides the ones for pay and travel shown on the example. Pay could have been further broken down into such categories as course development, in-class instruction, reading fee, and counseling and advising. Travel might have been described by location (local, in-state, out-of-state) or by type (airfare, per diem, automobile, hotel, and so on). Note that if the course is cancelled for any reason, we owe these instructors nothing, so there is no instructor compensation entry in the "sunk" column.

Our example shows only a few other expenses; there could be many more. Figure 2.12 is an expanded list of possible expense categories, and even it is by no means exhaustive. In our example, we had to determine whether part or all of each cost was fixed or variable and whether it would be expended (sunk) before the

Figure 2.12. Other Costs.

Audiovisual equipment
  Film, videotape rental or purchase
  Equipment rental, use charge
  Delivery, mailing charge
Course materials
  Textbooks, other books (including freight)
  Reproduction costs
    Copyright license fees
    Printing
      Offset
      Mimeo
      Xerox
      Typesetting costs
      Typing charges
    Collating
    Stapling
    Binding
    Delivery
Reader fee
Lab fee
Room, facility rental
Security service
Janitorial service
Ushers, crowd, traffic control
Coffee, refreshments
Lunches, meals
Staff expenses
  Couriers
  Cashiers
  Programmer on-site time
  Travel, per diem
  Meals
  Incidentals
Entertainment
Registration costs
  Registration pack
  Hotel charges
  Name tags

decision to hold the course was made. We had to produce some course materials before the date of that decision at a cost of $300, but we found that we could order books from the bookstore at the last moment. Thus the reproduction costs are fixed and sunk, but the book cost is variable. We computed that food for the students would cost $46 per person for the two-week period and found that we had to place a nonrefundable food deposit of $500 with the expedition organizer. Thus the food cost is variable and partly sunk. We also added some costs unique to this course—the cost of the pack train, special insurance costs, and the shuttle bus.

We have already discussed the desirability of calculating and showing explicitly an estimate of the amount and cost of the time that the programmer will spend in developing a particular course, and we set one of the levels of financial success at a point that included this cost. Note that in our current example, the programmer estimated that the cost of the time he would spend on this course was $1,000, of which $500 would be "sunk" (spent before the final decision about holding the course is made).

As we learned earlier, indirect costs can be applied to individual courses in a number of ways. In our example, registration indirect costs are applied on a per student basis, and other indirect costs are applied on the basis of a percentage of total income. Thus there are both fixed and variable elements in this indirect cost calculation. However, most CE organizations use only one method of assigning indirect costs.

The budget format given in our example is intended only as a suggestion. It was designed partly to illustrate concepts presented earlier in a different form. Once a programmer understands this budget's theoretical framework, he or she should be able to adapt this budget format to the requirements of particular organizational situations. This format can also be adapted for use on microcomputers with commonly available spreadsheet programs. Figure 11.4 shows this same budget as produced by such a program.

Summary

Developing a course involves making a series of decisions. The preparation of a course budget helps decision making by presenting a financial standard against which changes can be judged. The explanations and examples in this chapter were intended to render course budgeting more useful by giving programmers the facility to manipulate and understand the financial effects of new or changed conditions.

Course planning involves some natural financial decision points. One is the decision to promote a course, because promotion generally involves out-of-pocket expenditure. Another is the decision, based on the latest enrollment figures, to either cancel or continue a course. Formulating budgets before making these decisions is highly desirable. At all times, however, the programmer should be aware of the continuous flow of expenditures, including the cost of programmer time, into the category of sunk costs. Considering these costs can help a programmer determine the number of enrollments necessary for a course to achieve different levels of financial success.

In addition to the "hard" or quantifiable information that the programmer must assess (enrollment projections, forecast costs, and so on), there are other factors that are not as clear but must enter the decision-making process. An assessment of opportunity costs and a balancing of rewards and risks is almost automatic with most programmers, though these elements rarely are specifically calculated.

The dynamic nature of the course development process means that any course budget format is going to fall short of the ideal. Most of the time a course budget will be prepared only once, with changes and adjustments being mentally factored in. Even so, a properly prepared and formatted budget can bring together a number of the considerations necessary for careful course planning.

In the next chapter, we will apply the theoretical background developed in this chapter to some problems commonly faced by programmers.

Bibliography

Anthony, R. N., and Welsch, G. A. *Fundamentals of Management Accounting.* Homewood, Ill.: Irwin, 1974.

Buskey, J. H. "Program Planning in Continuing Higher Education." Unpublished manuscript, 1985.

Farlow, H. *Publicizing and Promoting Programs.* New York: McGraw-Hill, 1979.

Houle, C. O. *The Design of Education.* San Francisco: Jossey-Bass, 1972.

Larimore, L. K. "Break-Even Analysis for Higher Education." In D. Borst and P. J. Montana (eds.), *Managing Nonprofit Organizations.* New York: AMACOM, 1977.

Lauffer, A. *Doing Continuing Education and Staff Development.* New York: McGraw-Hill, 1978.

Nadler, L. *Designing Training Programs: The Critical Events Model.* Reading, Mass.: Addison-Wesley, 1982.

Noel, J. "Break-Even Analysis: A Practical Tool for Administrators of Continuing Education Programs." *Continuum,* 1982, *46* (1), 21–27.

Rados, D. L. *Marketing for Nonprofit Organizations.* Boston: Auburn House, 1981.

Seekings, D. *How to Organize Effective Conferences and Meetings.* London: Kogan Page, 1981.

Simerly, R. *How to Plan and Administer Successful Budgets for Non-Credit Continuing Education Programs.* Urbana-Champaign: Office of Continuing Education and Public Service, University of Illinois, 1981.

Strother, G. B., and Klus, J. P. *Administration of Continuing Education.* Belmont, Calif.: Wadsworth, 1982.

Talbot, G. *Achieving Success in Continuing Education, A Basic Financial Guide.* Provo, Utah: Division of Continuing Education, Brigham Young University, 1983.

=3=

Evaluating Cost Options
and Pricing the Program

The model of the course-planning and budgeting process that we have been building in the last two chapters can have immediate practical applications. Sound budgeting practice based on the concepts we have been discussing can help a programmer decide about whether to offer a particular program or which of a number of possible programs represents the best investment opportunity. These are the most important fiscal decisions in a continuing education enterprise, for the financial and educational health of the CE organization rests upon them. But many other decisions go into the presentation of a course, and the decision/process model can be of help in making these decisions, too. In this chapter we will examine a number of issues that programmers typically face during the course development process, including the following:

- fee determination: How much should we charge for a course?
- promotion costs: How can we make better decisions about the way a course is promoted?
- cost mixes: What is the effect of different proportions of fixed to variable or sunk to unsunk costs?
- instructor compensation: How much should an instructor be paid, and how should negotiations with instructors be conducted?

- indirect cost allocation: How do different methods of applying indirect costs to courses affect our decision-making process?
- cosponsorship and partial services: How should we split costs and income when two or more agencies are presenting a program, and how should we price services to outside agencies?

Finally, we will discuss how a programmer in a continuing education enterprise can develop an overall strategy to achieve the goals and the objectives of the organization. Our recommendations in this chapter are based on the idea that it is desirable to maximize financial return, even in educational settings where financial return may be a secondary goal. We try to indicate where and how entrepreneurial and educational interests may be unified to mutual advantage.

Determining Fees

Deciding how much to charge for a course is usually one of the more difficult tasks a programmer faces. Of course, in organizations where fixed rates per unit or per contact hour have been established, the fee-setting process is simple. But in a less structured environment, arriving at the fee can be as troublesome as it is important. It must take into account a number of factors, some of which must be estimated on the basis of very little information.

In this secton we will examine some of these factors, including cost, the market (or competition in supply and the elasticity of demand), and price as a perceived indicator of quality. In addition we will explain why the fee is only a part of the total cost of the course to the student and discuss how different ratios of course fee to total cost can affect fee determination. We will discuss how the notion of consumer surplus can help in setting differential fees. Finally, we will talk about the value of consistency in fee setting and about ethical considerations that can affect the establishment of fees.

Cost. In the last chapter we described the way programmers usually set course fees: They first determine how much the course will cost, then estimate the number of people expected to attend, and finally divide the cost (including, of course, all indirect costs and perhaps an amount for a contribution to margin) by the estimated number of attendees to arrive at the fee. Actually this is usually a rather poor way to establish a fee, although it has the advantage of being relatively easy to compute and explain. It does not consider the market factors of supply and demand or of competition. It also may not take into account the "full cost" of presenting a course or the effects of the "hidden subsidies" we explained in the Introduction. Because costs covered by hidden subsidies are not considered in determining fees, a distorted financial picture and a budgetary shortage at the end of the accounting period can result. On the other hand, a course's indirect cost allocation may include charges for elements from which the proposed course will not benefit. For example, an in-house course for a local company may not use the registration process or the services of the promotion coordinator, so a calculation that includes these elements in course costs may produce a fee that is higher than it ought to be.

Even though the "cost workup" method of calculating a course fee is not a very good one, it is a useful first step in the fee-setting process: It establishes a floor beneath which the fee should not fall after market factors are considered. Let us turn now to these factors.

Market. To obtain a true proportional relationship between the cost of a course and what we should charge for it, we must consider the market factors of *competition* and *demand.*

Competition affects the supply side of the traditional market model, in which market equilibrium is expressed in the equation:

Supply = Demand

Supply refers to the quantity of a good or service available in a certain specified market and includes all those goods or services that can be considered as substitutes for the good or service being offered. In our case, other continuing education courses being offered in our area on the same general subject or directed to the same people are part of the supply that competes with us. These courses might be offered by other agencies or might even, in restricted markets, include some of our own courses. If the fee we charge for our course is markedly higher than the fees for other courses that our market views as equivalent, it will not matter how rationally that fee was developed; other things being equal, no one will come. On the other hand, if the cost workup method produces a fee considerably lower than the cost of alternatives to our course, we will not realize the full potential margin on our course.

It is important that the programmer consider the cost and availability of alternatives to a given course in a broad and realistic context. The market for weekend programs during the winter may be considerably influenced by the size of the snow pack on nearby slopes, for example, and potential students may weigh the price of a weekend course against the price of lift tickets and transportation to ski areas. Almost invariably we are competing for the time of our potential students who face a plenitude of other choices.

Demand, particularly the phenomenon known as elasticity of demand, also has a considerable influence on the fee-setting process. *Elasticity of demand,* in our context, is the relationship of course fee to the number of enrollments. Consider the following demand table for Course A:

Fee	Estimated Participants	Income
$80	20	$1,600
75	30	2,250
60	40	2,400
55	45	2,475
50	50	2,500
40	60	2,400

As we decrease the fee, we entice more people to enroll in the course. Because of this increased enrollment, gross income continues to increase even as we reduce the fee—until the fee in our example course drops below $50. Beyond that point, further reductions in the fee will not attract enough additional students to result in higher gross income. Some courses are more elastic than others—that is, fee variations will significantly affect enrollment. A course in which a change in the fee will not result in a significant change in the number of students enrolled (say, when it is the only course of its kind and all potential students must take the course) is said to be "inelastic."

Since deregulation of airline fares by the federal government, the airlines have been experimenting continuously with their fare structure in an attempt to maximize their returns. They face problems similar to those faced by many CE programmers. Airlines provide a time-limited service in which the variable costs per passenger are a relatively small portion of the total costs they have to cover. Once the plane takes off, no return can be gained on empty seats. Business travelers, who make up a sizable portion of airline customers, probably have no real alternatives to flying, so their demand is relatively inelastic; they will fly even when fares are high. Recreational travelers, on the other hand, represent a market with fairly elastic demand. There are many competitors for that recreational dollar, and the airlines have learned that a decrease in fares will markedly increase traffic. The combination of empty seats and a public willing to pay lower fares to obtain those seats has caused the airlines to develop strategies to retain the higher-margin business traveler and at the same time to sell the otherwise empty seats to the recreational traveler. Standby fares and fare reductions for advance registration have been part of this strategy.

Continuing education professionals face similar problems. Empty seats in a classroom are much like empty airline seats, and students usually have motivations of varying strengths for enrolling in a course. We will return to this issue shortly when we discuss the concept of consumer surplus.

Price as a Perceived Indicator of Quality. Until now we have presumed a certain rationality in the choices students make among educational alternatives. However, a number of factors may go into buyer decision making that hardly seem to suggest scientific analysis. When a buyer is unfamiliar with a product or when the item being purchased cannot be inspected or approved in advance, price may become a symbol or an anticipator of quality. This factor can affect consumers' choice of restaurants, over-the-counter medicine, and continuing education courses. Thus, if we charge a price higher than that charged by our competition, we may attract students who view the higher price as an indication of higher quality. This effect can be further reinforced by a promotion approach that features, say, a higher quality brochure or personal letters, or by careful choice of course location and instructors. Granted, these measures may increase cost and, therefore, our risk. Again, balancing these factors leads to success in course development.

   Course Price as a Percentage of Total Cost to the Student. Often ignored in discussions of setting course fees are the other costs, both out-of-pocket costs and opportunity costs, that the student or the student's sponsor will have to pay. In some cases these costs are so substantial that the course fee becomes relatively unimportant, perhaps even trivial, in comparison.

   Take the case of Robert Shakalot, an engineer who works for a company in Moving, Florida. Mr. Shakalot has determined that a seminar on earthquake engineering to be presented in San Francisco next month will help him a great deal in an upcoming engineering project. The course begins with a cocktail party on Sunday evening and lasts through lunch on Friday.

   Shakalot's company requires him to prepare a budget showing all the costs associated with attending professional courses. He therefore prepares the following budget for the earthquake engineering seminar:

	Amount	*% of Total*
Cost of course	$ 750	14.1
Round-trip airfare	680	12.8
Per diem expenses—$50/day	300	5.6
Cost of employee time (salary)	1,000	18.8
Value of employee time at est. billing rate ($500/day)	2,500	46.9
Other costs	100	1.8
Total	$5,330	100.0

In this example, which is fairly typical of high-level professional courses, the course fee is a small percentage (14 percent) of the total cost of this education to the company. An increase of $50 in the fee would increase the total cost to the company by only 1 percent and would probably not influence the company's decision about whether to send Mr. Shakalot to the course.

In addition to these quantifiable monetary costs, there are other costs that are often hidden or not measurable in terms of dollars but may nevertheless be very important to the student. In this example, Shakalot will have to pay his own price to attend this program even though, if his company pays his way, he will not put out any money. Since the course begins on Sunday, he will have to leave home sometime on Saturday, completely upsetting his weekend (his company will not pay him or give him compensatory time off for travel to and from the conference when such travel is outside of normal working hours). Furthermore, because of the time change, there are no convenient flights out of San Francisco on Friday afternoon. This means that Shakalot will either have to leave early, on Friday morning perhaps, thus sacrificing some of the value of the conference, or will have to take a flight late Friday evening (a red-eye special) or Saturday morning. Either way, a good part of the next weekend is also shot. The personal cost to Shakalot thus is significant, a further reason why (even if he were a private practitioner, paying for the whole thing himself) the course fee would probably not be a major factor in his decision about the course as long as it fell within a reasonable range.

This personal cost is important in many situations. Most people do have at least recreational alternatives to attending a course, and many place a very high value on their time. The length of the course and the manner in which it is "packaged" come into play here. Courses that tie up too much time or require an extended commitment, say, over a three-month period, might well be viewed by students as priced too high in terms of lost opportunities even if the monetary fee is reasonable. For this reason, courses (aimed at local students) that meet once a week for three hours per night might be viewed as more attractive than courses that meet twice a week for one and a half hours per night. Some programmers avoid scheduling courses on Monday nights in the fall because of Monday night football and on Friday nights at any time of year because weekend recreational alternatives exert too strong a pull on potential students.

Consumer Surplus and Differential Prices. The concept of consumer surplus is closely allied with the concept of elasticity of demand. Let's return for a moment to the demand table for Course A. If we decide to set the fee for this course at $50, those twenty people who were willing to pay $80 for the course have, in a sense, been given a "surplus" of $30 each. A surplus could also be computed for any other students who were willing to enroll at a price above $50. The realization of this fact has led to the creation of differential prices aimed at allowing providers to recapture some of this surplus for themselves. The introduction of different prices generally is accompanied by an attempt to differentiate between customers. Airlines, in requiring advance reservations and week-long visits in order to qualify for lower fares or in offering standby fares, are trying to differentiate between the business traveler (with inelastic demand) and the recreational traveler (with elastic demand). In continuing education this differentiation may take several forms, of which the following are the most common.

- *Differentiation according to reason for enrolling in the course:* Students who take the course for credit, presumably in order to apply that credit toward a degree, may pay a higher fee than those who take it for other reasons, even though their enrollment does not cost the organization more.
- *Differentiation according to student categories:* Since some people will always be willing to pay more than others for the same course, it is desirable to isolate those people in some way, charge them the higher fee, and charge a lower fee to those who are willing to pay only the lower fee. This can be tricky to pull off. Usually the best way to do it is to set a relatively high price and then give discounts, scholarships, or partial scholarships to those unwilling or unable to pay the full fee. Recent graduates, senior citizens, faculty and staff, or officially designated needy people are some typical examples of differentiated low-fee categories. Some of these categories are determined by the fact that it is often advantageous to give up part of one's immediate return in order to achieve a long-range economic or political gain. Recent graduates (because of a desire to influence their future buying behavior), alumni of the institution, and

significant potential benefactors are examples of such categories.

- *Differentiation by geographical location:* Fees are sometimes set differently for out-of-state students or students who reside outside a particular district in order to discourage outsiders from taking advantage of a service paid for by and intended for a specific constituency.
- *Differentiation by manner of enrollment:* It is often useful to try to influence the pattern of enrollment and even the means of payment by setting different fees. The last chapter's discussion on course planning no doubt made it clear that it is very desirable to be able to determine early whether a course is going to make it or not, before too many costs have become sunk. It is also important to get an early count of enrollments in order to speed up the ordering of books and materials, lunches, and rooms. For these reasons, people who enroll early are often charged a lower fee, while enrollees at the door pay a higher fee. Those who enroll using a credit card as payment may pay a different fee from those who do not. Those who enroll in an entire lecture series may pay a lower fee per lecture than those who attend and pay for only selected lectures. To encourage word-of-mouth advertising and spur enrollments, people who enroll as part of a group may be charged a lower fee than single enrollments.

Consistency in Fee Structure. Many continuing education organizations have preset fees per units, per hours, or per course. There are good reasons for setting fees in advance, but there are some dangers and disadvantages, too, as should be apparent from the preceding discussion. The main advantage in setting fees according to a prescribed schedule is that fee consistency is maintained. Students can easily understand and remember the fees charged by the organization, and they are likely to view those fees as consistent and rational. The disadvantage of a preset fee structure is that market factors, and sometimes even differences in costs, cannot really be considered. Thus, if the fee schedule indicates that a three-unit course should have a fee of $150, then all courses from, say, French 1 to Advanced Computer Science will have the same fee despite the fact that the computer course may cost twice as much to present as the French course does or that students may be willing to pay more for the computer course. Established fee schedules work best when the courses to which they apply are relatively homogeneous in cost and market appeal.

Ethical Considerations. The hard-boiled market approach to fee setting may seem, and probably is, inconsistent with the goals and purposes of many continuing education enterprises, especially those dedicated to helping the educationally disadvantaged or with a policy requiring them to price their services at the lowest break-even level. However, even in enterprises that receive full or partial subsidies, many of these same market principles apply. Take, for example, the case of a fully subsidized agency whose purpose is to provide vocational training to adults. Usually such an agency is held accountable for some measure of results—number of adults trained, number of adults placed in jobs, and so on. The agency will therefore want to do its best to recruit adults motivated to learn in areas where jobs can be obtained.

Even where direct subsidies do not exist, we are often still faced with the spectre of hidden subsidies. Take the example of the self-supporting continuing education enterprise. It is fully able to recognize in its fee structure the market elements previously described, and its programmers can set the fee for each course so as to maximize return. Certain categories of students, such as professionals, may pay a higher fee and generate a higher return than, say, students interested in cultural or literacy programs. The professionals thus are not only paying more than the other students but may even, if other programs are run at a loss, be directly subsidizing the less profitable programs. Is this fair? Is it fair to base fees on ability to pay? This question must be answered by each organization facing a partial or full self-support mandate.

It should be clear by now that setting the fee for a course is not a matter of exact science and must usually be done on the basis of a feeling for the market and the intended audience. Despite this inexactness, a programmer who understands the factors involved can become skillful in setting fees. Giving up a blind attachment to the cost workup method of fee setting is the most important step in achieving this skill. A complete, well-written discussion of the pricing of services is contained in Chapter Eight of *Marketing for Nonprofit Organizations* by David L. Rados (1981).

Promotion: Deciding How Much to Spend

We have already identified the decision to promote as one of the most important early decision points in the process of course development. The manner in which a course is promoted and the amount of money spent on promotion are crucial to the course's success. Unfortunately, decisions about promotion are difficult to make and involve much ambiguity and lack of information. Most of the information needed for promotion decisions cannot be gathered by a single programmer but must flow out of a general, systematic information system provided by the organization. In Chapter Eight we will deal in more depth with the structure of such information systems.

Two characteristics of promotion costs make them important in course budgeting and financial planning. First, they are almost always "sunk" costs and are therefore "at risk." Second, they have a functional relationship to income—that is, the amount of money (and time and effort) spent on promotion has (or should have) a direct effect on the number of participants attracted to a particular course and therefore on the amount of income the course generates.

Determination of Promotion Costs. Programmers obviously will choose the form or forms of promotion that they feel will be the most effective—but, alas, there is usually no definitive measure of promotion effectiveness. Effectiveness is hard to measure because, to begin with, it is very difficult to isolate all promotional expenditures. If we use the broadest definition of the term *promotion,* as it is desirable to do, we will realize that many line items on the typical course budget have elements of "promotion" in them. One of the most common of these is programmer time. The most successful programmers are always looking for opportunities to promote their courses and spend a good deal of time in direct promotional efforts. Often telephone calls to training directors or others with whom the programmer has developed relationships are the most effective possible promotion—yet the time thus spent usually is not added to or computed in the promotion budget of the course, even though the opportunity cost of such promotion can be quite high.

Almost every line item on a course budget may also contain an element of promotion cost. Take, for example, the item "room rent." If we are presenting a high-level course directed at professionals, we may choose to rent a room in a well-known hotel rather than use the auditorium of a local community college, even though the auditorium would serve just as well from a pedagogical point of view. The name of the hotel and the atmosphere it implies may well be selling points to our potential audience; thus, theoretically, the difference in cost between the hotel room and the college auditorium might be classified as a promotion expense. In practice, such fine points are usually not reflected in the course budget, but the programmer should consider them in planning the course.

Marginal Cost. Another reason why promotion expenditures are difficult to isolate is that some portion of promotion expenditure can be viewed as marginal cost. It was apparent from Chapter Two's calculation of the several levels of financial success that, assuming a relatively low variable cost, additional enrollments beyond a certain point will produce a significant contribution to margin. Suppose we have a course that will reach its break-even point (level C) at twenty-five enrollments, that the variable costs per student total $15, and that the fee is $100. This means that each student contributes $85 ($100 – $15) to fixed costs and, once the break-even point is reached, to margin. Let us further suppose that we are very confident that the proposed promotion budget will attract twenty-five students. How much more should we be willing to spend to attract the twenty-sixth student?

This is the concept of *marginal cost*. Since the twenty-sixth student will bring an extra $85, we should be willing to spend up to a limit of $85 to generate more margin. In other words, once we reach the break-even point, we can calculate a new break-even point for the justification of further expenditure.

To continue our example, suppose our original promotion budget is $400. We also have an opportunity to advertise the course in the local paper at an additional cost of $500. If this additional expenditure produces six or more enrollments for the course, it is worth making, since at six enrollments we would be taking in more than we spent on the additional promotion ($85 × 6 = $510).

Suppose that ten additional enrollments result from the newspaper advertisement. Certainly our original promotion plan was more effective (and more cost effective) than the newspaper advertising, since it produced twenty-five enrollments at a cost of $400, while our newspaper ad produced only ten enrollments at a cost of $500. However, the expenditure of that extra $500 produced a contribution to margin of $850 ($85 × 10), leaving us $350 ahead ($850 – $500).

Applying the marginal cost concept to the measurement of promotion cost effectiveness can make measurement very difficult; for instance, in the preceding example we had to apply different standards of effectiveness to different promotion methods for the same course. Using the marginal cost concept to justify additional promotional expenditures is also dangerous. Remember that it is difficult to predict the exact number of enrollments any particular promotional scheme might produce and also that promotion money is risk money. The more a programmer spends on promotion, the higher the risk. Further, since, by definition, promotion money spent in pursuit of a marginal return is not as effective as that spent to produce the full return, the risk associated with marginal promotion cost is higher.

Quantitative Methods. In confronting promotion decisions, programmers often rely at least partly on quantitative methods that try to measure promotion effectiveness in hard dollar terms. The following are examples of quantitative measures:

Promotion cost expressed as a percentage of income:

$$\frac{\text{Promotion cost}}{\text{Gross income}}$$

Cost per thousand:

$$\frac{\text{Promotion cost}}{\text{Number of people (households) reached}/1,000}$$

Cost per inquiry:

$$\frac{\text{Promotion cost}}{\text{Number of inquiries}}$$

Cost per enrollment:

$$\frac{\text{Promotion cost}}{\text{Number of enrollments}}$$

Number of times margin earned:

$$\frac{\text{Margin}}{\text{Promotion cost}}$$

These measures have two characteristics in common: They are useful only through comparison to a tested standard of performance, and they must be interpreted with great care. If we computed that the promotion cost expressed as a percentage of income for a particular course was 17 percent, we would not know whether this was good or bad unless we compared it either to another course or to some previously established standard. Even were we to discover that another course had a 14 percent promotion cost, we might not be able to say that the first course was promoted less effectively than the second. The first course might have been more "promotion intensive" than the first—that is, it might have depended more on promotion than on other cost elements for its success. The first course might have produced more margin than the second course, with marginal cost elements thus coming into play. In fact, the second course might have been more successful if a higher percentage of its income had been spent on promotion.

Quantitative measures usually depend to a large extent on some sort of "tracking" system whereby enrollments, inquiries, and so on are traced to the promotional method that produced them. Tracking methods are seldom 100 percent effective, however, since some students will not be able to tell how they heard about a course or will enroll in a way that makes tracking impossible. For example, some may have heard about the course from a friend, but the source of that friend's knowledge is undeterminable.

Another problem is that quantitative measures usually are directed only at the short run, calculating the effectiveness of the promotion for a particular course without incorporating the possible future effects or the institutional effects of such promotion. Even if a brochure does not result in an immediate enrollment, for example, it may make a potential student aware of the institution, which, in combination with future promotion activity, may produce a future enrollment. A more complete discussion of quantitative measures of promotion effectiveness appears in Chapter Eight.

I do not mean to imply that quantitative measures are not useful; I am merely saying that they must be used in a broad context that relies upon both the intuition of the individual programmer and the ability of the CE organization to establish institutional guidelines concerning promotion effectiveness. The use of quantitative measures combined with an understanding of the market might be said to produce "informed intuition" in the programmer. Such informed intuition is a far more realistic goal than scientific, quantitative accuracy when dealing with promotion decisions.

In spite of the ambiguities involved, risk related to promotion can be reduced, and the return on the investment of a particular promotion expenditure can be increased, when time and effort are spent in setting up promotion evaluation measures. Programmers may establish tracking systems, ask enrollees and inquirers how they heard about a course, interview training directors about advertising effectiveness, and seek information about promotion effectiveness in many other ways. Evaluation is especially important when new promotion techniques are used. Evaluation of promotion effectiveness is worth the effort because of the crucial importance of promotion costs.

Evaluating Cost Alternatives

Fixed and Variable. Programmers must sometimes decide whether to make a particular cost fixed or variable. Take, for example, the situation in which an instructor is willing to (or demands to) negotiate his compensation. He is willing, he says, to take a flat (fixed) $300 for teaching the course or, alternatively, $25 per student (making instructor compensation a variable cost). In suggesting this per student compensation scheme, the instructor is offering to participate in the rewards and risks of the course. He is gambling that the course will attract twelve or more students, since at twelve students his compensation of $25 per student will equal his offer of a fixed $300 ($300/25 = 12). The programmer must decide whether to accept that same gamble. If more than twelve students show up, the programmer would have gained more by giving the instructor the fixed fee. On the other hand, under the variable instructor compensation arrangement, the risk of loss with small enrollment is also decreased.

Let us expand on this example a little. Suppose the course fee is $75. The programmer calculates the budget for the course under the two instructor compensation methods: Alternative 1, where the instructor gets a flat $300 for teaching the course, and Alternative 2, where he receives $25 per student. In both cases we will assume that, in addition to teacher compensation, fixed costs are $540 and there is a $5 per student variable cost for materials. A summary of the alternative budgets looks like this:

	Alternative 1	*Alternative 2*
Course fee	$ 75	$ 75
Variable costs		
Materials	$ 5	$ 5
Instructor compensation	0	25
	$ 5	$ 30
Fixed costs		
Instructor compensation	$300	$ 0
Other	540	540
	$840	$540

These alternatives are displayed graphically in Figure 3.1.

In these two alternatives, the break-even point is the same—twelve students—since that is the point at which the total cost, including instructor compensation, equals income in both alternatives. However, there are important trade-offs involved in choosing between these alternatives. To illustrate one of them, let us calculate the loss under both alternatives that would result from six enrollments (shown by the dotted line AB on each graph in Figure 3.1).

	Alternative 1	Alternative 2
Income ($75 × 6)	$450	$450
Expense		
Variable costs		
Alt.1 $5 × 6	30	
Alt.2 $30 × 6		180
Fixed costs	840	540
Total costs	$870	$720
Loss	($420)	($270)

Clearly the risk of loss is greater with Alternative 1, since the instructor is not sharing in the downside risk; his compensation is the same no matter what the enrollment. Under Alternative 2 the instructor would receive only $150, exactly half of what he would receive under Alternative 1, so the loss on the program would be $150 less ($420 – $270). From the programmer's point of view, Alternative 2 would be preferable under these circumstances.

Now let us see what our margin would be in each alternative if twenty people enrolled.

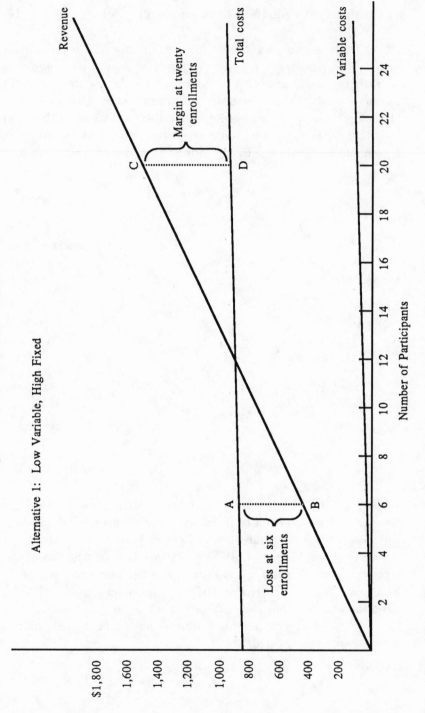

Figure 3.1. Effect of Different Cost Mixes.

Alternative 1: Low Variable, High Fixed

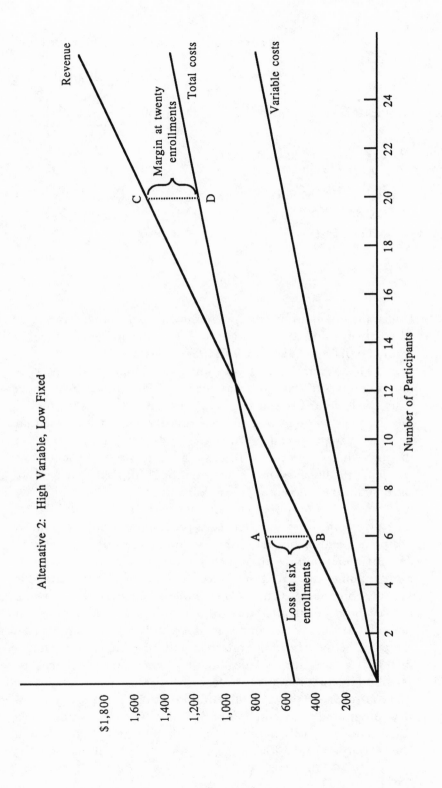

Alternative 2: High Variable, Low Fixed

	Alternative 1	Alternative 2
Income ($75 × 20)	$1,500	$1,500
Expense		
Variable costs		
Alt.1 $5 × 20	100	
Alt.2 $30 × 20		600
Fixed costs	840	540
Total costs	$ 940	$1,140
Margin	$ 560	$ 360

Under these conditions the programmer would obviously prefer Alternative 1, since the reward generated by the higher enrollments would not have to be shared with the instructor.

This example illustrates the most important aspect of differing mixes of fixed and variable costs: The higher the variable costs, the lower the risk and the lower the reward, while the higher the fixed costs, the greater the risk and the greater the potential reward. A programmer faced with the kind of decision presented in the preceding example will have to estimate the chances of achieving the break-even position and then will have to determine the desirability of accepting the risk involved.

Sunk and Unsunk. The mix of "sunk" and "unsunk" costs may also sometimes be altered. A programmer may be able to postpone spending or committing certain funds until after the final decision about holding the course has been made. If, for example, a programmer can avoid or reduce the amount of nonrefundable meeting room deposits (a good example of sunk costs) or arrange to pay the deposits after the go, no-go decision, the amount of potential loss (and thus, in a way, the risk) is reduced. In this case there is a net benefit to the program with no compensating trade-off. That is not always true, however. For example, it may be possible for a programmer to order materials three weeks in advance of a course for $20 per student, while a rush order, requiring a two-day turnaround, may cost $30 per student. The programmer may decide either to order ahead and gamble that enough people will show up to make the lower rate pay off or to play it safe and pay the higher rate when a much better estimate of final enrollments can be made, thus making it less likely that unneeded copies will be ordered.

Determining and Negotiating Instructor Compensation

In many organizational settings, programmers do not have to (or are not allowed to) negotiate with instructors about compensation; instructors are paid according to established schedules. This is particularly likely to be true where the educational program is relatively homogeneous and compensation can be based on credit hours. This saves time and aggravation but may be too inflexible for noncredit courses or courses that depend upon instructors who are well known or in high demand.

Where programmers do negotiate instructor compensation, such negotiations are often difficult. Cold-blooded dickering over compensation may seem inappropriate in an educational, service-oriented setting. By the time such discussion takes place, the programmer and the instructor often have already worked together for some time, with the instructor providing valuable ideas at no charge. It is then awkward at best for the programmer to quibble over compensation, let alone offer the teaching job to someone else who has not made the time investment but is willing to teach the course for less. In addition, many programmers have not developed negotiation skills and are uncomfortable with the bargaining process. However, our decision-process model, combined with some commonsense negotiation strategies, can make the process easier.

Options

There are many ways to calculate the compensation an instructor will receive. The following are among the most common:

Fixed Rate. An instructor is paid a fixed amount, established ahead of time, for teaching the course. The amount may be arrived at by negotiation, reference to a schedule of published compensation rates, or by some other means. This is probably the most common compensation method.

Per Student Rate. Here, instructor compensation is tied to the number of students who enroll in the class. The rate may be the same for all students, say $25 per student, or it may vary according to the category of student or the number of students. For instance, an instructor may be paid $25 for every regularly enrolled student and $15 for each student who audits the class, or he or she may be paid $25 for each student up to thirty students and $15 for every student in excess of thirty. Many variations of this kind of arrangement are possible. We studied some advantages and disadvantages of this option as compared to the fixed rate option when we looked at instructor compensation as a mix of fixed and variable costs.

Percentage of Income. This is essentially a variation of the per student method, in which an instructor is paid a stated percentage of the gross income generated from the course—say 25 percent. This method may be preferred over the per student method where the number of students is more difficult to determine than the total amount of income or where several fees apply to the course.

Percentage of Net. In this method, the instructor is paid a stated percentage of the net margin of a program. This requires a careful definition of net margin and accurate bookkeeping. Net may be defined as income minus direct expenses, income minus both direct and indirect expenses, or in any other way that makes sense and is clearly understood by both parties.

Sharing of Development and Sunk Costs. Where extensive development costs are involved, higher risks can be shared in a number of ways. Suppose an instructor is willing to develop a course for you for a fee of $500 and subsequently to teach the course, if it meets enrollment standards, for an additional $500 (Alternative C). Alternatively, she is willing to develop the course at no immediate charge, with the understanding that if the course meets enrollment standards and is presented, she will teach the course and be paid $1,500 (Alternative D). Under Alternative C, the instructor will be certain to receive $500 and will have a chance to receive a total of $1,000 if the course is successful. Under Alternative D, she is not certain to receive anything but has a chance of making $1,500 if the course is successful. Thus there is a trade-off between sunk and subsequent costs, and the programmer will have to estimate the risks involved and the potential for reward. Under Alternative C, the programmer will have to risk $500 in the hope of gaining a return of $500 later if the course is successful, whereas under Alternative

D, there is no upfront risk (no sunk costs associated with program development) but the eventual return will be lower.

Combination Methods. Two or more of the methods just described may be used together. For instance, the fixed rate may be combined with the per student rate, such that an instructor may be paid, say, $300 plus $25 per student for every student in excess of thirty. Alternatively, the instructor may be paid a fixed rate of $300 plus 15 percent of net margin. Combination methods are frequently used to produce more equitable reward/risk sharing.

In addition to these kinds of compensation arrangements, there is the situation in which an instructor is on an established monthly salary and is given course assignments according to established work load standards—an increasingly common circumstance where continuing education is integrated with traditional instructional programs. This is really a variation of the fixed rate method, but it presents some particular problems. First, it may be difficult to appropriately allocate salary and fringe benefits to the CE course, especially where work load standards are complex. Faculty teaching assignments may vary from one term to the next, and faculty may be assigned nonteaching duties, such as counseling and committee work, to which it is difficult to assign a value. Second, compensation varies among faculty, so each faculty member will have a different rate. Both of these circumstances make teacher compensation difficult to compute and to assign to the CE course and therefore difficult to budget. Also, teacher compensation under these circumstances, fully burdened with fringe benefit costs, may be too high for CE courses in self-supporting institutions.

Considerations

How, then, can a programmer decide which compensation method is best in a given situation? The determination of a fair compensation rate requires several factors to be considered, most of which are not quantifiable. These considerations involve both the programmer's perspective and an estimate of the instructor's attitudes. Some of the more important considerations are discussed in the following paragraphs.

Reward/Risk Ratio. As described in our discussion about cost mixes, if an instructor demands a share in the possible reward that a course may produce, he or she should usually also expect to share in the risk of presenting the course. This reward/risk sharing is best accomplished by using either the per student method or the percentage of net income or percentage of net margin method. The proportion of the reward/risk ratio that the instructor shares can be adjusted by setting the rate at different levels or by using a combined method. For instance, in a course with a break-even point at twenty students, we might set the instructor compensation rate at $25 per student for the first twenty students and $15 for every student thereafter. This would allow the instructor a larger amount of compensation for a marginal or an unsuccessful course, to a certain extent protecting him and compensating him for his investment of time and effort in preparing for the course, but allowing him less of a share in a successful program. Alternatively, we might agree to pay $10 per student for the first twenty students and $30 per student for each enrollment above that number. This pushes more of the risk to the instructor but allows him to share in a higher proportion of the potential reward. The programmer should be well aware of these trade-offs from his or her own point of view; the aggressive programmer is willing to accept a certain amount of risk as long as that risk is balanced by potential reward.

Relative Contribution. This factor involves estimation of the relative value of contributions to the success of a program. Some courses, for example, are "promotion intensive"; promotion is the most important factor in their success. Therefore, the promotion effort (whether its cost is high or low) makes a higher relative contribution than other factors. In other cases, a programmer may have come up with such a "hot" idea for a course that the idea is the contribution of greatest relative value. In either of these examples, it may not matter very much who teaches the course as long as the instruction is reasonably competent, so the programmer would not be very inclined to allow high instructor compensation for the course. On the other hand, some courses are "instructor intensive" and rely to a great extent on the name and reputation of the instructor(s) for their success. In these cases the programmer might be more inclined to offer or accept a relatively high instructor compensation rate and also to assume what would otherwise be a disproportionate share of the risk. This recognizes the fact that, in continuing education as well as in the motion picture industry, there are "stars" whose very appearance reduces risk and assures success.

Incidentally, the contribution of the organization to a course's success also should not be undervalued. The organization, which can answer students' questions, organize promotion efforts, and handle the many details of course development and presentation, has, by itself, considerable value; yet at times it is taken for granted both by instructors and by programmers. We will come back to this issue later in the chapter when we discuss the pricing of partial services.

Supply and Demand. Supply and demand issues are closely related in some ways to relative contribution. The same supply and demand factors that applied to course pricing also apply to instructor compensation. For many courses, the supply of instructors exceeds the demand for their services. At present this is true in most humanities subjects; in urban areas it is usually fairly easy to find competent instructors for French or Spanish or for literature survey courses who are willing to teach for reasonable compensation. In other subject areas—computer science, for example—there is a shortage of instructors. Those who are capable are often busy with other projects, so the opportunity cost to them of teaching a course is very high. Programmers can expect that these scarce instructors will demand and receive a premium for their services.

Nonmonetary Considerations. Programmers should be aware of the motivations of potential instructors and should structure compensation schemes and negotiations to maximize the potential benefit these motivations can generate. After all, teaching bestows a number of psychological rewards. Many people enjoy imparting knowledge to others and expounding on their favorite subject. Instructors may also take pride in being associated with a particular institution or organization or in fulfilling an impulse to serve the community. Whatever these motivations, be they ego-serving or selfless, they are part of the implicit equation programmers should use in calculating instructor compensation.

This "nonmonetary" category might also include an important consideration that has financial implications but is difficult to compute. For a number of professionals—accountants, lawyers, architects, insurance salespeople, dentists, physicians, and many more—teaching a course, especially one promoted widely and prominently featuring the instructor's name and qualifications, is a valuable form of advertising. The value of teaching the course to these people may thus far exceed the direct compensation they receive. This value should be recognized by the programmer and maximized in compensation negotiations.

Opportunity Costs. In bargaining with instructors, programmers should establish limits beyond which they will not go. This is called the *walk-away position.* There are two main opportunity costs connected with walking away from negotiation with an instructor. First, the programmer might have to abandon the program, losing all potential for return. Second, he or she will have to spend time, effort, and perhaps money to find an alternative instructor. That instructor may be less qualified than the first choice, which in turn has its cost to reputation, to established standards, and possibly to the direct financial return of the course if the change of instructor results in a decrease in the number of participants. As with all opportunity costs, these are difficult to calculate, but some sort of calculation must be made.

Organizational Considerations. Most CE programmers work for organizations, and they are expected to support those organizations' purposes. Furthermore, the very existence of the organization, as noted earlier, has a value for individual programs. Effective programmers recognize this value and can place their own programs and program development in the broader context of the organization. They recognize that the relationships they establish with their instructors influence the way the organization as a whole is viewed and that the organization's reputation in turn has a direct effect on its ability to attract competent instructors and, ultimately, participants. They see that there is real utility in maintaining consistency in instructor compensation policies, even if such consistency is maintained at the expense of a particular course. Programmers in the same organization who pay different rates to instructors, unless they can show good reason for doing so, can threaten the entire fabric of instructor relationships, lead to instructor dissatisfaction, and ultimately produce higher costs.

In a related vein, instructors who have taught regularly for a particular organization in the past and who have demonstrated institutional loyalty are likely to expect that their faithfulness will be recognized by an increase in pay. Increases in pay for past loyal service may serve an organization's future interests by encouraging such loyalty. Of course, an instructor who sells services to the highest bidder, including competing organizations, may not deserve an increase in pay no matter how long he or she has been associated with an organization; indeed, there may well be an institutional advantage in denying such a person an increase.

Present compensation negotiations may also be influenced by considerations of the future. We may agree to pay an instructor at a lower rate for his first few courses in anticipation that, as the program builds, he will have a heavier teaching load and will be paid more. On the other hand, we may agree to pay an instructor more than our standard in the beginning in order to establish a continuing relationship with her that will result in substantial returns over the long term.

There may be other organizational reasons for paying "above scale." Regular faculty of an institution are often paid at a higher rate than are outside or adjunct faculty, for example. This establishes a distinction that many faculty members, some of whom may now or later exercise some review function over continuing education, find congenial. There may be other categories of people to whom it is organizationally desirable to pay higher rates even if these cannot be justified on the basis of the course budget. These extra costs should simply be considered as part of the cost of belonging to an organization.

Negotiation Strategies

The art of negotiation is currently a very popular subject, and several books on it have appeared (see Cohen, 1980, and Fisher and Ury, 1981). There is not room here to develop a full discussion of strategies that might be employed in negotiating instructor compensation, but several points arising from the preceding sections are worth noting briefly.

Mention Compensation Early. It is often useful to address the subject of compensation rates very early in discussions with potential instructors. This can often take the form of what professional negotiators call "lowering expectations." It may be done obliquely, through remarks such as "I'm not sure we'll be able to get anyone to teach this course for what we can afford (are allowed) to pay," or "I'm concerned that we will not be able to pay the instructor for this course what he or she is really worth." It may also be done directly by saying to a potential instructor, "I'm excited about this course, but I'm wondering if a competent instructor such as yourself would be willing to teach the course at our established rate of $30 per contact hour."

This sort of early warning serves several purposes. First, it alerts potential instructors to the fact that, even if they expend great time and effort, they may not receive especially high compensation for teaching the course. Second, it demonstrates that there are rules regarding instructor compensation that the programmer cannot be expected to alter. This may subtly lower the expectations of the instructor who, caught up in the enthusiasm of the early stages of course planning, may begin to see dollar signs that are not there. Third, such frank, early introduction of the subject may clear the air for future discussions, eliminating much beating around the bush that can be embarrassing and frustrating to both parties.

Do Your Homework. In every negotiation it is important to know as well as possible beforehand where you stand. Knowledge really is power. The more knowledge a programmer has about the financial structure of a proposed course and about the personal financial situation and teaching motivations of the potential instructor, the more successful a negotiator that programmer is likely to be. The decision/process model, combined with the considerations and options discussed earlier in this chapter, can give the programmer a substantial advantage in instructor negotiations. Prior to discussions with the instructor, the programmer can compute the course's break-even point under varying assumptions, establish a rough calculation of the reward/risk ratio and the amount of risk the organization is willing to assume, determine the instructor's relative contribution to the program's success, and assess the supply and demand situation. The programmer should then be able to establish both the maximum compensation that the organization would be willing to pay (walk-away position) and the amount of compensation with which to open negotiations. Having established these two points, the programmer can proceed with some confidence, knowing when to yield and when (and how) to argue.

Plead Limited Authority. A very common tactic in negotiations is pleading limited authority. This can be used to gain time, to reorganize strategy, to rethink alternatives, and to put pressure on the other party. To plead limited authority, simply say that whatever the results of the present negotiations, they must be reviewed and approved by a higher authority. Since virtually every programmer has some kind of boss and belongs to some kind of organization, such a plea will sound legitimate. Even if a programmer has authority for determining instructor compensation, it is usually a mistake to admit this in negotiations. Since an instructor, who presumably has the authority to make his or her own decisions, can rarely counter with a similar tactic, the smart programmer can get the instructor to commit to a position, revealing real motivations and an initial bargaining position. The programmer can then retreat and compute at leisure a counterproposal that tries to address the instructor's concerns but results in a compensation basis more favorable to the programmer's organization.

Talk About Reward/Risk Ratios. Although it is sometimes counterproductive to talk about risk and reward ratios during compensation negotiations, shrewd instructors will inevitably force the issue. Usually, in arguing for higher compensation, they will select an estimate of the total enrollment in a course (the higher the better, from their point of view) and then show, using a very low estimate of total course costs, how unconscionably high the net return to the organization will be compared with the relatively paltry compensation they will receive. If the programmer has a clear notion of the relative risk of the course and has the latitude to negotiate, he or she can answer this ploy by suggesting a risk-sharing plan. Since the instructor has already made his or her own notion of a reasonable enrollment figure known (and remember, it is likely to be on the high side), a bargaining position has been established around which a per student rate can be set. This launches a discussion of reward/risk considerations and forces the instructor to take those factors into account. Although it has its dangers, the reward/risk concept can be a powerful tool in the hands of an astute programmer.

Know When to Defend the Budget. If negotiations necessitate a discussion of the course budget, the programmer is often placed in an inferior bargaining position. Remember that most course budgets are prepared on the basis of an enrollment number that means success for the program. What we have called the dynamic factors—reward/risk, opportunity costs, and the informal subsidization of losers by winners—do not appear on most budgets. Further, the concepts of cost and value of programmer time are completely foreign to most instructors. The instructor, by carefully ignoring or minimizing these factors, may attempt to persuade you by reference to the budget that he or she is being offered too small a share in the course's financial rewards. The instructor may also argue that the overhead is too high or that the pools upon which the overhead rate is based do not apply to this particular course. The only effective method of dealing with such tactics is to keep from assuming a defensive attitude about the budget and remind the instructor of the counterarguments. Again, a clear understanding of the issues is invaluable in dealing with instructors who insist on going into the course budget in detail.

The Effects of Overhead Allocation Methods

Early in Chapter One we introduced the notion of direct and indirect costs, and in Chapter Two we illustrated one method of allocating indirect costs to particular courses. Usually, but not always, indirect costs are allocated to cost objects (courses) on an easily calculable basis associated with the purpose of each indirect cost. For instance, the costs of a cashiering station may be allocated among programs on the basis of gross income received, on the theory that a higher income means more work for the cashier. The costs associated with the student enrollment process might be allocated on the basis of the number of students who enroll in each course.

Methods. In Chapter One we listed several common methods of allocating indirect costs to courses and course budgets. These included the following:

- *Percentage of total income.* This method makes indirect cost a variable cost and is equitable when the indirect cost pools are related to the amount of income generated.
- *Fixed dollar figure per student.* Again, this means that indirect costs are variable costs in course budgets. Where indirect costs are associated mostly with enrolling and dealing with students, this method is often the most equitable.
- *Percentage of total expense.* Using this method makes indirect costs both variable and fixed in direct proportion to the ratio of fixed and variable cost in the program. It tends to exaggerate the effect of different cost mixes.
- *Fixed dollar figure per course or program.* This method makes indirect costs a fixed cost.
- *Combination of two or more of the preceding methods.*

Trade-Offs. All these methods, inevitably, are to some degree arbitrary and inequitable. After all, indirect costs are classified as such precisely because they are impossible to attribute to a particular course or because the effort and cost involved in assigning such costs would not be worth the increased accuracy. In dealing with indirect costs, organizations always face this trade-off. Usually, the easier it is to calculate the overhead allocation, the less equitable the allocation will be. For instance, a per student allocation method burdens, perhaps unfairly, the low-fee, high-enrollment course. On the other hand, the percentage of income method may be inequitable to a course that carries a high fee but will enroll few people. Those who program noncredit courses where no records of enrollment are kept may object to paying part of an overhead pool that includes the cost of maintaining student records and issuing transcripts. To avoid these problems, organizations may adopt more and more complex combination allocation methods; but as methods increase in complexity, they also increase in cost, so again there is a trade-off. The management of an organization must weigh the trade-offs and choose whatever seems the best compromise. Programmers in turn must understand the nature of this compromise, the reasons behind it, and the effect it may have on their financial decisions.

Take, for example, a programmer who is thinking about offering a course that will generate both high income and a significant margin but will cost a great deal to put on. Overhead is allocated to this course on the basis of total income. The course budget, with and without the indirect cost allocation, is summarized as follows:

	Before Overhead	After Overhead
Income	$100,000	$100,000
Expense		
Direct expense	75,000	75,000
Indirect expense (30% of gross income)	—	30,000
Margin (loss)	$ 25,000	($ 5,000)

In this case the overhead allocation method has thrown the course into a deficit position, but—an important "but"—not to proceed with the course would decrease the amount available for overhead by a significant $25,000. If the programmer involved cannot persuade a higher authority to allow the course to be held, the organization and the programmer may suffer loss of a profitable opportunity.

On the other hand, given the facts that overhead costs *must* be assigned to courses and that all allocation methods contain at least some inequities, some form of special pleading could be made for just about any course. The programmer who constantly tries to beat down the overhead rate or avoid its full impact usually does the organization a disservice. The programmer who can understand the reasoning behind an overhead allocation method and the compromise it implies is the one who can help the organization minimize the difficulties of dealing with indirect costs.

Arranging Cosponsored Programs and Pricing Partial Services

Cosponsored programs present the programmer with a special set of problems. Cosponsorship usually requires careful definition of the roles and responsibilities of each of the sponsoring agencies and often means that considerable time and effort must be spent in coordinating activities and in negotiation regarding programmatic and financial issues.

Programmers are also sometimes asked to provide consulting services and/or conference services to others outside their unit. This may occur when, for example, an internal campus department that is sponsoring a conference looks to the continuing education organization for logistical help. Such situations involve considerations a bit outside the scope of our analysis so far, but the concepts we have covered can clarify some of the issues and provide a straightforward course of action.

Cosponsorship. Sponsoring a program with another agency can have real advantages, and programmers should be alert to cosponsorship opportunities. Often continuing education enterprises can gain market exposure and reach special markets easily and cheaply through cosponsorship arrangements. Other agencies often possess the subject matter knowledge required to organize the content of a course and the ability to attract competent instructors. For instance, the local Department of Public Health may have considerable experience in dealing with alcohol abuse in the community. It may welcome another qualified agency's offer to present a public course on alcohol problems and, because education is one of its missions, might want to lend its name and its support to such a program.

The issues involved in arriving at a cosponsorship agreement are usually fairly clear:

- Which agency will do what, when?
- Which agency will pay for what, when?
- How will student enrollments and processing be handled? Who will collect the money?

- How will the decision about holding the course be reached? Who will make the decision, on what basis? If the decision is to be made jointly, what process will be used to arrive at the decision?
- How will losses or margins be divided, and by what date will settlement take place?

Working out the first issue usually involves a realistic appraisal of the strengths and weaknesses of each agency and the coordination of contributions to ensure the success of the program. This is a necessary preliminary to working out financial arrangements, since they will normally hinge partly on the relative contributions of each agency.

The third issue is really an elaboration of the first, but it is important. The agency to whom the student must send the course fee is more likely to be identified with the course than other cosponsors, but such an identity carries the cost of handling enrollments with it, and this cost (normally covered through an overhead allocation) should be included in the overall financial arrangement.

Working out financial arrangements is usually the most difficult and time-consuming issue confronting cosponsors. Defining financial relationships tends to aid in defining programmatic relationships; the two are intertwined.

A desirable first step is the preparation of a course budget. This budget should be prepared in as much detail as possible, preferably in a format similar to that shown in Chapter Two. Initially the goal should be simply to list all costs and all sources of income, regardless of which agency is ultimately made responsible for them. Costs should include the costs of programmer time, programmer clerical support, and staff time as well as the cost of the time of those from the agency who will be involved in the program. In some situations it may also be appropriate to include the value of programmer time, although this concept is sometimes difficult to explain. In addition, it is usually appropriate to have the initial budget provide for indirect costs at whatever rate and upon whatever basis each of the sponsors customarily uses. This at least puts the overhead issue on the table for consideration and can help the negotiators arrive at an equitable arrangement.

After the initial budget is drawn up and presented to each party, the responsibilities and separate contributions can be assigned. At this point it is sometimes useful for all parties to agree to exclude certain costs from the calculation. Prime candidates for exclusion are costs that are relatively equal in value and costs that present potentially controversial points. For example, where staff effort will be contributed in roughly equal amounts by both agencies, the cost of staff time is often excluded from the direct cost base for the purposes of coming to an agreement, although it certainly should not be ignored in the independent calculation the programmer must make to determine the financial viability of the course. Overhead elements, because of the built-in inequities previously mentioned and because of a lack of comparable cost pools and allocation bases, are also often eliminated from the financial agreement. When this happens, the programmer should make sure that the respective organizations are sharing the cost of functions used by the program but which, under normal circumstances, would be included under the overhead allocation.

For instance, usually one agency or the other takes responsibility for enrolling the students. If the cost of enrolling students is normally charged to the program through overhead allocation and if, in the sponsorship negotiations, the parties agree to eliminate overhead rates, then the enrolling agency will not be compensated for the cost of enrolling the students. This cost could be put back into the calculation as a direct cost, say of $15 per student, by mutual agreement. In any event, the programmer should plan if at all possible to recapture any costs given up before calculating the bottom line, the eventual return to the organization.

Often cosponsorship involves extensive negotiations. Many of the negotiation strategies and considerations described in our discussion of instructor compensation are also applicable to cosponsored programs. Certainly reward/risk ratios are involved. Which agency puts up what, when, is crucial. To equalize the risk and to avoid inequities caused by incorrect estimates of costs, agencies will often agree to bear the risk equally or in fixed proportions, regardless of which agency actually pays the cost, and settle up at the completion of the course when all cost figures are in. If this kind of arrangement is not in place, great care should be paid to the distribution of sunk, fixed, and variable costs and their effect on the possible outcomes of the course.

The concept of relative contribution is also very important in these negotiations. Although hard dollars and cents contributions can be easily specified, the value of the name and reputation of the agencies involved or of access to a particular mailing list or newsletter are much harder to describe in monetary terms. As a rule, continuing education enterprises, especially those associated with institutions, tend to sell themselves too cheaply, undervaluing the marketing advantages that a cosponsored program will enjoy by being associated with the name and reputation of their institution.

Deciding in advance how the final decision about holding the course will be reached is very important. Cosponsoring agencies are likely to have unequal stakes in the success of the program. In addition to differences in financial investment and in the share of financial risks, the risks of embarrassment and loss of reputation that the organizations run may be quite different. Take, for instance, the situation in which two agencies are cosponsoring a large national conference on alcohol abuse. One is a continuing education arm of a local university, and the other is a large community hospital with the reputation of having one of the most successful alcohol treatment centers in the country. Leaders in the field from all over the country have been invited to present papers and serve on panels. The success of the program is much more likely to be important to the hospital's reputation than to that of the university. The embarrassment of contacting all the invited participants and informing them of a cancellation of the conference, after having prevailed upon them to organize their schedules with the conference in mind, is bound to have far more negative ramifications for the hospital than for the university. Thus the hospital's impulse to "save" the conference, even in the face of financial disaster, would be much stronger than the university's. This built-in conflict should be fully explored ahead of time, and both parties should have a clear and explicit understanding about how and under what circumstances the conference will be cancelled.

The easiest way is to agree that enrollments must reach a certain figure by an established date or the course will be cancelled.

The final financial question to be resolved concerns the division of the residual loss or margin on the conference. We have already discussed most of the factors to be considered in deciding upon an equitable split. Usually division formulae require that each agency be compensated for costs incurred on behalf of the program and that the residual (either plus or minus) be allocated on a percentage basis. This obviously requires a clear definition of costs and careful bookkeeping. Whatever division method is used—percentage of gross income, per student amount, percentage of expense contribution, or others—an initial meeting of the minds between the two agencies is required. A programmer informed by our previous discussions and the decision/process model will be able to sort out the issues quickly and see clearly where institutional self-interest lies.

Partial Services. The issues involved in the pricing of partial services are very similar to those connected with cosponsorship. In many organizational settings the continuing education function is involved with a wide range of related activities, from managing conference facilities and hotels or dormitories to providing audiovisual services to the parent organization. A common service allied with the development of courses has to do with conference logistics. Agencies that regularly provide this service, handling the hundreds of details involved in presenting a conference, usually have the financing of the activity well worked out. The conference service may be subsidized by outside funds, through a user tax such as a particular amount per conference participant, or through direct recharges according to published rate schedules. On the other hand, for those continuing education enterprises, and particularly for those programmers, who do not provide conference services on a regular basis, a request for help in planning and organizing a conference raises particular problems. Most of those who request help with conferences—say, an eminent faculty member who wants to host a national conference on campus—have no idea what is involved in organizing conferences or what it costs. In fact, being enthusiastic about the prestige and honor such a conference will bring to the campus, they will often expect that the institution,

specifically the continuing education organization, will at least
partially subsidize the conference by providing organization services
more or less free of charge.

Faced with this situation, the programmer must be careful to
detail all the costs involved even if, in the end, some subsidy is
required. First, the programmer will have to develop some estimate
of the demands such a conference will make on the time of people
in his or her organization. The cost and the value of each person's
time should then be calculated in the way we described in Chapter
One. The programmer should bear in mind that although the
concept of the *cost* of an employee's time is usually understood by
outsiders, the concept of the *value* of time, really a way of
establishing a value for the opportunity costs involved, is much less
likely to be appreciated. He or she may have to explain that "doing
conferences," by soaking up what otherwise would be margin-
productive time, can destroy the financial performance of a
programmer or a continuing education enterprise unless these
opportunity costs are covered.

This last point can be illustrated in another way. Often
conferences are subsidized by gift or grant money, and many
continuing education organizations are involved with federal or
state contracts and grants. A usual characteristic of such contracts
is that the organization cannot "make money" on them. They are
usually cost reimbursable: A contract provision specifies that the
government will pay only what it costs to present the course or
program. Costs incurred prior to the awarding of the grant or
contract, particularly the costs associated with proposal preparation, usually are not reimbursable. Thus, such contracts usually are
net losers. They may help to hold staff together during hard times
by subsidizing payroll costs, but over the long run, unless they lead
to income-productive activity, they will hurt the organization.

The first caution in pricing partial services, then, is to be
aware of opportunity costs, which often can be conveniently
expressed as the value of time. The second caution is to make sure
that the full pro rata share of overhead costs is being considered.
This is often difficult for a programmer, who may not know how
overhead rates are calculated. Proper pricing of partial services
demands not only a knowledge of how overhead rates work but also

a detailed understanding of the actual costs of providing the services. For instance, let us say that the Center for the Study of Irrelevant Information in Society approaches a programmer and asks that the participants in an upcoming conference cosponsored by the Center be awarded continuing education units (ceu), which the continuing education organization records on student record cards. The director of the Center asks the programmer how much it will cost to perform this service. The programmer is at a loss. He knows that he is charged $25 per student in courses that he organizes, but he also knows that this charge covers all student processing, including enrollment, money collection, and so on. The proper way to calculate this cost from a cost accounting standpoint is to identify the appropriate cost pool, which in this case may be a portion of the salary and benefits of the person who maintains student records plus an amount for related supplies and other expenses including supervisorial time, and divide the resulting sum by the total number of ceu's granted in the time period covered by the costs. Usually this kind of detailed calculation is beyond the expertise of the individual programmer, who would have to consult with the person responsible for finances to obtain a fair rate. The programmer may be able to avoid having to make the calculation simply by naming a rate adequate or more than adequate to cover the cost—say, in this case, the full $25 per student.

Developing an Overall Strategy

Until now this part of the book has dealt primarily with the economics and decision-making processes related to single courses. However, most programmers are involved with the development of many courses throughout the year and will be held financially accountable on an annual basis. Although most decisions made in dealing with a block of courses involve the same sort of reasoning needed for handling a single course, there are some additional considerations worth noting.

Faced with an appropriately negotiated budgetary goal, that is, a goal set high enough to stretch performance but low enough to be reasonably attainable, the programmer must make some hard choices about how to invest the available resources, particularly his or her own time and effort. In many situations this requires a balancing act of some complexity.

The first balance that must be struck is the one between adventure and safety. In any group of potential programs there are some that are tried and true, attract thirty enrollments term after term, and take almost no time to set up. These are like money in the bank—for awhile. Every experienced programmer knows how quickly and suddenly the market for a particular course or group of courses can turn down. For example, single-day management training seminars showed a sharp decline in the 1980–1982 recession as corporate training budgets dried up. As the dollar strengthened in early 1983, the bottom dropped out of most domestic English as a Second Language programs. As they view these market vicissitudes, wise programmers learn constantly to look for new markets, new programs. Entering any new area involves higher risk in the short run, but the riskiest strategy of all is to depend on traditional winners to keep on being winners. Thus the best strategy is to spend part of the available resources on the new and untried while relying on the more tested courses to provide the short-run floor of stability that is necessary for confident adventuring.

The programmer should have an overall plan into which to fit the opportunities that present themselves. Part of that plan should be an internal allocation of "venture capital" or "risk capital" for new programs or ideas. This may be expressed in terms of person-hours or number of programs rather than dollars. The size of the proportion devoted to these new schemes will vary from programmer to programmer, but if it grows so large that failure of the new programs would seriously jeopardize the position of the programmer or imperil the financial position of the enterprise, then the programmer had better gain the consent of superiors before proceeding. Most enlightened organizations recognize the need for risk taking and will provide the latitude for it; but just as individual programmers must balance risk and stability within a specific program group, so must the organization balance the overall quantity of risk.

A balance must also be struck between long-term and short-term goals. For example, we spoke earlier about the potential effectiveness of a programmer's personal involvement in the promotional effort for a course. Normally this is a short-term project—but in the process of chasing down enrollments, the programmer may be making contacts or running across ideas that will aid future programming efforts. The allocation of time between current operations and long-term planning and research and development is done most effectively as a result of a conscious plan.

Summary

Many programmers may feel that the discussion in this chapter contained more description and detail than was necessary or even useful. If a programmer had to calculate the fee, negotiate instructor compensation, evaluate promotion effectiveness, consider the pros and cons of making each cost element either fixed or variable, and determine the effects of overhead allocation methods for every course, there would be little time for the other parts of the development process. In real life, institutions usually work out policies and practices to make financial decisions about courses relatively easy and uniform, so many of these decisions will be made by the institution rather than the programmer. Similarly, the evaluation of promotion effectiveness is usually dependent on an organization-wide accumulation of tracking data and information on promotion costs (see Chapter Eight), and overhead allocation schemes are generally planned by management to meet organization goals (see Chapter Nine). Nonetheless, programmers do sometimes have to make some of these decisions, and doing so competently requires not only an understanding of the situation involving a particular course but also a broader knowledge of the possible, of the practices in other institutions and the theoretical background behind locally prescribed options. Special situations such as cosponsorship may also call on this deeper understanding.

The preceding three chapters were intended to present programmers with a comprehensive understanding of the economics involved in budgeting and accounting for individual courses of instruction. Such an understanding cannot be complete, however, without the additional understanding of the principles and considerations that go into the development of an overall budgeting system for the continuing education organization. Such an understanding allows the programmer to place in an appropriate context the decisions that have to be made. The next part of this book takes up these broader considerations.

Bibliography

Bagge, I. G. "Promotion: Extending the Market Mix." *Continuum,* 1983, *47* (4), 30–41.

Cohen, H. *You Can Negotiate Anything.* Secaucus, N.J.: Lyle Stuart, 1980.

Farlow, H. *Publicizing and Promoting Programs.* New York: McGraw-Hill, 1979.

Fisher, R., and Ury, W. *Getting to Yes.* New York: Penguin Books, 1981.

Lamoureaux, M. E. "A Review of Pricing Theories and Procedures for Continuing Education Programmers and Administrators." Unpublished manuscript, 1979.

McGee, J. A., and Ward, C. S. "You Guys Don't Pay Enough." *Continuum,* 1981, *46* (1), 25–27.

Prakash, P. "Cost-Benefit Approach to Capital Expenditure." In G. Zaltman (ed.), *Management Principles for Nonprofit Agencies and Organizations.* New York: AMACOM, 1979.

Rados, D. L. *Marketing for Nonprofit Organizations.* Boston: Auburn House, 1981.

⟾ *Part Two* ⟾

Budgeting for the Continuing Education Organization

This part of the book is designed for readers who are responsible for directing a continuing education organization. This would include deans and directors of such organizations and also their budget and financial managers and business managers. (In our discussion we will use the term *director* to refer to all people in charge of CE organizations.) This part might also be of interest to those in higher authority to whom the head of continuing education reports, and to the appropriate budget or fiscal officer of the larger institution. As pointed out in the Introduction, higher authorities are increasingly concerned with continuing education as it steadily grows in importance as both a possible source of funds and a possible problem area.

This part builds upon the foundation laid in Part One and assumes a knowledge of the concepts covered in that part, particularly the decision/process model. Most elements of this model can be applied to the continuing education organization as a whole as well as to individual courses, as we will show.

After reading this part, you should be able to

- plan a comprehensive budgeting system for a continuing education organization;

133

- establish an effective budgeting process in your organization;
- establish an effective budget monitoring (feedback) system and a system of meaningful financial reporting; and
- understand the effects of the budgeting process on the organization.

Chapter Four begins by describing the environmental factors that influence the structure and usefulness of the budgeting process in a CE organization. It then discusses several preliminary decisions that must be made before a budget system can be introduced or changed.

Chapter Five discusses the first steps in the budgeting process—the setting of targets and the issuing of the budget call. It provides examples of budget preparation worksheets and discusses the mechanics of the initial preparation of the budget.

Chapter Six covers the remaining, "interactional" steps of the budgeting process. The importance of negotiation is discussed, and some budget strategies commonly used by programmers are described. The process of coordination and review is then covered in some detail, as are final approval and the presentation of the budget to higher authority, including presentation strategies and preparation for reactions from superiors. Finally, we discuss the importance of the distribution of the budget.

Chapter Seven is devoted to the extensive and complex last "step" in the budgeting process, feedback and control. Several considerations and criteria for designing a feedback system are discussed first, followed by a description of characteristics that have a bearing on the form of the budgeting process common to most CE organizations. Then control in two budget contexts—fixed resource and variable resource—is discussed. We use several examples to illustrate statement presentation at different levels of the organization. We then explore the concept of analysis of variance and illustrate procedures for calculating a number of variances. This discussion leads naturally to a discussion of variable (flexible) budgets and the introduction of flexibility in budgeting.

Part Three will cover special applications of the concepts we have learned.

4

Establishing
an Effective
Budgetary System

Budgeting for an organization is much more difficult and less precise than budgeting for a course because it involves more complex issues, particularly issues of human behavior. In Part One we discussed mainly the behavior of costs; in this part we will talk mainly about the behavior of *people* under a budgetary system.

As we mentioned in the Introduction, the budget serves an important integrating function in effective organizations. It links the managerial concerns of planning, organizing, controlling, and motivating in a way visible to everyone in the organization. The budget is not only involved in the reward system but (at its best) is an important communication tool, helping both supervisor and subordinate sharpen goals and objectives, lay out plans and implementation strategies, and evaluate success or failure.

The pervasiveness of the budgeting process in organizational life means that the establishment of a new budget system or changes in an existing system must be planned carefully by the organization's leaders. They must consider environmental factors that affect the budgeting process and then make basic decisions about the budget system's structure and roles in the organization.

Sooner or later, all organizations face the need to establish or change their budget system. The change agent may be a new organizational arrangement, new financial requirements, a decrease in subsidy, poor financial results, or a change in leadership in the CE organization or its parent institution. This chapter is written for the director facing such a change. It also can help directors understand factors that affect their present budget system.

The first step in introducing a new budgeting system is understanding the environmental factors that influence the structure and effectiveness of the budgeting process. Once these elements are clear, basic decisions about the process can be made. Environmental factors affecting budgets can be divided into three categories: external, institutional, and internal. Figure 4.1 shows a representation of these factors.

External Environment

External factors are influences on a CE budget system that lie outside both the continuing education organization and the institution (parent) within which it may exist. Usually these external factors are beyond the control of the organization and therefore must be accepted as givens (although adjustments, accommodations, and counterattacks may be made). The following are among the most important external factors that can influence the structure of a CE budget system.

The Economy. For both self-supporting enterprises and those with subsidies, the state of the economy strongly affects decision making in continuing education, including decisions having to do with budget systems. In good times, when many students are willing to pay for an education, a self-supporting enterprise may adopt a flexible budget system with relatively loose controls. In hard times, where cost control is emphasized and decisions affecting even relatively small amounts of money are important, a more rigid system may be necessary. (However, it should be noted that a bad economy may sometimes mean an increase in students, even for a self-supporting enterprise, because more people have more time and are willing to spend money to make themselves more attractive in the job market.)

Subsidized or partly subsidized organizations also are directly affected by the economy, although in ways different from those

Figure 4.1. Environmental Factors Affecting the Budgeting Process.

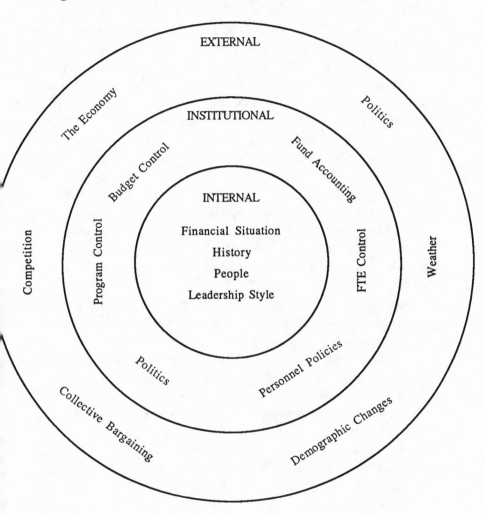

affecting self-supporting organizations. A declining economy may mean lower public revenues and lead to reduced subsidies. On the other hand, as government looks for ways to attract jobs and industry to a depressed region, it may increase support for programs that train workers and upgrade their skills. In any case, the economic climate will affect political decisions and ultimately therefore exercise a profound influence on the life of the CE organization. Thus, it must be recognized in the budget system.

Political Environment. The external political environment can also be an important influence on the CE budget. This is certainly true for subsidized organizations in which all or part of the subsidy comes directly from public funds. Tax revolts, the vagaries of state and local governments, and the public attitude toward education, particularly toward continuing education, can all have powerful effects. Self-supporting organizations may also be profoundly influenced by the political climate. On the one hand, budget cuts in subsidized continuing education can improve the market for self-supporting units. On the other, CE organizations may be asked by parent institutions to make up budget shortfalls.

The form of the CE budget system may also be significantly affected by the external political climate. Where education budgets are subject to public scrutiny and debate, the budget process may be rigid and formal, with much attention paid to detailed costs and charges and great time and effort spent on budget defense and justification. In a more favorable political environment, the budgeting process may be more open and venturesome.

Competition. The nature and extent of the competition facing a particular continuing education organization is also important. Effective organizations analyze their competition and adjust their goals and objectives, their marketing strategies, and their budget systems with this competition in mind. For instance, an organization may decide not to compete in an area, geographical or professional, where the competition is well established and strong. On the other hand, where the competition is assailable, the organization may well establish market share goals. For instance, it may set itself the goal of achieving a 20 percent share of the business and management courses given in its geographical area within a year. Meeting this goal may require extraordinary expenditures for promotion and marketing for the year and result in the hiring of highly paid professionals to develop and teach the courses. Thus competition has exercised a powerful (and not necessarily negative) effect on the organization's budget and budgeting process.

Other External Factors. Other factors influence the budgeting process, some directly and some indirectly. *Collective bargaining* comes into play when budgets and financial performance are part of the wage administration policy. Even *weather* may influence budgeting: for example, courses may be attended heavily in the fall and spring terms and more lightly in the winter, a fact that has obvious financial implications. Less obviously, the winter may be seen as a relatively slack period during which the annual budget may be prepared; thus the weather can influence the timing of the budgeting process. *Demographic changes* might also have an effect on the process as programs and marketing efforts are adjusted to recognize changes in the age and nature of the local continuing education audience.

Institutional Setting

Institutional factors have a more immediate effect on the CE budgeting process. Continuing education organizations are usually part of larger institutions and must operate within a framework of rules, regulations, and goals set by those institutions. This plainly is true in higher education institutions, where continuing education is usually organized either as a separate entity (centralized) or as a part of a department or school that is responsible for continuing education in its particular subject area (decentralized). The choice of a centralized or decentralized structure has obvious financial impact, and sound budgeting may well reveal which choice is the more economical and efficient for a particular institution. Continuing education is also part of a larger whole in many other institutions—museums, community centers, religious institutions, service organizations, and professional societies—and thus is influenced by institutional factors. Some of the more important institutional factors and their possible effects on the CE budgeting process are as follows.

Budget Control. The most immediate influence that an institution can exert on the continuing education organization is direct budget control. Usually the parent institution can exercise absolute control over budget line items and can impose spending limitations as it wishes. In reality, this control is rarely exercised to the limit; the director of continuing education usually has some flexibility in making budgetary adjustments and in developing budget systems suited to the needs of the organization. The relationship between responsibility and authority is important here. If the director is ordered to "make money," to make the CE organization fully self-supporting, or even to serve a specified number of students per term, then the parent institution should invest that director with enough authority, including budgetary authority, to carry out the assigned responsibility.

In some organizations, an expense budget is given to the continuing education unit, and the director of that unit has the responsibility of limiting spending to the amount allocated. (Sometimes restrictions are even more severe; the director must not only keep within the budget but actually go below it by meeting a "savings target," often in the form of "salary savings.") In these situations the director's main job is to allocate the budgetary resources among programs and services. Organizations falling into this pattern are called *fixed resource* organizations.

This restrictive case can be contrasted with the opposite end of the spectrum—the *variable resource* (usually self-supporting) organization. Such an organization typically has two sides to its budget, income and expense, and the amount available for expenses varies with income. Again, the resources of the organization must be allocated among programs, but here there is the additional task of generating the resources required. Variable resource organizations and their budgets have to be flexible so that they can adjust to market conditions, contracting when the market shrinks and expanding when market opportunities arise. Directors of variable resource CE organizations therefore usually have more autonomy and more opportunity to make budget adjustments.

In reality, pure examples of either type of organization probably do not exist. Most continuing education organizations are funded from a number of different sources, and these sources often have different budgetary restrictions attached to them. Student fees may be relatively free of expenditure restrictions, for example, while subsidies from the parent institution and monies received from contracts and grants, gifts, endowments, and tax revenues may be tightly controlled. In Chapter Five we will discuss some ways to handle the special problems of such "montage funding."

Another form of budget control by parent institutions, more subtle than direct financial control, is the imposition of charges (sometimes quite ingenious) for services provided or the more candid requirement that the continuing education organization return money directly to the parent institution. The assessment of indirect costs (overhead) is a further example of "parental" control. Such charges may be for personnel services, administrative space, library use, or other aspects of the institution used by the CE organization. However expressed, these charges burden the continuing education budget, removing funds from the control of the CE director and, in bad times, contributing to budget deficits, thereby giving higher authority an excuse to impose even greater budgetary restrictions. On the other hand, as CE organizations become more important in the financing of parent institutions' operations, meeting recharge payments or a targeted budget surplus often means greater autonomy, freedom, power, and influence for continuing education. The ideal is a relationship between the CE organization and the parent that is based on a full understanding of the underlying economics of the CE market.

Before a budget system is introduced or changed, the degree and nature of budget control by a parent institution should be understood and taken into account.

Fund Accounting. Closely related to the question of institutional control is the matter of fund accounting, to which most CE enterprises must adhere for at least part of their funding. The basic tenet of fund accounting is that where special restrictions or conditions attach to the transfer or giving of an amount of money, that money should be segregated and accounted for separately. This means that a separate accounting entity must be established on the books of the organization and that each expenditure of funds must be examined to make sure it is in accordance with the terms and conditions under which the organization was given the funds. Fund accounting therefore has a profound effect on the form and process of the budget system. In Chapter Five we will develop techniques for keeping track of different funds.

Obviously, the legal requirements that fund accounting reflects can severely reduce a CE organization management's ability to act. For instance, money given under government contract to train medical technologists may not be used to train medical librarians, even if the latter are more urgently needed.

Funds fall into several categories in fund accounting. *Restricted* funds must be dedicated to a particular purpose. *Unrestricted* or *discretionary* funds may usually be expended as management wishes. A *general operating* fund is usually an unrestricted fund used to support the overall operations of the organization.

Funds may also be *lapsing* or *nonlapsing*. Lapsing funds terminate either at the end of the organization's fiscal year or at the end of a special term provided for in the funding agreement. This means that all money unspent at the end of the term must be returned to the funding source. Nonlapsing funds, on the other hand, may be carried over and spent in subsequent periods. Lapsing funds present management with severe restrictions and often dictate decisions about courses. The presence of lapsing funds in an organization usually means that the budget system and the accounting system must be comprehensive, accurate, and timely.

FTE Control. A specialized form of budget control, called here FTE (for "full-time equivalent" employees) control, is sometimes imposed upon continuing education organizations, especially those associated with higher education institutions. In colleges and universities not only are dollars, including payroll dollars, carefully budgeted, but the number of employee positions are also subject to strict budget control. The department that commands the most FTE, especially the most academic FTE, is typically the most powerful and often commands the greatest share of the institutional budget. Standard budget allocation formulae used by institutions of higher education are based on proportionate FTE: Each FTE, by formula, brings with him or her an increment in the supplies budget, the photocopying budget, the telephone budget, the secretarial support budget, and so on. Elaborate budget controls and much paperwork surround the addition or transfer of FTE from one budgetary unit to another. This may be acceptable in the larger institution, where the primary budget task is to allocate a fixed amount of resources among budget units, but it can devastate a CE organization expected to be fully or partially self-supporting, for which flexibility and ability to respond to market opportunities are essential to success. The necessity of responding to institutional requirements of FTE control can have a far-reaching impact on the CE budgeting process.

Personnel Policies. The personnel policies of the parent institution are also important in shaping the CE organization's budgeting process. Where unions or civil service traditions rule, any attempt to change the budget system may change what are considered "conditions of employment" and may fall under the "meet and confer" category of issues, subject to negotiation. This is particularly true where the budget system is (as it should be) tied to the employee reward system. Pay raises for employees, both performance related and cost-of-living related, are often part of official policy. For example, cost-of-living adjustments for many state-supported institutions are determined by the legislature, often well after the beginning of the fiscal year, resulting in retroactive payments to employees. Such adjustments typically apply to all employees of the institution, no matter from what source they are paid; thus, self-supporting CE organizations are often burdened with large increases in payroll costs without a budget allocation to fund them.

The director of a continuing education organization, then, is responsible for paying employees at rates consistent with those in other parts of the parent institution but often has no say in what those rates should be. More often than not, the director is granted no additional funds to pay salary increases, other than those generated by the CE organization itself. Furthermore, the director is almost always constrained by policy in matters of firing or disciplining unproductive workers, establishing limits on job authority, or changing work assignments. These limitations can have a considerable effect on establishing or changing a budget system.

Programming Restrictions. Beyond direct budget control, the most common and powerfully restrictive institutional factor affecting CE budgeting is the ability of the parent institution to exercise programmatic control over the CE organization—that is, control over the nature and subject matter of instruction. Such control can take a number of forms. Most direct is an explicit order not to do certain types of programs. For instance, a major research university may not allow its continuing education division to set up courses in automobile repair, deeming such courses inappropriate to the mission and image of an institution of higher education. In another case, a museum may not allow its continuing education unit to present programs not directly related to a current or upcoming exhibit.

Sometimes agreements between institutions prevent a particular institution from programming in a certain area. Perhaps it has been agreed that the community college in a given city will offer all the courses in woodworking and the YMCA will offer photography courses. Such agreements, especially in areas requiring considerable investment in capital items and facilities, can serve the public interest by concentrating community resources and thereby providing better services. This same kind of agreement can exist within an institution. For example, the continuing education arm of a major university may be prohibited from offering courses in business and management because courses in this subject area are given by an institute attached to the school of business administration.

Other forms of programming control are less direct but still important. An institution may insist that only regular faculty teach courses in CE, or it may establish implausible requirements for the hiring of faculty. In a new field such as computer education, institutional policy may require instructors to have a degree that is actually irrelevant to the field. Institutional policy may also influence decisions about whether to hold some courses. Often summer session faculty contracts must be honored, for instance, no matter how many students enroll in a course.

It is easy to see that institutional control over programming can have far-reaching indirect effects on the CE budgeting process. It may require careful, and frequently costly, program review by both the parent institution and the CE organization. Sometimes potentially profitable courses may not be attempted or a course is made too costly for financial success. Bitter wranglings about educational quality may sidetrack budget hearings. Academic authority will call the quality of the continuing education program into question, while the continuing education director asks for more money to assure and maintain quality.

Politics. More often than not, continuing education is looked on as a bit outside the main mission of a parent institution. Thus the CE organization is usually politically weak and vulnerable to attack from "mainstream" units. When resources become scarce, continuing education is often one of the first units to have funding reductions (in subsidized situations) or to have additional charges assessed against it (in full or partial self-support situations). Of course, the more the parent becomes dependent on the stepchild for dollar support, the more influential the stepchild may become; but this progression is hardly assured, especially when the parent's financial expectations are not met.

The budgeting process is both profoundly affected by institutional politics and a powerful instrument in such politics. Political considerations may dictate that the director keep the CE budget a little obscure—"What they don't know won't hurt them" or, more often to the point, "What they don't know about my operation can't be used to hurt me." On the other hand, the political situation may require a comprehensive and detailed budget system. Knowing that the budget will be inspected carefully by the officers of the parent institution, a CE director will want to be "squeaky clean" in the budget presentation. He or she should have sufficient backup information to support all requests represented in the budget and fend off anticipated attacks. Often the form of the budget presentation, complete with neat schedules and fully explained requests, will prove more important than the budget's substance. In Chapter Six we will consider some strategies the CE director might employ in presenting a budget to superiors.

Internal Environment

Assessing the internal or intraorganizational factors that can influence the budgeting process requires detailed knowledge of the organization and the personalities involved. Such assessment is often difficult, but it must be made if a budget is to be really useful.

Here are some of the most common internal factors that can affect budgeting.

Financial Situation. Recent events, including a fluctuating economy, have placed financial strains on education institutions, with the result that most CE organizations are either experiencing a financial crisis or will face one shortly. Most budgeting systems are born of financial crisis, and the alert manager can use concern about a possible crisis to institute tighter budget controls or to change an existing system. Unfortunately, it all too often happens that by the time the organization sees the need for a more comprehensive and accurate budgeting system, the crisis is already at hand.

It is better to plan and gain employee support for budget reforms while the organization is still on a firm footing. For one thing, the footing may not be as firm as it seems. Not all successful organizations are well managed, just as not all unsuccessful organizations are poorly managed. An organization may be successful because of a happy accident of geography and lack of competition—external factors not under the control of the management—and gross management errors may be hidden behind the mask of success. If an incident suggests a reason for increasing financial control that will make sense to the rank and file, the astute manager will take advantage of the occasion to prevent trouble later on.

History. The history of the organization, particularly with regard to budgeting and financial control, is an important variable when a new budgeting situation arises. Many academics view budgeting or anything having to do with money as distasteful. Furthermore, many people have grown up with the idea that education ought to be free to those who wish it and that educational institutions should provide their services at nominal cost to the individual. In a CE organization, this attitude can be a significant barrier to acceptance of a budget system.

Another kind of problem arises if the organization has a long history of budgetary control that has failed. When budgets are not compared with actual results or used to evaluate performance, they become mere empty forms that many employees see (perhaps correctly) as a waste of time and energy.

Even when an organization has had a positive history of budgetary control, it may need a change in its budget system. It may have become accustomed to a system that is really an empty form but is so much a part of organizational life that it is no longer resented. In these cases, changes in the budget system, even if obviously desirable, often will be resented and resisted. The changes must be introduced slowly and their differences from the old system deemphasized.

People. The people in an organization are an important factor in the success or failure of a budget system, but it is difficult to describe the many ways in which this "variable" can affect budgeting. Certainly the ages of the members of an organization, their length of employment, and their attitudes toward the organization and toward budgeting and financial control will all be important. When introducing budgetary (or any other) change, a manager must be sensitive both to the needs of the organization and the needs and perceptions of the people who make up that organization. Meeting both kinds of needs can be exceptionally difficult in matters of budgeting and financial control.

Leadership Style. Finally, leadership style has an important effect on the form and texture of the budgeting process. The budget system chosen by an organization is usually very much an extension of the style and philosophy of the organization's managers. Directors of CE organizations should be self-aware enough to identify their own leadership styles and figure out how those styles can be carried through in the budget system.

The literature on leadership styles categorizes these styles in several ways. White and Lippett (1960), for example, describe authoritarian, democratic, and laissez-faire leadership styles. Authoritarian leaders are control oriented, dictating relatively narrow ranges of action for subordinates, setting all policies, and directing work tasks very actively. Budgeting under authoritarian leaders also tends to be control oriented, with clearly defined rewards or sanctions attached to positive or negative deviations from the budget. Democratic leaders, on the other hand, encourage participation by all members of the organization, work toward consensus, and motivate through a common knowledge and understanding of the goals and objectives of the organization.

Budgeting under democratic leaders tends to be characterized by much participation and negotiation. Overall results rather than details are regarded as important, and, perhaps paradoxically, rewards for doing well may be somewhat undefined or even internalized. The third style, laissez-faire "leadership," represents almost an absence of leadership, with the leader making minimal contributions to the organization or group process unless directly called upon to do more. Budgeting under this kind of leadership is likely to be either nonexistent or the product of a group process undirected by the manager.

Leadership styles may also be classified as relations oriented or task oriented. Relations-oriented leadership is characterized by the leader's effort to maintain a supportive, friendly atmosphere in the organization and to pay careful attention to the needs of individuals (Borst and Montana, 1977). The task-oriented style concentrates on "getting the job done" and places emphasis on achievement rather than on the feelings of group members or the process by which the task is accomplished.

Budget systems, too, can be authoritarian or democratic, rigid or flexible. They can concentrate on small details or on overall objectives. They can be used punitively or as part of a reward system. They can support the leadership style of the director, or they can decrease leadership effectiveness by sending mixed messages to the organization. For these reasons, leadership style is an important influence on the budget system.

Defining a Budgetary Context

Once the outside factors we have discussed have been taken into account, preliminary decisions about the budget system may be made, either by the director alone or through a participative process in the organization. We will now discuss these basic decisions and some factors to consider when making them.

Organizational Goals and Objectives. Most management systems are based on a more or less clearly articulated set of organizational goals and objectives. Every process and every part of the organization, including the budget system, must in some way advance the organization toward its stated objectives. Although the process of setting goals and objectives can be overemphasized or carried to extremes, it is, nevertheless, a logical starting point for the development of a budget system. The following are examples of broad objectives for a continuing education enterprise:

- to present courses of instruction of the highest possible academic quality to the citizens of Cimmaron County;
- to provide the nurses of the state of Nevada with the most up-to-date continuing professional education programs;
- to generate a surplus of income over expense of at least $10,000 each year; and
- to provide continuing education programs at a cost not to exceed the annual budget approved by the board of directors.

Objectives can be much more detailed, specific, and complex. Examples of more specific objectives include the following:

- to provide at least 150 course hours of continuing education to the radiology technicians of the Boise metropolitan area in the current fiscal year.
- to gain at least a 30 percent share of the market for continuing education courses directed at accountants in the San Diego area.
- to provide a $20,000 excess of income over expense for programs offered in the west county area after a full proration of overhead costs.

All these objectives, both general and specific, have definite budget implications. For instance, gaining a 30 percent market share of accounting courses may require hiring an accounting specialist, increasing the promotion budget, or spending money to develop an accounting curriculum. The budget serves an organization's objectives by providing an implementation plan directed toward achieving them. Budgets can also be an expression of the financial objectives of the organization, and "living within the budget" is often an organizational goal.

Degree of Control. Another basic decision the director must make is the determination of the level and degree of managerial control that the budget will represent. "Control" here means, first, control over setting the budget objectives themselves. Who will set those objectives, and with what specifications and restrictions? In a large CE organization, with several departments composed of several programmers each, the budget targets may be set for the department chairs, who are then left to implement the targets, distributing the load among their subordinates; or targets may be set individually by the director for each programmer. Centralized organizations tend to have more detailed and specific goals, whereas decentralized organizations usually establish general goals and leave their implementation to a lower level of management. For instance, in a centralized structure the director might set a target for a programmer of a year-end "available for overhead" figure of $20,000 but might also place a limit of $15,000 on promotion expenditures and require that at least 100 courses be offered in the year. In a decentralized organization, the same end result ($20,000 available for overhead) might be specified, but no restrictions would be placed on how that goal should be achieved. Theoretically, if the programmer were to meet the goal by presenting only one extremely successful course, the director would be satisfied.

A second form of control represented by the budget has to do with its monitoring or feedback function. In order to be effective, a budget process must compare actual results against the budget and reinforce performance that meets or exceeds budget standards. But who is to make the comparison—the programmer, the programmer and the department chair, the director and the programmer? When is the comparison going to be made?—every month, every term, twice a year?

The control represented by the budget can be exercised either before or after basic program decisions are made. For instance, programmers may be required to prepare course budgets before spending any significant amounts on proposed courses. If these budgets are subjected to a rigorous review before the programmer can proceed, then control is being exercised before the fact, and the reviewer is very much participating in decisions about the course. On the other hand, if course budgets are either not required or not carefully reviewed before a program is attempted, control may be exercised after the fact when results are examined and compared with the budget. Rewards or sanctions can be meted out on the basis of performance, and the certainty that accounts will be compared is usually enough to influence behavior in the desired direction. In this case the programmer has a greater decision-making responsibility, and the organization can be said to be decentralized in terms of program decisions, even though management still exercises control. In another example, two organizations might establish similar limitations on promotion costs. One organization might ensure compliance by requiring that each proposed promotion expenditure be approved in advance. In the other, performance might be evaluated and compared with the standard at the end of the year when all promotion figures can be added up. Predecision control is tighter but generally uses a lot of administrative time and effort, which is expensive to the organization. Such tight control may well be necessary. however, in organizations where the record shows consistently unsound financial decisions.

Finally, it should be noted that the mere existence of a system designed to hold people to account, to compare actual results with what they were required to do, is often enough to assure compliance with organizational standards. To the extent that this is true, the system of control *is* the control, and management need exert little energy in exercising control.

Organization Segmentation. Every organization is composed of parts, and, as managers, directors of CE organizations need to know how those parts are performing. The way authority in an organization is divided should be reflected in the structure of the budget, since the budget determines what information will be available to managers.

Organization segmentation is an element in what is called "responsibility accounting." This idea began in corporate organizations where authority was distributed in the traditional hierarchical, bureaucratic way. Managers of these organizations wanted to be able to attribute success or failure to particular, well-defined segments of the organization. They wanted to be able to assign clear responsibility for results to individual managers and to structure reward systems that were related to these results. This philosophy has to some extent been replaced by a tendency toward more participative organizations that emphasize teamwork, consensus building, and group processes, but responsibility accounting is no less important for these latter organizations: Management and the work group or team still need to know how each part of the organization is performing.

Control and responsibility go together—or they should. The director who reviews and approves all course budgets before expenditures are made must assume a degree of responsibility for the success of those programs. If control is very tight, the director can hardly place full blame for failure on programmers. On the other hand, programmers who have more autonomy to make decisions about course presentation must accept more responsibility for making "good" decisions.

As mentioned in the Introduction, the review of course budgets is part of the responsibility structure of an organization. The responsibility structure serves three purposes:

- to divide an organization into smaller parts so that the work of the organization can be divided into more manageable steps;
- to assign authority, resources, and responsibility for success to specified individuals or groups of individuals; and
- to permit objective evaluation of performance of individuals or groups of individuals against clearly defined goals.

In this context, organization segments are called "responsibility centers." There are three general types of responsibility centers. In *cost centers,* managers have the responsibility for controlling costs but do not have any responsibility for generating income. Examples of cost centers in CE organizations include the registration office, the director's office, and the business office. In *profit centers,* on the other hand, managers are concerned not only with controlling costs but also with generating income and, in a business environment, with maximizing the excess of income over costs. Self-supporting segments of CE organizations generally fall into this category.

The last type of responsibility center is only infrequently encountered in continuing education. It is called an *investment center,* and its object is to measure and, presumably, maximize the return on investment of a defined group of assets. CE organizations involved in the management of endowment or other asset-based funds may have investment centers. It is also possible to create investment centers whenever significant resources are directed toward a particular end. A computer lab or a downtown center, through lab charges or room rental fees, could become an investment center because the return on the investment involved in it could be computed.

Development of a useful and realistic organization segmentation plan should begin with the present organizational structure. CE organizations can usually be segmented into two general categories—service departments and programming (operating) departments.

Service departments provide the support services necessary to carry out the presentation of continuing education programs but are not responsible for programming courses. Typical service departments and their functions include the following:

- *Director's Office:* CE director and director's immediate staff and clerical support. Provides overall administration of the CE organization, usually not directly involved in programming; includes director's salary and salary of immediate support staff.
- *Cashier's Office:* Handles cash receipts and depositing; may have responsibility for registration input and accounting of income and accounts receivable.
- *Personnel Services:* Provides services to staff and academic employees and sometimes to instructional staff; processes paperwork related to employment; counsels employees on benefits and employment opportunities; may provide staff training and be involved in employee disputes; may handle recruitment.
- *Business Office:* Processes purchase orders; provides invoice approval, coding, and payment; may handle instructor payroll, contract and grant accounting, student refunds, inventory accounting, and insurance.
- *Financial (Accounting) Services:* Prepares periodic financial statements, financial analysis, budgets; is responsible for systems design and monitoring.

- *Registration Office:* Handles walk-up and telephone enrollments, requests for information, course enrollment tallies, and preparation of enrollment cards.
- *Student Records:* Maintains student record (transcript) files, issues transcripts, posts grades to transcripts.
- *Program Processing:* Handles room assignments; processes course and teacher approvals; orders books; maintains file of course outlines and examinations.
- *Reprographics (Print Shop):* Handles production of course and promotion materials.
- *Promotion (Marketing) Department:* Administers in-house or outside contractors in promotional art, layout and design, pasteup, editing, mailing list maintenance and coordination; secures paid advertising; produces enrollment tracking reports; and analyzes promotion effectiveness.
- *Computer Center or Laboratory:* May have instructional functions and administrative functions separated or combined. Instructional functions may include classroom and/or open lab provisions. Administrative functions may relate to registration, cashiering, promotion, and so on.
- *Conference Facility:* Includes all costs associated with operating and maintaining a conference center including salaries, utilities, janitorial services, repair and maintenance, rent, and so on.

Most CE organizations will need all the service functions in this list, though they may be arranged for in different ways. Some may be provided by a parent organization free or through a fee-for-service arrangement. Personnel services and registration functions may be handled under administrative auspices not controlled by the CE director.

When designing a new budget system, the CE director has a chance to rearrange the segmentation of service functions. For instance, the director may decide to budget the promotion department as a single department or to handle it at a greater level of detail, with separate budgets for the art department, the editorial department, and so on. More detailed budgeting provides an opportunity for more precise evaluation of individual segments, but at a cost. Multiple budget units require more attention from the whole administrative apparatus—more budgetary review, more accounting and bookkeeping services, more statement presentation and analysis. Thus, detailed segmentation may not be necessary or desirable for service units that are relatively stable and present few managerial problems, but it may be worth the expense for units that are likely to develop problems or to be subjected to periodic cost scrutiny.

The promotion department is an example of this latter category. Promotion expenditures are both volatile and important, so they should be under constant review. Many services provided by the promotion department could be provided by outside organizations, so there is likely to be pressure to justify the cost of maintaining the services in house. Thus a budgeting/managerial system that provides information for periodic analysis of promotion costs may well be worth the cost of maintaining the additional detail.

Once service departments have been defined and the level of detail of their segmentation has been determined, the next step in budget system planning is to decide how the service departments will relate to the programming departments. On the surface, service departments appear to be cost centers rather than profit centers, since they generally do not involve the generation of income. However, just about any cost center can become a profit center through a *transfer pricing* system. Under transfer pricing, a service center establishes prices for the services provided and charges users, in this case other departments within the same organization, according to this pricing schedule. Thus, the registration office might charge programming departments $15 per student for registration services, the reprographics department would have a price list for various types of reproduction services, and so on. Transfer pricing is one method of *cost allocation,* which we will describe briefly later in this chapter and in more detail in Chapter Nine.

Segmentation of *programming departments* presents a different set of complexities, especially in regard to information gathering. Determining current and forecasting future information requirements is more crucial for programming departments than for service departments because, by and large, decisions made in programming departments are more important to the overall health of the organization. Financial information, including that generated through the budget process, helps programmers and management stay in touch with changing market conditions as well as monitor the effectiveness of decision making.

Careful segmentation can greatly aid information gathering. Take, for example, a departmental segment labeled "Business and Management." As it stands, budgeting and accounting for this department provide only very general information to management because the group of courses it covers is so large. If "Business and Management" were divided into "Real Estate," "Accounting," "MBA Prerequisites," and "Personal Financial Planning," however, the results from all these segments could be tracked, and opportunities and downturns in the markets served by the individual segments could be discerned. Again, the trade-off is the increased cost of maintaining and analyzing the additional information.

Other *subject matter* departments could be segmented similarly. For an Arts and Sciences department, the second order of segmentation might begin with "Art," which, depending on the extensiveness of the organization, might be further broken into "Art History," "Studio Art," and "Art Appreciation."

There are many other possible bases of segmentation of programming departments. The traditional or functional approach reflects the difference in the organizing tasks involved in mounting credit courses and noncredit conferences and institutes (C & I). This can be called segmentation by *credit classification*. It might be valuable where the parent institution is interested in these categories or they seem to reflect market structure.

Another basis for segmentation is *curriculum groupings*. The "MBA prerequisites" category in our earlier example might be a curriculum grouping. Multicourse certificate programs or degree programs might also be in this category. Such a basis for segmentation makes sense primarily where there is a homogeneity of student motivation for taking the courses. If, for instance, there were an accounting course in the MBA prerequisites category that regularly enrolled students with no interest in the MBA degree, the category would carry less value as a segmentation basis.

A variation of this method might relate to the parent institution. Where individual courses can be related to a specific department of the parent, say, the School of Business Administration, and where there are other good reasons for it, this segmentation scheme may be called for.

So far the segment categories we have talked about might be termed program categories, since they reflect attributes of the programs being presented. They can be contrasted with responsibility categories—categories that reflect the responsibility structure of the organization. The individual programmer and associated clerical support staff make up an obvious responsibility center. This kind of segmentation makes sense when programmer performance evaluation is based, at least in part, on financial results.

Another responsibility segmentation scheme might relate to *course format*. This is something like the credit classification division mentioned earlier. The traditional CE conferences and institutes (C & I) division, separated from degree and credit programs, might be further segmented into one-day programs, programs for a national (as opposed to local) audience, and programs in which the CE division serves as a facilitator or logistical coordinator for sponsoring units elsewhere in the parent institution.

Still another responsibility center segmentation method might relate to *geographical location*. It is often desirable to track separately the budgets and finances of programs located in different geographical parts of the CE service area. A downtown location may serve a market segment distinctly different from that served by a suburban or campus location, even when both offer the same courses. When this is true, a geographical segmentation scheme could provide valuable information.

Clearly, there are many other possible segmentation schemes besides those just described; nor are the methods described here mutually exclusive. The director should choose the segmentation plan that provides the most useful financial information and is most responsive to the organization's style of control. For instance, where an individual programmer has the exclusive right to program in a specific subject matter area and that subject matter area is the only one with which the programmer is involved, the individual responsibility segment and the program or subject matter segment will coincide. On the other hand, if two programmers representing two separate responsibility centers both decide to program, say, computer courses, the director may have to choose between responsibility center segmentation and program-related segmentation.

Judicious planning can aid in the choice of the best segmentation scheme. One important step in this planning is determining what might be called the "lowest common denominator" cost or budget object. In the Introduction we defined the cost object as anything for which an organization wishes to accumulate costs. Similarly, budget objects are those defined units within an organization for which budgets are prepared. Organization segments, however they are determined, are budget objects. The "lowest common denominator" budget object is the smallest entity for which a budget is prepared. Identifying this smallest entity defines the level of detail and of combinatory flexibility of the organization's budget system. For instance, a CE organization might prepare a budget for each department and also for each programmer within a department, thus making the programmer the smallest budget object. The department budget should exactly equal the sum of the individual programmer budgets. However, if circumstances warranted, the financial results of programmers in different departments could be combined to produce new budgetary and financial groupings unrelated to the departmental structure.

In our subsequent discussion we will use the course as the lowest common denominator budget object, because doing so allows us to use several different segmentation schemes simultaneously. By attaching a number of attributes to each course—subject matter classification, curriculum grouping, parent institution department, credit classification, programmer, and so on—we can combine the budgets and financial results of individual courses to produce information that can be classified according to different segmentation schemes. However, we have to make sure that each segmentation scheme includes the entire universe of courses: We must not be able to double-count or avoid counting any course.

Thus, every course must be given every attribute and carry only one classification within that attribute.

Classifying information according to a number of different segmentation schemes simultaneously can be time-consuming, even if the integrity of budget and financial detail is rigorously maintained. With the advent of computerized accounting systems, particularly those involving microcomputers and prepackaged software, however, the cost in both time and money of performing such multiple calculations has been greatly reduced. This technology makes it possible to create a data base that can incorporate many course attributes and produce reports containing information sorted in many different ways. We will discuss the structure of such data bases in more detail in Chapter Eleven.

Several other issues associated with organization segmentation should be mentioned here. The first is the *cost-benefit ratio.* Even with the most efficient computer system in the world, the larger the number of segmentation schemes and the greater the level of detail of the segmentation, the higher the cost of the resulting analysis will be because more work will have to be done to prepare budgets, code income and expenses, define segments, and classify budget objects. This work must be done carefully, furthermore, because unless someone places budget objects into consistent categories, the organization will incur the cost of decisions that are poor because they are based on imprecise, sometimes meaningless, information. The cost of maintaining an excessively elaborate information structure thus may well exceed the information's value to the organization. Information from a budgeting and accounting system must be not only interesting but useful in shaping decisions or performing other tasks that pay a real return to the organization. Too much information can be as hard to interpret as too little.

This brings up another problem related to information systems and organization segmentation: the *"unquenchable thirst for information."* All financial information, no matter how detailed and precise, gives rise to a need for additional information. This is because all financial information requires some form of interpretation, and each successive iteration of interpretation in turn requires further objective verification.

For instance, let us suppose that a self-supporting CE organization is experiencing a decline in income. Segment analysis determines successively that the general decline is due primarily to a decline in the Business and Management department, that Programmer A (a responsibility center) is not doing as well as last year, and that the Real Estate program is the primary reason for Programmer A's poor showing. This certainly narrows and defines the problem, but the director might still feel the need to know more. Part of that need might be satisfied by the existing accounting and budgeting system, but part might require information that would have to be obtained outside the system. For instance, the decline might be isolated to one-day programs directed at practicing professionals. This information could be obtained easily if the organization happened to be segmented according to course format, but if not, further analysis would be necessary. Alternatively, it might turn out that downtown one-day programs were thriving but courses on campus were in trouble. In this case, there would be a need for further analysis if the segmentation scheme did not include geographical location. And even with the most comprehensive and detailed segmentation plan, management is still likely to be left with the question: Why the decline? Is the programmer at fault for failing to design exciting new courses that will attract sophisticated urban professionals? Has competition moved in with a slick promotional campaign? Has something occurred in the urban real estate market that the programmer has not yet incorporated into course offerings? Whatever the reason, outside investigation will probably be needed to uncover it.

After each successive analysis of a financial problem, the pressure to provide further information becomes more intense because the final answer seems ever closer at hand. The "unquenchable thirst for information" thus really cannot be avoided. All a director can do is try to strike a balance between the lower cost and lesser precision of a lower level of segmentation and the higher cost, but greater discriminatory power, of a higher order of segmentation.

One other factor to keep in mind when developing a segmentation plan is the *value of historical data*. Budgetary and financial data become most useful when they are compared both with future actual results and with the results of a prior period. When new systems are being planned, there is a tendency to emphasize the inadequacies of the predecessor process, sometimes to the extent of complete abandonment of the former structure of financial and budget analysis. If this happens, the organization has at least temporarily lost the use of its history.

For instance, suppose a director decides to reorganize a CE organization, adopting a responsibility center segmentation scheme based on individual programmers in place of an older scheme that was composed of departments based on course format. During the next year, current financial results will not be comparable to prior year results; thus the kind of comparison proposed earlier for the real estate program, for example, would not be possible without extensive analysis. The problem could be avoided if either the prior year's results were restated in terms of the new organization structure or the current year were restated in terms of the structure of the past year. It is usually easier to develop a segmentation plan that incorporates the previous structure than to go back and restate prior years. In any event, casting out old systems too completely usually costs something in terms of management information.

A good job of organization segmentation greatly facilitates the process of *management by exception,* which I defined in the Introduction. As Drucker (1979) repeatedly points out, one of an organization's scarcest and most valuable resources is the time and attention of management, and this time and attention must be allocated carefully. Priority in such allocation usually should be given to areas of exceptional opportunity or difficulty. A well-conceived and properly utilized organization segmentation scheme can help to identify both opportunities and problems.

Line Item Classifications. In Chapters Five and Six we will examine in some detail the format of worksheets that can be used in the budgeting process. In these worksheets, organization segments are shown in the columns going across the top of the worksheet. Typically, these columns represent either the program or the responsibility center classification scheme. Down the left side of the worksheet, known as the "stub," budget *line items* are listed. (Line items were defined in our discussion of traditional budgeting in the Introduction.) For instance, a payment to an instructor might be an expense associated with a real estate program. The program (columnar) classification of this expense would be "real estate," and its line item classification would be "teacher compensation." A typical budget worksheet is shown in Figure 4.2.

Establishing or changing line item classifications is usually easier than establishing or changing organization segments, but the selection of line items is nevertheless important. They should be chosen with present and anticipated information needs in mind. What kinds of expenses will it be necessary to keep track of? What kinds of decisions regarding expenses will have to be made? Might we be forced to cut the travel budget by 50 percent during the next budget crisis, for example, or effect a 10 percent salary saving in the last half of the year? If so, we will need to know what our budget for travel is and how much we have spent to date, and who is being paid how much. Of course, the usual trade-off must be kept in mind: As with organizational segmentation, the more detailed and specific the line item classification scheme is, the more information can be gained from it but the more costly and difficult it is to maintain and monitor.

A detailed and categorized listing of possible line items appears in Figure 4.3. It would be very unusual for an organization to use every item listed, but the list can be adapted and rearranged to suit a variety of institutional settings and managerial purposes. It incorporates all the line items listed in the course budget worksheets in Part One and adds a number of others.

Cost Allocation Basis and Method. Determination of the basis for and the method of allocating indirect costs is an extremely important preliminary decision because these methods can significantly affect the behavior of staff members and the relationships between various organizational segments as well as between responsibility center managers and the director. Cost allocation in a CE organization consists primarily of allocation of service department costs to programming or operating departments.

It is easy to see why service department costs are usually indirect costs. For instance, registration office costs (composed of payroll costs, telephone costs, office supplies expense, and so on) would be very difficult to associate directly with a course or a responsibility center. We could not very well have each person in

Figure 4.2. Typical Summary Budget Worksheet.

Line Items	Total	Program Departments A	B	Service Departments
mber of programs	80	50	30	
mber of enrollees	2,000	1,000	1,000	
come	$120,000	$40,000	$80,000	
pense				
Direct costs				
Promotion	$ 7,000	$ 3,000	$ 4,000	
Teacher compensation	25,000	7,000	18,000	
Program-related expenses	7,000	2,000	5,000	
Subtotal	$39,000	$12,000	$27,000	
Responsibility center costs				
Programmer salaries	$40,000	$15,000	$25,000	
Clerical salaries	25,000	5,000	10,000	$10,000
Fringe benefits	4,500	1,000	3,000	500
Other costs				
Telephone	3,500	500	1,000	2,000
Travel	1,400	400	1,000	
Office supplies	1,800	300	500	1,000
Subtotal	$76,200	$22,200	$40,500	$13,500
Total direct costs	$115,200	$34,200	$67,500	$13,500
ailable for overhead	$4,800	$5,800	$12,500	($13,500)
direct cost allocation		(4,500)	(9,000)	13,500
rplus (Deficit)	$4,800	$1,300	$3,500	

te: Indirect costs are allocated pro rata on the basis
     of total income.

Figure 4.3. Typical Organization Budget Line Items.

Volume measures
  Number of programs
  Number of enrollments

Income
  Student fee income
  (Less) Pass-through costs
  Net student fee income
  Transcript fee income
  Conference accommodation income
  Subsidy income
    Federal contracts and grants
    State contracts and grants
    Private contracts and grants
    Endowment fund transfers
    Institutional support payments
  Other income
    Conference facility rental income from outsiders
    Book sales

Expense
  Expenses associated directly with courses
    Promotion expenses
      Advertising costs
        Categorized by media
          Radio
          Television
          Newspapers
          Magazines
          News releases
        Categorized by natural classification
          Space costs, spot costs
          Production costs
            Writing
            Printing
            Distribution costs
            Actors' fees
            Audiovisual equipment rental
            Other
      Production costs
        Categorized by type of piece
          Catalogue
          Brochure
          Flyer
          Poster
          Newsletter
          Letters

Figure 4.3. Typical Organization Budget Line Items, Cont'd.

Categorized by natural classification
  Editing
  Layout
  Pasteup
  Illustration
  Cover design
  Author fees
  Copyright fees
  Typesetting
  Printing
  Paper
  Envelopes
  Staff time
Mailing costs
  Postage (perhaps by mail class)
  Mailing label purchase
  Mailing label extraction
  Mail house (handling charges)
    Folding
    Binding
    Stuffing
    Sorting
    Affixing labels
    Pickup and delivery
    Warehouse and storage charges
    Administrative costs and profit
Other promotion costs
  Displays/exhibits
    Fees
    Production costs
    Setup costs
    Staff time
  Press kits
  Hospitality, entertaining
  Telephone selling
Teacher compensation
  Instructor compensation (perhaps categorized by instructor
    classification)
  Reader and teaching assistant compensation
  Course development compensation
  Instructor travel
    Local
    National
    International

Figure 4.3. Typical Organization Budget Line Items, Cont'd.

Other direct course costs
  Audiovisual equipment
    Film, videotape rental, purchase
    Equipment rental, use charge
    Delivery, mailing charges
  Course materials
    Textbooks, other books (including freight)
    Reproduction costs
      Copyright license fees
      Printing
        Offset
        Mimeo
        Xerox
        Typesetting
        Typing
        Layout, design
      Collating
      Stapling
      Binding
      Delivery
  Lab fees
  Room rental
  Security service
  Janitorial service
  Ushers, crowd, traffic control
  Coffee, refreshments
  Lunches, meals
  Staff expenses
    Couriers
    Cashiers
    Programmer on-site time
    Travel, per diem
    Meals
    Incidentals
  Entertainment
  Registration costs
    Registration package
    Hotel charges
    Name tags

Expenses associated directly with responsibility centers
  Payroll costs
    Programmer salary and fringes
    Clerical support salary and fringes
    Occasional assistance wage and fringes
  Unallocated (to courses) promotion

Figure 4.3. Typical Organization Budget Line Items, Cont'd.

Travel
Telephone
Office supplies
Office machine maintenance, rental
Computer charges
Entertainment
Reproduction costs
Space rental
Incidentals
Other costs

Indirect cost allocations—to be derived from the worksheet technique developed in Chapter Six.

---

the registration office keep track of his or her time and try to associate it with service to the students of a particular department. Even if that were possible, such an accounting system would be exceedingly expensive to maintain. However, by adding up all registration office costs and dividing by the total number of students served, we could arrive at an average cost per student. Knowing how many students enrolled in each course or in courses offered by each department would give us a basis upon which to allocate registration costs to the desired cost object.

Of course, this method may not be fair to every department. The students of one department—say, the Adult Literacy Department—may take a disproportionate share of the time and attention of registration personnel. Using average cost per student as a basis for allocation would therefore give a break to this department and unfairly burden the others. However, as was pointed out in Part One, every cost allocation scheme has some element of inequity built into it. The best a director can do is try to minimize inequity and avoid distorted behavior on the part of the staff.

When an organization is segmented into responsibility centers, there is always the possibility that what is good for one part of the organization is not good for the organization as a whole. For instance, using the example just described, let's say that the Computer Science Department, seeing the advantage obtained by the Adult Literacy Department, protests the registration office charge and insists that instead of paying for the services of the registration office, it will establish its own registration function—in effect, secede from the union. Even if this department could demonstrate that it could provide registration for itself at a cost lower than what it is now paying, the organization as a whole would suffer: Students might be confused, and the decrease in volume in the main registration office might change the economy of scale of that operation so that the average per student costs for all the remaining departments would markedly increase.

Another example of distorted behavior occurs when programmers adjust their programming to take advantage of the allocation formula. Again using the registration example, programmers might be more inclined to program high-fee, low-enrollment courses than relatively low-fee, high-enrollment courses because of the per student charge. This distortion could be avoided if the basis of allocation were changed from a per student basis to a percentage of total income: That is, total registration costs would be divided by total income to obtain a percentage that could be applied against course and departmental income. Unfortunately, changing the basis might simply lead to a different distortion, skewing programming toward low-fee, high-enrollment courses. Of course, it might happen that management wants to encourage, say, higher enrollments, and changing the allocation basis would be one way to encourage this trend. In any case, the director who is choosing a cost allocation method should try to predict the behavior a given method is likely to produce and consider whether that behavior is desirable.

An organization that accepts the premise that responsibility should be clearly articulated (and this presumably applies to nearly every CE organization) faces a particular problem with regard to cost allocation schemes. There are two dominant philosophies governing cost allocation. The first is called *full* or *absorption costing*, which we mentioned briefly in Chapter One. Under this philosophy, the end product should have built (absorbed) into it all costs, including all possible indirect costs, associated with its production. Thus, the cost of a course under full costing would include a portion of the director's salary, a portion of the costs of any utilities that the organization has to pay, a portion of the cost of the computerized registration system, and so on—in other words, a pro rata share, based on some rational allocation method, of every indirect cost element in the organization. The great advantage of a full costing system is that it allows one to see the total effect that a particular course had on the "bottom line" of the organization. The total of the surpluses and deficits of all the courses offered should equal the organization's surplus or deficit.

Full costing has some disadvantages, however. First, it is sometimes expensive to maintain because of the added detail necessitated by the allocation process. More importantly, it can be destructive to the responsibility structure of an organization. The basic tenet of responsibility accounting and the segmentation scheme is that responsibility should be clearly assigned to individuals or groups. Where the responsibility center is either a cost center or a profit center, the responsible party, which here we will call the manager, should theoretically have control over all the elements included in the responsibility center. However, the manager of a responsibility center usually has virtually no control over either the amount of indirect costs or the method of their allocation. Under these circumstances it is hard to hold the manager fully responsible for the "bottom line."

To preserve the responsibility structure, a second costing philosophy, called *incremental costing,* was developed. Under this philosophy, only those cost elements that can be directly associated with the responsibility center are charged to it, and the responsibility center is theoretically responsible only for the increment in indirect costs caused by its inclusion in the organization. Thus, in our example where the computer department sought to avoid being charged on a per student basis for registration costs, incremental costing would allow the department to be charged for only the amount that the indirect costs of the registration office would decrease if the department were to pull out. These costs are called *separable fixed indirect costs,* since they can be "separated" from the organization along with the responsibility center. The costs that remain are called *common fixed indirect costs,* since they cannot be identified with the incremental volume brought by any one responsibility center.

These common fixed costs are also sometimes referred to as "ready-to-serve" costs, since they bring the organization into a position where it is ready to serve its individual units.

One disadvantage of incremental costing is the difficulty of computing separable and common cost elements. Such costs have to be estimated subjectively, which usually means that they become subject to negotiation and debate. A greater disadvantage is that the "bottom line" for the whole organization can become dissociated from the financial results for each of the organization's parts. Each segment, in trying to maximize its own margin, seeks to avoid common costs that, in the end, must be paid by the organization. As long as the segment margins are sufficient to cover the common costs, the organization will be served, but budget planning and the monitoring of budget targets may become very complex.

Various combinations of full and incremental costing have been devised to preserve the advantages of each system. Responsibility center costs can be divided into two parts, "controllable" and "noncontrollable." Controllable costs, logically, are costs over which the manager of the responsibility center has control. The manager will be held responsible only for financial results that involve these elements. If the noncontrollable elements, including the indirect cost burden, are added to the controllable costs in all financial statements, the full-cost "bottom line" can also be calculated.

Figure 4.2 illustrated this method. In that example, the managers of programming departments A and B might be held responsible for producing the "available for overhead" line, which shows $5,800 and $12,500 respectively. The noncontrollable (at least from the managers' point of view) indirect costs are then subtracted from these figures to arrive at full-cost bottom lines of $1,300 and $3,500, which, when added together, equal the organization's bottom line of $4,800.

A final point to bear in mind is that cost allocation schemes involve both a *method* of allocation and a *basis* for allocation. One example of a method might be a period-end blanket allocation of costs performed by the accounting staff; another might be a transfer pricing system. An example of an allocation basis is number of enrollments or percentage of income. In Chapter Nine we will explore possible methods and bases for cost allocations and the implications of their use in more detail.

Degree of Budgetary Flexibility. One problem with preparing budgets is that as soon as they are prepared, they are obsolete. Some event occurs or some condition changes, and the carefully prepared budget plan that presumed to project the future suddenly becomes an historical document. The change may be internal to the organization, as when a budget is based on the continued services of a programmer who subsequently decides to leave the organization. The "hole" left in the budget is unlikely to be filled in exactly the same way by another programmer. Or the change may be external, as when a change in tax laws creates an opportunity for a large program on taxation that had not been anticipated in the budget or, conversely, a weakening dollar causes a drop in overseas travel program enrollments. A third kind of change results from a simple deviation from the budget plan. For instance, a programmer might have planned in the budget to present thirty courses during the fall term but end up presenting only twenty; or enrollment projections may be off.

These last two examples result in what are called *volume deviations.* Budgets are usually based on a specified volume of activity. If the volume estimates (in this case, number of courses or number of enrollments) are either not met or exceeded, there will be deviations in all variable-cost budget items. For instance, presenting ten fewer courses in the fall will probably result in lower teacher compensation expense, which in budgetary terms is a positive or favorable variance. This favorable cost variance is probably more than offset, however, by an unfavorable income variance. On the other hand, if the programmer presented forty courses instead of the projected thirty, income might exceed expectations, but so probably would the line item for instructor compensation. Furthermore, it may be possible for the programmer to achieve the same "bottom line" result with twenty courses as with the budgeted thirty courses. Theoretically, if management were primarily concerned with the bottom line, the budget target could then be met despite these volume variances.

The ability to adjust the budget for volume variances is one aspect of budgetary flexibility. Computers, particularly microcomputers with spreadsheet programs, have greatly enhanced the flexibility of budgets by increasing the speed with which the effects of change can be computed. In Chapter Eight we will examine some specific techniques for developing budgetary flexibility.

Whatever the reason for actual or potential deviations from the budget, management, especially the director, will have to decide what to do when they occur. It is always possible to recast the budget, and it is sometimes desirable to do so; but frequent revision of a budget can be time-consuming and expensive and can decrease the value of the budget as a standard against which performance is to be judged. For instance, to allow the programmer in our example to revise the budget on the basis of twenty programs rather than thirty somehow lets the programmer off the hook and mitigates the value of the standard. Even such an external factor as the weakening dollar perhaps should have been foreseen by the programmer of the travel programs. To some extent, that programmer is responsible for the fact that the budget was prepared on an incorrect premise. Deviations from budgets are facts, and facts should not be hidden. The alternative to frequent budget recastings is to allow the deviations to occur and record reasons for them as they become apparent.

As the preceding discussion suggests, the role of the budget as a standard of comparison for actual results and its role as a forecasting and planning instrument can come into conflict. Before establishing a budget system, management should define the kinds of circumstances that will require a budget revision and the sorts of budget deviations for which managers will be held accountable. The ability of a budget to maintain its usefulness as both a standard and a planning document in the face of changing conditions is another form of budgetary flexibility. This form of flexibility is established through custom, personality, stated policy, and/or experimentation. Management's attitude toward revisions and deviations suffuses the budget process, especially the part involving feedback or monitoring, which we will discuss in Chapter Seven.

Degree of Integration with Reward System. Another factor that must be determined before a budget system is introduced is the relationship, if any, that will exist between the organization's budget system and its reward system. In many CE organizations, management's ability to formally reward desirable behavior or favorable operating results is rather restricted. There may be budgetary restrictions on employee compensation, or the salary and wage administration policies of the parent institution may not recognize the criteria for reward established in the CE organization. When formal reward is not possible or very limited, informal symbols of recognition—the figurative "pat on the back"—are called for. Even where it is possible for the director to reward employees with raises or promotions, it is unlikely that such rewards will be granted solely on the basis of financial or budgetary performance. Scholarship, teaching ability, community service, and the educational quality of courses offered are often accorded equal or superior status in performance evaluations, especially of programming staff.

Nonetheless, ideally at least, achieving or failing to achieve budgetary goals should somehow be related to the reward system. Such a relationship can go a long way toward establishing the legitimacy of the budget system and assuring its success. The mechanisms of interaction between the two systems should be carefully worked out in advance and clearly communicated to those who will assume budget responsibility.

Handling of Hidden Subsidies. In Part One we discussed the budgetary options in dealing with a course that enjoyed a partial subsidy from a sponsoring agency. The temptation is to prepare a budget that does not include the subsidy either as income or as expense. The same issue arises in budgeting for a CE organization as a whole. For instance, in many CE organizations the salary of the director is paid through a funding source not associated with the CE cost center, or the fringe benefits of employees are paid from fund sources outside the CE budget. Because these items are not part of the CE budget, they tend to be ignored in the budgeting process. Other common hidden subsidies were listed in the Introduction.

Hiding of subsidies is often even more pronounced when the parent organization, by diverting CE-generated funds, develops a source of funding less restricted in its use than other funds available. An example of this might be the CE division of an academic department of a university. Often academic departments are short of funds, particularly of discretionary funds—funds that may be used for things like travel, office furnishings, or additional teaching assistants. Student fee income from CE courses is often unrestricted. Thus, where the costs of the CE enterprise can be handled by more restrictive fund sources, more money can be shifted into the discretionary category. This means that often clerical and even instructional costs related to the CE enterprise are paid from other fund sources.

The existence of these hidden subsidies makes interinstitutional cost comparisons difficult and casts considerable ambiguity on the term "self-supporting." More important, such subsidies obscure the true cost of the CE organization from the management of the parent institution and even from the management of the CE enterprise itself. As described in the Introduction, hidden subsidies often lead to distorted financial statements and ultimately to poor management decisions. There are often good practical and political reasons for not recognizing these hidden subsidies in the formal budget; for example, bringing attention to such subsidies during a period of tightening resources may lead to their disappearance. But, at least in the informal financial planning that goes on around the formal process, these subsidies should be taken into account. Somebody, somewhere, should know what is really going on.

Other Factors. The CE director should consider at least two other issues before launching a new or revised budget system. The first is the question of openness versus secrecy. How open a process is budgeting going to be? Are budget targets for each responsibility center going to be universally known? Are comparisons of actual results to budgets going to be available to everyone in the organization? Are rewards and sanctions going to be known? How will decisions regarding budgets and financial issues be made and communicated? Who should know "how things are going," when, and from whom?

The second issue is the question of who does what, when. The introduction and maintenance of a budget system are time-consuming and difficult tasks requiring careful coordination of the efforts of a large number of people. Clear assignment of tasks and establishment of deadlines are essential ingredients for success.

Once all these preliminary decisions are made, the budget system itself can be set up. Our next three chapters will explain in detail the stages in developing and implementing a budget for a CE organization.

Summary

The revision or introduction of a budget system represents a significant change for an organization, and change never takes place in a vacuum. A new or revised organizational budget system must be consistent with the environment it is supposed to serve and compatible with the goals and objectives of the organization's management. Narrowly conceived budget systems, directed at correcting a transitory problem or merely increasing managerial control, are unlikely to succeed. The planning of a budget system must involve examination of the organization's history, its place *vis-a-vis* the parent or other organizations, its external environment, and, above all, its people and their attitudes.

This examination of the organizational environment must guide important preliminary decisions about the way the budget system will be structured. Perhaps the most important decision concerns the way the organization will be segmented or divided so that responsibility for the performance of the parts will be clearly defined. The relationship of the budget system to the employee evaluation and reward system is also important. Budgets will not be effective unless they *mean* something—unless they are compared with actual results and used as a basis for decisions and employee evaluation.

Another vital decision concerns control. Budgets are unquestionably part of the control structure of an organization, and the control aspect of any potential budget system should be carefully considered by management. A budget system that is too heavy-handed in its control will create resentment and fear in employees, while a budget system that is too flexible and easily altered may not be sufficiently effective as a standard.

Before instituting or revising a budget system, a CE organization's management should be clear on these and other issues and incorporate them in a clearly articulated implementation plan. A budget system can be controversial, especially in its early and fragile stage when it is likely to be looked upon with suspicion and apprehension. Early errors—those of tone and style as well as those of substance—can severely damage the future effectiveness of a budget system. Only a very broad view of the budgeting process, one that includes its effect on people and their perceptions of their jobs and the organization they work for, can lead to successful budget system design.

Bibliography

Anthony, R. N., and Herzlinger, R. E. *Management Control in Nonprofit Organizations.* (Rev. ed.) Homewood, Ill.: Irwin, 1980.

Borst, D., and Montana, P. J., (eds.). *Managing Nonprofit Organizations.* New York: AMACOM, 1977.

Drucker, P. "A Day with Peter Drucker." A lecture presented by the University of California, Berkeley, University Extension, San Francisco, Apr. 26, 1979.

Holder, W. W., and Ingram, R. W. "Flexible Budgeting and Standard Costing: Keys to Effective Cost Control." In R. W. Ingram (ed.), *Accounting in the Public Sector: The Changing Environment.* Corvallis, Ore.: Brighton, 1980.

Knox, A. B. "Creative Financing of Continuing Education." In T. Shipp (ed.), *Creative Financing and Budgeting.* New Directions for Continuing Education, no. 16. San Francisco: Jossey-Bass, 1982.

Sullivan, T. J. *How to Budget in a Service Organization.* New York: American Management Association, Extension Institute, 1982.

Titard, P. L. *Managerial Accounting: An Introduction.* Hinsdale, Ill.: Dryden Press, 1983.

White, R., and Lippett, R. *Autocracy and Democracy.* New York: Harper & Row, 1960.

5

Setting
Realistic Guidelines
and Targets

With preliminary considerations out of the way, we can now turn to the actual budgeting process. Although budgeting varies greatly from organization to organization, certain steps can be identified as belonging universally to the process. These steps are:

1. Establishing budget guidelines
2. Setting sales/volume targets
3. Budget call and initial preparation
4. Negotiation
5. Coordination and review
6. Final approval
7. Distribution
8. Feedback and monitoring

Steps three, four, and five represent the bulk of the work in the budgeting process and may be repeated several times as the budget takes shape. Step Eight, feedback and monitoring, is very important but is often not recognized as part of the process, because it is carried out after the original budget is prepared.

We will examine the first three steps in detail in this chapter, using as an example a CE organization that is partly self-supporting, has many service departments and programming departments, and has segmented the latter into a number of responsibility (profit) centers. We will continue to assume that the smallest budget object is the individual course. This model will not exactly describe all or even perhaps most CE organizations, but it represents the most comprehensive and complex organization structure and is therefore useful for expository purposes. The explanations presented in connection with it can be applied fairly easily to a large variety of CE organizational forms, including fully subsidized organizations.

Establishing Budget Guidelines

The first step in the budgeting process proper is establishing planning guidelines. This follows the preliminary steps, described in the last chapter, of adopting an organization segmentation plan, choosing appropriate budget line items, and establishing an indirect cost allocation basis and method.

Deadlines. Deadlines are an important element in budget guidelines. Usually the budget for a CE organization must be presented to its parent institution for approval and inclusion in the institutional budget, and the deadline for this submission is often used as a date by which other deadlines can be determined. A Gantt chart showing a typical budget preparation schedule with deadlines is pictured in Figure 5.1.

Our chart indicates that the parent institution has established a May 1 deadline (item 7 on the chart) for budget submission, presumably in preparation for a July 1 fiscal year. Backing up from that date, we can establish deadlines and time periods for each stage of the budgeting process. Under this schedule, preparation starts about February 1 with the issuing of budget guidelines. By March 1 the sales/volume targets are established, and the budget call can go to those responsible for generating operating budgets. In this chart, the entire month of March is allowed for initial preparation. This may be more time than is needed in some cases, but management has a stake in careful and serious preparation of budgets and should be sure to allow enough time. Coordination and review are allowed two weeks; in relatively

Figure 5.1. Gantt Chart: Typical Budget Preparation Time Schedule.

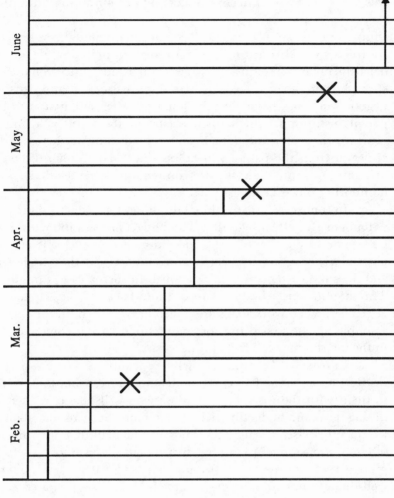

1. Preparation of Budget Guidelines
2. Estimating Sales/Volume Targets
3. Budget Call
4. Initial Preparation
5. Review, Coordination
6. Further Negotiation
7. Submission to Parent
8. Recast for Parent Approval
9. Final Approval
10. Distribution
11. Feedback, Monitoring

simple organizations this may be more than enough, but where indirect cost allocations have to be reconciled and service department budgets adjusted, two weeks may not suffice. Some time should then be allowed for final adjustments and further negotiation—for "balancing the budget." After submission to the parent institution, which often occurs in the form of a budget hearing, there may need to be further adjustments before final approval from the parent can be obtained. That done, the now-official budget(s) can be distributed and the feedback and monitoring process can begin.

In some cases, institutional deadlines for budget submission will not mesh well with deadlines for budget preparation within the CE organization. For instance, programmers' work loads may be particularly heavy during March, when the spring term is underway and the summer term is being planned. In such a case it might be desirable to push budget preparation back, perhaps even to December, when work loads are not so heavy. Then, in the spring, a simple update to account for changes that have become obvious in the interim may be all that is necessary.

In cases like this, or where deadlines set by parent institutions are not a factor, the budgeting process should be timed to fit in with the work load of those who will take part in it. If timing is poor, budgeting will seem more burdensome than it would otherwise. Because the budget is a planning instrument, often a long-range planning instrument, it is most usefully prepared when time and reflection can be spent in developing a well-thought-out look at the future. It should be prepared early enough to be able to influence the future, but not so early that implementation is at too far a remove from the development of the plan. In some organizations, a budget prepared in March and April for a fiscal year beginning in July would have to include a summer program that had already been prepared. This is obviously unwise, since the value of the budget as a plan is lost if it includes a portion that, in effect, has already been implemented.

Basic Assumptions. Those asked to prepare budgets must be given basic assumptions upon which to base their estimates of activity. These assumptions may involve some of the environmental factors described in the last chapter, including the economy and market conditions. Such assumptions may be broadly and simply stated, or they may relate to specific markets and anticipate complex relationships. An example of a general assumption might be: "For the purposes of this budget, market and economic conditions will be assumed to be unchanged for the coming fiscal year." Another more specific assumption might be: "The market for courses in real estate, following the decline in the real estate market, will decline by 10 percent through the third quarter of next year and then recover at a 10 percent per quarter rate for the next three quarters." Other examples can be seen in Figure 5.5 (p. 201).

One element of the economy, the rate of inflation or general price level change, is particularly important where detailed expense justifications have to be prepared. Of course, for self-supporting organizations, the rate of inflation will also have an impact on the price charged for courses. Usually the relevant budget assumption will designate an inflation rate that should be applied to costs calculated in terms of current dollars, for example: "Assume a rate of inflation of 5 percent for the next fiscal year." Care should be taken, however, not to ignore changes in the prices of specific items that are expected to differ from general price level changes. For instance, several years ago price increases for paper were greater than the general rate of inflation. Paper is a significant expense for CE organizations, since it is used not only for administrative purposes but also for mail promotion; thus, failure to recognize this increase could have resulted in cost overruns. Another significant cost element for CE organizations is postage, and postage increases rarely coincide exactly with inflation rates.

In addition to cost changes created by external economic conditions, there are a number of possible cost increases from internal or institutional sources. A common example of this is payroll costs; cost-of-living adjustments and even so-called merit increases are often mandated by institutional policy. Other examples might be computer time provided by the parent institution and instructor compensation rates. Internal service department recharges will also come under this classification. (Such recharges will have to be calculated as a separate part of setting the guidelines, as we will discuss later.) All necessary assumptions about internally or institutionally caused cost changes should be provided to the budget preparers.

Another kind of budget assumption relates to changes in subsidy. When a CE organization is granted funding by the parent institution or by outside agencies, any expected changes in this funding should be specified in the budget guidelines. It is sometimes useful here to make the distinction between "hard money" and "soft money." *Hard money* is funding from a regular source—money that can be depended upon from year to year. It may be given to the CE organization by a funding agency, or it may be a source of income from a very stable internal program. Despite the basic dependability of the source, there may nevertheless be changes in the amount of the funding from year to year. These changes, known or predicted, will have to be specified before budget preparation. If the amount of the changes is not precisely known, different calculations reflecting alternative assumptions about them must be requested. For instance, the preliminary plan might ask a manager to prepare budgets using three assumptions: (1) no change in funds, (2) a 10 percent increase in funding, or (3) a 10 percent decrease in funding. The manager would have to compute individual line items and program changes under each of these.

Soft money is funding from sources that are relatively short term or uncertain. Traditionally, this label has been applied to funding sources such as government contracts, which generally are granted from year to year at the pleasure of the Congress or the state legislature; but other kinds of funding may also be called soft money. Although it may be necessary to state some assumptions about soft money sources in the overall budget guidelines, it is often more appropriate for individual managers, who may be closer to relevant information, to generate these assumptions.

To meet increases in costs or for other reasons, management may want to call for course fee increases. If the CE organization uses a course fee schedule and changes in the schedule are planned, the revised schedule can be presented as an assumption in the budget planning guide.

Management may also want to prescribe some program changes in the budget assumption list. These may specify the discontinuance or addition of a particular program, curriculum, or subject matter grouping of programs. They may reflect the balance of rewards and risks, status quo and adventure, that characterizes the particular organization.

Specific facility availability may also be an item in budget assumptions. A particular classroom may have become available at a specific price, a computer lab may have been developed, or a woodshop in a local high school may not be available any more. Changes in availability or cost of use of specific installations should be specified in budget assumptions.

One final assumption that should be specified, but for which specification is difficult, might be termed "level of optimism" or "level of reality." Each budget preparer brings to the process his or her own personal feelings about the future and the purpose of budgeting. Some will forecast a rosy future or set unrealistically high goals for themselves, while others will consistently underestimate their financial prospects or try to work the budget process to their advantage by setting themselves very low targets. It is possible to head off a resulting lack of consistency by making some general statements about the future in the budget assumptions.

Ideally, budgets should set goals that are difficult but not impossible to achieve, and they should be realistic about the future. Too optimistic or pessimistic a forecast may lead to poor management decisions and damage the budget's usefulness as a planning tool. Even worse, when different parts of the budget are prepared on different bases, both the planning function and the integrity of the goal-setting process are all but destroyed, since, in effect, different standards are being applied to different sectors of the organization. These problems can be minimized by statements such as: "Projected enrollments more than 10 percent lower or higher than last year's must be supported with a narrative justification." The "evening out" of levels of optimism or pessimism is a major task of the budget step called coordination and review, which we will discuss in Chapter Six.

Estimates of Indirect Costs. A starting point for many CE budgets is estimation of the total amount of indirect or overhead costs that have to be covered from operations. This is obviously of great importance to self-supporting units, but it is really of equal importance to subsidized units in spite of superficially less distinction between their overhead or service departments and their programming or operating departments. A parent institution may charge indirect costs to a CE organization on any one of several bases, including a flat amount for the budget period, a percentage of total income or expense, or a given amount per enrollment or per employee. Indirect cost charges of this type, which are "givens" to the CE organization, should be built into the budget guidelines for the organization's subunits. For instance, the subunits could be instructed to budget 10 percent of total expense as institutional overhead.

Another level of indirect cost arises from the CE organization itself. In the last chapter we listed a number of service departments that might be associated with a CE organization. Funds for these services have to come from somewhere. In self-supporting units, that "somewhere" is obviously the programming departments. The first step in calculating what the organization will have to generate in "available for overhead" is to estimate what that overhead will be—in other words, how much each service department will cost in the next budget period.

To aid in this task, preliminary budgets for the service departments should be prepared. Fortunately, costs in service departments (with the possible exception of the promotion or marketing department) generally are rather stable. Payroll costs usually constitute the bulk of their expenses, and, unless the number of employees is likely to change significantly, these costs (based on the payroll increase assumption of the budget) can easily be estimated. Unless the organization is rapidly expanding or contracting, other line item costs for service departments usually can be estimated from the actual results of either the current year or the last full fiscal year.

In preparing these preliminary budgets, planners are presented with two options. First, they can do a "quick and dirty" cost estimate, hoping to arrive at a reasonably good approximation, and then request individual service center budgets along with the rest of the responsibility center budgets. Alternatively, they can ask service department managers to prepare budgets in relatively great detail, based on volume or use estimates that they either supply or allow the managers to specify. These budgets can then be added together to arrive at the total costs. Figure 5.2 is an example of a careful estimate of the costs for the service departments of a CE organization.

Please note the form of the worksheet in Figure 5.2: we will use it again and again. It shows the responsibility centers in columns across the top and the line item expenditures down the left side, thus allowing the expenditure budgets and the program budgets to be shown simultaneously. Note also that income associated with a particular service center, such as transcript fees for the Student Records department (column f) and outside rental income for the Downtown Classroom Facility (column h), is shown at the top and serves to reduce the total cost of the service center. In a similar fashion, two departments, Promotion (column g) and Reprographics (column i), whose total costs are recharged to programming departments and thus end up in programming department costs, show "income" equal to their total costs. The total of all expenses for all departments ($767,000) is shown in column a on the "Total expense" line. The next line shows total expense less total income, producing a total net indirect cost of $460,000. Later we will talk about the process of reconciliation between these amounts and the amounts that programming department budgets provide for these services.

As we have stated, financial data for any single period is of limited use unless it is compared to some similar set of figures. Thus, an estimation of the current year's figures is shown on the worksheet, below the figures for the previous year. Significant deviations from the previous year should be explained in footnotes on the schedule where possible.

Computerized spreadsheet programs make the generation of worksheets like this very rapid and, because of the flexibility they offer in generating reports in different formats, give a new dimension to financial analysis. For instance, the budget and the actual results for each department with a better or worse column could be generated as shown in Figure 5.3. This figure is also an example of the kind of worksheet that might be needed to generate the worksheet shown in Figure 5.2. Certainly the "other costs" category on that worksheet would be of interest.

Figure 5.2. Annual Budget: Service Department Summary.

Budget Year	(a) Total	(b) Director's Office	(c) Business Office	(d) Cashier's Office	(e) Reg. Office	(f) Student Records	(g) Promotion Dept.	(h) Downtown Facility	(i) Reprographics	(j) Parent Recharges
Income										
Internal recharges	$252,000						$152,000		$100,000	
Transcript income	15,000					$15,000				
Outside income	40,000							$30,000	10,000	
Total income	$307,000					$15,000	$152,000	$30,000	$110,000	
Expense										
Staff payroll	$424,500	$90,000	$36,000	$30,000	$56,000	$28,000	$100,500	$22,000	$62,000	
Fringe benefits	84,800	18,000	7,200	6,000	11,200	5,600	20,000	4,400	12,400	
Total payroll	$509,300	$108,000	$43,200	$36,000	$67,200	$33,600	$120,500	$26,400	$74,400	
Supplies and expenses										
Office supplies	$ 10,300	$ 500	$1,000	$ 500	$2,000	$2,000	$ 4,000	$ 0	$ 300	
Telephone	7,300	1,000	500	300	2,000	500	2,000	500	500	
Travel	2,700	2,000			200		500			
Printing, repro.	24,500	1,500	2,000	500	3,000	1,500	15,000	500	500	
Other	212,900	1,000	500	1,000	2,000	500	10,000	133,600	34,300	$30,000
Total S & E	$257,700	$6,000	$4,000	$2,300	$9,200	$4,500	$31,500	$134,600	$35,600	$30,000
Total expense	$767,000	$114,000	$47,200	$38,300	$76,400	$38,100	$152,000	$161,000	$110,000	$30,000
Net service dept. costs	$460,000	$114,000	$47,200	$38,300	$76,400	$23,100	$152,000	$131,000	$110,000	$30,000
Contingency	250,000									
Total	$710,000									

Current Year Projected

Income	$250,000					$15,000	$125,000	$12,000	$98,000	
Expense										
Payroll	$358,750	$73,500	$32,000	$25,750	$47,000	$24,500	$74,000	$18,000	$64,000	
Fringe benefits	71,750	14,650	6,400	5,200	9,400	4,900	14,800	3,600	12,800	
Total payroll	$430,500	$88,150	$38,400	$30,950	$56,400	$29,400	$88,800	$21,600	$76,800	
Supplies and expense										
Office supplies	$ 9,000	$ 500	$ 700	$ 400	$1,800	$1,800	$ 3,500		$ 300	
Telephone	6,500	800	500	300	1,800	400	1,800	$ 400	500	
Travel	2,000	1,500	100				400			
Printing, repro.	23,000	1,400	1,800	500	2,900	1,400	13,500	500	1,000	
Other	190,000	1,000	500	1,200	500	300	6,000	125,000	28,500	$27,000
Total S & E	$230,500	$5,200	$3,600	$2,400	$7,000	$3,900	$25,200	$125,900	$30,300	$27,000
Total expense	$661,000	$93,350	$42,000	$33,350	$63,400	$33,300	$114,000	$147,500	$107,100	$27,000
Net service dept. costs	$411,000	$93,350	$42,000	$33,350	$63,400	$18,300	($11,000)	$135,500	$9,100	$27,000

Figure 5.3. Downtown Facility: Budget Compared to Actual.

	Budget 19A-B	Actual Projected This Year	Budget Better (Worse)	Actual Prior Year	Budget Better (Worse)
Income					
Classroom rental	$6,000	$1,000	$5,000	$4,000	$2,0●
Auditorium rental	7,000	3,500	3,500	4,500	2,5●
Special events	13,000	7,000	6,000	7,000	6,0●
Office rental	4,000	500	3,500	1,500	2,5●
Total	$30,000	$12,000	$18,000	$17,000	$13,0●
Expense					
Payroll-Superintendant	$22,000	$18,000	($4,000)	$28,000	$6,0●
Fringe	4,400	3,600	(800)	5,000	6●
Total payroll	$26,400	$21,600	($4,800)	$33,000	$6,6●
Supplies and expense					
Office supplies					
Telephone	$500	$400	($100)	$400	($1●
Travel				500	5●
Printing, repro	500	500			(5●
Other					
Janitorial	$44,000	$40,000	($4,000)	$37,000	($7,0●
Security	30,000	28,000	(2,000)	27,000	(3,0●
Utilities	15,000	14,000	(1,000)	13,000	(2,0●
Minor repairs	5,000	5,800	800	3,200	(1,8●
Major repairs	34,600	29,600	(5,000)	15,500	(19,1●
Garbage	3,000	2,600	(400)	2,500	(5●
Other	2,000	5,000	3,000	2,000	
Subtotal other	$133,600	$125,000	($8,600)	$100,200	($33,4●
Total S & E	$134,600	$125,900	($8,700)	$101,100	($33,5●
Total expense	$161,000	$147,500	($13,500)	$134,100	($26,9●
Net cost	$131,000	$135,500	$4,500	$117,100	($13,9●

Note: Payments for janitorial and security services are to outside
      contractors.

Once indirect costs have been estimated, a contingency provision can be added to them. For example, the contingency amount of $250,000 is shown added to the total budgeted costs in Figure 5.2. The contingency amount provides a cushion against a shortfall anywhere in the budget, such as a cost overrun in a service department or the failure of an expected source of income. Prudent managers always provide a contingency factor, and putting it in at this stage of the budgeting process means that it will be built into the whole budget plan. The amount of the contingency is a matter of managerial judgment but should probably be at least 5 percent of the total budget. Of course, contingencies get tucked into all kinds of places in the budget as each manager provides a certain amount of "fat"; but it is a good idea to make explicit this overall contingency.

The addition of a contingency factor to the indirect cost calculation can also be used to build into the budget system a "profit" or "available for overhead" amount assessed by the parent institution. Figure 5.2 shows indirect costs from the parent institution in the last column. In what follows we will assume that the CE organization is required to "break even," with a small surplus going into a reserve to prevent an overall deficit. However, profit targets can easily be incorporated into the budget planning process.

Estimating indirect costs near the beginning of the budgeting process can lead to a special problem that we will mention here and discuss more fully in Chapter Six when we talk about coordination and review. Service department costs are, in part, based on estimates of volume—number of enrollments, number of programs, number of student class hours, and so on. These volume estimates come from the programming departments and are not really available until after their department budgets are developed. Once programming departments have prepared their budgets, the original volume estimates upon which the service department budget estimates were based can be compared with those in the new programming department budgets. When this information is fed back into the service department budgets, the latter may have to be revised. For instance, the estimation of registration office costs is based in part on the number of enrollments anticipated during the next budget period. If, after the preparation of the programming department budgets, it becomes apparent that there will be a significant deviation from that estimate, the registration office budget will have to be changed.

Indirect promotion costs are usually more highly volatile than, say, registration costs. What the programming departments contemplate for the next budget period has a major effect on the budget of the promotion department. Thus it is highly likely that the initial promotion department budget will have to be revised after preparation of the programming department budgets. For departments providing services on a transfer pricing basis, the total amount of the costs will have to be reconciled with the amounts upon which program department budgets are based.

The problem of hidden subsidies also comes up again here. Even if the subsidies are not hidden, in a self-supporting organization the tendency is to ignore any costs that are not part of the self-support budget. This results in budget entities that do not correspond to operating entities, which makes managerial decision making difficult. One way of making sure that subsidized units are seen as part of the whole organization is to include them on budget worksheets along with the others, with the amount of the subsidy shown as "income." An example of this is shown in Figure 5.4, which is simply Figure 5.2 recast under the assumption that the registration office is fully subsidized.

The column positioning in Figure 5.4 has been altered from that in Figure 5.2 to show a subtotal for the self-supporting part of the budget (column c), to which is added the subsidized registration office (column b) to get the total budget (column a). A new line labeled "Subsidy" has been added in the income section, and "income" amounting to the total registration office costs has been entered here. Thus the registration office "nets out" to a zero figure. This worksheet technique shows all the relevant information while preserving a sense of the whole. The same technique can be used for programming departments when, for example, one program is subsidized or funded from a government grant. It can prove very handy when dealing with montage funding.

Preliminary Targets. Having estimated what the service departments will cost for the budget period, budget planners can now go about setting preliminary targets for the programming departments. This process can be either simple or complex, depending on the situation.

The simplest tactic is for management to set no targets at all, allowing each programming department to come up with what it believes to be a reasonable financial goal for the next year. If the

Figure 5.4. Service Department Summary Showing Treatment of Subsidized Department.

Budget Year	(a) Total	(b) Reg. Office	(c) Subtotal Self Support	(d) Director's Office	(e) Business Office	(f) Cashier's Office	(g) Student Records	(h) Promotion Dept.	(i) Downtown Facility	(j) Repro- graphics	(k) Parent Recharges
Income											
Internal recharges	$252,000		$252,000					$152,000		$100,000	
Transcript income	15,000		15,000				$15,000				
Outside income	40,000		40,000						$30,000	10,000	
Subsidy	76,400	$76,400									
Total income	$383,400	$76,400	$307,000				$15,000	$152,000	$30,000	$110,000	
Expense											
Staff payroll	$424,500	$56,000	$368,500	$90,000	$36,000	$30,000	$28,000	$100,500	$22,000	$62,000	
Fringe benefits	84,800	11,200	73,600	18,000	7,200	6,000	5,600	20,000	4,400	12,400	
Total payroll	$509,300	$67,200	$442,100	$108,000	$43,200	$36,000	$33,600	$120,500	$26,400	$74,400	
Supplies and expenses											
Office supplies	$10,300	$2,000	$8,300	$500	$1,000	$500	$2,000	$4,000		$300	
Telephone	7,300	2,000	5,300	1,000	500	300	500	2,000	$500	500	
Travel	2,700	200	2,500	2,000				500			
Printing, repro.	24,500	3,000	21,500	1,500	2,000	500	1,500	15,000	500	500	
Other	212,900	2,000	210,900	1,000	500	1,000	500	10,000	133,600	34,300	$30,000
Total S & E	$257,700	$9,200	$248,500	$6,000	$4,000	$2,300	$4,500	$31,500	$134,600	$35,600	$30,000
Total expense	$767,000	$76,400	$690,600	$114,000	$47,200	$38,300	$38,100	$152,000	$161,000	$110,000	$30,000
Net service dept. costs	$383,600		$383,600	$114,000	$47,200	$38,300	$23,100		$131,000		$30,000
Contingency	250,000										
Total	$633,600										

departments are conscientious and honest and it is relatively easy for the organization to meet financial expectations, this tactic can be effective. However, if extensive revisions later become necessary in order to "balance the budget," this managerial failure to set targets can lead to a great deal of wasted time and effort.

Another relatively simple tactic is to set "available for overhead" targets based on the service department costs. For instance, the amount of $710,000 calculated in Figure 5.2, which included a contingency figure, could be allocated to programming departments on some basis, say a proportional allocation based on the actual contribution to overhead made by each programming department in the prior year. In our example CE organization, there are five programming departments, several of which have more than one programmer. Although this organization is segmented largely along subject matter lines, there is one "functional" department called "Conferences and Institutes" (C & I), which handles special programs covering a wide range of subjects, usually in conjunction with other departments of the parent organization. Service department costs are allocated to these programming departments as follows:

Arts and Sciences	$380,000
Business Management	150,000
Education	10,000
Engineering	150,000
Conferences and Institutes	20,000
	$710,000

Each of these departments has the responsibility to develop a budget that, after all costs associated with the department have been covered, provides an excess of income over expense of at least the amount specified. The advantages of this "available for overhead" tactic are that it can be simple to calculate, concentrates quite directly on the "bottom line," and does not involve a great deal of subsequent reconciliation. Its disadvantages are that it may be too simple, ignoring important factors and resulting in poorly established goals. It also does not relate the volumes upon which the service department costs were based to the volumes anticipated in the programming department budgets. For instance, Arts and Sciences may plan to achieve its budget by offering 20 percent more courses for the next budget period than for the last, which would mean that those service departments whose costs are related to enrollments (Registration, Cashier, Student Records) and number of programs (Program Processing) might be underbudgeted.

The next level of tactical complexity would be to set targets that recognize the relationships between service department costs and program activity and also intradepartment cost-income relationships for the programming departments. Thus, programming departments might be asked to provide 5 percent of total income for registration costs and, in addition, to budget 35 percent of expected direct promotion costs for indirect promotion, which would be recharge income to the promotion department. Once it is understood by staff, this approach is less complicated than it may sound. Methods of computing these relationships and communicating them to the programming departments are described in more detail in the section of this chapter that deals with setting the enrollment/volume target.

Other kinds of preliminary targets relate to elements other than service department costs or sales volume. Fully or partially subsidized organizations often ignore enrollment volumes altogether, since their main budget task is to allocate given resources among a number of departments. For these organizations and even for self-supporting units, management may wish to establish expenditure caps on budget line items, either in absolute terms (for example, total instructor compensation may not exceed $15,000) or as percentages (instructor compensation may not exceed 40 percent of the total budget).

Some budget targets may be nonfinancial. Such targets are important for many subsidized organizations, which do not have the external measure of success—market acceptance—that most self-support organizations have. Quantitative targets might include the number of students served, the number of courses or student hours provided, or, where absenteeism is a factor, the number of student contact hours provided. Qualitative targets might be the number of students who successfully pass courses or graduate from programs or might be related to learning goals measured by standard tests.

Of course it is possible to relate these nonfinancial targets to financial targets. For instance, a target might be established on the basis of the cost per student hour or per (incremental) point of learning achievement. In such cases, the total budgeted costs of a program would be divided by the expected volume of student hours or student learning improvement points to arrive at the target.

Now let us look at a more complex target-setting process.

Setting the Enrollment/Volume Target

Estimating income or enrollment is the most crucial and also the most difficult part of budget preparation for a self-supporting CE organization. It is difficult because it depends in part on estimates of market and economic forces outside the control of management. It is crucial because so much of the rest of the budget is a direct function of total income. The variable costs of instructor compensation and direct program expenses are obviously directly related—they "follow" enrollment volume. For fixed costs, too, enrollment or income will define a "relevant range." We spoke earlier about establishing service department budgets based on an estimate of the volume of expected activity, and total sales can give us a basis for that estimation. Promotion expenses, too, are directly related to total income and enrollment, though they precede enrollment rather than follow it. All these costs and their relationship to total enrollments can directly and radically affect the "bottom line."

The income budget can be drawn up by top management as part of the preliminary goal-setting process, by the programming departments as part of the initial preparation of the budget, or both. Management needs to do some kind of income estimation in any case, for two reasons. First, such an estimate can be used to test the validity of service department budgets and to establish the "relevant range," as previously described. Second, management needs to develop a standard against which to evaluate programming department income budgets. Whether this standard is imposed as a preliminary target or remains unknown to the department chairs until their budgets have been prepared is a matter of management choice.

At whatever level the income budget is prepared, the process remains approximately the same. The first step is to look outside the organization and make some estimate of potential sales—the income forecast. It should be noted here that the income forecast and the income budget are not the same. The income forecast is a projection of the income level that the organization *could* achieve if the budget is effective. The income budget is the plan—including promotion cost elements and strategies, pricing strategies, and program or product strategies—for achieving the forecast.

Estimating sales potential is always difficult; there are no really reliable methods of doing it. One method involves examining patterns of past enrollment growth and decline in defined markets. For instance, as the economy worsens, the market for one-day training courses in employee supervision may dry up because businesses tighten their training budgets. Conversely, as the economy picks up, the market for these courses may return.

Given an accurate projection of major trends, it is usually easier to forecast income for larger organizations and those with a wide variety of offerings than for smaller or more narrowly focused organizations because the larger and more diversified the organization, the more likely it is to reflect the general situation. Taking advantage of this characteristic, a CE manager may forecast total sales for the organization in two ways. First, the pattern of income for the entire unit can be calculated according to the overall assumptions about the economy and the market that are being applied to the budget. Second, the organization can be broken into smaller units, and the income for each unit can be calculated according to assumptions about the individual market that the unit serves. The income of these units can then be added together and compared with the estimate under the first method. Reconciliation of the two methods of calculating sales can provide a more reliable forecast than either one by itself.

The second step in preparing the income budget is to look inward at elements affecting income that are under the control of management and decide how they should be shaped. The most important of these elements have sometimes been called the three

Ps. *Price* is of particular importance: How courses are priced can have a significant effect on total income, especially where there is competition and "elasticity of demand." Fee schedules should be carefully examined and compared with prices set by the competition and other market conditions. The *product* should also be examined, since the subject matter offering, course format, instructor quality, academic level, evaluation techniques employed, classroom facility utilized, location and time of the offering, and many other factors can influence the total sales of an organization. For instance, although one-day seminars on employee supervision held on weekdays may be on the decline, the same seminars, aimed at people seeking to gain a certificate in personnel management and held on Saturdays, may be successful.

The third "P" is *promotion*. The amount spent on promotion and, more important, the way that money is spent will have a profound effect on total sales. The simplest way to develop the promotion budget is to "peg" promotion as a percentage of total sales. Conceptually, this method does not coincide with reality, since sales should be a function of promotion rather than the other way around. However, this conceptual discontinuity may not result in any significant distortion in the decision-making process. At the other extreme, a detailed marketing and promotion campaign could be developed, and the effect of each element of the plan on total income could be estimated. Again, individual subunit promotion budgets could be developed, added together, and compared with the results of the first method. However the promotion budget is developed and at whatever level of the organization, it is one of the most important budget elements because it is "up front," almost totally discretionary, and can have a direct effect on income generation.

One "quick and dirty" way of estimating what the total sales of the organization or subunit will have to be in order to cover indirect costs and contingency provisions involves the break-even analysis technique described in Part One. Carrying forward the example we began earlier, we will assume that our organization's top management is performing this calculation for the organization as a whole and that the estimate obtained will not be communicated to the subunits until the coordination and review stage.

Management could, of course, perform the same calculations to arrive at subunit income and enrollment expectations and targets, and certainly each subunit manager could do the same.

The first step in making the calculation is to estimate total fixed costs. We have already computed the fixed costs associated with the service departments in Figure 5.2. The fixed costs of each programming subunit also have to be estimated. This is usually not too difficult; most of these fixed costs relate to payroll, and, given a reasonably stable program with known or estimated payroll increases, payroll costs (exclusive of instructional costs) can be easily estimated. Other fixed costs of the subunits, such as departmental supplies, telephone costs, and the like, can also be estimated. Let us say that, for the next budget period, total subunit payroll costs for our example organization are estimated to be $1,000,000, and other departmental costs will be $340,000.

The next step is to estimate the percentage of income represented by variable costs. Again, for relatively large units this is usually not too hard to determine from history, plus adjustments for known factors. For instance, we may know that instructor compensation last year was 30 percent of income, but this year we are raising our prices by an average of 10 percent and increasing instructor compensation by 15 percent. The new estimated percentage for instructor compensation, all other factors (including, most importantly, class size) being equal, would then be 31.36 percent. This result is obtained by taking the original ratio of 30/ 100 and multiplying the instructor compensation rate by 1.15 and the sales amount by 1.10 to get a new ratio of

$$\frac{34.5}{110} = 31.36\%$$

Other elements of direct cost can be similarly calculated, using, perhaps, a general price level (inflation) index. We will assume an inflation rate of 5 percent for all other direct program costs in our example. If these other costs equaled 12.5 percent of sales in the previous year, we can calculate as follows:

$$\frac{12.5 \times 1.05}{100 \times 1.1} = \frac{13.125}{110} = 11.9\%$$

Finally, for our example we will say that promotion cost is pegged at 14 percent of sales (making this, too, a variable cost).

The break-even point for our example organization, expressed in total sales dollars, can now be calculated. Where S = total sales, the computation is as follows:

$S = (.3136 + .119 + .14)S + 710,000 + 1,000,000 + 340,000$
$S = .5726\ S + 2,050,000$
$S = 4,796,443$

This break-even point can be converted into measures other than total sales, given further information or assumptions. For instance, if the average fee per student were known or could be estimated, the break-even in total enrollment could be computed. If the average income per course were known, the total number of courses needed to break even could be computed. Or, given the number of courses and the total enrollment, management could compute the average class size needed to break even. Whatever measures are used (and one should probably use as many as make sense in the situation), the results should be compared to the estimates of what is really possible for the budget period. A calculated break-even point that markedly exceeds the actual results for the previous year strongly suggests that either the basic financial structure of the organization, the assumptions under which the budget has been prepared, or both should be reconsidered.

Later, when the budgets from the subunits are submitted, the budgeted income can be compared with break-even income. When budgeted income exceeds break-even income, the difference is a cushion; when it is less, the budget usually has to be reexamined.

We now turn to the next step in the budgeting process: the budget call and initial budget preparation.

Issuing the Budget Call

Having established guidelines and targets, we can now issue the call for the budget and request managers of successively lower levels of the organization to prepare their budgets. We will describe this process in terms of our example CE organization, with its five programming departments of Arts and Sciences, Business and Management, Education, Engineering, and Conferences and Institutes. Managers of these departments are assigned targets for the "bottom line"—the amount "available for overhead." The department managers in turn are responsible for assigning "available for overhead" targets to the programmers who report to them. Assigning indirect costs this way helps keep our example simple. However, the budgets for the service departments will still have to be reconciled with the volume assumptions that come from the program departments. Later, we will use promotion costs in a detailed illustration of this reconciliation process.

The manager of each department is also given certain other information: the present name and salary level for each employee in the department, the total departmental supplies and expense figure as projected for the current year, and the amount of promotion overhead that the department will have to bear. In our example, most promotion costs are charged directly to the programming departments on a per job basis, according to a rate schedule established at the beginning of every year. The programmers estimate their promotion costs by using this rate sheet. The amount of unrecharged costs is also estimated for budget purposes and assigned to departments. Promotion costs are very carefully reconciled between the programmers' anticipated use and the promotion service department budget.

In contrast to promotion costs, the amounts charged to the programming departments by the reprographics department are not closely reconciled. The costs of reproducing materials are not controlled as a budget line item; rather, they are built into the programming department budgets in a number of places and cannot be pulled out. However, since the reprographics department has a strict cost control system and since prices for the department's services can be compared with those of outside vendors, the reconciliation is not as crucial as with promotion.

Nature of the Budget Call. The budget call serves three purposes. First, it communicates budget assumptions and targets. Second, it provides the preparers with some of the information they need to prepare the budget. Third, it gives them worksheets in formats that, when completed and returned, will facilitate the consolidation, coordination, and review of the budget. These worksheets are useful both in conveying information (such as projected payroll) and in structuring information that is requested.

The budget call is the issuance of the worksheets and instructions for preparing the budget. Instructions to department managers in our example organization are given in Figure 5.5, and instructions to the programmers are given in Figure 5.6. I suggest that you read these instructions carefully, since they establish the premises of the example situation. The worksheets provided to department heads and programmers (shown filled in in Figures 5.9, 5.10, 5.11, 5.12, 6.1, 6.2, 6.3, and 6.4) illustrate the successive levels of detail on which the budget summaries are based. Each schedule "ties in" to the schedules above and below it, as shown in Figure 5.7. We will use Arts and Sciences for our sample department and Cindy E. for our example programmer (responsibility center) within the department.

Initial Preparation. Once the budget call has been issued, budget preparation can begin. Each manager makes the required computations and assigns targets to the programmers. The programmers then begin preparing the detailed estimations upon which the whole budget rests. In our example the programmers will compute individual estimated course budgets for each term, but in reality, this is often impractical—there are too many unknowns, especially in the most distant term. Groups of courses or "average" courses can be estimated, or programmers may be able to predict their results for the term more accurately without going to course detail estimates. Figure 5.9 shows the worksheet in Figure 5.8 as it was filled in by the department manager (columns d-1). Note that the department manager does not anticipate any changes in his programming staff, but he does expect Karen M. to quit and Quentin S. to go to a half-time position; they will be replaced by

Figure 5.5. Budget Instructions to Department Managers.

To: Department Managers
From: Budget Officer
Re: 19A–B Annual Budget

Here is the call for the 19A–B budget computation for your department. It should be completed and returned to me by April 1, 19A. The budget should be prepared in accordance with the following assumptions and instructions.

Budget Assumptions. For the purposes of this budget you should assume that economic conditions will remain the same as last year, except that there will be a 5 percent inflation rate. Market conditions will remain the same except where you have information to the contrary. Fees are to be increased by 10 percent, and instructor compensation rates are to be increased by 15 percent. Promotion costs should be computed by using the present promotion cost guide increased by 10 percent. The budget for each responsibility center should reflect a goal that, if achieved, represents more than satisfactory performance. Adjustments to reflect realistic expectations should be made in the adjustment column of the Department Budget Summary Worksheet.

Budget Targets. The costs for the service departments have been calculated as follows:

Director's Office	$114,000
Business Office	47,200
Cashier's Office	38,300
Registration Office	76,400
Student Records	23,100
Downtown Facility	131,000
Administration	30,000
Contingency	250,000
Total	$710,000

The Director has allocated these costs, based on projections for the current year and on market conditions, as follows:

Arts and Sciences	$380,000
Business and Management	150,000
Education	10,000
Engineering	150,000
Conferences and Institutes	20,000
Total	$710,000

You should allocate the target for your department to your responsibility centers, setting appropriate goals for them and adding whatever contingency you feel is appropriate.

Figure 5.5. Budget Instructions to Department Managers, Cont'd.

Responsibility Center Allocations. Before issuing the budget call to your responsibility centers, you should compute the payroll costs for each center based on the enclosed worksheet [Figure 5.8]. Make adjustments to these calculations based on your own information or plans and allocate the salary of each person to the appropriate responsibility center. Then post the salary figure to the Programmer Term Summary Worksheets [Figure 5.11]. Also post the amount of fringe benefits, which should be calculated as 20 percent of total salaries.

Several other allocations should also be made. First, you should calculate the amount of "departmental" promotion—promotion costs that cannot be allocated to any one responsibility center. Unrecharged promotion department costs, which should be included in departmental promotion, have been calculated to be $50,000 and have been allocated as follows:

Arts and Sciences	$13,000
Business and Management	15,000
Education	5,000
Engineering	13,000
Conferences and Institutes	4,000
Total	$50,000

Departmental supplies and expenses should also be allocated to the Programmer Term Summary Worksheets. As a guide, the actual supplies and expense figures for last year are given below:

Arts and Sciences	$32,000
Business and Management	30,000
Education	11,000
Engineering	27,000
Conferences and Institutes	63,000

Please make these calculations and allocations and distribute the programmer worksheets as soon as possible. If you or your programmers need assistance in filling out these worksheets, let me know.

Figure 5.6 Budget Instructions to Programmers.

To: Programmers
From: Budget Officer
Re: 19A-B Annual Budget Preparation

Here is the call for the 19A-B budget computation for your responsibility center. The Director, after reviewing the projected costs of the service departments, has set the margin target for each department. The department chair, in turn, has set the available for overhead target for each responsibility center. This target appears on the last line of column e of the Programmer Term Summary Worksheet [Figure 5.11]. After you have completed your calculations, you may wish to discuss your target with your department chair. Also allocated to you in column e is your share of payroll costs, departmental promotion, and departmental supplies and expense. Unless there is a compelling reason to do otherwise, you should allocate these costs equally to the four terms. Although we expect some balance in programming volume among terms, it is not necessary to break even or exceed break-even every term as long as the total available for overhead target is attained.

You should complete a Programmer Course Summary Worksheet [Figure 5.12] in as much detail as possible for each term, then post the totals of each worksheet to the top part of the Programmer Term Summary Worksheet (columns a-d). This year we are paying particular attention to promotion costs. You should calculate promotion costs according to the latest promotion cost guide, increasing all rates by 10 percent. Promotion costs for each program (or group of programs) should be calculated using the worksheet called Programmer Promotion Summary by Course [Figure 6.2]. The totals of these worksheets should then be posted to the Programmer Promotion Summary Worksheet [Figure 6.3].

The deadline for submission of these worksheets to your department chair is March 20, 19A. If you have questions or need assistance in filling out these worksheets, please let me know.

Figure 5.7. Relationship of Budget Worksheets.

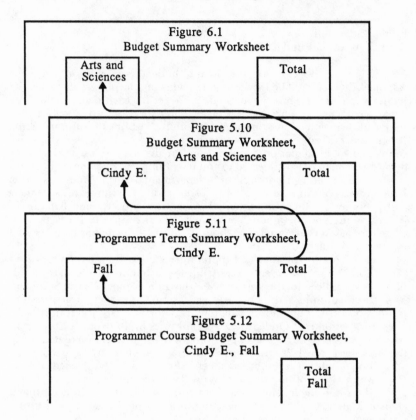

two new employees. The department manager has also distributed total payroll costs to the various responsibility centers in columns f through l.

Figure 5.10, the Arts and Sciences Budget Summary Worksheet, represents the next level of detail. The responsibility centers for the Arts and Sciences department, which in this case are programmers, are listed across the top of the page and totaled in the last column. This total will be carried forward to a worksheet summarizing all programming departments, which we will see later (Figure 6.1).

The "adjustments" column enables the department manager to adjust the totals turned in by the programmers. In this instance,

Figure 5.8. Programming Department Payroll Worksheet, Arts and Sciences (Uncompleted).

Name	(a) Current Salary	(b) Calculated Increases	(c) Estimated Salary	(d) Adjust-ments	(e) Revised Estimate	(f) Allocated to: Cindy E.	(g) Debbie F.	(h) Ernie G.	(i) Freddie H.	(j) Gary I.	(k) Hubert J.	(1) Dept. Admin.
Program salaries												
Cindy E.	$ 30,000	$2,000	$ 32,000									
Debbie F.	30,000	2,000	32,000									
Ernie G.	21,000	1,000	22,000									
Freddie H.	19,400	600	20,000									
Gary I.	22,800	1,200	24,000									
Hubert J.	31,200	600	31,800									
Total	$154,400	$7,400	$161,800									
Staff salaries												
Irene K.	$ 13,300	$1,000	$ 14,300									
John L.	15,200	1,000	16,200									
Karen M.	10,900	800	11,700									
Larry N.	12,400	400	12,800									
Mark D.	12,000	1,000	13,000									
Nora P.	15,400	600	16,000									
Orville Q.	9,400	400	9,800									
Pam R.	9,200	800	10,000									
Quenton S.	10,000	1,000	11,000									
Robert T.	10,300	500	10,800									
Total	$118,100	$7,500	$125,600									

Figure 5.9. Programming Department Payroll Worksheet, Arts and Sciences (Completed).

Name	(a) Current Salary	(b) Calculated Increases	(c) Estimated Salary	(d) Adjustments	(e) Revised Estimate	Allocated to: (f) Cindy E.	(g) Debbie F.	(h) Ernie G.	(i) Freddie H.	(j) Gary I.	(k) Hubert J.	(l) Dept. Admin.
Program salaries												
Cindy E.	$ 30,000	$2,000	$ 32,000		$ 32,000	$32,000						
Debbie F.	30,000	2,000	32,000		32,000		$32,000					
Ernie G.	21,000	1,000	22,000		22,000			$22,000				
Freddie H.	19,400	600	20,000		20,000				$20,000			
Gary I.	22,800	1,200	24,000		24,000					$24,000		
Hubert J.	31,200	600	31,800		31,800						$31,800	
Total	$154,400	$7,400	$161,800		$161,800	$32,000	$32,000	$22,000	$20,000	$24,000	$31,800	
Staff salaries												
Irene K.	$ 13,300	$1,000	$ 14,300		$ 14,300			$13,000	$ 1,800			
John L.	15,200	1,000	16,200		16,200							$16,200
Karen M.	10,900	800	11,700	($11,700)	0							
Larry N.	12,400	400	12,800		12,800				9,000			3,800
Mark D.	12,000	1,000	13,000		13,000					$13,000		
Nora P.	15,400	600	16,000		16,000			1,000			$15,000	
Orville Q.	9,400	400	9,800		9,800				9,800			
Pam R.	9,200	800	10,000		10,000	$10,000						
Quenton S.	10,000	1,000	11,000	(5,500)	5,500				5,500			
Robert T.	10,300	500	10,800		10,800		$ 2,000	8,800				
New hire				9,400	9,400		9,400					
New hire				12,000	12,000			3,000				
Total	$118,100	$7,500	$125,600	$ 4,200	$129,800	$10,000	$11,400	$25,800	$26,100	$13,000	$15,000	$20,000

Figure 5.10. Budget Summary Worksheet, Arts and Sciences.

	Cindy E.	Debbie F.	Ernie G.	Freddie H.	Gary I.	Hubert J.	Adjust.	Total
Number of programs	25	30	30	40	50	60		235
Number of students	1,620	1,500	1,500	1,200	1,600	1,700		9,120
Income	$373,000	$350,000	$280,000	$225,000	$392,000	$340,000	($60,000)	$1,900,000
Less pass through	58,000				42,000			100,000
Adjusted income	$315,000	$350,000	$280,000	$225,000	$350,000	$340,000	($60,000)	$1,800,000
Expense								
Direct expenses								
Promotion	$ 50,000	$ 47,000	$ 45,000	$ 35,000	$ 50,000	$ 68,000		$295,000
Teacher compensation	80,000	97,000	77,000	47,000	88,000	71,000	$33,200	493,200
Other direct	30,000	45,600	63,000	11,400	9,000	3,000		162,200
Total direct	$160,000	$189,600	$185,200	$93,400	$147,000	$142,000	$33,200	$950,400
Gross margin	$155,000	$160,400	$94,800	$131,600	$203,000	$198,000	($93,200)	$849,600
Department indirect								
Payroll								
Programmer	$32,000	$32,000	$22,000	$20,000	$24,000	$31,800		$161,800
Staff support	19,000	11,400	25,800	25,600	13,000	15,000		109,800
Dept. admin.	4,000	4,000	2,000	2,000	4,000	4,000		20,000
Fringe benefits	11,000	10,000	12,000	13,000	14,000	12,000		86,200
Subtotal payroll	$66,000	$57,400	$61,800	$60,600	$55,000	$62,800	$14,200	$377,800
Dept. promotion	9,000	6,000	4,000	4,000	9,000	9,400		41,400
Dept. S & E	8,000	7,000	4,000	4,000	9,000	5,800		37,800
Total dept. indirect	$83,000	$70,400	$69,800	$68,600	$73,000	$78,000	$14,200	$457,000
Total expenses	$243,000	$260,000	$255,000	$162,000	$220,000	$220,000	$47,400	$1,407,400
Available for overhead	$72,000	$90,000	$25,000	$63,000	$130,000	$120,000	($107,400)	$392,600

Figure 5.11. Programmer Term Summary Worksheet, Cindy E.

	(a) Total Fall 19A	(b) Total Winter 19B	(c) Total Spring 19B	(d) Total Summer 19B	(e) Total Year 19A-B
Number of programs	5	7	10	3	25
Number of students	530	400	600	90	1,620
Income	$128,000	$88,000	$88,000	$69,000	$373,00
Less pass-through	28,000	10,000		20,000	58,00
Adjusted income	$100,000	$78,000	$88,000	$49,000	$315,00
Expense					
Promotion	$15,000	$13,000	$16,000	6,000	$ 50,00
Teacher compensation	25,000	13,000	27,000	15,000	80,00
Other direct expense	11,000	6,000	4,000	9,000	30,00
Total direct	$51,000	$32,000	$47,000	$30,000	$160,00
Gross margin	$49,000	$46,000	$41,000	$19,000	$155,00
Departmental indirect					
Payroll					
Programmer	$ 8,000	$ 8,000	$ 8,000	$ 8,000	$32,00
Staff support	4,750	4,750	4,750	4,750	19,00
Depart. admin.	1,000	1,000	1,000	1,000	4,00
Fringe benefits	2,750	2,750	2,750	2,750	11,00
Total payroll	$16,500	$16,500	$16,500	$16,500	$66,00
Department promotion	2,250	2,250	2,250	2,250	9,00
Department S & E	2,000	2,000	2,000	2,000	8,00
Total dept. indirect	$20,750	$20,750	$20,750	$20,750	$83,00
Total expenses	$71,750	$52,750	$67,750	$50,750	$243,00
Available for overhead	$28,250	$25,250	$20,250	($1,750)	$72,00

Figure 5.12. Programmer Course Summary Worksheet, Cindy E., Fall.

	Course 1	Course 2	Course 3	Course 4	Course 5	Total Fall 19A
Number of students	300	70	30	100	30	530
Income	$33,000	$14,000	$5,000	$19,000	$57,000	$128,00
Less pass through	3,000			1,000	24,000	28,00
Adjusted income	$30,000	$14,000	$5,000	$18,000	$33,000	$100,00
Expense						
Promotion (see attach.)	$4,500	$1,000	$ 600	$2,900	$ 6,000	$15,00
Teacher compensation	3,000	3,000	1,000	6,000	12,000	25,00
Other direct	1,000	800	300	900	8,000	11,00
Total direct	$8,500	$4,800	$1,900	$9,800	$26,000	$51,00
Gross margin	$21,500	$9,200	$3,100	$8,200	$7,000	$49,00

the manager felt that the totals were too optimistic. Since the budget target was exceeded and the manager did not want to interfere with the self-imposed program targets, the manager used the adjustment column to pull down income by $60,000, increase instructor compensation by $33,200, and increase fringe benefits by $14,200. This left Arts and Sciences with a budgeted "available for overhead" of $392,600, very close to the targeted amount.

Figure 5.11 shows the projected activity, by term, for one of the Arts and Sciences programmers, Cindy E. Again the total column will be carried forward to the next worksheet, and each column is supported, in turn, by a separate worksheet such as the one shown in Figure 5.12, which shows the detailed calculations made by Cindy E. in estimating her fall term activity down to the "gross margin" point. Her course planning for that term has apparently progressed far enough that she can be specific in estimating the costs of the five courses she shows on this worksheet. Such specificity of detail is desirable, but it is rarely possible for distant terms.

The programmer budget gives the programmer an opportunity to forecast and plan the future. This involves an understanding of the time and resource allocations it will take to achieve the budget goal. In order to be useful, these allocations should be based on reasonable calculations that are expressed in written form so that they can later be compared to actual events and results.

Legitimate budgets, even though based on estimates, represent quasi-contracts. Programmers, department managers, and directors are bound to fulfill them to the best of their abilities or to explain why they were not fulfilled. This contractual characteristic gives rise to the next step in the budgeting process, *negotiation*, which we will discuss in the next chapter.

Summary

The budget call, the first formal step in the budget process, provides estimations and assumptions and the targets upon which the budget preparers will base their budgets. It usually is preceded by a number of calculations of indirect costs and some preliminary allocations. The purpose of the budget call is to set in motion a process that will result in a balanced, strenuous, but achievable budget, prepared according to explicit and uniform assumptions and incorporating both financial and nonfinancial goals.

The preparation of the budget ideally proceeds in building block fashion, with programmers first thinking carefully about the programming they will do in the next budget period. If they can plan each term course by course (as assumed here), estimated course budgets will become the lowest accounting entity upon which the whole budget is based. If it is not possible to estimate the details of future courses, as is often the case, more global estimates must be made.

All course budgets for one programmer for one term will be added together, and the total will be combined successively with totals for other terms and other programmers within the department to arrive at a departmental budget—and so on until the whole budget is developed. It is important that the budget call establish a form for worksheets so that this summation can be done easily and quickly. As the budgets pass from one level of the organization to another—in our example, from programmer to department manager and then from manager to director—the budgeting process proceeds to the next steps: negotiation, review, and coordination.

Bibliography

Anthony, R. N. *Financial Accounting in Nonbusiness Organiza-tions.* Stamford, Conn.: Financial Accounting Standards Board, 1978.

Anthony, R. N., and Herzlinger, R. E. *Management Control in Nonprofit Organizations.* (Rev. ed.) Homewood, Ill.: Irwin, 1980.

Anthony, R. N., and Welsh, G. A. *Fundamentals of Management Accounting.* Homewood, Ill.: Irwin, 1974.

Borst, D., and Montana, P. J., (eds.). *Managing Nonprofit Organizations.* New York: AMACOM, 1977.

Matkin, G. W. "Living and Learning with Inflation: How to Be a Winner." *Continuum,* 1981, *45* (3).

Shipp, T. (ed.). *Creative Financing and Budgeting.* New Directions for Continuing Education, no. 16. San Francisco: Jossey-Bass, 1982.

Strother, G. B., and Klus, J. P. *Administration of Continuing Education.* Belmont, Calif.: Wadsworth, 1982.

6

Achieving Consensus
in the Budget Process:
The Human Element

So far, the various parties involved in the budgeting process have not had much interaction. Management has gone about the tasks of setting guidelines and targets and making indirect cost estimates with little formal contact with those who are primarily responsible for budget preparation. Of course, there may be—there should be—a great deal of interaction between management and the programmers and department heads, but, in our example at least, such interaction has not been named as a part of the process. This chapter describes the steps in the budgeting process that explicitly involve the interplay between budget preparers and budget approvers, an interplay that is the essence of budgeting as a form of communication for both organizational and individual goals and expectations.

Negotiation

In many ways negotiation is the most crucial aspect of the budgeting process. Negotiation can take place at many stages of the process, but I have chosen to discuss it here because in most CE organizations, the most important negotiation is that which takes place between the programmer and the department manager.

The ability of the manager to establish realistic targets that motivate programmers and provide a standard against which performance can be measured is extremely important. Too ambitious a goal can lead to frustration and bitterness, and too easy a goal can undermine the budget and the managerial control system. The quality of the negotiation between manager and programmer is also important. Programmers should be able to present reasonable arguments for target reductions if their calculations and expectations indicate that they cannot attain their targets, but "game playing" and irresponsible ploys, such as those described at the end of this section, should be discouraged. The manager can help to establish a healthy negotiating atmosphere by supporting the chosen targets set with calculations and documentation. Financial results from the recent past can usually be used as a standard upon which to base targets for the upcoming period, with appropriate adjustments being made to reflect anticipated changes.

The departmental target-setting process is particularly difficult when differential targets must be established. Just as it was unreasonable for the director in our example to expect the Education Department to produce as much available for overhead as the Business and Management Department, it is often unfair to expect all programmers to produce the same bottom line. Thus the manager is often put in the position of having to defend not only the targets themselves but also the differences between them. Supporting calculations and a clear rationale are even more important in this situation.

In addition to negotiations regarding the actual level of the targets, there may be negotiations about the methods that will be used to reach the goals. Here managers should look for a balancing of risks and rewards. For instance, a programmer may propose to reach her target by producing just three blockbuster programs during the year. The manager may decide that reliance on only three programs represents too great a risk of failure and thus will require the programmer to schedule more programs. Alternatively, a programmer may not be venturesome enough, relying on tried and true programs when, in fact, those programs are showing a declining trend. The manager in this situation may require the programmer to add some new programs to bolster the old.

Finally, the timing of the financial results may come under discussion. The programmer who expects to do poorly for the first two quarters of the budget year and then make it all up in the last two puts the organization at risk, since no adjustments can be made if the last two quarters also fizzle out. Thus the manager is likely to require a reasonably even distribution of results.

The desired outcome of the negotiating process is "goal congruence" and a commitment by the programmer to achieving the goals set by agreement between programmer and manager. Ideally, the manager, in approving the programmer (responsibility center) budget, has agreed that the programmer will have done a "good job" if the budget goal is met, and the programmer has agreed that the goal is achievable.

Upon reaching agreement with each of the programmers in the Arts and Sciences Department, the department manager in our example organization adds up all the budget goals for the programmers on the A & S Summary Worksheet (Figure 5.10). Finding that the programmer targets add up to more than the target for his department as assigned by the director, the A & S manager, unwilling to reduce the targets the programmers have agreed to, builds in a contingency by adjusting income, instructor compensation, and fringe benefits—areas where experience tells him that the budget has not provided enough. If the department budget had come up short of the target set for it, the manager would have the choice of going back to the programmers and asking for more or negotiating in turn with the director for a lower target.

Programmer Strategies

The ideal budget negotiation involves a programmer of good will who is honestly trying to achieve the assigned budget goal, accepts the manager's challenge, and is willing to discuss openly any problems expected to be encountered in achieving the goal. Programmers who fall short of this ideal usually fit into one of several categories, each of which has its special ploy. Managers should be aware of these common strategies so that they can be ready with suitable counterploys.

"Tell Me How." A programmer in this category works out a very detailed budget that does not meet the assigned goal and then enters the negotiation by asking how the department manager would change the budget in order to reach the goal. Every suggestion for change is then countered with arguments that the change will not achieve the desired results. A programmer using this tactic has not really accepted the goal and is hoping either that the goal will be lowered or that the manager will impose the goal upon the programmer so that the programmer can deny that the goal was personally acceptable.

The most effective counter to this ploy is simply not to accept it. A firm insistence that the goal must be met and that finding the means to do so is the programmer's responsibility is the best way to avoid being co-opted by the programmer into doing the hard work of budgeting.

The Alternative Presenter. A variant of the "tell me how" type is the programmer who prepares not one budget but several, each under a slightly different set of assumptions. Usually only a few of the alternatives actually meet the budget goal, and these few are based on such tenuous assumptions that they are unlikely to be successful. The manager is asked to choose one of the alternatives.

Again, the most effective counter is simply not to play the game. Instead, the manager should ask the programmer to choose the best budget and then argue this alternative on its merits.

The Unrealistic Optimist. This type is out to impress—on paper. He or she is filled with enthusiasm and confidence and seems to find the exercise of putting numbers on paper, of planning the future, invigorating and fulfilling. No matter that the budget shows a doubling of activity and a marked decrease in expense; the fact that it is down in black and white is somehow assurance that it can and will happen. Although optimism can be a very positive quality, it can also lead to unrealistic projections that ultimately destroy the integrity and usefulness of the budgeting process.

Since an unrealistic optimist usually presents a budget that in some way does not make sense, the most effective counter is to reject the proffered budget and require that the final budget presented bear some reasonable relationship, either in absolute dollars or in expense ratios, to results from prior periods.

The Lowballer. The programmer who understands that performance evaluation and rewards are based on whether or not budget targets are met may try to have the targets reduced. Such a programmer will present a budget considerably below the established target and will resist all efforts to raise estimates. The appropriate counter is to compare the budget with actual results from the same programmer and other programmers in the past, pointing out that decreases in productivity are not reasonable or acceptable. The inability of any programmer to "pull his or her weight" should have sanctions attached to it, and the manager may find it appropriate to invoke the threat of these sanctions when faced with the lowballer. In extreme cases the target has to be imposed on the lowballer, since the actual results will almost always be better than the budget anyway.

The Gambler. This type presents a budget that has a chance of being achieved but presents significant risks. The gambler wants to take the risks but also wants the manager to know and approve the risk taking, at least to the extent that he or she will let the programmer off the hook if the gamble fails. Dealing with gamblers is tricky because organizations do indeed have to take risks to survive and move forward. However, those risks should be calculated carefully, and gambles that will potentially yield the highest reward should be chosen first. Some of these may be gambles that more conservative programmers are forced to take, rather than those presented by the gambler type. The gambler should be required to present careful calculations of the risks involved and the potential rewards—how much time and effort the proposed project will take, what else will not be done because of it (opportunity costs), and how much up-front (sunk) costs the gamble will incur, and a realistic estimate of the possible return. A second counterploy is to discuss the personal consequences if the gamble fails. Will the programmer be completely off the hook or, say, fail to get an expected raise? The final response is not to accept the gamble and to insist that the budget be redrawn on a firmer footing.

"I Can Do It, If . . ." This type of programmer presents a budget predicated on the occurrence of some particular event or condition, the implication being that if the specified circumstance does not happen, the programmer cannot be held responsible for a failure to achieve the budget target. Possible conditions ending the "I can do it, if . . ." sentence include the following:

- ". . . something happens in the outside world (beyond my control)." "Somethings" in this category range from a continued favorable economic climate to the passing of mandatory relicensing laws. A counter to this approach is to request a contingency plan based on the assumption that the external condition does not occur and to establish a deadline for determining whether the condition has in fact occurred. The contingency plan should also achieve the budget target, and it may be adopted instead of the original plan if it is more feasible.
- ". . . I get something." Programmers sometimes use the budgeting process to express their own demands. Instead of accepting the usually implicit assumption that if the budget is achieved, they will be rewarded, they want the reward spelled out very clearly; they may even demand the reward before they have achieved the success. This last is a kind of blackmail, implying that if the programmer does not get the reward, he or she will not make a full effort toward achieving budget goals. The counter to this is, of course, for the manager to reject the proposal out of hand, spell out clearly his or her understanding of the threat implied in the proposal, and make it plain that a failure to achieve the budget will be regarded as a failure on the part of the programmer to perform—thus countering threat with threat.
- ". . . someone (or some department) elsewhere in the organization does a good job." Programmers with personal axes to grind or strong opinions about others in the organization may use the budgeting process to point the finger. An example might be the promotion or publicity department. In most CE organizations there is a certain tension, at best a creative one, between programmers and the promotion department. Proper promotion is so important to the success of most programs and yet such an unknown that programmers often want to be relieved

of the responsibility for promotion decisions. If they are looking for someone on whom to blame possible failure of a program, the promotion department is a prime candidate. A counter to this is to push the responsibility back on the programmer, rejecting the idea that someone else is responsible and requiring that any instance of a failure in another party be brought up immediately for discussion and review.

• ". . . you allow me to spend money." Programmers will often try to tie their ultimate results to the approval of specific line items in the budget they present. Again, promotion expenditure is a good example. Since everyone knows that "you have to spend money to get money," and since promotion expenditures are usually carefully controlled, programmers often want to protect this line item from cuts. Alternatively, they may suggest that they will have to entertain more, travel more, or be away from the office more in order to achieve the success represented by the budget they present. The only counter to this kind of request is to treat each suggestion on its merits, referring to recent history or establishing controlled experiments to test the validity of each dubious assertion. For instance, promotion costs might be allowed to exceed the norm for one term to see whether a better financial result will occur.

• ". . . you keep someone out of my territory." This ploy often appears in organizations where there are jurisdictional disputes. Programs related to computers are common examples. Virtually every field of endeavor is feeling the impact of computers, and programmers specializing in many different fields are presenting programs related to this subject. Programmers who have specialized in computer-related courses often see these other programmers as invaders. It is natural for them to try to resist claim jumping, sometimes using the budgeting process to do so. The only real counter to this is to be as clear as possible about territorial boundaries and to have a dispute resolution system that can help avoid damaging jurisdictional warfare.

The Context Questioner. This type of programmer objects to the entire budgeting and target-setting process. This attitude may arise when the programmer identifies more with the audience served than with the CE organization or when the programmer perceives overhead as being too high. Such a programmer will ask, "Why do I (or my audience) have to support the (dean's office, registration office, or whatever)?" Alternatively, the programmer may question the target distribution process, citing another department as having a lower target and claiming inequity. In countering this ploy the manager should take care to avoid defensiveness. The organization has a value to everyone, and belonging to an organization carries with it certain duties, including paying for a portion of the overhead costs. Context questioners should be made aware that they work within a context that they *must* recognize and respect and that no part of the organization can escape its responsibilities.

The Sacrificer. This type is willing to do what is asked but also wants more recognition than normally is given. Such a programmer will make it very clear that the budget he is presenting will strain him to his limits, will involve giving up the kind of programming he really wants to do, or will be done in the face of personal (medical, familial, professional) sacrifices above and beyond the call of duty. The sacrificer may hope to establish an excuse for possible failure or, if goals are reached, gain an increase in reward. Often the anticipated reward may simply be verbal recognition; sacrificers are seldom satisfied with the rewards given, but, at the same time, they appreciate very much whatever comes their way. If the sacrificer plays rather lightly on the theme, the manager need not actually do anything, knowing that the programmer will do his or her best anyway and recognizing that the expected extra reward will not really cost much. When the sacrificer carries the role to an extreme, or when real negative feelings may be generated when expected extra rewards are not forthcoming, the manager should make clear that the organization rewards success on the same basis for everyone.

The Expert. This type of programmer resists any questioning of the presented budget by claiming a superior knowledge of the market or subject area. He or she adopts a take-it-or-leave-it attitude and raises even the smallest question or suggestion for improvement to the level of a crisis of confidence. The expert appears particularly often in professional fields such as law, medicine, architecture, which traditionally have had a measure of independence and autonomy. One counter to this type is to call the bluff and suggest that if the program does not meet the standards set for it, it will have to be abandoned. If this counter is not realistic, the manager should carefully analyze the budget and raise specific questions based on past history or comparisons. Persistent questioning, even in the face of animosity, will eventually reveal the weaknesses, if any, in the "expert's" budget presentation.

Having examined negotiation strategies in some detail, let us now turn to the next step in the budgeting process: coordination and review.

Coordination and Review

Having collected all the department budgets, the director or budget officer is now ready to put the whole budget together. In our example, this is done with the Budget Summary Worksheet, shown in Figure 6.1. This worksheet adds all the programming departments (columns a through e) together in column f, then adds the total of the service department budgets from the Service Department Budget Summary Worksheet (Figure 5.2, column a) to get the total budget for the CE organization. Note that each line item of expense has been calculated as a percentage of adjusted income. This facilitates both comparisons between departments and comparisons of a single department's performance over several years.

With the entire budget in view, the managers can begin the coordination and review process. The process has the following goals:

- to determine, to the extent possible, whether assigned targets will be met;
- to determine whether the budget represents a realistic estimation of the future;
- to reconcile the interrelated parts of the budget; and
- to "balance" the budget, making sure it represents a plan acceptable to, or at least worthy of presentation to, those who must approve it at a higher level.

Adjustment of Targets

The first and easiest task in reviewing the budget is to determine whether all the assigned targets have been met. The review of each department's budget may require a hearing in which the manager of the department has an opportunity to voice opinions about the chances of attaining the goal. If the goal cannot be met, negotiation must occur so that a realistic goal can be agreed upon. If an earlier hearing has not been held, departments that have not met their assigned targets must be questioned. In each case the director or the budget officer should examine the process by which the department manager arrived at conclusions in order to determine whether it was thorough and whether the conclusions are justified. Assuming that they are, the director and the manager must decide what to do next: revise the goal downward or take some action that the manager failed to take and that seems likely to make possible the achievement of the goal.

Reality Tests

Once the director has determined that all the assigned targets have been either met or equitably adjusted, the entire budget can be reviewed to determine whether it presents a realistic forecast of the future. This is done by comparing against a given set of standards both the actual figures and the relationship between figures for departments and for line items. One fairly common procedure involves comparing the details of departments and line items in the budget with the actual results for prior periods and then comparing appropriate segments of the organization with others in budget terms. When, as in our example, the budget is prepared by adding parts together, there is a high probability that a particular line item will be systematically under- or overstated, and such an error should show up when comparisons are made with prior periods. For instance, many programmers budget too little for promotion. If total promotion costs in the budget are considerably lower than the total for the prior year, it is likely, barring some known reason for the decline, that promotion is underbudgeted and some adjustment will have to be made. Not only should the totals for line items be

Figure 6.1. Budget Summary Worksheet.

	(a) Arts and Sciences Amount	%	(b) Business and Management Amount	%	(c) Education Amount	%
Number of programs	235		200		96	
Number of students	9,120		9,000		2,156	
Income	$1,900,000		$1,550,000		$300,000	
Less pass-through	100,000		50,000			
Adjusted income	$1,800,000	100.0%	$1,500,000	100.0%	$300,000	100.0%
Expenses						
Direct expenses						
Promotion	$295,200	16.4%	$214,000	14.3%	$ 42,000	14.0%
Teacher compensation	493,200	27.4%	541,700	36.1%	128,000	42.7%
Other direct	162,000	9.0%	180,000	12.0%	30,000	10.0%
Total direct	$950,400	52.8%	$935,700	62.4%	$200,000	66.7%
Gross margin	$849,600	47.2%	$564,300	37.6%	$100,000	33.3%
Departmental indirect						
Payroll						
Programmer	$161,800	9.0%	$128,700	8.6%	$27,000	9.0%
Staff support	109,800	6.1%	120,300	8.0%	23,000	7.7%
Dept. admin.	20,000	1.1%	18,000	1.2%	5,000	1.7%
Fringe benefits	86,200	4.8%	53,400	3.6%	11,000	3.7%
Total payroll	$377,800	21.0%	$320,400	21.4%	$66,000	22.0%
Dept. promotion	41,400	2.3%	37,000	2.5%	9,000	3.0%
Dept. S & E	37,800	2.1%	60,000	4.0%	15,000	5.0%
Contingency						
Total dept. indirect	$457,000	25.4%	$417,400	27.8%	$90,000	30.0%
Total expenses	$1,407,400	78.2%	$1,353,100	90.2%	$290,000	96.7%
Available for overhead	$392,600	21.8%	$146,900	9.8%	$10,000	3.3%

Figure 6.1. Budget Summary Worksheet, Cont'd.

(d) Engineering		(e) Conferences and Institutes		(f) Total Programming Depts.		(g) Total Service Depts.	(h) Total	
.mount	%	Amount	%	Amount	%		Amount	%
80		12		625			625	
,000		500		26,775			26,775	
40,000		$550,000		$5,240,000		$307,000	$5,547,000	
40,000		50,000		240,000			240,000	
00,000	100.0%	$500,000	100.0%	$5,000,000	100.0%	$307,000	$5,307,000	100.0%
28,800	14.3%	$ 10,000	2.0%	$ 690,000	13.8%		$ 690,000	13.0%
17,000	24.1%	200,100	40.0%	1,580,000	31.6%		1,580,000	29.8%
88,000	20.9%	30,000	6.0%	590,000	11.8%		590,000	11.1%
33,800	59.3%	$240,100	48.0%	$2,860,000	57.2%		$2,860,000	53.9%
66,200	40.7%	$259,900	52.0%	$2,140,000	42.8%	$307,000	$2,447,000	46.1%
60,500	6.7%	$ 27,000	5.4%	$ 405,000	8.1%		$ 405,000	7.6%
58,000	6.4%	83,900	16.8%	395,000	7.9%	$424,500	819,500	15.4%
10,000	1.1%	27,000	5.4%	80,000	1.6%		80,000	1.5%
25,700	2.9%	23,700	4.7%	200,000	4.0%	84,800	284,800	5.4%
54,200	17.1%	$161,600	32.3%	$1,080,000	21.6%	$509,300	$1,589,300	29.9%
32,000	3.6%	20,600	4.1%	140,000	2.8%		140,000	2.6%
30,000	3.3%	67,200	13.4%	210,000	4.2%	257,700	467,700	8.8%
						250,000		
16,200	24.0%	$249,400	49.9%	$1,430,000	28.6%	$1,017,000	$2,447,000	46.1%
50,000	83.3%	$489,500	97.9%	$4,290,000	85.8%	$1,017,000	$5,307,000	100.0%
50,000	16.7%	$10,500	2.1%	$710,000	14.2%	($710,000)	$0	

compared, but each department's budget should also be compared with a prior period, line by line, to make sure that the budget appears reasonable.

Ratio analysis can also be used to compare present to prior periods and to make comparisons between departments. The worksheet in Figure 6.1 shows each item of expense expressed as a percentage of income. The ratio of promotion expense to total income for Arts and Sciences is 16.4 percent, higher than for any other department. This would probably require some explanation, as would the very low percentage for the Conferences and Institutes Department.

Internal Reconciliation

In our example, the budgets for the service departments were developed first, based on estimates of the volume of activity that would be generated by the programming departments. An important task in coordination and review of the budget is to make sure that those volume estimates were sound. For instance, the registration office budget was based on an estimate of the total number of enrollments for the budget period. Figure 6.1 indicates that the programmers are projecting enrollments of 26,775 (column h). If this estimate is significantly different from the estimate used in calculating the registration office budget, that budget may need to be revised. This revision, especially if it is upward, might send the whole budget out of balance and require increasing targets or reducing costs in other places. If targets have to be revised, the total enrollment figures might again change, so the registration office budget again would need revision. A certain amount of this back-and-forth process is usually unavoidable whenever the budget is put together in interrelated parts. However, revisions that take place after negotiations (often long and hard) have resulted in realistic targets for all responsibility centers can be demoralizing and time-consuming for everyone concerned. If such iterations are anticipated in the beginning, extensive revisions may sometimes be avoided by building more into the contingency or providing some flexibility in the service department budgets. We will return to this problem in the section on balancing the budget.

We have chosen promotion to illustrate the detailed computations that are sometimes involved in reconciling the various parts of the budget. Promotion costs are so important to control and yet dependent upon so many individual decisions that they usually have to undergo careful review. In the worksheets provided with the budget call in our example, each programmer was asked to support the promotion budget for each term with a worksheet called "Programmer Promotion Summary by Course" (shown completed by our example programmer, Cindy E. in Figure 6.2) and to add up all the terms on the worksheet called "Programmer Promotion Summary Worksheet" (Figure 6.3), with data from the total column in Figure 6.2 showing as the first column in Figure 6.3. It should be clear from these worksheets that Cindy characteristically presents large programs that require heavy promotion expenditures not typical of most CE courses. This sort of program, however, provides a good example of the complexities of promotion budgeting and reconciliation.

After Cindy and the other programmers fill out their worksheets, the next step is for the results of all the programmer promotion summaries to be added together to get the departmental promotion summary. This is done on the Department Promotion Summary Worksheet (Figure 6.4). Note that, as is typical, not all promotion costs can be assigned to individual responsibility centers. Our example organization handles this by having a "Department" column. Further, it is often necessary to build a contingency factor into service department budgets that does not fit into the normal line item classification of expense. Here, this contingency is handled as a "share of unrecharged" line item just above the total line.

Once this kind of worksheet is prepared by every department, the departmental estimates for promotion costs can be summarized and compared with the estimation that was done in the beginning to arrive at preliminary promotion cost estimates. This estimate summary is shown in the Promotion Department Recharge Distribution Worksheet (Figure 6.5).

On this worksheet (Figure 6.5) the promotion department is divided into subunits by columns, and the line items are listed down the left side, as usual. Note that the promotion department has an

Figure 6.2. Programmer Promotion Summary by Course.

Programmer: Cindy E.
Term: Fall, 19A

	Course 1	Course 2	Course 3	Course 4	Course 5	Tot..
Catalogue costs	$ 400	$ 400	$600	$ 600	$ 800	$ 2,▮
Advertising	800	600			300	1,
Typesetting	500			400	800	1,
Printing	1,000			800	2,500	4,.
Mailing						
Postage	400			400	1,000	1,▮
Mail lists/labels	200			300	200	
Coordination	150			150	150	
Processing	250			250	250	
Staff time						
Art	600					▮
Editorial & processing	200					▮
Total	$4,500	$1,000	$600	$2,900	$6,000	$15,▮

Note: Catalogue costs are based on estimates of the cost per catalogue
       page; other costs are estimates based on published
       guidelines from the promotion department.

Figure 6.3. Programmer Promotion Summary Worksheet.

	Fall 19A	Winter 19B	Spring 19B	Summer 19B	Tota▮
Catalogue costs	$ 2,800	$ 3,800	$ 4,000	$3,600	$14,▮
Advertising	1,700	1,500		2,000	5,▮
Typesetting	1,700	1,000	1,500		4,▮
Printing	4,300	3,000	3,000		10,▮
Mailing					
Postage	1,800	1,800	3,000		6,▮
Mail lists/labels	700	300	800		1,▮
Coordination	450	250	1,000		1,▮
Processing	750	350	700		1,▮
Staff time					
Art	600	800	1,200	200	2,▮
Editorial & processing	200	200	800	200	1,▮
Total	$15,000	$13,000	$16,000	$6,000	$50,▮

Figure 6.4. Department Promotion Summary Worksheet, Arts and Sciences.

	Cindy E.	Debbie F.	Ernie G.	Freddie H.	Gary I.	Hubert J.	Subtotal	Department	Total
Catalogue costs	$14,200	$15,000	$15,200	$13,000	$18,000	$25,000	$100,400	$ 9,400	$109,800
Advertising	5,200	3,000	4,000	1,000	4,000	10,000	27,200	7,000	34,200
Typesetting	4,200	2,000	3,000	4,000	8,000	5,000	26,200	1,000	27,200
Printing	10,300	8,000	7,000	5,000		10,000	40,300	5,000	45,300
Mailing									
Postage	6,600	8,000	6,000	4,000	8,000	4,000	36,600	2,000	38,600
Mail lists/labels	1,800	4,000	1,800	2,800	3,700	5,700	19,800	2,000	21,800
Coordination	1,700	500	200	200	300	300	3,200		3,200
Processing	1,800	1,500	4,000	3,000	3,000	2,000	15,300	2,000	17,300
Staff time									
Art	2,800	3,000	1,800	900	3,000	4,000	15,500		15,500
Editorial & processing	1,400	2,000	2,000	1,100	2,000	2,000	10,500		10,500
Share of unrecharged								13,000	13,000
Total	$50,000	$47,000	$45,000	$35,000	$50,000	$68,000	$295,000	$41,400	$336,400

Note: Catalogue costs are based on estimates of the cost per catalogue page; other costs are estimates based on published guidelines from the promotion department.

Figure 6.5. Promotion Department Recharge Distribution Worksheet.

	Total Promotion Dept.	Catalogue Costs	Advertising	Mail Coordin.	Staff Time Art	Staff Time Editorial	Costs Not Distributed	Other Direct
Staff payroll								
Zack A.	$ 24,000	$ 2,000	$1,000		$ 8,000	$ 1,000	$12,000	
Yorell B.	11,000	9,000		$1,000			1,000	
Xenon C.	23,000		2,000			1,000	20,000	
Warren D.	12,000		1,000			11,000		
Vernon E.	16,000				16,000			
Ulysses F.	14,500			4,000	5,000	5,500		
Subtotal	$100,500	$11,000	$4,000	$5,000	$29,000	$18,500	$33,000	
Fringe benefits (20%)	20,000	2,200	800	1,000	5,800	3,600	6,600	
Other costs (1)	31,500	3,500	1,200	1,600	9,000	5,800	10,400	
Subtotal recharges	$152,000	$16,700	$6,000	$7,600	$43,800	$27,900	$50,000	
Other direct costs								
Advertising costs	45,000		45,000					
Typesetting	100,000	22,000						$78,000
Printing	210,000	120,000						90,000
Mailing								
Postage	176,000	30,000						146,000
Mail/lists/labels	60,000	10,000						50,000
Processing	47,000							47,000
Total	$790,000	$198,700	$51,000	$7,600	$43,800	$27,900	$50,000	$411,000

(1) Other costs include supplies and all other costs and are
distributed to the cost centers on the basis of total payroll.

in-house staff and in-house expenses, here totaled on the "subtotal recharges" line, and also goes to outside vendors for services, here labeled "direct costs."

The Promotion Summary Worksheet (Figure 6.6) adds up all the promotion costs from the departments and, in columns g and h, compares the sum of the programming department promotion costs with the previously developed promotion department budget. The entries in column g come from the Recharge Distribution Worksheet (Figure 6.5) and are either the totals of the columns or entries in the "other direct" column.

In our example, the sum of programming department estimated promotion costs is $40,000 more than was initially estimated and budgeted. The programming department estimates are based on a promotion cost rate schedule that incorporates both direct and indirect promotion costs. Careful analysis of the differences between current programmer estimates and the original estimates is necessary because the promotion budget, particularly the indirect promotion budget, may have to be revised. For instance, Figure 6.6 shows that the programmers expect to spend $11,900 more on catalogues than the original promotion budget had anticipated. This may mean that the catalogues will have to be larger. Where such an increase in size results in increased costs paid to outside vendors, such as for typesetting, printing, and postage, the difference between the two estimates will have little impact on the balancing of the budget; increases in recharges will be passed on to the program departments directly. Where the increase means more work for the promotion department, however, the budget for that department may have to be augmented to provide additional help.

The catalogue cost is a rather complex example. The original budget provided for $11,000 in payroll costs related to the production of catalogues. In light of the estimated increase in catalogue use, is this enough? If not, how should management adjust? They could shift staff from other areas (advertising, perhaps, where the volume will be slightly less than anticipated), adopt a policy limiting the programmers to the resources originally proposed, or add staff. Adding staff, of course, would add cost, and that cost would have to be covered from somewhere.

Figure 6.6. Promotion Summary Worksheet.

	(a) Arts and Sciences	(b) Business and Management	(c) Education	(d) Engineering	(e) Conferences and Institutes	(f) Total Per Programming Depts.	(g) Per Programming Promotion Budget	(h) Per Programming Dept. (Over) Under
Catalogue costs	$109,800	$ 59,700	$27,000	$ 14,100		$210,600	$198,700	($11,900)
Advertising	30,200	13,000		3,800		47,000	51,000	4,000
Typesetting	23,200	46,300	3,200	10,000	$ 2,300	85,000	78,000	(7,000)
Printing	53,300	20,700	4,700	15,700	3,600	98,000	90,000	(8,000)
Mailing								
Postage	38,600	48,700	2,000	54,500	13,200	157,000	146,000	(11,000)
Mail lists/labels	21,800	13,300		8,900	2,000	46,000	50,000	4,000
Coordination	3,200	1,200	400	8,100	1,500	14,400	7,600	(6,800)
Processing	17,300	9,400	700	9,600	1,000	38,000	47,000	9,000
Staff time								
Art	15,500	12,700	2,800	12,500	1,500	45,000	43,800	(1,200)
Editorial & processing	10,500	11,000	5,200	10,800	1,500	39,000	27,900	(11,100)
Share of undistributed	13,000	15,000	5,000	13,000	4,000	50,000	50,000	0
Total	$336,400	$251,000	$51,000	$161,000	$30,600	$830,000	$790,000	($40,000)

Each line item in the budget should be analyzed in a similar way to determine its effect. The large outside cost differences in typesetting, printing, and postage do not concern us, since these costs "pass through" the promotion department. However, the large differences in coordination and editorial services should give us some pause, since it appears that the programmers expect to use more of these services than was anticipated and that the amount provided for these in-house costs therefore will not be enough. Again, management will have to decide how to provide the additional services or else curtail their use.

If reconciliation of the interrelated parts of the budget reveals potential problems, these will have to be dealt with in the last step in coordination and review: balancing the budget.

Balancing the Budget

Using the phrase "balancing the budget" to describe the process that concludes the coordination and review function can be misleading because a budget in which income and expenses match exactly is not its goal. The desired end product of the budget review process is a budget that presents the organization with an attainable goal and is acceptable to the higher authority to whom it is presented. As pointed out earlier, effective budgets must provide room for contingencies—unforeseen or unexpected events or conditions that could cause one or several parts of the organization to fall short of their budget goals. The size of this cushion, or margin of safety, may vary, but it must be present. The budget that is carefully "balanced" between income and expense is in balance only on paper and for a very short time. Determining the appropriate size for the contingency reserve, and having the nerve—sometimes under great counterpressure—to resist decreasing that reserve, is an important test of the director's ability to understand and control the organization.

Having put together the budgets from all the programming departments and performed the internal reconciliations, management can now review the organization budget to see whether it represents a realistic plan, using something like the Budget Summary Worksheet shown filled out in Figure 6.1. All of our example organization's departments met, or came close to meeting, their targets, so there is really no need for further action in this case. In reality, however, it rarely happens that the budget comes so close to what was originally planned. Targets may have been renegotiated, the internal reconciliation process may have disclosed factors that change the budgets of the service departments, or events may require a change of assumptions. Circumstances may have made the contingency larger or, more likely, smaller (maybe much smaller) than was planned.

Let us take the happier circumstance first. Suppose that when everything is added up, instead of the $710,000 that our organization's management had planned for the programming departments to produce, the final figure is really $800,000. They learn that the higher available for overhead is due primarily to the Engineering Department, which projects four very large conferences that the director had not taken into account in setting the budget targets. The director now has several options. If it appears that the Engineering Department's projection is unrealistic—that the proposed conferences are too risky to base the increase on or that the department's costs will have to increase excessively to handle the additional volume—the department's manager might be required to revise the department budget to a more realistic proportion. After all, the organization's credibility is at stake; if the budget is too optimistic and cannot be achieved, the whole organization will suffer, even if only a part was at fault. Alternatively, the director might let the Engineering Department budget stand and adjust the total budget, either by increasing the contingency factor (appropriate considering that the projected increase comes from a risky source) or by reducing the Engineering Department's budget on budget reports submitted to higher authority but retaining the department's original submission for internal purposes. This course has the advantage of leaving a strenuous goal for the Engineering Department—which, after all, had been set by the department itself—and, at the same time, rendering the overall budget reasonably realistic and conservative. It also is likely to take less time and involve less negotiation.

Now let us look at the more common experience. Suppose that instead of the $710,000 that was anticipated, the final figure is $680,000, and the reconciliation process indicates that the promotion department budget is going to have to be increased by $15,000. This means that there is a shortfall in the budget of $45,000: $710,000 – $680,000 = $30,000 and $30,000 + $15,000 = $45,000. Again, the director has several choices:

Reduce Overhead Costs. It may be possible, given projected reductions in volume, to reduce either the costs in the service departments or the contingency. If, however, the service department budgets were prepared carefully and a reduction in the contingency is not justified, reducing overhead will be difficult.

Increase Targets. Another possibility is to go back to the programming departments and ask them to come up with more available for overhead. This alternative can be very destructive, however, especially if the preceding steps were done with care. Such a request will appear to be evidence of bad faith, or at least bad planning, by the management. However, where there is a large difference between income and expense, it may be necessary to redo the budget in all its steps.

Eliminate Unprofitable Segments. Where a segment shows a deficit or a relatively minor contribution to the available for overhead, it may be desirable to eliminate the unit or reorganize it to effect a saving in service department costs. In our example, both the Education Department and the Conferences and Institutes Department appear to be only marginally productive. Together they contribute over 16 percent of the income and over 10 percent of the enrollments but only about 3 percent of the available for overhead (refer to Figure 6.1). If, by eliminating these two programming departments, management could reduce service department costs by more than the $20,500 that the departments are scheduled to contribute, the budget deficit would be lessened. However, many other factors have to be considered before making such a serious policy decision. It is always painful to eliminate programs. The morale of the employees throughout the organization might be damaged by a decision to close down departments (although carrying losing programs can also be damaging to morale). Political considerations may make program elimination difficult, and it may hurt the public's perception of the CE organization to see its "product mix" become less extensive and varied.

In a case like this, management must also consider whether eliminating a large segment of the organization will change the economies of scale for the service departments, making the per unit costs increase to a point where some departments can no longer operate efficiently. For instance, Education is scheduled to pay about 13 percent of the cost of the catalogues (see Figure 6.6). If this department is eliminated, the overhead costs included in the catalogue costs will have to be spread over a smaller pool, increasing the price of catalogues to other users. Similarly, there may be "embedded" overhead costs that have to be considered. Note that Education was scheduled to pay $5,000 and Conferences and Institutes to pay $4,000 of the undistributed promotion costs (Figure 6.6). If promotion department overhead costs could not be reduced by at least this much, the gain from the department elimination would not be as great as it might at first appear.

Another consideration is that in eliminating a program or department, management is eliminating the possibility for a return that may exceed budget expectations, either in the long run or the short run. Experienced CE professionals are well aware of the cyclical nature of the popularity of certain subject matter areas. Education and teacher training, which had been the mainstay of many continuing education organizations from the 1930s to the early 1970s, fell off drastically after 1975 throughout the country, but they will probably regain some strength in the mid- and late 1980s. External conditions change so rapidly that it is difficult to predict where the next market opportunity may spring up.

Of course, it may be that only a particular segment of a department is unprofitable and should be eliminated. A detailed enough budget and accounting system can provide the information necessary to make such a determination. Finally, the cost of closing a department and phasing out its operations has to be considered. Severance pay or extensive paid but unproductive time may be necessary, students currently in structured programs may have to be served by programs and courses that are not economically viable, and much time and managerial effort may have to be spent in carrying out the reductions. Despite all these possible drawbacks, it may still be necessary, after a hard look at all the factors, to take the step of eliminating an unprofitable department.

Reduce Line Items. A traditional way of dealing with prospective budget deficits is to attempt to reduce line items in "across-the-board" budget cuts. In examining line items for potential savings, it usually makes sense to look first to the largest items as having the most potential for savings—barring known inefficiencies in the smaller items, of course. For instance, it is tempting to try to reduce departmental supplies and expense, since these expenditures all take place inside the organization. However, they amount to only 4.2 percent of the example budget (refer to Figure 6.1). To save 1 percent of the budget ($50,000), management would have to reduce departmental supplies and expense expenditures by 25 percent, which might be extremely difficult, especially if the expense budgets were developed in good faith by the managers. On the other hand, to save the same amount the instructor compensation budget would have to be decreased by only 3 percent, perhaps by eliminating the payment for local travel or by not paying instructors for meeting the first class in courses that cancel. Of course, reducing any aspect of instructor compensation is likely to be a visible and widely challenged decision.

Payroll costs are also likely to constitute a high percentage of a CE organization's budget. Some reductions in staff and payroll costs are usually possible through attrition and "salary savings" (that is, savings effected by unpaid leaves of absence, by gaps in the time between the leaving of one employee and the arrival of a replacement, or by replacement of a highly paid employee with a new employee paid at a lower rate). If the amount of the budget deficit is great, however, real staff cuts may be necessary—cuts that actually eliminate performance of certain tasks. Care should be taken that such losses do not cut into the "muscle" of the organization or sap morale too badly, and that the cost savings effected by the cuts will not be more than offset by a decrease in the organization's ability to generate income.

Reductions in line items are often delegated to the department managers, who are asked to effect a percentage reduction either in particular line items or anywhere in their budget. In some departments it may be easier to reduce staff than to reduce instructor compensation, for example; or fees may be raised in some courses to provide the targeted available for overhead. Again, this is difficult to do after negotiations have been held. Certainly the director should know exactly where the savings or additional income will come from in order to evaluate the validity of the proposal and should establish a monitoring system to see that the cuts or additional income sources are effective.

Combine Approaches. Most directors facing prospective budget deficits will use some combination of the approaches described. Whatever approaches are chosen, care must be taken that the interrelated parts of the organization remain in balance and an objective view of the possible is maintained. Managers and programmers, driven to an extreme, are likely to be less conservative than in their initial calculations and less inclined to take the hard steps that they are being asked to take. They are more likely simply to revise their estimates of income or class size upward to accommodate the difference.

Reorganize and Negotiate for an Acceptable Deficit. In cases where the prospective budget deficit is very large, the budget system may be indicating that the organization is seriously off track and that no simple reduction method is going to be enough. In this situation, a complete reshaping and probably an adjustment of the scale or size of the organization may be necessary. A director of an organization in this position needs time—time to rethink and reshape the organization and time to see the results of that reshaping in financial returns. Usually a deficit is unavoidable in the interim period, and certainly a new budget reflecting the phase-out, phase-in period and the eventual desired organizational structure is going to be required. In most organizational settings, such reorganization will have to have the sanction of higher authority, and that authority will have to recognize that a budget deficit is unavoidable on the way to what will hopefully be a brighter future.

Once the director is satisfied that the budget as prepared and adjusted fulfills the four goals of the review process—meeting the established targets, being realistic and attainable, having internal integrity so that all of the interrelated parts of the budget reconcile, and being at least minimally acceptable to those in higher authority—the next step in the budget process, final approval, can be taken.

Final Approval

In most cases the CE director does not have the authority to approve the final budget. Such authority usually resides with the administration of the parent institution or the board of directors of the CE organization. This means that, after having worked hard to produce a budget that meets all appropriate criteria, the director must now defend that budget and the methods used to produce it. It is important that the CE director have confidence in the budget at this point—the sort of confidence that can come only from thorough prior review. Directors with extensive budgeting experience develop a "feel" for the process and can sense when a budget is realistic and when it is not.

Often the form in which the budget must be presented to higher authority does not coincide with the form in which it was developed. Indeed, when the presentation form is dictated by the parent institution, it may create an inaccurate picture of the CE organization because it ignores factors important in self-support undertakings. If this happens, the CE director should try to structure the presentation in a way that follows institutional practices when possible but also points out where following such practices may lead to faulty decision making.

In this section we will look at several standard budget presentation formats and then discuss some strategies that may be used by those who review the CE organization budget. Knowledge of these strategies can help the CE director prepare the budget, including special schedules, for presentation and defense.

Standard Budget Presentation Formats

Of the two standard budget formats, the *line item format* is more familiar to most institutional budget officers because it is the same as the format usually used in colleges and universities for reviewing subsidized programs and departments. An illustration of

Figure 6.7. Annual Budget, Line Item Format.

	(a) Projected 19A – B Budget Amount	%	(b) Projected Results This Year Amount	%	(c) Better (Worse) (a–b)	(d) Actual Results Last Year Amount	%	(e) Better (Worse) (a–d)
Number of courses	625		597		28	549		76
Number of students	26,775		25,350		1,425	24,568		2,207
Income	$5,547,000		$5,400,000		$147,000	$5,100,000		$447,000
Less pass-through	240,000		200,000		(40,000)	200,000		(40,000)
Adjusted income	$5,307,000	100.0%	$5,200,000	100.0%	$107,000	$4,900,000	100.0%	$407,000
Expenses								
Direct expenses								
Promotion	$ 690,000	13.0%	$ 650,000	12.5%	($ 40,000)	$ 600,000	12.2%	($ 90,000)
Teacher compensation	1,580,000	29.8%	1,430,000	27.5%	(150,000)	1,400,000	28.6%	(180,000)
Other direct	590,000	11.1%	600,000	11.5%	10,000	550,000	11.2%	(40,000)
Subtotal direct	$2,860,000	53.9%	$2,680,000	51.5%	($180,000)	$2,550,000	52.0%	($310,000)
Gross margin	$2,447,000	46.1%	$2,520,000	48.5%	($73,000)	$2,350,000	48.0%	$97,000
Departmental indirect								
Payroll								
Programmer	$ 405,000	7.6%	$ 400,000	7.7%	($ 5,000)	$ 380,000	7.8%	($ 25,000)
Staff support	819,500	15.4%	800,000	15.4%	(19,500)	770,000	15.7%	(49,500)
Dept. admin.	80,000	1.5%	75,000	1.4%	(5,000)	60,000	1.2%	(20,000)
Fringe benefits	284,800	5.4%	280,000	5.4%	(4,800)	242,000	4.9%	(42,800)
Subtotal payroll	$1,589,300	29.9%	$1,555,000	29.9%	($ 34,300)	$1,452,000	29.6%	($137,300)
Dept. promotion	140,000	2.6%	180,000	3.5%	40,000	170,000	3.5%	30,000
Dept. S & E	467,700	8.8%	500,000	9.6%	32,300	515,000	10.5%	47,300
Contingency	250,000	4.7%		0.0%	(250,000)		0.0%	(250,000)
Total dept.indirect	$2,447,000	46.1%	$2,235,000	43.0%	($212,000)	$2,137,000	43.6%	($310,000)
Total expenses	$5,307,000	100.0%	$4,915,000	94.5%	($392,000)	$4,687,000	95.7%	($620,000)

the line item format, using information from the example we have been following, appears in Figure 6.7.

Note that the proposed budget (which is taken from the last column of Figure 6.1) is compared with the projected results of the current fiscal year and the actual results of the previous fiscal year. The comparison is carried out in actual dollars and also through ratio analysis by computing the percentage that each category of expense bears to total income.

The other commonly used presentation format is the *program or departmental format.* This format shows the financial results for each segment of the organization. An example of it is shown in Figure 6.8.

The advantage of the departmental format is that the rise and fall of departments (at least over the three years presented here) can be seen easily, and the financial results of the same department can be compared over a number of periods. For instance, it appears that the Arts and Sciences and Engineering departments in our example organization are growing steadily, Business and Management is stable, Education is in a steady decline, and Conferences and Institutes is having ups and downs.

The worksheet format used in Figure 6.1 can also be used to present a budget, since it combines both of these formats by showing programming departments in the columns and line items down the side of the worksheet. However, it does not show historical comparisons clearly, and it presents so much data in such a compact form that reviewers unfamiliar with the organization may not be able to interpret it readily.

Summary schedules in any format can be supported by more detailed schedules, some being the same worksheets we have already seen and some being developed separately to answer anticipated questions. For instance, a question is likely to come up about Conferences and Institutes in Figure 6.8. Why did expenses decrease so drastically between the prior year and the current year ($603-$490), and why, with decreased income in the budgeted year ($530-$500), do expenses not also decrease ($490-$490)? The director might want to prepare supplementary schedules that isolate the cost problems and indicate some of the interrelationships of income and expenses

Figure 6.8. Annual Budget, Departmental Format (in Thousands).

	Proposed Budget 19A-B	Projected Current Year	Better (Worse)	Actual Prior Year	Better (Worse)
Income					
Arts and Sciences	$1,800	$1,750	$ 50	$1,680	$120
Business and Management	1,500	1,490	10	1,240	260
Education	300	300	0	350	(50
Engineering	900	880	20	800	100
Conferences and Inst.	500	530	(30)	600	(100
Other	307	250	57	230	77
Total Income	$5,307	$5,200	$107	$4,900	$407
Expense-Program Depts.					
Arts and Sciences	$1,407	$1,367	($40)	$1,379	($ 28
Business and Management	1,353	1,354	1	1,151	(202
Education	290	271	(19)	310	20
Engineering	750	750	0	707	(43
Conferences and Inst.	490	490	0	603	113
Total Expenses	$4,290	$4,232	($58)	$4,150	($140
Available for Overhead					
Arts and Sciences	$393	$383	$10	$351	$42
Business and Management	147	136	11	130	17
Education	10	29	(19)	40	(30
Engineering	150	130	20	102	48
Conferences and Inst.	10	40	(30)	(3)	13
Total Available	$710	$718	($8)	$620	$90
Less Service Depts.					
Director's Office	(114)	(93)	(21)	(90)	(24
Business Office	(47)	(42)	(5)	(40)	(7
Cashier's Office	(38)	(33)	(5)	(31)	(7
Registration Office	(77)	(64)	(13)	(60)	(17
Student Records (net)	(23)	(18)	(5)	(19)	(4
Promotion		(11)	11	(15)	15
Downtown Facility	(131)	(136)	5	(117)	(14
Reprographics		(9)	9	(10)	10
Parent Indirect	(30)	(27)	(3)	(25)	(5
Contingency	(250)		(250)		(250
Total	$0	$285	($285)	$213	$213

in this department, which may be different from those in other departments.

So far we have been following an example of a self-supporting CE organization. The budget process for subsidized organizations is often considered to require a different approach and be governed by different considerations, but such an assumption shows lack of understanding of the real purposes of budgeting. For instance, in a fully self-supporting organization, the acceptance or rejection of the budget by higher authority is likely to be based upon the degree of realism in its appraisal of market conditions and the soundness of its management's implementation strategies. In fact, some version of the "market test" should be employed in evaluating subsidized budgets as well. In a self-support situation, the question might be: Has the manager correctly evaluated the market potential for CE courses? In a subsidized situation, this same question might become: Are we providing our target clientele with what they want or need? Self-supporting organizations have automatic feedback on this question—a program either makes money or it does not. In a subsidized situation, other evidence must be gathered, such as number of enrollments, number of completions, client evaluations, external evaluations, or client learning outcomes.

Similarly, as explained in the Introduction, the budget review process in subsidized organizations often uses the incremental approach. Under this approach, the budget of the current year is considered the base, and budget review concentrates primarily on changes (or increments) to this base. A budget presentation in an organization that uses this approach usually calls for a defense of the base and a plea for funds to be added to it, both supported by appropriate arguments and evidence. A version of the incremental approach can also be usefully employed in the budgeting of self-supporting or "variable resource" organizations. Portions of the self-support budget can be identified as being stable and dependable producers of income and margin, and the total of these programs can be considered to be the base. The budget review can then concentrate on the less stable, more risky programs—the "increment."

Budget Review

Just as programmers negotiate with the department chair over responsibility center budgets, the CE director will probably have to negotiate with those to whom the organization budget is presented. In such negotiations, the director has the advantage of knowing the organization and its budgeting process far better than the reviewers are likely to. However, reviewers have the power to ask a broad range of questions and demand changes in the budget without warning. If the CE director is not prepared to answer these questions or counter these suggested changes, the advantage of superior knowledge is lost. It is important, therefore, that the CE director anticipate the behavior of the budget reviewers. Reviewers' questions and challenges are likely to fall into the following categories.

Questions About Budget Schedules. In preparation for any budget review, each schedule to be presented should be carefully scrutinized so that questions can be anticipated and answers prepared. For instance, if Figure 6.1 were used in a presentation, a reviewer might ask why both Education and Conferences and Institutes budgeted instructor compensation as such a high percentage of income; why such a small amount was budgeted for promotion in Conferences and Institutes; or, more broadly, why Arts and Sciences has such a high percentage of income available for overhead compared to the other departments, especially to Business and Management, the department that comes closest to the size of Arts and Sciences and, according to conventional wisdom, should do better financially than an Arts and Sciences department. It is a good practice to allow someone unfamiliar with the organization to review the budget schedules and raise questions that are likely to occur to outsiders but may be neglected by those who deal with budgetary matters every day. All possible or likely questions should be written down, and answers, including supplementary schedules where appropriate, should be prepared. The surest way to "sell" a budget is to demonstrate an obvious grasp of all its aspects, and diligent preparation is absolutely necessary to achieve this mastery.

Across-the-Board Cuts. One strategy traditionally used by reviewers in institutional settings is to require that proposed budgets be reduced by a stated percentage, say 5 percent. This suggests a certain desperation, an unwillingness to make tough budget decisions personally, or both, on the part of the reviewers. In subsidized organizations, the CE director who suspects or is faced with such a strategy should prepare an alternative budget, indicating how and where the cuts will be carried out. The consequences of the cuts should also be clearly spelled out. One slightly Machiavellian counterstrategy is to propose to cut a program that the reviewers regard as important in the hope that the cut will be restored. Of course, this strategy can backfire and create greater problems.

Across-the-board cuts can be particularly troublesome in self-supporting organizations. Income and expense are interrelated, and to reduce expense may also mean a reduction in income. Directors of such organizations should be prepared to remind reviewers of this fact and to show that cuts anywhere will ultimately directly affect income. Across-the-board cuts mean that the organization reduces its ability to serve its students and thus also reduces its ability to generate income. The best strategy for countering across-the-board cuts is to choose the least harmful element for reduction and then outline the consequences of the reduction as clearly as possible to the reviewers.

Discontinuation of Programs or Departments. Another possibility is for the reviewers to request or suggest that a particular program or department be discontinued just as a director faced by an unbalanced budget might do. For instance, in our example, the reviewers might suggest that the Conferences and Institutes Department be discontinued in light of the small available-for-overhead amount it generates in relation to its size. We have already discussed some of the problems associated with removing a segment of an organization. If such a suggestion is likely to arise, the director should make careful calculations indicating the effect of the reduction on indirect costs and estimating the cost of the phaseout (severance pay, redistribution of service to present students, and so on). It may also be important to discuss the effect that the discontinuance will have on the organization's product mix and public image.

Alternative Scenarios. Sometimes the reviewers require several budgets to be presented, each prepared under a different assumption. For instance, they may require one budget that assumes a 10 percent increase, another that assumes no change from the previous year, and a third that assumes a 10 percent decrease. This approach requires that the director identify new targets of opportunity that might be pursued if the budget were increased and cuts that might be made if the budget had to be reduced. This is probably something the director should do anyway, and it can lead to productive discussions with budget reviewers; in fact, the CE director might be the one to suggest it. If this approach is planned or expected, three separate budgets might be built from the ground up, or the director might develop a budget according to one set of assumptions and then adjust it to reflect others. Sometimes this strategy simply attempts to hide the reviewers' intention to reduce a budget, but it can represent a real opportunity to inform those in higher authority about the CE organization, and the wise director will exploit it as such.

Line Item Attacks. Another frequently encountered set of questions, likely to come particularly from reviewers used to analyzing subsidized budgets, concerns the appropriateness of individual line items. For instance, a reviewer examining Figure 6.7 might ask why less is budgeted for departmental supplies and expense in the current year than was spent in the previous years. Another reviewer might require that budgeted promotion expense, which shows an increase, be reduced. In some cases, an attack on line items may require such extensive revision that the whole budget must be redone. Line item defense, like defense of budget schedules as a whole, requires careful preparation and anticipation of possible attacks.

Increases in Fees. Especially in colleges and universities, the CE organization budget is often reviewed by people who are not familiar with the market aspects of continuing education. Such reviewers often propose a seemingly quick and simple answer to any budget difficulty: raising fees. Assuming that the fee structure has been carefully considered in the budgeting process, the best way to counter this suggestion is to provide the reviewers with a schedule of the fees of competitors in the area. The reviewers should be reminded that the CE organization does not exist in a vacuum and that the fee structure cannot be adjusted without careful consideration.

In presenting the organization budget to higher authority, the CE director must be able to articulate clearly the consequences of changes in that budget, either positive or negative. In subsidized organizations, the director should have a clear idea of the levels of service that the budget represents and the effect on those levels of increases or decreases in funding. In self-supporting organizations, the director should have a clear understanding of the broader aspects of the markets being served and the relationship of various items of expense to the production of income. The wise director views the budget hearing as an opportunity to gain the approval not only of the budget but of the management decisions that are revealed through it. It is a chance to educate those who are in charge of continuing education and to include them in the decision-making process.

Once approval is obtained from higher authority, the director can distribute the budget, the next step in the budgeting process.

Distribution

Distribution of the approved budget is an important element in the budgeting process. The director who does not formally express approval to those who worked so hard to achieve a reasonable budget by giving them copies of the final product has missed an opportunity to validate the whole process and to bring the budget preparation phase to an official completion. He or she has also missed the chance to make very clear the nature of the contract that the budget for each responsibility center represents. Finally, the distribution step is useful for providing each person involved in the process with an understanding of the whole that might not have been apparent during budget generation. It is important that each responsibility center see itself and be seen as a part of the organization.

Although distribution is the last step in the preparation of the budget, it is not the last step in the budgeting process. The budget should provide decision makers with a framework in which the interrelationships of all the organization's parts have been considered and a standard against which actual results can be judged. If the budget is to have this kind of continuing importance, an effective way of monitoring progress toward the budget goal and evaluating results as they occur is needed. Thus, the last "step" in the budgeting process is really a walk—a continuing series of steps throughout the budget period that provide those responsible for performance with the feedback they need to understand whether they are fulfilling, exceeding, or falling short of their "contract." We will discuss this feedback process in the next chapter.

Summary

Negotiation of budget targets is the first and usually most intense of the interactions between budget preparers and budget reviewers. It is the step where most of the communication between management and those responsible for carrying out the aims of the organization takes place. Ideally, negotiation occurs in an atmosphere of openness and cooperation, with both sides coming to a common understanding of operational goals and objectives. When negotiation falls short of this ideal, certain common ploys may come into play. The director or budget officer should recognize these ploys and be prepared to counter them, channeling the budgeting process back into a productive course.

Coordination and review of the budget is the next step. First, submissions from operational units are collected and added together. Then internal reconciliations are performed to make sure that initial estimations of service department costs are still valid in light of the projected activity of the programming departments. Reconciliation of promotion indirect costs is particularly important. The goal of the review process is a "balanced" budget that establishes reasonable targets for each identifiable operating unit, has internal integrity, and will be acceptable (or at least defendable) to those who must ultimately approve it. If the budget does not "balance," a number of steps can be taken to adjust it.

The process of attaining final approval of the budget is analogous to the negotiation step described earlier but takes place at a higher level of organizational authority. Here, too, certain predictable patterns can be recognized and prepared for. At its best, the budget approval process can be an opportunity for the management of the CE organization to inform those in higher authority about the special peculiarities of CE financing and concerns.

The distribution of the approved budget is often overlooked as a step in the budgeting process, but it is important because it can serve as a reminder of established targets and a symbol of the importance of budgeting in the organization. It can help those who have prepared parts of the budget to see the whole picture and how their own portion fits in.

Although the budget is usually prepared just once a year and revised only a few times, the budgeting process continues throughout the year as the budget is systematically compared with actual results and guides the hundreds of day-to-day operating decisions that must be made. We now turn to this process of feedback and control.

Bibliography

Anthony, R. N., and Herzlinger, R. E. *Management Control in Nonprofit Organizations.* (Rev. ed.) Homewood, Ill.: Irwin, 1980.

Powell, R. M. *Management Procedures for Institutions.* Notre Dame, Ind.: University of Notre Dame Press, 1979.

Strother, G. B., and Klus, J. P. *Administration of Continuing Education.* Belmont, Calif.: Wadsworth, 1982.

Wildavsky, A. B. *The Politics of the Budgetary Process.* (2nd ed.) Boston: Little, Brown, 1974.

7

Monitoring and Reporting on Financial Performance

Although presented here as a step in the budgeting process, feedback and control in a CE organization should extend beyond the budget framework and be integrated with other functions. The establishment of a budget system for a CE organization is typically the first step in developing a management information system (MIS). Its value is that it requires segmentation of the organization. The establishment of "responsibility centers" in the budget becomes the basis of the organization's control structure, and this structure in turn determines the kind of information that management will receive and prescribes the flow of information within the organization. Although in this section we will be dealing primarily with information systems as they relate to the budgeting process, such systems must also relate to the enrollment process, the process of institutional financial accounting, and many other internal and external activities.

The purpose of any management information system is to provide managers with the information they need to make decisions. Although we usually think of computers and numbers when we think of MISs, such systems may contain qualitative as well as quantitative elements and have both formal and informal aspects. The qualitative or informal aspects are hard to describe because they are composed of individual and group interaction patterns. The way an individual or a small group (say, a department) translates organizational goals into action and the extent to which it reflects the ideals of educational quality and appropriateness are within the "informal" sphere. The budget system, by contrast, is part of the "formal" system of control, composed largely of quantitative standards and measures. An unfavorable variance from the budget standard is a signal to management for corrective action, while a favorable variance is a signal for reward and recognition.

Considerations in Designing a Feedback System

Budget monitoring requires an accounting system that accumulates income and expenses in meaningful categories and timely fashion. In this context, categories are "meaningful" when they correspond to the organization segmentation plan upon which the budget was based, clearly assign responsibility for results to individuals, match or bracket income and expense in defined time periods, and, most importantly, provide management with the information it needs to make decisions. Let's now examine these and some additional considerations relevant to the implementation of an effective accounting system or MIS.

Congruence Between Budget and Accounting Systems. An accounting and reporting system must reflect the form and structure of the budget system in order to be an effective feedback or control mechanism. Ideally, the budget system and the accounting system should be developed together so that financial reporting will serve the budget system.

Cash and Accrual Accounting. Many CE organizations (and their parent institutions) employ the *cash accounting* method; that is, they base financial measurement on the in- and outflow of cash, paying little attention to the difference between the point at which the income is earned or the costs incurred and the actual receipt or payment of money. The principles of fund accounting encourage the use of this method, since accounting funds in most institutions act like bank accounts, with increases in appropriations acting like deposits and with expenditures of funds and decreases in appropriations acting like withdrawals.

The cash method may be used by a CE organization that is fully subsidized, although there are problems associated with accounting for commitments. For self-supporting organizations, however, the cash system is inappropriate. The typical pattern of fund flow for CE organizations has three distinct phases: first, money is spent on planning and promotion; then income for the course is received; and finally, after the course is either well under way or completed, its presentation costs (instructor compensation, room rent, and so on) are paid. Because of the long lead times required to plan and promote the course and the sometimes long delay in initiating payment for course costs, several accounting periods (months or terms) may be involved. Therefore, particularly where there is a significant fluctuation from period to period, the accrual accounting method is more appropriate.

The *accrual* method requires that costs be associated or matched with the income that the incurring of those costs helped to produce and that both income and associated costs be reported in the same accounting period. Thus, planning and promotion costs might be "deferred" (carried forward) to the following accounting period, when the income for a given course will be recorded; or the costs of presenting a course, expected to be paid in a future period, might be "accrued" (counted) in the present period. Alternatively, both the planning and promotion costs and the income might be deferred to the period in which the presentation costs are paid. The accrual method, properly applied, preserves a true "bottom line" and gives managers a clear picture of the financial results of an operation. Unfortunately, this method is not commonly used in CE organizations, primarily because parent institutions usually do not use it and having an accounting system different from that of the parent presents practical problems that are sometimes costly to solve. The dissociation of income from its related expense is perhaps the greatest common barrier to informed decision making by CE directors. Later in this chapter we will examine some inexpensive ways of implementing accrual accounting where it is appropriate.

Production of Useful Information. The idea that an accounting system or management information system should provide management with information useful for making decisions might at first seem simplistic and obvious, but in fact, such information systems far too often generate a great deal of information that is interesting without being the slightest bit useful. An example in continuing education might be enrollment information. A programmer might decide that if the enrollment in a particular course is less than thirty-five one week before the course is to begin, the course will be cancelled. The programmer might very well be interested in what the enrollments are two weeks before the beginning of the course, but, since no decision will be based on the earlier enrollment figure, that information is not truly useful or meaningful. It may also be interesting to know how much telephone costs have increased over the last ten years; but again, assuming that everything reasonable has already been done to keep phone costs to a minimum, the information is not really useful because it will not lead to any decision. Of course, it is possible to conceive a situation in which either of these kinds of information would lead to a decision, but it is usually not desirable to develop a financial accounting system that produces information useful only in special and limited circumstances. This point brings up two further considerations.

Avoidance of Information Overload. The increasing availability of computers makes it possible to generate a great deal of information inexpensively. Unfortunately, managers have a finite ability and a finite amount of time to interpret data. The more information is produced, the more time and effort are required to consider and interpret it. Irrelevant data tend to cloud management decision making, at times hiding what is relevant. For instance, a large CE organization recently installed a comprehensive promotion tracking system that produced each month for each course a complete profile of the source of enrollments, broken down by individual mailing list, promotion piece, and categorized by home and work zip code, with optional resorting by interest code. Each month's report was several inches thick. It was soon obvious that only a small portion of this monstrous document was ever used to make decisions. Even where the report could have been useful, it was not used because extracting relevant data from it was too time-consuming. Inevitably, the old "seat of the pants" methods for evaluating promotion effectiveness were being used instead.

There are several ways to avoid information overload. The most obvious is simply to limit the amount of information produced to what is relevant to decision making. Just as most closets contain some clothes that are never worn and never will be worn, most systems, no matter how carefully conceived, produce some information that is never used. Eliminating this information increases the efficiency of the system.

Another common way to avoid overload is to construct a data base from which relevant information can be extracted as needed for decision making. However, this requires a careful definition of each decision and the kind of information relevant to it. Such a degree of preplanning is uncharacteristic of many managers, who prefer to "browse" in the data, shopping for relevance as they walk along the aisles of the data base. They often lack a clear understanding of how the data base is structured and how data can be extracted from it.

Another way of avoiding information overload is to aggregate data at different levels of detail for different levels of management. For instance, members of upper management probably need to know only that, say, promotion costs are increasing as a percentage of income and that most of the increase appears to be in the cost of mailing lists. On the other hand, operating personnel—the mailing list coordinator, for instance— would need to have more specific information (on the relative response rate to specific mailing lists, perhaps) so that the least cost-effective lists could be discontinued. This detailed information would be irrelevant to upper management personnel because they would not be involved in the individual decisions that would go into correcting the cost increases. The more detailed the information and the lower the level in the organization to which it is directed, the less subject to interpretation and the more clearly presented the information must be.

Cost-Benefit Ratio. It is clear that information has both a value and a cost. Its value lies primarily in the improved decision making it can produce. Figure 7.1 shows typical cost and value curves for a management information system.

The "true" value of relevant and accurate information can seldom be measured precisely, just as the correctness of a decision is difficult to measure. The cost of information is also difficult to

Figure 7.1. Cost-Benefit Analysis of Any System.

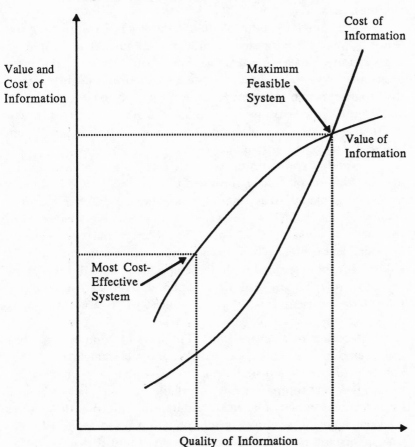

determine. We may be able to tell how much it costs to physically produce a particular report from a data base, but often we cannot properly attribute all the relevant costs of maintaining and inputting the data. An accounting system that requires the use of 100 expense classifications or codes is bound to be less expensive than one requiring 1,000 expense codes, both because the coding process will probably be more time-consuming in the larger system and because there is more chance for error in the more comprehensive plan, and faulty conclusions caused by such errors can cost an organization dearly. On the other hand, the 1,000-code system will allow for more detail and precision, which might "pay" in some circumstances.

Decisions must be made about the level of complexity and detail an accounting system should incorporate. Too simple an aggregation of data—for instance, down only to the department level—may invalidate a budget system that requires detail down to the programmer (responsibility center) level, while too complex an aggregation may cost more than it is worth. The cost-benefit calculation is an extremely important consideration in the design of a useful accounting system.

Timely Reports. Information delivered after the making of a decision that it could have informed is as useless as if it had never been generated and, in addition, has probably cost the organization resources that cannot be recovered. An accounting/management information system thus must be able to deliver accurate information on time. When this does not happen, the fault may lie either with the system or with decision makers who did not allow enough time for information to be delivered. An effective information system must have a consistent as well as timely reporting schedule.

Accuracy of Interpretation. The level of complexity of the interpretation that any report requires must be matched with the ability of the readers of the report to make that interpretation. A financial report comparing the "available for overhead" produced by two programmers, one in the humanities and one in business and management, would defy interpretation by someone who did not understand both the programs involved and the organization that produced them. This is one argument against a widespread dissemination of financial results of responsibility centers in CE organizations, where wide variation between programs is often expected. Those unfamiliar with the markets addressed and the costs and difficulties of presenting particular programs are likely to make straightforward but invalid comparisons.

Characteristics of CE Accounting

Having examined some considerations and criteria for establishing information systems that can provide effective feedback and control, let us turn to several common characteristics of the accounting environment of CE organizations that affect their information needs.

Lack of a Balance Sheet and Double-Entry System. Those unfamiliar with the principles of accounting often use accounting terms rather loosely, and the terms "balance sheet" and "double entry" are often misunderstood. A *balance sheet* is a listing of the assets, liabilities, and owners' share of a particular accounting entity. It reflects what is known as the basic accounting equation:

$$\text{Assets} = \text{Liabilities} + \text{Owners' Equity.}$$

This is simply a way of saying that whatever things of value currently exist in a business (assets) were put there either by creditors (which "putting" is recorded as a liability) or by owners. Since owners "own" either the profits or the losses of a business, the difference between income and expense in any one period belongs to them. Thus the basic equation can be expanded to:

$$\text{Assets} = \text{Liabilities} + [\text{Owners' Contributions} + \text{Income} - \text{Expense}]$$

The "income minus expense" part of this equation, for a defined period of time, is called the income or operating statement. The rest of the equation, with total income minus expense for all the periods during which the business has been in operation summarized in one number, is the balance sheet.

This equation is the logic behind the *double-entry system* of accounting. It allows each financial transaction to be recorded in its two components. For instance, if a business borrows money, it records the transaction as an increase in its asset, cash, and also as an increase in its liabilities. If it sells something to a customer on account, it records an increase in its asset, accounts receivable, and an increase in its income.

This double-entry system, when combined with the accrual method defined earlier, allows businesses to measure their operating and financial results accurately and consistently. Unfortunately, most CE organizations do not have control or even knowledge of their own balance sheets, so the double-entry system will not work for them. They are limited to the single dimension of the income statement.

This characteristic can lead to distorted managerial behavior. Suppose a CE organization is contemplating the development of a computer classroom. Under normal business conditions, a company might go to a bank, borrow the funds necessary to build and equip the classroom, and then, once the classroom was completed, charge the cost of the development of the facility against the income of future periods through depreciation expense. The CE organization, lacking a balance sheet on which to post the increase in the asset of computer equipment, must either (1) absorb the entire cost in the current period, (2) identify an external, nonoperating source of funds that can be used for the development, (3) lease the equipment from an outsider, or (4) abandon the project. The first two choices will lead to future periods in which none of the cost of the initial purchase is charged against the income it is helping to generate. The lease possibility has the same effect as depreciation expense— it spreads the cost over the useful life of the asset—but it may be more costly than normal financing. Without a balance sheet to absorb timing differences between the expenditure of funds and the incurring of costs, directors of CE organizations are continually faced with very difficult financial decisions, particularly where a current investment is required in order to provide the organization with a long-run advantage.

CE directors must also deal with the many distortions presented by income and expense statements in which expenses may be hidden. For instance, a large CE organization was able to purchase a very expensive computerized registration/student records system, using reserve (nonoperating) funds. The efficiency gained from this system, coupled with the fact that none of the initial cost of the system came from or was charged to operations, resulted in a very low cost per enrollment—until the equipment had to be replaced or improved. Then, because the reserve funding source was lacking, enrollment costs began to increase rapidly. It came as quite a shock when the organization's managers realized that their inadequate system (or, rather, lack of a system) had hidden the factors that brought about the sudden surge of costs.

This lack of a balance sheet and double-entry bookkeeping is perhaps the largest single barrier to the adoption of "business-like" practices by CE organizations. It prevents the utilization of management systems that have evolved over the years to serve private businesses.

Antiquated or Misdirected Parent Systems. As has been noted, the fact that CE organizations usually exist within larger institutions means that they must often conform to reporting and accounting practices not useful to the purposes of a CE administration. The principles of fund accounting, designed to assure that the fiduciary duty of the parent institution is carried out, are not well suited to the information needs of CE management, particularly where the CE organization is self-supporting. Where CE is part of a college or university, the supporting accounting systems are usually geared to a slower pace and a longer periodicity than the CE organization is comfortable with, since the parent does not need information as crucially or as quickly for decision making. Where the CE organization may need monthly or quarterly reports and may need enrollment information daily, the parent may be satisfied with reports on a semester or biyearly basis and may pay real attention to financial matters only near the year's end. All these factors usually mean that the CE organization must develop a separate management information system to meet both institutional requirements and its own needs.

Need for Standards. Standards, including budgetary standards, are both exceptionally important and exceptionally difficult to set in the relatively volatile environment of continuing education. History often is not a reliable guide, so budget standard setting must depend heavily on the skill and knowledge of the CE director. Budgeting in the self-supporting or variable resource CE organization exists in a different context than in most service organizations, since income and expense must be considered in close relationship to one another.

Lack of Information. Another characteristic of the control structure of CE organizations, albeit not unique to them, is the continuous need for management to make decisions without adequate information. No matter how detailed and responsive a management information system is, it can never describe the external world so completely that decision making becomes automatic. The CE director who does not recognize this will become frustrated with any information system that is developed. A good MIS can provide relevant information, but it can never substitute for management's wisdom and judgment.

Feedback in Fixed Resource Organizations

Throughout this book we have been comparing subsidized and self-supporting CE organizations and drawing our examples mainly from the latter. For our present discussion, however, better categories for comparison might be "variable resource" and "fixed resource" organizations. In a *variable resource* organization, the amount of resources available to the organization in any period is, at least to some extent, unknown at the beginning of the period and is usually dependent upon the performance of the organization. Variable resource organizations usually incorporate both the income (source) and expense (outflow) sides into their budgeting and planning process and closely resemble traditional profit-oriented businesses. In *fixed resource* organizations, the amount of resources available to the organization in any period is fixed and known at the beginning of the period. Budgets in such organizations therefore deal only with expenses (outflows).

Although most "self-supporting" organizations are variable resource organizations and most subsidized organizations have fixed budgets, a significant number of CE organizations are self-supporting but have fixed budgets: The parent institution imposes a fixed expense budget, requiring that the organization support itself out of its own income but removing any surplus of income over expense and, presumably, funding any deficits. Where this form exists, the CE director is under a particular difficulty because inflows and outflows are artificially dissociated from one another, with the parent serving as a buffer. The director is therefore forced into a fixed resource mentality when a variable resource structure is more appropriate.

Fixed resource organizations face different controls and thus different feedback problems from those of variable resource organizations. Because a significant number of CE organizations are fixed resource organizations, either in reality or artificially, we will begin with a description of possible feedback and control structures that these organizations may employ.

The objective of most fixed resource organizations is to spend exactly what is provided for in the budget. To exceed the budget is to fail to live up to one's financial responsibility and is the cardinal sin in organizations of truly fixed resources. Overspending in one area thus must be made up by underspending in another whenever possible. Paradoxically, however, underspending also often carries sanctions. If the amount provided is not completely spent by the end of the period, it will often lapse—that is, not be available for future periods. Further, it may signal to authorizing bodies that budgeted amounts should be reduced in the next fiscal period. This failure to provide incentive for economy and efficiency is the greatest failure of fixed resource budgeting.

Fixed resource organizations generally employ pure fund accounting methods. The objective of spending no more and no less than is budgeted shapes the feedback and control structure. The main problem is to keep track of "discretionary" funds—the amount of uncommitted money that remains in the accounting period. This means that commitments for future expenditure of funds as well as present, actual expenditures must be accounted for.

Expenditures, Encumbrances, and Commitments. Accountants use precise terminology in describing the status of actual and prospective outlays of funds. An *expenditure* is a fully completed actual outlay of funds. An *encumbrance* is a legally executed, fully completed transaction requiring the future outlay of funds. Budgeted funds are "encumbered," that is, reserved for a future payment, when a legal or formal commitment has been made. For instance, the purchase of a typewriter is legally completed when a fully authorized purchase order is issued, even though the machine might not yet actually be paid for. An encumbrance becomes an expenditure when payment is made. A *commitment* is a planned and definite outlay of funds that will occur before the end of the budget period. It differs from an encumbrance in that it is not legally binding, but it usually has the same effect as a legally binding contract because it has been deemed necessary for the mission of the organization to be carried out. For instance, a CE organization must employ instructors in order to present courses to the public. It is therefore committed to paying instructors in the future, even though no legally binding employment contracts are presently in force. Sometimes the distinction between encumbrances and commitments is not carefully maintained. This usually does not result in major problems unless severe cutbacks are necessary in mid-term, in which case the legal status of commitments can become important.

Keeping track of commitments, and even encumbrances, can be a difficult task, since there is often no documentation automatically generated to support them. The director of a project or organization may know that certain amounts must be committed for future outlay, but unless those commitments are recorded in a way that can be recognized and incorporated into the accounting system, they will have a tendency to be "lost" until it is too late and the budgeted provision is exceeded.

It is also difficult to match expenditures with related encumbrances and commitments so that the encumbrances and commitments can be relieved (reduced) when payment is made. Failure to reduce the encumbrances and commitments will incorrectly reduce the discretionary funds available to the organization. For instance, when payment for the typewriter in our example is made, how will the payment clerk know that the encumbrance that was created when the purchase order was signed should be reduced? Similarly, how will a payroll clerk know that the instructor compensation commitment should be reduced when payment is made to an instructor?

Commitments are often estimates and may differ substantially from the amount that is finally paid out. Thus there may be differences between encumbrances and expenditures. For instance, the purchase order for the typewriter might not have provided for sales tax, so that the final expenditure exceeded what was anticipated; or the estimate of the instructor compensation commitment might have been lower than what is actually being paid. In the first instance, a single transaction unrelated to others, the actual payment represents only a small increase over the expected payment and therefore requires only a small adjustment to the uncommitted balance of funds (although, of course, we will want to make sure that in the future, sales tax is included in our encumbrances). However, the instructor compensation case, which may involve many future transactions, may require an upward adjustment of the instructor compensation commitment, with a concomitant decrease in discretionary (uncommitted) funds. A method must be devised to relate all the stages of a particular transaction so that the amount of funds remaining available is always known.

A final difficulty is keeping track of expenses that, escaping the encumbrance and commitment process, flow directly into the expenditure category. These may be expected, or they may be surprises. There must be some way of making sure that these items decrease the discretionary balance.

A Reporting System for Fixed Resource Organizations. In order to properly manage fixed resource organizations, directors must be provided with up-to-date reports that clearly show the amount of funding remaining available and also indicate where commitment balances must be adjusted. This usually requires a budget that establishes a rate-of-expenditure plan. Such a plan divides the budget for a particular period (such as a year) into smaller periods (say twelve months) so that expenditure rates throughout the larger period could be monitored.

A number of budgeted items may be expended uniformly throughout the period. Payroll costs for regular staff employees usually fall in this category. Total budgeted payroll costs for the year, then, might be divided by twelve to come up with what the monthly payroll expenditure would be. However, if employees receive midyear range or merit increases, a more precise calculation would have to be made. Other costs for which expenditure rates are either stable or difficult to estimate in advance might be divided evenly over the entire year. Telephone costs or noncontracted machine maintenance might be examples of such costs. On the other hand, there are usually a number of costs that definitely do not occur at a uniform pace throughout the year. The cost of temporary help for periods of heavy enrollment around the beginning of the academic terms is an example. Promotion costs, especially where promotion utilizes periodic catalogues or course announcements, are also good examples of nonuniform rate expenditures. Reports that simply relate the percentage of the amount spent to date to the percentage of the budget period that has elapsed, or which take each line item in the budget and divide it evenly throughout the period, ignore the effect of these nonuniform expenditures and are likely to mislead management.

The preferable approach is to analyze the rate of expenditure for each budget item and prepare a time-distributed budget such as that shown in Figure 7.2. This figure closely resembles the traditional cash flow statement, which we will examine more closely in Chapter Ten.

Figure 7.2. Time-Distributed Annual Budget for a Fixed Resource Organization.

	Total Approved Annual Budget	July	Aug.	Sept.	Oct.
Number of courses begun	700		3	270	
Number of students	17,500		75	6,750	
Teacher compensation	$700,000		$200,000	$ 3,000	
Teacher travel	10,000	$ 800	800	800	$ 80
Classroom costs	42,000	3,000	1,400	5,000	5,00
Course material costs	57,000	12,000	4,000	10,000	10,00
Other course costs	15,000	1,250	1,250	1,250	1,25
Total course costs	$824,000	$17,050	$207,450	$20,050	$17,05
Payroll					
Director salary	$ 38,000	$ 3,033	$ 3,033	$ 3,033	$ 3,03
Assistant director	28,000	2,266	2,266	2,267	2,26
Prog. coord.-Humanities	26,000	2,167	2,167	2,167	2,16
Prog. coord.-Business	29,000	2,400	2,400	2,400	2,40
Prog. coord.-Health	29,000	2,400	2,400	2,400	2,40
Program support staff	72,000	6,000	6,000	6,000	6,00
Registration staff	60,000	5,000	5,000	5,000	5,00
Temporary staff	30,000			10,000	
Total payroll	$312,000	$23,266	$23,266	$33,267	$23,26
Office costs					
Telephone	$ 6,000	$ 500	$ 500	$ 500	$ 50
Postage, mailing	10,000	800	800	800	90
Office supplies	4,000	400	300	300	30
Machine maintenance	1,000	80	80	80	9
Rent, janitorial costs	4,800	400	400	400	40
Utilities	5,000	400	400	400	40
Other	30,000				
Total other	$60,800	$2,580	$2,480	$2,480	$2,59
Total budget	$1,196,800	$42,896	$233,196	$55,797	$42,90

Figure 7.2 shows the annual budget for a fixed resource CE organization that has three terms per year, beginning in September, January, and June. Because the resources are fixed or given, there is no "income" line on this schedule. The cyclical nature of the organization's activity means that there is an uneven flow of expense from month to month. For instance, instructors are generally paid once, at the end of the term. This means that there are large outflows in August, December, and April, with little or no outflow for instructor compensation in other months. Course material costs tend to be heaviest at the beginning of the term but

Nov.	Dec.	Jan.	Feb.	Mar.	Apr.	May	June
2		220		3	2		200
50		5,500		75	50		5,000
	$272,000				$223,000	$2,000	
$ 800	1,000		$ 800	$ 800	800	2,600	
5,000	1,000	$ 4,500	4,500	4,500	3,500	1,600	$3,000
1,000	600	8,000	8,000	1,600	500	500	800
1,250	1,250	1,250	1,250	1,250	1,250	1,250	1,250
$8,050	$275,850	$13,750	$14,550	$8,150	$229,050	$7,950	$5,050
3,034	$ 3,034	$ 3,300	$ 3,300	$ 3,300	$ 3,300	$ 3,300	$ 3,300
2,267	2,267	2,400	2,400	2,400	2,400	2,400	2,400
2,167	2,167	2,167	2,167	2,166	2,166	2,166	2,166
2,400	2,400	2,434	2,434	2,433	2,433	2,433	2,433
2,400	2,400	2,434	2,434	2,433	2,433	2,433	2,433
6,000	6,000	6,000	6,000	6,000	6,000	6,000	6,000
5,000	5,000	5,000	5,000	5,000	5,000	5,000	5,000
		10,000					10,000
23,268	$23,268	$33,735	$23,735	$23,732	$23,732	$23,732	$33,732
$ 500	$ 500	$ 500	$ 500	$ 500	$ 500	$ 500	$ 500
800	800	800	900	800	800	900	900
400	300	300	400	400	300	300	300
80	80	80	90	80	80	90	90
400	400	400	400	400	400	400	400
450	400	450	400	450	400	450	400
					30,000		
$2,630	$2,480	$2,530	$2,690	$2,630	$32,480	$2,640	$2,590
33,948	$301,598	$50,015	$40,975	$34,512	$285,262	$34,322	$41,372

are usually paid out in the month following the first month of the term. Payroll costs, except for temporary help needed at the beginning of each term, are uniformly distributed over the months, but several employees are shown with small raises effective January 1. Most of the office costs are uniformly distributed over the year. The "other" item, which in this case is remodeling of the office, is expected to take place in April. It is positioned late in the year so it can be cancelled or modified if other line items go over budget. By holding off such major discretionary items, management builds in a contingency factor much like the contingency that was built into the variable resource budget of our previous example. Note that this distributed budget relates to the rate of *expenditure* and does not include encumbrances and commitments, although certainly some of the line items, particularly in payroll, are records of commitments.

Figure 7.3 shows the results of operations for the first three months of the fiscal year in our example organization compared to the distributed budget. It also shows a revision of the original budget based on the actual results of the first three months of the year.

Analysis of Variance. When actual results vary from those projected in the budget, the variation can be one of two types. It may be a "real" variation between estimated and actual expenditure, or it may be caused by differences between the time when the budget estimated that items would be paid and the time when they were actually paid. Timing differences usually do not influence the final, year-end result, but true variations often do. The first column in Figure 7.3 (column a) shows the actual expenditures for the three months. Column b shows the adjustments for timing differences. For instance, it was determined that $7,000 of the instructor compensation for the summer term had not yet been paid out, although the budget had anticipated that all the summer instruction should have been paid for by September 30. To make a true comparison between the budget and actual expenditures, this $7,000 must be encumbered or added to the outflow. All the entries in the adjustment column result from delayed payment of items that the budget had anticipated would be paid by September 30, with the exception of office supplies, which shows a reduction from actual.

	(a) Actual Expenditures	(b) Adjustments	(c) Revised Expenditures (a+b)	(d) Budget	(e) Better (Worse) (d-c)	(f) Revised Projected Year-End	(g) Original Budget	(h) Better (Worse) (g-f)
Number of courses begun	262		262	273	(11)	689	700	(11)
Number of students	7,200		7,200	6,825	375	17,875	17,500	375
Teacher compensation	$185,050	$ 7,000	$192,050	$203,000	$10,950	$689,050	$700,000	$10,950
Teacher travel	2,175	600	2,775	2,400	(375)	11,125	10,000	(1,125)
Classroom costs	10,000		10,000	9,400	(600)	44,000	42,000	(2,000)
Course material costs	24,750	4,000	28,750	26,000	(2,750)	58,750	57,000	(1,750)
Other course costs	4,000		4,000	3,750	(250)	15,000	15,000	
Total course costs	$225,975	$11,600	$237,575	$244,550	$6,975	$817,925	$824,000	$ 6,075
Payroll								
Director salary	$ 9,099		$ 9,099	$ 9,099		$ 38,000	$ 38,000	
Assistant director	6,799		6,799	6,799		28,000	28,000	
Prog. coord.-Humanities	6,600		6,600	6,501	($ 99)	26,396	26,000	($ 396)
Prog. coord.-Business	7,200		7,200	7,200		29,000	29,000	
Prog. coord.-Health	7,200		7,200	7,200		29,000	29,000	
Program support staff	16,500		16,500	18,000	1,500	70,500	72,000	1,500
Registration staff	14,500		14,500	15,000	500	59,500	60,000	500
Temporary staff	11,000	$500	11,500	10,000	(1,500)	31,500	30,000	(1,500)
Total payroll	$78,898	$500	$79,398	$79,799	$ 401	$311,896	$312,000	$ 104
Office costs								
Telephone	$1,000	$ 475	$1,475	$1,500	$ 25	$ 6,000	$ 6,000	
Postage, mailing	2,500		2,500	2,400	(100)	10,000	10,000	
Office supplies	1,600	(600)	1,000	1,000	0	4,000	4,000	
Machine maintenance		240	240	240	0	1,000	1,000	
Rent, janitorial costs	800	400	1,200	1,200	0	4,800	4,800	
Utilities	1,100	500	1,600	1,200	(400)	6,600	5,000	($1,600)
Other						30,000	30,000	
Total other	$7,000	$1,015	$8,015	$7,540	($475)	$62,400	$60,800	($1,600)
Totals	$311,873	$13,115	$324,988	$331,889	$6,901	$1,192,221	$1,196,800	$4,579

This rarely happens except when there is a major advance payment for something. In this case the organization was able to purchase a large supply of paper, estimated to last for the entire year, at a good price. Since future periods will be benefited, an adjustment downward was made in the present period's expenditures. Column c shows expenditures revised for timing differences so that they can be legitimately compared with the budget as calculated for the first three months of the year (July–September from Figure 7.2).

The resulting variation, although interesting in itself, has more relevance if its effect is carried to a projection of the results for the end of the year. This is done in columns f, g, and h. In recalculating the year-end projection, our organization's management must determine what a variation in the first three months really means. Sometimes it does not indicate any change in subsequent months. For instance, eleven fewer courses were begun and 375 more students were served than the original budget had estimated. Does that indicate anything about the next two terms? In this case, management assumed that it did not; thus, the revised projection for number of courses and students reflects adjustments only for the variations in the fall term. Instructor compensation was lower than projected originally, probably due to the smaller number of courses offered. Again, since this reduction was not expected to carry into the next terms, the year-end estimate of instructor compensation is revised only by the fall variance. The same is true with course material costs, but not with instructor travel and classroom costs. In these two items it appears that the negative variance was not due to the difference in number of courses or number of students but rather to a real increase in costs that will be carried into subsequent terms. It appears that the negative $375 variance in instructor travel for fall will expand to a negative $1,125 by the end of the year. Classroom costs are now reestimated to jump up $2,000 over budget, and lower in the report, we see that utilities are also expected to be higher than budget. In the payroll section, salary savings caused by the departure of an employee in the program support section (and the delay in hiring a replacement) and a leave of absence without pay by an employee in the registration office are reflected as a difference that will ultimately show up as a reduction in the year-end balance. Note, however, that there appears to be a partly compensating increase in temporary staff costs, which will also carry over to the year's end.

This sample report illustrates most of the financial control and monitoring problems and mechanisms faced by fixed resource CE organizations, although in larger, more complex organizations the process can be considerably more difficult, particularly in identification of timing differences and projection of trends from current actual data.

We might note briefly here the effect of a variation between estimated and actual volume of activity, which will be very important in our later discussion of variable resource organizations. As we saw, the decrease in the number of courses begun and the increase in the number of students served had an influence on the budget. How can we determine the real effectiveness of the organization when there is a difference in volume?

Part of the answer lies in ratio analysis. We can determine the budgeted cost per course and cost per enrollment and compare these ratios to the actual ratios. These calculations for our example situation are shown below:

	Actual	*Budget*	*Better (Worse)*
Cost per course:			
$\dfrac{\text{Total course costs}}{\text{Number of courses}}$	$\dfrac{\$237,575}{262} = \$906$	$\dfrac{\$244,550}{273} = \$895$	($11)
Cost per enrollment:			
$\dfrac{\text{Total course costs}}{\text{Number of students}}$	$\dfrac{\$237,575}{7,200} = \$33$	$\dfrac{\$244,550}{6,825} = \$36$	$3

Although $11 more was spent per course than was budgeted, $3 less was spent per student. Only someone very familiar with the organization and its service mission could accurately interpret these ratios and decide whether management was doing a satisfactory job, but it should be clear that a simple dollar better or worse figure is usually not enough to allow sound judgments.

This brings us to another significant difference between fixed resource and variable resource CE organizations. Lacking the relationship between the inflow and outflow of resources, the fixed resource organization must look to external, nonfinancial measures to gauge its effectiveness. Without these external measures, the budgeting process becomes sterile and unrelated (except in a mechanical way) to the mission of the organization. But where, through the use of ratios or a reporting format that incorporates retention rates, the budget can be tied to the achievement of learning objectives, the number of people served, the expression of satisfaction from students, or other nonfinancial measures, it can take on a deeper meaning.

Feedback in Variable Resource Organizations

Although it is possible for self-supporting CE organizations to be budgeted like fixed resource organizations, such organizations are usually variable resource. Their financial objectives may range from spending no more than is taken in to making as much profit as possible.

Unlike the fixed resource organization, in which the purpose of the feedback and monitoring system is to keep track only of outflows—expenditures, the rate of expenditure, commitments, and the ultimate effect on discretionary funds—the variable resource organization must track both inflows and outflows. This usually requires that the organization be segmented into small parts and that the responsibility for the financial performance of those parts be clearly assigned to individuals. We discussed this earlier in Chapter Four when we established the structure of the budgeting process. The feedback and control system should mirror this budget structure.

Cost Structure

The establishment of the control or responsibility structure of an organization, of which the financial reporting process is an important instrument, requires understanding of the concepts of controllable costs, noncontrollable costs, discretionary costs, and committed costs. As has been noted, an individual cannot fairly be held responsible for costs *noncontrollable* by that individual, such as organization overhead in the case of individual responsibility center managers in a CE organization. Other costs, however, are *controllable* by managers to various degrees. Costs controllable entirely by the manager, as promotion costs are in many circumstances, are called *discretionary costs*. The ability of a manager to correctly balance such costs with the income they are supposed to produce should be a significant factor in evaluation of his or her performance.

Some costs seem, in a strict sense, to be controllable, but they may not be entirely discretionary. Take, for example, the situation in which instructor compensation per course is fixed: Every instructor is paid exactly the same for every course taught. In this case, the amount of instructor compensation is a function of the number of courses offered and is not directly discretionary. The manager may be able to vary the number of courses offered and determine minimum enrollments and maximum class sizes, but these parameters only indirectly influence instructor compensation totals. If compensation rates were not established, so that the manager or the programmers determined the rate of compensation for each instructor individually, instructor compensation would become more discretionary.

Feedback and control structures also must comprehend the nature of *committed or sunk costs*. Like courses, individual responsibility centers and whole CE organizations have sunk costs—either costs already paid for or future costs to which the organization is obligated. Promotion costs are common examples; once it has been determined how a course or group of courses will be promoted, the costs associated with the promotion campaign become committed. Payroll costs also are usually committed costs, since only under unusual circumstances will the number of employees be reduced during a budget period. The distinction between committed and uncommitted costs is important because decisions about the incurring of these costs are made at different times. For example, decisions about staffing levels and the amount to be spent on promotion are usually made earlier than decisions about expenses involving the actual presentation of courses—room rental, course material costs, entertainment, and so on. Because committed costs are givens, they often have more impact on the overall level of operation and the financial success of the organization than do other kinds of costs. Decisions to commit costs are therefore very important.

Timing

All feedback systems must somehow deal with the fact that financial results take time to become clear, and managers (and programmers) are constantly pressed to make decisions before these results are available. Because of long preparation and promotional lead times, it is typical that planning for the spring term, for instance, must be complete before the results of the fall term are known. Thus a course that proves to be an utter failure in the fall might be included in the spring catalogue because of an early promotion deadline. (Of course, it is possible that the spring course will be a roaring success, in which case the programmer can take credit for perseverance.) Feedback systems must incorporate the natural timing of financial transactions and the trade-offs that are necessary between comprehensiveness and precision, on the one hand, and timeliness and relevance to decision making on the other.

Figure 7.4 is a graphic representation of the timing and transaction flow of a typical CE organization.

The major categories of transactions pictured in this figure are as follows:

- *Staff costs and other continuing expenses.* These tend to be expended uniformly over time, with little variation from one period to the next. They are often indirect (overhead) costs and are allocated in some way to the appropriate income-producing segment and time period.
- *Planning and promotion costs.* The costs of planning a course or group of courses precede all other transactions related to those courses, and although the bills for promotion costs may come in later, promotion costs are committed during this early period.

Figure 7.4. Timing and Transaction Flow in a Typical CE Organization.

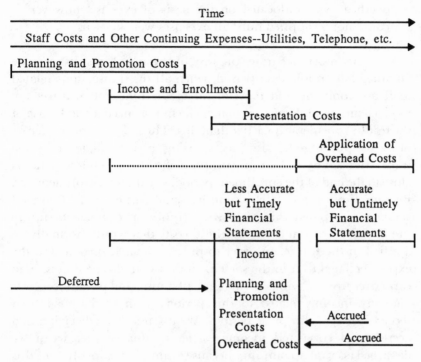

- *Income and enrollments.* Income and enrollments are received during periods immediately preceding the starting of the courses. Because they are the first real indications of the success or failure of a program, levels of income and enrollment are usually watched closely.
- *Presentation costs.* Once it has been determined that the course or courses should be held, the costs of actually presenting the course(s)—instructional compensation, room rental, course materials, and so on—are committed.
- *Application of overhead costs.* The timing of the application or "billing" of overhead costs to the responsibility centers can vary greatly from organization to organization. The allocation may be a function of income or expense in some way and thus may be applied when all other transactions are completed, or it may be applied as transactions occur. For instance, overhead might be allocated on a per student basis, in which case it would be

possible to apply the overhead as each student enrolls. If overhead were allocated on the basis of expense, however, it could not be applied until all expenses were known.

The most accurate picture of financial results can be obtained late in a budget period, when all the transactions related to it are complete and most or all of the bills and invoices are received and paid. However, management may need a good sense of the results considerably earlier than this. Thus, the financial picture must be put together in pieces, using best estimates of some transactions. The earliest practical time for this piecing together is close to the end of the enrollment period, when total enrollment and income figures are fairly complete and accurate. A financial statement prepared this early will require an estimate of future presentation costs and any overhead costs that would normally be applied in the future. In order to properly match income and the expense related to it in the same period, it will also be necessary to carry over from previous periods any planning and promotion costs and any income related to this period's courses that had been received or spent in prior periods. We discussed the deferring and accruing of costs and income earlier in this chapter when we described accrual accounting. Because estimation is involved in this method, there is the possibility of error, and one of the problems in rendering financial statements that involve accruals is the necessity of reconciling the estimates with actual results when they are finally available. For a further discussion of the timing of financial decision making, see Strother and Klus (1982, p. 50).

Types of Reporting Systems

Many of the decisions involved in setting up a financial feedback and reporting system mirror those made (and already discussed) in connection with setting up the budget system, since the feedback system and the budget system must coincide in order to provide accurate and useful information. These decisions include the timing of the reporting period and the choice of the lowest organizational level for which data will be aggregated. As we have noted, choosing the course as the common denominator gives us the advantage of aggregating data in many ways; for instance, if we have a financial statement for each course, we can potentially add together the financial results of all the courses presented by one programmer in one term, all computer courses, all the courses in a particular geographical area, or all courses with a particular presentation format. This flexibility is not possible if the data are collected at a level that does not provide enough detail to allow discrimination among these categories.

The following are examples of financial reports that might be useful for a self-supporting, variable resource CE organization. The list, of course, is not exhaustive. Each organization will have to develop for itself a reporting system timed to its own operating rhythms and pitched at a level of detail that balances the trade-off between the costs of maintaining it and the benefits of more detailed and timely information.

The "Inventory" Report. This kind of report compares the amount of program activity (measured in number of programs, income, and enrollments) projected in the annual budget with the actual activity as shown in a summary of course budgets. You will recall that the programmer we followed in our earlier example, Cindy E., was asked to summarize her planned activity for each term for the annual budget. The worksheet she filled out for the fall term is shown in Figure 5.12. This worksheet may have been prepared as early as the preceding April, assuming a fiscal year beginning July 1. Cindy's calculations at that time may have included many guesses, and by the time she is ready to make final plans for the fall term, say, in May or June, she might wish to consider changes that have occurred. For example, she may have added or deleted courses, changed fees, reconsidered expenses, and/or come up with new estimates of enrollments. If these changes were reflected in course budgets prepared reasonably close to the point at which promotion plans were approved, the sum of those budgets represent an "inventory" of the courses that Cindy has scheduled for the fall term. Her "inventory," added to those of other programmers, can be compared to the annual budget to make sure it is sufficient to maintain the potential for achieving the budget objective. This comparison is really a comparison between two plans, one prepared on relatively up-to-date information (the course budgets) and one against which performance will ultimately be measured (the annual budget). An example of an inventory report for all the programmers in the Arts and Sciences Department is shown in Figure 7.5.

We see from this report that Cindy has increased to six the number of courses she plans to present in the fall, reduced the number of enrollments she expects, increased her estimate of total income, and hopes to do $4,000 better on the bottom line than she had previously anticipated. This increase in expectation is something that a manager likes to see, since it adds to the margin of safety in the original budget and allows for some slippage without damaging the original budget goal. Debbie F., on the other hand, expects to fall short of her budget goal for the fall term. In fact, her expected shortfall pulls the entire department below its original budget. This is not good news, but it is still useful, because it gives higher management an early indication that this responsibility center is in trouble and may not be able to achieve its goal. Armed with that information, management can attempt to improve the situation.

Note that this report deals with the top part of the budget—the income part—and the bottom line; it does not deal with expenses at all. The report could be expanded to include expenses at this point, since annual budgeted expenses are known and the sum of the expenses in the course budgets could be obtained. However, the details of the expenses probably would not add much to the information that managers need to make decisions.

Budgeted Income Compared with Actual. The next logical step in the feedback process is to compare actual income, enrollments, and number of programs with the projected figures in the budget. This can usually be done soon after enrollment for a particular period is determined, and it is the earliest indication of what is actually happening during the budget year. Figure 7.6 is an example of such a comparison.

From this report we can see that Cindy offered exactly the number of courses she expected to at the time the annual budget was drawn up. She apparently had to cancel the additional one she had later planned on offering, and she fell just a bit short on the number of enrollments and income. Debbie, as expected, and Gary, perhaps unexpectedly, were considerably below their budget goals

Figure 7.5. Fall Course Inventory Compared to Budget,
Arts and Sciences.

Programmer	Per Course Budgets	Per Annual Budget	Better (Worse)
	Number of Programs		
Cindy E.	6	5	1
Debbie F.	6	10	(4)
Ernie G.	11	9	2
Freddie H.	18	15	3
Gary I.	18	18	0
Hubert J.	26	22	4
Totals	85	79	6
	Number of Students		
Cindy E.	500	530	(30)
Debbie F.	350	500	(150)
Ernie G.	400	300	100
Freddie H.	400	300	100
Gary I.	600	600	0
Hubert J.	650	700	(50)
Totals	2,900	2,930	(30)
	Income		
Cindy E.	$110,000	$100,000	$10,000
Debbie F.	55,000	85,000	(30,000)
Ernie G.	95,000	75,000	20,000
Freddie H.	105,000	95,000	10,000
Gary I.	102,000	100,000	2,000
Hubert J.	130,000	115,000	15,000
Totals	$597,000	$570,000	$27,000
	Available for Overhead		
Cindy E.	$53,000	$49,000	$4,000
Debbie F.	10,000	27,000	(17,000)
Ernie G.	19,000	18,000	1,000
Freddie H.	33,000	30,000	3,000
Gary I.	36,000	36,000	0
Hubert J.	39,000	38,000	1,000
Totals	$190,000	$198,000	($8,000)

Figure 7.6. Fall Actual Activity Compared to Annual Budget, Arts and Sciences.

Programmer	Actual	Per Annual Budget	Better (Worse)	
Number of Programs				
Cindy E.	5	5	0	
Debbie F.	6	10	(4)	
Ernie G.	10	9	1	
Freddie H.	16	15	1	
Gary I.	12	18	(6)	
Hubert J.	24	22	2	
Totals	73	79	(6)	
Number of Students				
Cindy E.	500	530	(30)	
Debbie F.	370	500	(130)	
Ernie G.	350	300	50	
Freddie H.	325	300	25	
Gary I.	450	600	(150)	
Hubert J.	780	700	80	
Totals	2,775	2,930	(155)	
Income Compared to Annual Budget				
Cindy E.	$ 97,000	$100,000	($ 3,000)	97.0%
Debbie F.	64,000	85,000	(21,000)	75.3%
Ernie G.	87,000	75,000	12,000	116.0%
Freddie H.	100,000	95,000	5,000	105.3%
Gary I.	83,000	100,000	(17,000)	83.0%
Hubert J.	150,000	115,000	35,000	130.4%
Totals	$581,000	$570,000	$11,000	101.9%
Income Compared to Sum of Course Budgets				
Cindy E.	$ 97,000	$110,000	($13,000)	88.2%
Debbie F.	64,000	55,000	9,000	116.4%
Ernie G.	87,000	95,000	(8,000)	91.6%
Freddie H.	100,000	105,000	(5,000)	95.2%
Gary I.	83,000	102,000	(19,000)	81.4%
Hubert J.	150,000	130,000	20,000	115.4%
Totals	$581,000	$597,000	($16,000)	97.3%

Management had previously been warned about Debbie from the inventory report, but this is the first financial indication of the evident decline in Gary's programs.

Notice that this report does not tell anything about either expenses or the bottom line. To estimate expenses so soon after courses have begun might be difficult, time-consuming, and not worth the effort. Also, it is usually true that income is a reasonably good surrogate for the bottom line. Expenses in any particular program tend to be fairly stable, so that if the income target is achieved, the bottom line target probably also will be achieved. In this case, where course budgets are reviewed and approved individually, the chance of a major problem developing in expense would be slight. Expense overruns are a problem only when expenses are extraordinarily out of line, as may happen occasionally with self-willed or inexperienced programmers.

It is important, however, to use some care in extrapolating from income to the bottom line. Cindy's $3,000 shortfall in income would probably translate into a smaller decline in the bottom line, since the shortfall is apparently caused by fewer enrollments than she expected, and variable costs associated with those enrollments probably did not have to be paid. Similarly, enrollments beyond what was expected are likely to have additional costs, so that a "better" condition, such as indicated by Hubert's income, also will not be maintained intact all the way to the bottom line.

The information at the bottom of the report, labeled "Income Compared to Sum of Course Budgets," shows a comparison of the actual results of income and the total of the course budgets in Figure 7.5. This comparison would generally be less important than the comparison with the original annual budget because the budget encompasses the organization for the entire period and is the basis for evaluating performance. However, it is interesting to see how accurate the programmers are at preparing course budgets, and this information may be useful in the next term when the "inventory" report is prepared. For example, note that although Debbie fell considerably below her annual budget target, she exceeded the expectations represented in her course budgets. This may indicate that her problem is with the smaller number (volume) of courses she is offering rather than with the financial quality of the courses she does offer.

Actual Results Compared with Budget by Course and by Term. The first two reports merely painted the outline of the financial picture, generally indicating problem and boom areas, opportunities and trends. They avoided the cost (expense) side of the equation. Adding actual expenses to the reporting scheme brings a significantly greater level of complexity and difficulty to the feedback process. The timing problem we discussed earlier becomes important. Unless the expense schedules were prepared well after the courses had been completed, it would be necessary to accrue expenses as well as to keep track of costs already expended on the course or group of courses. Additionally, overhead costs must be assigned to appropriate income-producing segments of the enterprise.

Figure 7.7 begins the comparison of actual results with budget at the lowest level of aggregation, the course.

Figure 7.7. Course Actual Compared to Course Budget.

Programmer: Cindy E.
Course: 1

	Actual	Budget	Better (Worse)
Number of students	310	300	10
Income	$31,000	$33,000	($2,000
Less pass-through	3,100	3,000	100
Adjusted income	$27,900	$30,000	($2,100
Expense			
Promotion	$3,758	$4,500	$742
Teacher compensation	3,100	3,000	(100
Other direct	1,511	1,000	(511
Total direct	$8,369	$8,500	$131
Gross margin	$19,531	$21,500	($1,969

This figure shows the actual results of one of the courses Cindy planned for the fall term (Course 1 from Figure 5.12). When the results of all Cindy's courses for the term are added together and compared with her fall term budget, we can generate a report at the programmer level, which is the next logical level of aggregation of data. This is shown in Figure 7.8.

Figure 7.8. Comparison of Actual with Budget, Fall, Cindy E.

	(a) Actual	(b) Per Annual Budget	(c) Better (Worse)
amber of programs	5	5	
amber of students	500	530	(30)
acome	$123,000	$128,000	($5,000)
Less pass-through	26,000	28,000	2,000
djusted income	$ 97,000	$100,000	($3,000)
xpense			
Promotion	$16,000	$15,000	($1,000)
Teacher compensation	26,000	25,000	(1,000)
Other direct	8,000	11,000	3,000
Total direct	$50,000	$51,000	$1,000
ross margin	$47,000	$49,000	($2,000)
Departmental indirect			
Payroll			
Programmer	8,000	8,000	
Staff support	4,475	4,750	$275
Fringe benefits	2,300	2,750	450
Total payroll	$14,775	$15,500	$725
rogrammer margin	$32,225	$33,500	($2,725)
Dept. admin.	700	1,000	300
Dept. promotion	2,182	2,250	68
Dept. S & E	1,854	2,000	146
Total dept. indirect	$19,511	$20,750	$1,239
otal expenses	$69,511	$71,750	$2,239
vailable for overhead	$27,489	$28,250	($761)

As forecast in the inventory report, Cindy did slightly below what she had projected in the annual budget. To show the complete picture, the report adds overhead elements, shown at the bottom (beginning with "dept. admin."). Three levels of overhead are incorporated here, the first of which is the responsibility center, or programmer, level. Programmer and staff support payroll and related fringe benefits are overhead items at this level. They are classed as overhead because it is too much trouble to charge time directly to individual courses. The annual payroll budget was simply divided by the number of terms in the year (four) and compared to the actual experience for the period. In this case, Cindy's secretary took some time off without pay, thereby creating a "better" situation in staff support, and there was a big savings in fringe benefits due to a miscalculation in the annual budget. Because of the importance of this level in isolating the direct costs of the programmer responsibility center, "dept. admin." payroll costs have been pulled out of the payroll section and added below and a new line, "programmer margin," has been added.

The next level is departmental overhead: administrative payroll, promotion, and supplies and expense at the departmental level. Departmental administrative payroll proved to be lower than expected, and this advantage was passed on to the programmers on a pro rata basis. Departmental promotion is allocated pro rata to all programmers on the basis of total adjusted income, and departmental supplies and expense are allocated on the basis of total payroll costs. In both expense categories, Cindy shows up a bit "better" than projected, probably due to lower volume.

This example illustrates the concept of responsibility accounting we discussed earlier. Note that at the gross margin line, Cindy is $2,000 worse than her budget, but at the bottom line, she is only $761 worse. The improvement is due to lower payroll costs in Cindy's responsibility center and to lower administrative costs. The lower payroll costs are legitimately ascribed to Cindy, and she should get full credit for effecting them. However, the savings in the departmental overhead line items were not the result of anything Cindy did, except, negatively, to have lower pro rata income. Thus, Cindy should not be given credit for the $514 "better" condition in these accounts; her performance should really be evaluated on the basis of the "programmer margin" line.

The third level of overhead dealt with here is organizational overhead, which is incorporated in the bottom "available for overhead" line. This represents Cindy's actual and expected contribution to the costs that we summarized first in Figure 5.2. An alternative to this treatment is to create a line item or items for these costs also, coming out with a responsibility center that is "fully burdened" with overhead costs and that will have a bottom line corresponding to the true profit or loss statement of a businesslike enterprise. In this example, because different programmers are expected to produce different amounts available for overhead, we stopped the analysis at this point.

Actual results can be compared to the budget in a format similar to that of Figure 7.8 for successively higher levels of the organization. For instance, the results of all the responsibility centers (programmers) can be added together to get a departmental statement, and the results for all the departments can be added together to get a financial statement for the entire organization for each term.

Annual Reports. This aggregation of data reaches its ultimate form in annual reports, which summarize the results for the whole organization for the whole year. The actual results for the year could first be summarized in the format used in Figures 5.2 and 6.1. These reports, of course, would need to be supported with a number of schedules summarizing financial results for lower levels of the organization.

Although they are useful in providing a definitive summary of results, however, these annual reports are not in a form that would allow management to compare the results with the budget or with the results of the prior year to provide the feedback on the budgeting process that we are seeking. For comparisons we have to develop reports using the budget that was approved at the beginning of the year. The first example of such a report is shown in Figure 7.9.

This report compares the operating budget, term by term, for Cindy E. (which she calculated in Figure 5.11) with her actual operating results for each term. The results for the whole year are

Figure 7.9. Summary of Program Activity by Term, Actual Compared with Annual Budget, Cindy E.

	(a)	(b)	(c)	(d)	(e)	(f)	(g)	(h)	(i)
		Fall			Winter			Spring	
	Actual	Per Annual Budget	Better (Worse)	Actual	Per Annual Budget	Better (Worse)	Actual	Per Annual Budget	Better (Worse)
Number of programs	5	5		9	7		8	10	(2)
Number of students	500	530	(30)	450	400	50	580	600	(20)
Income	$123,000	$128,000	($5,000)	$109,000	$88,000	$21,000	$85,000	$88,000	($3,000)
Less pass-through	26,000	28,000	2,000	15,000	10,000	(5,000)			
Adjusted income	$ 97,000	$100,000	($3,000)	$ 94,000	$78,000	$16,000	$85,000	$88,000	($3,000)
Expense									
Promotion	$16,000	$15,000	($1,000)	$19,000	$13,000	($ 6,000)	$13,000	$16,000	$3,000
Teacher compensation	26,000	25,000	(1,000)	20,000	13,000	(7,000)	25,000	27,000	2,000
Other direct	8,000	11,000	3,000	7,000	6,000	(1,000)	7,000	4,000	(3,000)
Total direct	$50,000	$51,000	$1,000	$46,000	$32,000	($14,000)	$45,000	$47,000	$2,000
Gross margin	$47,000	$49,000	($2,000)	$48,000	$46,000	$2,000	$40,000	$41,000	($1,000)
Departmental indirect									
Payroll									
Programmer	$ 8,000	$ 8,000		$ 8,000	$ 8,000		$ 8,000	$ 8,000	
Staff support	4,475	4,750	275	4,750	4,750		4,950	4,750	($200)
Fringe benefits	2,300	2,750	450	2,400	2,750	$350	2,500	2,750	250
Total payroll	$14,775	$15,500	$725	$15,150	$15,500	$350	$15,450	$15,500	$ 50
Programmer margin	$32,225	$33,500	($1,275)	$32,850	$30,500	$2,350	$24,550	$25,500	($950)
Dept. administration	700	1,000	300	1,000	1,000		1,300	1,000	(300)
Dept. promotion	2,182	2,250	68	2,500	2,250	(250)	1,000	2,250	1,250
Dept. supplies & expense	1,854	2,000	146	2,540	2,000	(540)	1,800	2,000	200
Total dept. indirect	$19,511	$20,750	$1,239	$21,190	$20,750	($440)	$19,550	$20,750	$1,200
Total expenses	$69,511	$71,750	$2,239	$67,190	$52,750	($14,440)	$64,550	$67,750	$3,200
Available for overhead	$27,489	$28,250	($761)	$26,810	$25,250	$1,560	$20,450	$20,250	$200

	(j)	(k) Summer	(l)	(m)	(n)	(o) Total	(p)
	Actual	Per Annual Budget	Better (Worse)	Adjustments	Actual	Per Annual Budget	Better (Worse)
Number of programs	4	3	1	(1)	25	25	
Number of students	150	90	60	(100)	1,580	1,620	(60)
Income	$80,000	$69,000	$11,000	($10,000)	$387,000	$373,000	$14,000
Less pass-through	18,000	20,000	2,000		59,000	58,000	(1,000)
Adjusted income	$62,000	$49,000	$13,000	($10,000)	$328,000	$315,000	$13,000
Expense							
Promotion	$ 7,000	$ 6,000	($ 1,000)	($2,500)	$ 52,500	$ 50,000	($ 2,500)
Teacher compensation	22,000	15,000	(7,000)	(5,000)	88,000	80,000	(8,000)
Other direct	12,000	9,000	(3,000)	(2,000)	32,000	30,000	(2,000)
Total direct	$41,000	$30,000	($11,000)	($9,500)	$172,500	$160,000	($12,500)
Gross margin	$21,000	$19,000	$2,000	($500)	$155,500	$155,000	$500
Departmental indirect							
Payroll							
Programmer	$ 8,000	$ 8,000		($2,000)	$30,000	$32,000	$2,000
Staff support	4,950	4,750	($200)	(1,262)	17,863	19,000	1,137
Fringe benefits	2,500	2,750	250	(625)	9,075	11,000	1,925
Total payroll	$15,450	$15,500	$ 50	($3,887)	$56,938	$62,000	$5,062
Programmer margin	$5,550	$3,500	$2,050	$3,387	$98,562	$93,000	$5,562
Dept. administration	1,300	1,000	(300)		4,300	4,000	(300)
Dept. promotion	2,500	2,250	(250)	(400)	7,782	9,000	1,218
Dept. supplies & expense	2,200	2,000	(200)	(553)	7,841	8,000	159
Total dept. indirect	$21,450	$20,750	($700)	($4,840)	$76,861	$83,000	$6,139
Total expenses	$62,450	$50,750	($11,700)	($14,340)	$249,361	$243,000	($6,361)
Available for overhead	($450)	($1,750)	$1,300	$4,340	$78,639	$72,000	$6,639

summarized in the last three columns. Cindy did a bit better than projected in the budget in every term except the fall, ending with an available for overhead line better than her budget by $6,639. The gross margin and the programmer margin lines represent the income minus the expense for all lines above them. This format may be an example of the "information overload" problem we discussed earlier; there is so much information on it that it is a bit hard to read.

The "Adjustments" column (column m) is usually necessary for several reasons. First, there may be timing differences in expenses or even income that have to be recognized. Second, there may be accounting errors or errors from other sources that have to be adjusted here. Third, it may be necessary to make adjustments for special arrangements with programmers. For instance, in this case the director asked Cindy to be responsible for a public service program in the summer that everyone knew would not meet budget standards but that the director wanted to do for political reasons. Cindy agreed to do the program, provided that the results of it were not included in her financial statements and that the value of the time that she and her support staff spent on the program was credited to her responsibility center. Thus the program, enrollment, income, direct expenses, and an allocated share of both payroll and departmental overhead were removed from Cindy's financial statement in the "Adjustments" column. Of course, this activity will have to go somewhere in order for the departmental activity summary to be complete. It could go in a separate report or on an adjustment column in the programmer summary schedule, for example.

The programmer summary schedule simply shows the last three columns of Figure 7.9 for every programmer and adds them all up to get the total departmental results. Service department results can be summarized on the form shown in Figure 5.3. Departmental results can then be combined to get summary results for the whole organization.

These summary results can and should be displayed in two ways. The first format, which might be called the Departmental Summary, is shown in Figure 7.10. It corresponds to the budget schedule shown in Figure 6.8.

Figure 7.10. Departmental Summary (in Thousands).

	Actual	Budget	Better (Worse)	Actual Prior Year	Better (Worse)
come					
Arts and Sciences	$1,702	$1,800	($ 98)	$1,680	$22
Business and Management	1,456	1,500	(44)	1,419	37
Education	281	300	(19)	271	10
Engineering	957	900	57	870	87
Conferences and Inst.	436	500	(64)	352	84
Other	342	307	35	282	60
Total Income	$5,174	$5,307	($133)	$4,874	$300
ense-Programming Depts.:					
Arts and Sciences	$1,402	$1,407	$ 5	$1,293	($109)
Business and Management	1,343	1,353	10	1,287	(56)
Education	290	290	0	256	(34)
Engineering	784	750	(34)	736	(48)
Conferences and Inst.	446	490	44	358	(88)
Total expenses	$4,265	$4,290	$25	$3,930	($335)
ailable for Overhead					
Arts and Sciences	$300	$393	(93)	$387	($87)
Business and Management	113	147	(34)	132	(19)
Education	(9)	10	(19)	15	(24)
Engineering	173	150	23	134	39
Conferences and Inst.	(10)	10	(20)	(6)	(4)
Total available	$567	$710	($143)	$662	($95)
ss Service Depts.					
Director's Office	(118)	(114)	(4)	(102)	(16)
Business Office	(43)	(47)	4	(40)	(3)
Cashier's Office	(37)	(38)	1	(34)	(3)
Registration Office	(73)	(77)	4	(74)	1
Student Records (net)	(25)	(23)	(2)	(20)	(5)
Promotion	(19)		(19)	(13)	(6)
Downtown Facility	(142)	(131)	(11)	(137)	(5)
Reprographics	(12)		(12)	(9)	(3)
Parent Indirect	(30)	(30)		(28)	(2)
Contingency		(250)	250		
tal	$ 68	$ 0	$ 68	$205	($137)

    This report format shows very quickly the results for the year in each department, comparing these actual results with the budget and also with the prior year. It is clear from this report that the organization did not do as well as was budgeted and that the reserve for contingencies was the major factor in allowing it to end up in the "better" category. The organization also did not do as well as last year; although income was up, expenses were up even more, so the margin of difference was smaller. A margin of only $68,000 was produced, as compared to the previous year's margin of $205,000.

    The second summary format is shown in Figure 7.11.

    This figure shows the "line item" or "natural classification" format, which is the usual format for institutional budget and financial presentation. Here we can see that in most line items our example organization did not do as well as budgeted, even in promotion and "other direct costs," which, because of lower income volume, we would expect to have done better than the budget. These cost items, along with departmental promotion, appear to be the major factors in the relatively poor showing for the year.

Analysis of Reports

    These summary reports and the detailed schedules that support them by giving the real information behind the summary figures can provide material for more analysis. Ratio analysis is one technique of making comparisons, especially when the volume of activity is markedly different from one comparison base to the other. In Figure 7.11 all expense items have been calculated as a percentage of adjusted income, and this gives us some general clues. For instance, promotion as a percent of income increased to 13.9 percent, from 13.4 percent a year earlier and the 13.0 percent budgeted. This tells us something we already knew, but perhaps more clearly the organization's promotion effort, at least by this measure, is less effective than it was last year and than it was planned to be in the budget. The situation may be less clear when it comes to instructor compensation. Some instructors might see these statements and, noting that instructor compensation was the only "better" item in direct cost, begin agitating for higher wages.

	(a) Actual 19A - B Amount	%	(b) Budget 19A - B Amount	%	(c) Better (Worse)	(d) Actual Results Last Year Amount	%	(e) Better (Worse)
Number of courses	594		625		(31)	581		13
Number of students	24,183		26,775		2,592	23,013		1,170
Income	$5,393,782		$5,547,000		($153,218)	$5,067,184		$326,598
Less pass-through	219,600		240,000		20,400	192,370		(27,230)
Adjusted income	$5,174,182	100.0%	$5,307,000	100.0%	($132,818)	$4,874,814	100.0%	$299,368
Expenses								
Direct expenses								
Promotion	$ 719,847	13.9%	$ 690,000	13.0%	($29,847)	$ 654,720	13.4%	($ 65,127)
Teacher compensation	1,556,700	30.1%	1,580,000	29.8%	23,300	1,436,780	29.5%	(119,920)
Other direct	623,620	12.1%	590,000	11.1%	(33,620)	557,042	11.4%	(66,578)
Subtotal direct	$2,900,167	56.1%	$2,860,000	53.9%	($40,167)	$2,648,542	54.3%	($251,625)
Gross margin	$2,274,015	43.9%	$2,447,000	46.1%	($172,985)	$2,226,272	45.7%	($47,743)
Departmental indirect								
Payroll								
Programmer	$ 393,000	7.6%	$ 405,000	7.6%	$12,000	$ 343,760	7.1%	($ 49,240)
Staff support	824,300	15.9%	819,500	15.4%	(4,800)	793,000	16.3%	(31,300)
Dept. administration	68,300	1.3%	80,000	1.5%	11,700	52,800	1.1%	(15,500)
Fringe benefits	274,800	5.3%	284,800	5.4%	10,000	243,182	5.0%	(31,618)
Subtotal payroll	$1,560,400	30.2%	$1,589,300	29.9%	$28,900	$1,432,742	29.4%	($127,658)
Dept. promotion	172,560	3.3%	140,000	2.6%	(32,560)	182,760	3.7%	10,200
Dept. supplies & expense	473,860	9.2%	467,700	8.8%	(6,160)	406,087	8.3%	(67,773)
Contingency			250,000	4.7%	250,000			
Total dept. indirect	$2,206,820	42.7%	$2,447,000	46.1%	$240,180	$2,021,589	41.5%	($185,231)
Total expenses	$5,106,987	98.7%	$5,307,000	100.0%	$200,013	$4,670,131	95.8%	($436,856)
Margin (Deficit)	$67,195	1.3%	$0	0.0%	($67,195)	$204,683	4.2%	$137,488

But ratio analysis shows that despite the "better" condition, the instructors received a larger share of the pie (30.1 percent) in the current year than was budgeted (29.8 percent) or than they received last year (29.5 percent).

Many other analyses using ratios are possible. One way of evaluating programmer productivity might be to divide the available for overhead produced by each programmer by the direct payroll costs of the programmer's responsibility center. Returning to Figure 7.9, we could compute Cindy E.'s "productivity index" as follows:

$$\frac{\text{Available for overhead}}{\text{Payroll costs}} \qquad \frac{\$78,639}{\$56,938} = 1.38$$

Cindy's index might be compared to that of other programmers to determine relative productivity. As with any financial data, however, these calculations must be interpreted with great care. Cindy's index, for instance, exceeds the index set for her in the budget. Another programmer might have an index higher than Cindy's but lower than budgeted. In such a case, a simple comparison between the two programmers might be misleading and thus might have to be extended to include a comparison with budgets or other factors.

Variable Budgeting and Analysis of Variance

Variable Budgeting. So far we have been dealing with what might be called a *static budget*—that is, a budget prepared for only one level of volume or activity. As mentioned earlier, a *variable budget* (sometimes called a *flexible budget*) is a budget or a series of budgets based on a range of activity. A programmer seldom does exactly the same number and kind of courses or has exactly the number of enrollments anticipated in the budget, and variations in anticipated volumes create variations in line items that are sometimes hard to evaluate. Where actual results are better than those projected in the budget, we say that there is a favorable variance, and where actual is worse than budget, there is an unfavorable variance. For instance, a greater enrollment in a particular course will create a favorable variance in the income of the course but, because of an increase in the variable costs of the course, an unfavorable variance in expenses. Because variable budgeting provides for budget standards over a range of activity, it takes into account the relationship between income and expense. It can be used effectively for both service and programming departments.

Let us use Cindy E.'s winter quarter as an example of variable budgeting. Figure 7.9 shows that Cindy did pretty well in that quarter, producing more "available for overhead" than she had budgeted. There is no question that, when we look at the bottom line, Cindy and her staff have done a good job; but it is a bit difficult to interpret some of the figures. For instance, we see that Cindy exceeded budgeted income by presenting more courses and attracting more students than she had expected. We can also see that Cindy had large unfavorable variances in her direct costs, part of which certainly is due to the increase in volume. Variable budgeting allows us to factor out the influence of the variation in number of courses and number of enrollments and base budget comparisons on per unit price or cost computations. Figure 7.12 is an illustration of how variable budgeting works.

Column a of this report shows the budget as originally approved (Figure 7.9, column e). The original budget was based on seven courses and 400 enrollments. We can restate this budget in terms of per unit measures. Column b indicates the per course measure, obtained by dividing each of the values in column a by 7, the number of budgeted courses. Column c shows the per enrollment figures, obtained by dividing each of the values in column a by 400. Column c shows a restatement of the original budget based on the actual volume achieved. Cindy actually programmed nine courses that attracted a total of 450 enrollments. For each of the line items, the appropriate per unit measure is selected and multiplied by the associated actual volume. For instance, the income items are more closely associated with enrollments than with courses, so each of the per enrollment measures is multiplied by 450 to come up with the revised budget.

Figure 7.12. Variable Budget Compared with Actual, Winter, Cindy E.

	(a) Winter Per Annual Budget	(b) Flexible Budget Per Course	(c) Flexible Budget Per Per Enroll.	(d)	(e) Budget Per Actual Volume	(f) Actual	(g) Better (Worse)
Number of programs	7				9	9	
Number of students	400				450	450	
Income	$88,000	$12,571	$220.00	E	$99,000	$109,000	$10,000
Less pass-through	10,000	1,429	25.00	E	11,250	15,000	(3,750)
Adjusted income	$78,000	$11,143	$195.00	E	$87,750	$94,000	$6,250
Expense							
Promotion	$13,000	$1,857	$32.50	C	$16,714	$19,000	($2,286)
Teacher compensation	13,000	1,857	32.50	C	16,714	20,000	(3,286)
Other direct	6,000	857	15.00	E	6,750	7,000	(250)
Total direct	$32,000	$4,571	$80.00		$40,179	$46,000	($5,821)
Gross margin	$46,000	$6,571	$115.00		$47,571	$48,000	$429
Departmental indirect							
Payroll							
Programmer	$ 8,000	Fixed	Fixed		8,000	8,000	
Staff support	4,750	Fixed	Fixed		4,750	4,750	
Fringe benefits	2,750	Fixed	Fixed		2,750	2,400	$350
Total payroll	$15,500	Fixed	Fixed		$15,500	$15,150	$350
Programmer margin	$30,500	$4,357	$76.25		$32,071	$32,850	$779
Dept. administration	1,000	143	$2.50	E	1,125	1,000	125
Dept. promotion	2,250	321	5.63	E	2,531	2,500	31
Dept. supplies & expense	2,000	286	5.00	E	2,250	2,540	(290)
Total dept. indirect	$20,750	$2,964	$51.88		$21,406	$21,190	$216
Total expenses	$52,750	$7,536	$131.88		$61,585	$67,190	($5,605)
Available for overhead	$25,250	$3,607	$63.13		$26,165	$26,810	$645

Note: Column (d) indicates the basis used, high column (c)...

For promotion and teacher compensation, however, which are basically (in this example) fixed costs of courses, the per course measure is used and is multiplied by 9, the actual number of courses presented. A code shown in column d indicates whether the per enrollment basis (E) or the per course basis (C) was used. Because payroll costs are reasonably fixed, at least over a "relevant range" of courses and enrollments, calculations of costs per course or per enrollment are not made for payroll.

This restated budget can now be compared to the actual figures. We see that Cindy still exceeded her budget expectations but not by as much as Figure 7.9 indicated. Her direct expenses still represent a problem. We can now see clearly that, although Cindy's income and her bottom line are definitely better than her original budget predicted, she paid out much more in instructor compensation and promotion than she had originally intended, and these two areas may warrant some attention in the next period.

Variable budgets can also be very useful in service departments. A simple example might be the registration office. It is reasonable to assume that registration costs should vary directly with the volume of enrollments. The original budget showed total registration costs of $76,400, based on enrollments of 26,775, or $2.8534 per enrollment (Figure 5.2). Actual enrollments turned out to be somewhat lower than expected—24,183. Based on this lower enrollment figure, we would expect the actual costs for the registration office to be $69,004 ($2.8534 × 24,183). However, actual costs turned out to be $73,400: better than originally budgeted but worse than the variable budget would have indicated. The problem may be that not all the costs of the registration office are directly variable with enrollments. Some element of payroll costs, telephone costs, and virtually every line item of expense is probably fixed. Thus, a worksheet similar to the one shown in Figure 7.12 is probably necessary for this department also. Further, there is often not enough time to react to lower than expected enrollments; the office has to schedule staff in advance, based on estimates of enrollments, and when those enrollments do not materialize, it is too late to send staff home and reduce costs. The unfavorable variance of the actual from the variable budget may be the cost to the organization of maintaining a registration office ready to serve, and the cost to the organization of understaffing that office, in lost enrollments and inconvenience to students, might add up to many more dollars than the unfavorable variance indicated in the budget comparison. As always, interpretation of these data must be done with care and an understanding of the organization as a whole.

Analysis of Variance. Although variable budgets are theoretically superior to static budgets, they are somewhat cumbersome to work with and costly to maintain. Most organizations prepare static budgets and then concentrate on any major variations from budgets that appear, performing on these items a deeper analysis called *analysis of variance* (not to be confused with the same term used in statistics). This kind of analysis is designed to determine the underlying causes for the variances so that subsequent estimates can be made more accurately and corrective action can be taken to avoid mistakes.

There are three kinds of budget variances: *price variances, volume variances,* and *mix variances.* Price variances occur in expenses when the price we expected to pay for some item of expense proves to be different from what we actually have to pay. When applied to income, which is done less frequently, "price variance" refers to a difference between the fee an organization expected to charge and what was actually charged. We are already familiar with volume variances, which occur because the actual volume of activity (usually the number of courses or enrollments) is different from what was budgeted. A mix variance occurs when the budget estimate of volume is based on a particular proportional combination of elements that is different from the proportion actually achieved. A mix variance can be considered a special combination of price and volume variances as we will see shortly.

The formulae for computing price and volume variances are as follows:

Price variance:
  (Actual price per unit – Budget price per unit) × Actual volume

Volume variance:
  (Actual volume – Budgeted volume) × Budget price per unit

We can illustrate each of these variances by referring back to Figure 7.7. Adjusted income for this course was $2,100 less than what was budgeted. This is an unfavorable variance because it will produce a smaller bottom line than was anticipated. It is a bit hard to understand, since there were ten more enrollments than was anticipated, which should have given a better result than budgeted. We can compute this better-than-expected result by using the standard formula for computing the volume variance:

$$(310 - 300) \times \$100 = \$1,000$$

The increased number of enrollments created a favorable variance of $1,000. However, the fee charged was not as high as had been budgeted. Thus, the 310 enrollments produced only $27,900, or $90 per person. We can also compute the price variance:

$$(\$90 - \$100) \times 310 = -\$3,100$$

There is an unfavorable price variance of $3,100, which combines with the favorable volume variance of $1,000 to produce the net unfavorable variance of $2,100.

A mix variance can be illustrated by a variation of this same example. Suppose that instead of a single fee, the fee had been set at $110 for those who desired academic credit and $80 for those who did not want credit. Let us say that the budget was based on this estimate of the number of enrollments in each category:

	200 @ $110 =	$22,000
	100 @ $ 80 =	$ 8,000
Total	300	$30,000

Suppose also that 310 people did show up but that the income was $27,920:

	104 @ $110 =	$11,440
	206 @ $ 80 =	$16,480
Total	310	$27,920

The "mix" or proportion of enrollments in each category was different from what was expected in the budget. Whereas the budget anticipated that two-thirds of the total enrollment would be at the higher fee, the actual proportion at the higher fee was only about one-third (104/310). In this case we can consider that there is a price variance because the average price per enrollment between budget ($100, or $30,000/300) and actual ($90, or $27,920/310) was different. Under this consideration the calculation of the price and volume variances would be exactly the same as the previous example. However, since we did not change the actual fee, we might consider that there was no price variance and that the entire variance is a volume variance caused by the different proportions of enrollment. The volume variance under this assumption has to be calculated in two parts:

$$
\begin{aligned}
(104 - 200) \times \$110 &= -\$10,560 \\
(206 - 100) \times \$\ 80 &= \underline{\$\ 8,480} \\
&\ \ -\$\ 2,080 \ \text{(unfavorable)}
\end{aligned}
$$

Thus the entire unfavorable variance ($30,000 - $27,920) is explained as a volume variance.

These same techniques can be applied to expenses. For fixed expenses (those that do not vary with the number of enrollments) the analysis is fairly straightforward. In Figure 7.7, instructor compensation shows an unfavorable total variance of $100. This variance could have been caused by paying one or more of the instructors at a rate higher than anticipated, which would be a price or cost variance. Alternatively, it could have been caused by adding one lecturer to the program and paying him or her $100; this would be a volume variance, where "volume" refers to the number of instructors. It could also have been a combination of factors, say, additional instructors but lower payments to each instructor.

For variable costs the issue is a bit more complex, since the volume we are talking about is again enrollments. Going back to our original example (Figure 7.7) and looking at "other direct expenses," we see a net unfavorable variance of $511. To analyze this variance we first have to determine its fixed and variable components. Suppose our analysis shows the following:

	Actual	Budget	Variance
Fixed	$581	$250	($330)
Variable	930	750	(180)
Total	$1,511	$1,000	($511)

Of the total unfavorable variance of $511, $331 relates to fixed expenses. This variance could be analyzed in a way similar to what we used with instructor compensation. The budget estimate for variable costs was based on 300 enrollments at $2.50 per enrollment ($750), whereas the actual variable costs turned out to be $930 for 310 enrollments, or $3.00 per enrollment. Again, the total variance consists of a volume variance and a price variance.

Volume variance:
$$(310 - 300) \times \$2.50 = \$25 \text{ (unfavorable)}$$
Price variance:
$$(\$3.00 - \$2.50) \times 310 = \$155 \text{ (unfavorable)}$$

These two variances, added together, equal the total unfavorable variance of $180. Note that these variances are unfavorable even though they are mathematically positive values. This is because we are dealing here with expense, and an increase in expense over budget decreases the margin.

This last example illustrates one of the problems of analyzing variances. The "unfavorable" volume variance of $25 was caused by ten more enrollments than had been anticipated, and it was more than offset by the favorable volume variance in revenue of $1,000. When variable cost budgets are exceeded because there are more enrollments than were expected, it is usually a positive rather than negative sign. A budgeting system that does not take this into account and imposes negative sanctions on programmers for exceeding line items of variable expense without relating those excesses to the increases in revenue associated with them is too rigid and will subvert the goals of the organization.

To be effective, all budgets must build in some flexibility. Variable budgeting is only one of several ways to accomplish this. There are other, less formal ways of achieving flexibility that may be less time-consuming, less costly, and more efficient. These other ways depend to a great extent on the knowledge, understanding, and interpretive skills of those responsible for monitoring the budget, and above all on their interpersonal skills. These skills hold the budgeting process together and keep it from becoming either so lax that it is ineffective as a standard or so rigid that it fosters resentment. When a programmer runs into budgetary trouble, he or she may need help, encouragement, more resources, or a kick in the behind—or all of these in some measure. Management has the responsibility for motivating employees, and there is no sure formula for successful motivation. A budget system supported by an effective feedback process is only one factor, albeit a very important factor, in achieving motivation; the most comprehensive and well-designed budget system will not be effective without managers who are skilled in human interaction.

Summary

The stage of feedback and control is an integral part of the budgetary process even though it takes place after the budget has been prepared. In order for the budgeting process to be effective, it must operate all year long, serving as both a standard and a planning tool.

Feedback and control systems in CE organizations must meet certain criteria and be devised with certain considerations in mind. First, they must coincide with the forms and categories that structured the budget, so that actual results can be compared to the budget. Second, a decision about the basic accounting method, cash or accrual, must be made. Although the accrual method is theoretically superior, there are some complexities and disadvantages in using it. Third, a feedback and control system must be developed with the needs of the users (programmers and managers) in mind. It should provide accurate and timely information in a form and at a level of detail sufficient for managers to make informed decisions. Too much information, an increasingly common phenomenon in our computer age, can lead to information overload and problems of interpretation. The trade-off between the cost and the benefits of a control system should be explored, and general guidelines for assessing the cost-benefit ratio of feedback systems should be developed.

In developing control systems, directors must take into account a number of characteristics common to CE organizations. Rarely is it possible for such organizations to develop a system similar to those used in business, because CE organizations are usually part of a larger institution and do not have a separate balance sheet. The practical consequences of this are far-reaching. The inability to deal with an operating period greater than one year severely inhibits the kind of long-range planning that is vital to the continuing financial health of an organization. It also means that the self-checking aspects of the double-entry accounting system often are not available to CE organizations. In addition, CE organizations often have control systems imposed upon them by the parent institution that are ill suited to their particular needs. Finally, directors often have to make decisions without adequate and timely information.

CE organizations may be involved in either fixed resource or variable resource budget contexts (or some of both). The structure and methods of budgeting in these two contexts differ, although we feel that the differences are not as great as traditional literature on the subject suggests. Fixed resource organizations have their resources "given" to them at the beginning of the budget period, and their main budgetary goal is not to either underspend or overspend this budget. Most service organizations and governmental or quasi-governmental agencies fit this pattern. Variable resource organizations must earn their resources as they go, much like a traditional business.

Budgets are either static, prepared for only one level of activity, or variable, prepared for a range of activity. Although variable budgets provide a greater range of detail for analysis, they are time-consuming and expensive to administer. Analysis of variance techniques, used to isolate price, volume, and mix variances, are important tools in helping managers discover the underlying reasons for exceptional (higher or lower than budget) performance.

Bibliography

Louderback, J. G., III, and Dominiak, G. F. *Managerial Accounting.* (3rd ed.) Boston: Kent, 1982.

Powell, R. M. *Management Procedures for Institutions.* Notre Dame, Ind.: University of Notre Dame Press, 1979.

Strother, G. B., and Klus, J. P. *Administration of Continuing Education.* Belmont, Calif.: Wadsworth, 1982.

Sullivan, T. J. *How to Budget in a Service Organization.* New York: American Management Association, Extension Institute, 1982.

Titard, P. L. *Managerial Accounting: An Introduction.* Hinsdale, Ill.: Dryden Press, 1983.

⟺ Part Three ⟺

Special Problems in Budgeting and Financial Control

This part extends the discussion in the earlier parts of the book to cover some common problems encountered in managing a CE organization and some special functions that often fall under the jurisdiction of CE management. Chapter Eight describes ways to measure the effectiveness of promotion, which is important because promotion costs can be a significant proportion of the CE budget and can have a direct relationship to the amount of income generated by the organization. Chapter Nine expands on the discussion of overhead cost allocation problems presented in Parts One and Two.

Chapter Ten discusses the budgetary aspects of a number of specialized functions. One is inventories and inventory accounting, which many CE organizations must deal with and which raises some issues not normally encountered in CE accounting and budgeting. The issues of cash and capital budgeting are important to some CE organizations, and an understanding of budgeting is incomplete without some knowledge of these functions. This chapter also deals with independent study, publications, and media-based services.

In Chapter Eleven we discuss computerization of CE budgeting and financial control systems. Computerization involves much more than selecting hardware; it places a significant strain on an organization and rarely can be isolated to do just a single task. Computerizing the budget, even on the smallest microcomputer using the simplest software, can have far-reaching implications. I take a "systems approach" to the issue of computers in budgeting, relating previous sections of this book to the process and outlining the considerations and steps involved in computerization.

8

Assessing
the Cost-Effectiveness
of Promotion

The Importance of Promotion Costs

In using promotion costs as illustrations in earlier pages, I have explained why promotion costs are at once so important and so difficult to measure. Promotion costs are (or should be) directly related to attracting students and producing income. Although other factors are certainly important, no one will attend a course if it is not publicized, and more will attend if it is both useful and publicized well.

Promotion costs are sunk or up-front costs. They must be expended before there are any real indications that a course will be successful. If only a few people enroll, it may well be possible to cancel the course, thereby avoiding costs of teacher compensation, room rental, course materials, and so on—but there is no way to avoid the promotion costs already expended.

Promotion costs are often a significant portion of the CE expense budget, typically ranging from 10 to 20 percent. Some CE organizations are "promotion intensive" and depend for success more on effective promotion than on any other line item of their budget. For instance, an organization with a relatively high proportion of its offering in noncredit courses directed at a widespread audience may well have to spend more for promotion and be more dependent on it than a school with high visibility offering an evening degree program.

Promotion costs are also likely to be highly discretionary, and decisions about promotion are likely to be distributed and decentralized. This follows from the fact that promotion is effective only when its potential audience is well defined and well understood. It is difficult for centralized authority to acquire the knowledge to make effective promotion decisions, so it makes more sense for the programmer, who is closer to the audience/market, and/or the promotion or marketing professional, who knows about promotion media and costs, to map a promotion campaign and decide (within reasonable limits) how much to spend. This means that knowledge about promotion has to be distributed widely throughout the organization and that control and monitoring of promotion budgets is important.

Promotion costs are also important to CE management because responsibility for promotion decisions rarely resides with only one individual. If a course fails, it may well be because of a failure of promotion, but this is often hard to determine. Even when failure can be directly attributed to promotion problems, whose failure is it? Except for small organizations in which the programmer is a jack-of-all-trades, not only the programmer but the promotion manager, mailing coordinator, and a number of others are likely to be involved in the decision-making process, and any one or all may be responsible for successes and failures. The inability to assign clear responsibility for promotion results presents managers with difficult issues of control and evaluation. It also makes programmers and promotion specialists reluctant to use data and measuring standards that may be misinterpreted or used to find them at fault. This reticence can be overcome only through greater understanding by everyone involved.

The characteristic of promotion that demands the attention of CE management most of all is the unpredictability of promotion results and the lack of standards, at least obvious ones, by which to judge the success or failure of promotion efforts. How much should be spent on promotion? How many enrollments should result from a particular promotion effort? These questions cannot be answered without experience and the use of both "hard" and "soft" evaluations.

Standards of promotion effectiveness can be developed through an evolutionary process in which one experience sheds light on the next and a simple measurement can be supplanted by a more complex one the next time around. In this way, the managers of each CE organization can develop standards uniquely suited to that organization. This chapter presents some common quantitative ways of measuring promotion effectiveness, starting with some relatively simple calculations and proceeding to more complex and comprehensive measures. At each level of complexity, evaluators must draw heavily on their interpretive skills and "informed intuition." Thus our recommended process combines both qualitative and quantitative elements.

Determining the cost-effectiveness of promotion involves the following steps:

1. identifying costs
2. attributing results
3. choosing and calculating methods of measurement
4. interpreting measurement

We will examine each of these steps in turn. In our discussion we will usually use the term *promotion campaign* to indicate a promotion effort designed to produce enrollments in a defined course or set of courses. Thus we will speak of the fall real estate course campaign, spring interior design course campaign, and so on, rather than a radio campaign or a newspaper campaign. Each course campaign may involve one or several media.

Identifying Costs

Many promotion costs can be identified easily, but identifying all the costs of promotion is impossible. For example, management can usually determine how much is spent on printing, postage, radio and newspaper advertising, and so on for a particular campaign, but there are almost always additional costs attributable to staff activities, some of which can play a crucial role in the success of a promotional effort, that are not so apparent. For instance, most programmers spend part of their time promoting courses, starting at the very beginning of course development. The contacts they make and the knowledge they gain about the market for a course are part of the promotional effort for that course. A few telephone calls to the training directors of several businesses in the area, say, may produce many enrollments, yet the cost of this effort is rarely recorded. Because such effort is so difficult to keep track of, we have to define the level of detail upon which we will base our definition of promotion cost. This definition should make clear which costs will be directly associated with a promotional campaign, which will be indirectly allocated to it, and which will not be recorded at all. For instance, in a promotional campaign consisting of a single brochure mailed to a mailing list of 30,000, management might "direct-cost" printing costs, mailing costs, mailing list costs, art and layout costs, typesetting, and so on. Editorial time could be allocated to the job based, say, on the number of words or the number of panels in the brochure; this would relieve editors of the task of keeping track of their time job by job. Finally, management might decide not even to attempt to keep track of the programmer time that goes into the production of the brochure—writing copy, collecting information, and so on.

Another issue in identifying costs has to do with the *method of indirect cost allocation*. We discussed some issues involved in choosing an indirect cost allocation method earlier, and in Chapter Nine we will examine this matter in greater detail. The same kinds of problems arise in regard to overhead allocation when the cost object is a promotion campaign as arise when it is a course of a CE organization. For instance, in the example just cited, it was the policy to allocate editorial time to brochures on the basis of number of panels. If some four-panel brochures required less editorial time than others, due to art work or mailing restrictions, or if some six-panel brochures required less editorial time than brochures with fewer panels, this allocation method would mask the "real" cost of producing the brochures and might lead to poor promotion decisions. Thus allocation methods should be chosen with care. In addition, everyone involved with the promotion decision process and the measuring of promotion effectiveness should be completely familiar with the allocation bases.

In identifying promotion cost we must also consider the concept of *relevant cost*—that is, costs relevant to a particular decision. Suppose a programmer has decided to experiment with two campaigns designed to attract new students to a course in interior design. One is a radio advertising campaign of twenty-five spots lasting twenty seconds each, and the other consists of a one-eighth page ad in a newspaper appearing twice a week for two weeks. The radio spots will cost $400, and the newspaper ads will cost $300. A tracking system has been devised so that the number of inquiries and of subsequent enrollments can be established for each promotion method. Respondents will be mailed a brochure, from which they can enroll in the program. Each brochure costs $1.18 to print and $.18 to mail.

To illustrate the concept of relevant cost in this example we will use two common measures of promotion effectiveness, *cost per inquiry* and *cost per enrollment*. The cost of the brochure is not relevant to evaluating the effectiveness of our two campaigns in generating *inquiries,* since everyone inquiring about the program will receive a brochure; it is constant per inquiry and therefore drops out of consideration. However, the cost of the brochure does become relevant when evaluating cost per *enrollment:*

	Radio		*Television*	
Number of inquiries	50		100	
Number of students	17		15	
	Total Cost	*Per Student*	*Total Cost*	*Per Student*
Cost of advertising	$400	$23.53	$300	$20.00
Cost of brochure	68	4.00	136	9.06
Total	$468	$27.53	$436	$29.06

Although the radio campaign cost more initially and resulted in fewer inquiries, more people who heard about the course through that medium enrolled, and the cost of the brochure tips the scales in favor of the radio campaign, at least within the narrow confines of this analysis.

As a rule of thumb, costs are not relevant when they remain the same *per unit* among all alternatives or cost objects. Thus, where indirect costs are allocated on the basis of per unit (per inquiry or per enrollment) calculations, they are irrelevant to most decisions.

As usual, however, things are often a bit more complex than this. Identifying the costs of a particular promotion effort is relatively easy when the campaign is short-lived, but it is more difficult to identify costs of long-term or progressive campaigns. For instance, in the example of the interior design campaign, there was a progression from radio and newspaper advertising to brochure mailing. This mailing might have been followed by a letter soliciting interest in the program. Names obtained from these two sources would probably be held until the next term, when another brochure would be sent out. Any enrollments that result from this long-term, progressive campaign obviously cost more to secure than the first set of enrollments; but it is difficult to distinguish between the short-term proximate cause of an enrollment and the effect that exposure of the program over a period of time had on the market, and it is certainly difficult to maintain cost records for long periods.

This introduces a point to which we will return several times in this chapter. Paradoxically, it is often the costs that cannot be identified and the results that cannot be properly attributed that, in the end, lead to an efficient and effective promotion system. Each promotion campaign places the institution's name in front of people, automatically increasing recognition of that name and, in effect, promoting all course offerings. At some point an economy of scale is reached, and the "spillover" effect becomes more and more important. Although results must be defined in relation to a particular campaign, the total promotion effort is always larger than the sum of its parts, and any measurement of individual campaigns will leave something out.

This concept of spillover can also be very important in internal relationships. Often the CE organization, by becoming highly visible through its promotion efforts, provides the parent institution with needed and valuable public exposure and thus brings internal attention to the CE function. When the president of the parent institution hears the CE organization's ad on the radio on the way to work, it *can* be important, and it *can* create a favorable climate within the parent institution. This sort of public exposure can also have favorable effects on the morale of CE employees.

There are always additional intangible and unmeasurable costs. CE organizations are often faced with "make or buy" decisions involving promotion. For instance, should the organization employ a full-time artist for brochure design and layout, or should it purchase these services from vendors and contractors? Some costs of these alternatives can be identified, such as the amount that the organization will have to pay the artist as compared with the contractors. But it is difficult to measure the amount of extra effort required to supervise the artist or oversee the work of several contractors or to set a dollar value on the fact that the in-house artist may be more responsive to deadlines and special requirements and may be able to develop a more consistent image for the promotional output of the organization. All the costs involved in these alternatives are real; we can identify them, but we cannot measure them.

Attributing Results

Just as costs of a particular promotion effort must be identified, so must the results of that effort be identified. Results in this context can mean a number of things. In the example we just used, "results" were defined first as inquiries and then as enrollments. Later we will see definitions that focus on other factors.

Most attribution schemes rely on "tracking"—that is, some system of adding up responses and enrollments for each defined promotion effort. Typically, tracking systems involve coding advertising in such a way that respondents automatically indicate which promotion effort they are responding to. For instance, the enrollment form on the back of a brochure or catalogue may have a preprinted or prestamped code located somewhere near the place for the student name that indicates which brochure and which mailing list were used. As enrollment forms come in, some record is made of the codes so that responses or enrollments produced from each combination can be counted. Where telephone responses are solicited, "coding" can be achieved by asking the respondents to ask for different people—Ms. Jones for one method, Ms. Smith for another. In cases where respondents may either send in a form or enroll by telephone, tracking can be more difficult. Registration personnel must be trained to ask for tracking codes so that as many responses as possible are traced to their source.

Measures of promotion effectiveness usually assume that untracked responses are distributed among alternatives in the same proportion as the responses that have been tracked. Thus, where two campaigns result in a total enrollment of 100 people, of which 30 enrollments are attributed to one campaign and 50 to the other, the remaining 20 are assumed to come three-eighths from the first campaign and five-eighths from the second. Of course, if all of the untracked enrollments actually resulted from the first campaign, this assumption could lead to erroneous conclusions. As a rule of thumb, schemes that are not able to track more than 80 percent of the responses or enrollments are likely to produce misleading data. The untracked responses need to be considered carefully in any case.

Responses may also be incorrectly tracked. This happens, for example, when respondents to one campaign use a method related to another campaign to enroll. For instance, a radio advertisement for a major university extension operation suggested that people could enroll either over the telephone or over the counter at several locations. Although the telephone enrollments were correctly traced to the radio, it was discovered that over-the-counter enrollees often used forms on the backs of catalogues placed in racks near the enrollment counter. Since these catalogues were coded as "over the counter," the full effect of the radio advertising was not measured because the walk-in enrollees were not attributed to it.

"Word-of-mouth" responses act on the decision process much like untracked items. People who "heard about your course from a friend" usually cannot tell you how the friend heard about the course, which means that the response is not tracked. Progressive campaigns and promotional efforts that utilize more than one method also present problems for tracking schemes, since only the method used for the response will be tracked. For instance, an organization might send out an early announcement of a course, followed by a detailed brochure and later a follow-up letter. Unless this campaign is conceived of as a whole, tracking will be difficult, since responses may come from any or all of the methods. Similarly, a potential student may hear about a course over the radio but use the form from the back of a brochure sent to her house to enroll. The mailing will get the credit, even though it was the radio that actually motivated the student.

Tracking schemes also have trouble in attributing responses due to the spillover effect. Radio advertising for an engineering course may suggest to a potential student that the same institution may offer courses he needs in management, for example. Institutional campaigns—promotional efforts designed to increase the recognition of the CE organization in the market rather than to spur enrollments in particular courses—may produce enrollments that cannot be attributed directly to the campaign.

Another common problem with tracking schemes is the necessity of separating the effects of the form of the promotion from those of the method of distribution. For instance, an art director may wish to determine the relative effectiveness of two brochures for the same course—one a two-page, eight-and-a-half-by-eleven piece and the other a four-panel, four-by-eight flyer. If these two pieces are sent to two different mailing lists, the validity of the test can be questioned, since the target audience as well as the brochure format is a variable. Validity would be increased if half the people on each list got one format, and half got the other, but even then, the art director would have to make sure that the lists were organized in a manner that did not bias the distribution method. If the lists were arranged alphabetically by last name, the test probably would be valid, but if they were organized by zip code, a third variable—socioeconomic status—might creep in.

Sometimes it is impossible to avoid having at least two variables in a comparative test. For instance, a commercial that sounds "right" on a country-and-western station may not be effective or appropriate on a classical music station, so a test of the relative drawing power of the two stations that holds the form of the message constant might not be valid. On the other hand, introducing two different messages adds the variable "message" to the variable "station" and makes the comparison logically invalid.

In spite of the limitations and problems of interpretation associated with tracking systems, such systems are useful, even indispensable, in measuring promotion effectiveness. In the example just given, one must have faith that two different messages, each equally appropriate to its auu.cuce, can be devised so that the relative effectiveness of the two radio stations can be validly compared. A healthy skepticism regarding the data must be balanced by a faith in one's own ability to sort through the effects of the uncontrolled variables to arrive at valid conclusions, even though these may be unsupported by formal logical or statistical analysis.

Measuring Effectiveness

Once data are collected, we can begin to make analyses. Even before the data are accumulated, however, we should have a clear idea of our purpose so that we can choose appropriate evaluation measures. No one measure can answer all our questions, and usually the more analyses we make, the more questions we will encounter.

A common error is to invest one measure with more importance than is appropriate. For instance, it is tempting to say that the promotion method that produces the most enrollments is the most effective. When the notion of cost-effectiveness is introduced, we might modify this view by saying that the campaign that produces the most enrollments at the least cost is the most effective. But even this statement turns out to be too simple when the concept of *contribution margin* is introduced. We first discussed this concept in Part One. Contribution margin is the difference between per unit revenue and per unit variable costs—the additional "available for overhead" provided by each additional enrollment. Thus, the contribution margin of one enrollment in a course with a fee of $100 and variable costs of $20 is $80, which goes, presumably, first to cover fixed costs and then to provide a surplus or margin for the organization. Theoretically, any expenditure, including promotion expenditures, that results in a per enrollment cost of less than $80 is contributing to the margin. Thus, two promotion methods, one of which produces 50 enrollments at a cost of $5 per enrollment and the other of which produces 10 enrollments at $25 per enrollment, both contribute to the success of the course, even though the second method cost five times more per enrollment than the first. This notion of contribution margin will be important to keep in mind as we examine specific effectiveness measures.

Prospective Measures

Prospective measures are made before promotion actions are taken. They deal with estimates of costs and results and thus, in a sense, do not measure anything. They are used primarily to compare one or more proposed alternatives of action. Often they are incorporated into or are reflected in the budget process.

Reward/Risk Ratios. We have already described one of the most important prospective measures, the ratio of reward to risk. As you may recall, this ratio is calculated as follows:

$$\frac{\text{Estimated margin}}{\text{Total estimated promotion costs}}$$

We saw this measure in slightly altered form in Figure 2.8, which showed a sample course budget. There the denominator of the equation was total sunk costs, including promotion costs. This measure is used to determine whether a course is worth spending money to promote or, given a fixed promotion budget, to decide between courses to present. As with most measures we will be examining, this one means little by itself and must be compared with similar calculations for alternatives. It is a good measure if used consistently because, unlike most other measures, it relates margin directly to promotion costs. However, because it deals in estimates, it is far from precise.

This kind of ratio also raises another problem common to most of the measures we will discuss: Interpreting it requires that the variable promotion intensiveness of courses be considered. As you may recall, promotion intensiveness is the degree to which a course depends upon its promotion for success, relative to other factors such as the names and reputations of its instructors. The promotion reward/risk ratios for two courses should not be blindly compared if one course needs very little "selling" and the other needs a great deal.

Cost per Thousand. This measure is traditional in the advertising industry. It is the cost to *reach* 1,000 people (or, more commonly, 1,000 households) with an advertising message. For newspapers, cost per thousand is calculated by dividing advertising rates by certified circulation figures and dividing again by 1,000. For radio and television, advertising rates are divided by the number of people listening and watching (as determined through rating services) and then by 1,000. Cost per thousand for something like a brochure can be calculated by dividing the cost of the brochure by the number of thousands of brochures distributed (on the sometimes unwarranted assumption that each brochure will reach a separate household or office). The general formula is:

$$\frac{\text{Advertising cost}}{\text{Number of people (households) reached}/1,000}$$

Cost per thousand is a fairly precise prospective measure, since circulation and ratings rarely change drastically between measurement periods and since mailing lists, if well maintained, usually do reach an unduplicated audience. However, it is not very useful because it does not incorporate a measure of results. Reaching an audience is not the same as causing it to respond—and the latter is the only thing that counts. Still, cost per thousand can be handy when it seems likely that alternative campaigns will result in a similar response rate and when it can be combined with some measure of results.

Indeed, this last comment applies to all prospective measures. Evaluations of promotion effectiveness require a continuous and organized process in which promotion decisions are made, their effects are measured, and information from those measures is "fed back" into the next decision process. Let us now look at retrospective measures, which help us evaluate results.

Retrospective Measures

Retrospective measures determine the results of past promotion expenditures, but their real purpose is to predict the future. Their usefulness is based on the assumption that the past is a good guide to the future, a notion that must be tempered by judgment. Retrospective measures can be divided into two categories, gross measures and detailed measures.

Gross Measures. Gross measures determine the effectiveness of large aggregations of costs and results. They are designed to help managers form overall judgments of effectiveness rather than decide on specific promotion strategies.

• *Production measures.* These measure the physical output of a promotion department much as one might measure the output of any production line. They measure effectiveness only in the narrowest sense. For instance, we might count the number of "jobs" processed in a year by a CE promotion department and then calculate the *cost per job* by dividing that number into total promotion department costs. We could calculate the cost per course or the cost per mailed piece in a similar way, in the latter case dividing the number of pieces into total mailing costs rather than total promotion department costs. This kind of measure is often useful in budget comparisons.

Analysis of variance, described in the last chapter, is also production oriented. The promotion budget for an organization is based on a certain level of predicted activity (number of courses promoted or number of brochures produced). If actual activity is different from the estimate, it may be useful to calculate volume and price variances.

Gross measures of production are appropriate for certain ranges of budgetary control, but, like prospective measures, they lack a way of determining results and therefore must be carefully interpreted.

• *Cost/income ratios.* Perhaps the best overall measure of promotion effectiveness is the *ratio of total promotion costs to total income.* This measure works best with larger organizations where the nature of the courses offered changes little from year to year, so that variables tend to average out. A cost/income ratio of from 15 to 20 percent is fairly common for a self-supporting, non-degree-granting CE organization. This ratio is most useful when it is employed to compare the effectiveness of the same organization from one year to the next. A decrease in the ratio, especially if it is accompanied by an increase in overall margin for the organization, is a very good sign, while an increase in the ratio could signal danger.

A variation of the cost/income ratio is the *average promotion cost per enrollment,* determined by dividing total promotion costs by the total number of enrollments. Here, too, a decline in the ratio is generally a good sign, while an increase may indicate trouble. Using these two ratios together can aid interpretation. For instance, a decline in the first ratio accompanied by an increase in the second may indicate that the course mix is changing in favor of high-fee, low-enrollment courses.

Gross measures, by taking into account large aggregations of data, are generally more valid than more detailed measures for indicating overall and long-range trends, but they are difficult to translate into managerial action. For instance, an increase in the cost/income ratio may mean danger, but what should be done? Answers to this question depend on more detailed analyses.

Detailed Measures. Detailed measures are often structured as comparisons between promotion alternatives: Which of several radio stations is most effective in generating enrollments? Is it better to advertise a particular course in a general catalogue or in a special brochure? Which mailing list is most effective in generating enrollments? Answers to questions like these can be determined most accurately by using a combination of some or all of the following measures.

• *Response ratio.* The prospective measure of cost per thousand included an estimate of the number of people an advertising message would reach. After all the responses to a particular promotion effort have been gathered, we can determine the response ratio by dividing the number of responses by the number of people (households) reached. The resulting ratio is usually expressed as a percentage. Response percentages vary greatly and, as with most of these measures, an organization must develop a history in order to determine an appropriate standard for comparison. Response ratios are a function of how well the audience is "targeted." They add actual results to the cost per thousand equation. However, they do not incorporate other cost comparisons that we need to make. For these we can use the next measure.

• *Cost per inquiry.* Instead of dividing total cost by the number of people or households reached, this measure divides the cost by the number of inquiries to determine the cost of stimulating each inquiry. It allows us to compare the cost-effectiveness of alternative advertising campaigns in terms of responses received. This is a step forward, but our ultimate objective is to generate enrollments, not inquiries. In fact, a promotion campaign that produces a large number of "window shoppers" who do not buy the product is doubly expensive, since it costs something to process responses. We therefore need the next measure.

• *Conversion ratio.* This measure is the ratio of the number of people who buy (in our case, the number of people who enroll) to the number of people who express interest. It finally measures a result, enrollments, that is of direct interest to us. As just mentioned, it can discriminate between campaigns that produce a large number of nonbuying window shoppers and those that produce actual customers. It can also demonstrate that an advertising message was misleading. For instance, an advertisement for an expensive course that does not mention the fee is likely to generate many more nonbuying responses than it would if the fee were named. However, like the response ratio, this measure ignores the cost of the promotion effort—so we need another measure.

• *Cost per enrollment.* This measure is the cost of the promotion campaign divided by the number of enrollments that can be attributed to it. It is clearly a useful and meaningful measure—but it, too, has limitations. As with other measures, this ratio is valuable only when it is calculated for a number of projects and then compared across projects. Even then, unless the course or courses compared are very similar in financial structure, there are likely to be problems in making the comparisons. For instance, a cost per enrollment of $45 for a course with a fee of $200 means something altogether different from the same cost per enrollment for a course with a fee of $35. Cost per enrollment is most useful when applied in conjunction with other measures.

• *Cost per enrollment derivatives.* For comparing campaigns involving individual courses, a possible further refinement of cost per enrollment that relates it to course fees may be appropriate:

$$\frac{\text{Course fee}}{\text{Cost/enrollment}}$$

Presumably, the higher the ratio, the more cost-effective the promotion campaign was. However, this measure is not easily applicable to comparisons where a number of courses with different fees are involved, say for comparing two brochures, each of which advertises several courses.

Even where it is appropriate, this refinement does not tell the whole story because course fee is usually not as good a measure of financial success as is contribution margin, which we discussed earlier. We might therefore want to do the same thing with contribution margin that we did with course fee to obtain a new ratio:

$$\frac{\text{Course fee – variable cost per enrollment (contribution margin)}}{\text{Cost/enrollment}}$$

The value of this ratio relative to some others we have discussed is illustrated in the following table:

	Course A	*Course B*	*Course C*
Cost per enrollment	$45	$45	$45
Fee	$200	$200	$100
Fee/cost per enrollment	4.44	4.44	2.22
Contribution margin	$35	$100	$55
Contribution margin/cost per enrollment	.77	2.22	1.22

If we looked only at cost per enrollment, we would say that the promotion efforts for all three courses were equally successful; if only at fee/cost per enrollment, we would say that the campaign for Course C was less effective than for the other two—that is, that an expenditure for promotion of $45 in Course C brought in income of $100, while the same expenditure in the other two courses brought in $200. However, when we look at contribution margin, we see quite a different story. The expenditure of $45 per enrollment in course A brought in only $35 in contribution, while in the other courses the expenditure brought in $100 and $65, respectively. Dividing the contribution margin by the cost per enrollment gives us an index of relative success by relating the two measures.

Another way of looking at these data is simply to subtract the cost per enrollment from the contribution margin:

	Course A	Course B	Course C
Contribution margin	$ 35	$100	$ 55
Cost per enrollment	- 45	- 45	- 45
Total	-$ 10	$ 55	$ 10

These last measures are perhaps the most comprehensive of all of the measures we have yet examined. They are also probably the most difficult to obtain, simply because they contain so much. Although by taking averages they can be used in comparisons involving more than one course, they have more validity when the comparisons involve single courses. Again, no measure tells everything, and this one leaves out residual effects.

• *Repeater rate.* It is tempting to restrict measurement of promotion effectiveness to a relatively short period of time, but this impatience costs us by excluding potentially valuable information, especially if we are measuring the effectiveness of institutional advertising. On the average, a *new* enrollment is probably worth more in the future than a repeat enrollment; thus, a promotion effort that brings in many new enrollments is more effective than one that brings mostly repeaters. This is especially true for courses that fit into multicourse curricula: A promotion effort that gets a student into the first course of a series should be given credit for the subsequent enrollments as well, even though the student may enroll in later courses by using forms from later catalogues or brochures.

The same thing holds true for inquiries. A promotion effort may create an inquiry (response) that does not turn into an enrollment immediately but sparks an enrollment in a later term. If inquiries are entered onto a mailing list with a special code and if subsequent enrollments from people on the list can also be recorded, the long-term effectiveness of the promotion campaign can be assessed. However, this requires a long-term tracking effort and organizational staying power of the sort that can be maintained only with a comprehensive tracking system. We can add subsequent enrollments on the same basis as initial ones or count a subsequent enrollment as less than a new one on the theory that later promotion material did, in some way, influence the enrollment.

In organizations that have high repeater rates, the relationship between new enrollments and repeaters might be calculated by dividing the number of new enrollments by the total number of enrollments. This can show which campaign is relatively more effective at generating new enrollments. Of course, it should be used in conjunction with the cost per enrollment measure, perhaps in a table such as this:

	Course A	Course B	Course C
Total promotion cost	$900	$1,000	$1,200
Total enrollments	30	30	30
Cost per enrollment	$ 30	$ 33	$ 40
New enrollments	1	6	23
% new enrollments	3%	20%	77%

If we look at cost per enrollment alone, we might come to the conclusion that Course C was not as well served by its promotion campaign as the other two courses were by theirs. When new enrollments are segregated, however, we see that Course C's campaign brought 23 new people into the student body. An organization with a high rate of repeat enrollments would value campaign C highly, since some of those 23 people could be expected to take subsequent courses, whereas the other campaigns were simply attracting students who had already taken courses from the organization.

Taking some liberties with logic and scientific analysis, we might do a further calculation. Suppose we could assume that half of all new enrollments will take at least one additional course with us in the future. In such a case, the calculations would be different:

	Course A	*Course B*	*Course C*
Number initial enrollments	30	30	30
New enrollments	1	6	23
Repeat ratio	.5	.5	.5
Expected later enrollment	.5	3	11.5
Total equivalent enrollment	30.5	33	41.5
Cost per enrollment	$29.50	$30.30	$28.92

Under this assumption, the Course C campaign was the most cost-effective if measured by cost per enrollment.

Problems of Interpretation

Usually, the more measures we use to calculate promotion effectiveness, the more accurate our results will be. However, all of these measures, even when used collectively, suffer from certain problems of interpretation.

Contribution Margin Effects. We have seen how important the concept of contribution margin is to our measures of effectiveness, and we also discussed, briefly, a problem always associated with contribution margin. Imagine an organization that promoted a course with four separate methods (that is, reached an unduplicated audience with a four-pronged campaign). The course had a break-even point of 50 enrollments and a contribution margin of $60 per enrollment (fee–variable costs), with promotion costs treated as fixed costs. The course was successful, enrolling 60 people. After the course, a careful analysis was performed with the following results:

	Total	A	B	C	D
Number of enrollments	60	40	10	5	5
Contribution margin	$60	$60	$60	$60	$60
Cost per enrollment	$36.60	$30	$40	$55	$65
Contribution margin – cost per enrollment	$23.40	$30	$20	$ 5	-$ 5
Total margin	$3,600	$2,400	$600	$300	$300
Cost of media	$2,200	$1,200	$400	$275	$325
Margin after promotion costs	$1,400	$1,200	$200	$ 25	-$ 25

It is clear that campaign A was the most successful and that campaign D was least so; if D had not been attempted, the overall margin would have been $25 higher. But what about B and C? B was much less effective than A, yet it did produce $200 in margin. Without this campaign, the course would not have reached its break-even point. Campaign C is a marginal case, producing only a little more than it cost. With hindsight the analysis is straightforward and the conclusions clear. And, assuming the same pattern, next time management would definitely use campaign A and search for new ways to spend the promotion money spent this time on C and D. But what about B? Although it produced a markedly lower total contribution margin than A, it nevertheless was important to the success of the course. Here, management is faced with a typical decision: Can an untested alternative produce a contribution margin larger than the tested campaign? The decision rests largely on an assessment of an unknown quantity.

This example also illustrates that analysis of contribution margin, contribution margin ratios, and contribution margin-cost/enrollment can establish relative effectiveness of campaigns and, at the extremes, clearly indicate whether a method should be used again. Yet these measures must take into account the effect on the whole: A simple comparison showing that one campaign is much less effective than another may hide the fact that, nevertheless, both were crucial to the success of the course.

Spillover Effects. These effects occur when one promotion campaign (or method) has effects on another. Most of the time, spillover effects cannot be or are not measured. For instance, a radio advertisement for an engineering course may be heard by someone who is reminded that he wants to take a course in accounting. Hearing the name of the sponsor, he calls for a catalogue and enrolls in an accounting course. Since most CE organizations have names that clearly indicate that they offer educational courses, the advertising of any specific program has aspects of institutional advertising. A particular campaign may also spill over into future periods. Advertising messages often depend on frequent repetition; by the time a student has heard about a program four or five times, he or she may be ready to enroll.

Since virtually any campaign will have some spillover effect, and since spillover effects are largely unmeasurable, they present significant obstacles to interpretation. It is common for an obviously ineffective campaign to be justified in terms of its supposed spillover effect. Such a justification is valid only where it can be shown that the spillover effect is likely to be much greater for the given campaign than in possible alternatives. If the spillover effect is considered to be present in all promotion efforts, it can often be ignored in decisions about individual methods, much as irrelevant costs are ignored.

Untracked Items. In the preceding section we mentioned the effect of untracked items on analysis. Where the percentage of untracked items is small, say less than 20 percent, we may be justified in assuming that these items are distributed equally among the alternatives we are comparing. However, a larger percentage of untracked items casts suspicion on the validity of all measures and can significantly skew results. It is therefore important that the number of untracked items be known and, intuitively at least, factored into promotion analysis. Whenever a comparison between campaigns is made, it is valuable to calculate what would happen if most of the untracked items came solely from one or another of the campaigns to see if the comparison would be influenced.

Unidentified Costs and Influences. Many of our analyses involved the cost per enrollment calculation and thus are particularly sensitive to the accuracy of the cost figure. As noted in the first section of this chapter, defining and accumulating costs is often difficult and subject to error. Relevant costs may not be included or even known. The same is true of other influences that affect enrollments. For example, the programmer making phone calls to training directors to generate enrollments, mentioned earlier, is an "influence" that probably would not be recognized in the promotion evaluation process. The credit for the enrollments generated by those calls might go to the brochure that was sent to the companies, thereby making that campaign appear more effective than it really was.

People hear about courses in many ways, some of which we can never know about. A radio station may pick up a public service announcement about our courses, an in-house newsletter may mention one of the courses, or some unforeseen event may occur that suddenly makes a particular course popular. Such occurrences generate enrollments that show up either as untracked or as attributed to a particular campaign that only indirectly produced them. Programmers and promotion professionals must always be alert to these influences and be aware that promotion analyses may not incorporate some important factors.

Unknown Repeater Rates. Although it may be theoretically possible to trace each enrollment back to the source of the initial contact with the student, few CE organizations actually have the resources to do it. Thus, the important influence of repeater rates often is not really included in the promotion effectiveness analysis because the spillover effect from term to term cannot be measured. This means that the true value of any particular campaign cannot be fully assessed. In situations where campaigns all have about the same repeat rate, this lack is not important, but in some cases analysis is likely to lead to decisions that are somewhat off the mark because of it.

Information Overload. Throughout this chapter we have stressed that measures should be used in conjunction with one another and that the gathering of data should be as comprehensive and detailed as is feasible. However, as explained earlier this can lead to so much data that analysis is actually hindered: It becomes more and more difficult to determine what the questions should be when so many answers are available.

Developing Informed Intuition

It should be clear by now that evaluating the cost-effectiveness of promotion expenditures is hardly a science. The measures you have learned are mainly useful as ways of informing yourself so that you can use your other skills in evaluation. There is no substitute for being close to students and potential students, knowing from personal contact what is important to them, what they need and want, and how to talk to them. All the quantitative techniques, questionnaires, and statistical analysis in the world cannot substitute for this kind of personal knowledge.

At the organizational level, too, it is important to accumulate and analyze promotion data in a comprehensive and organized way and at the same time to recognize the need to develop, exercise, and retain the intuitive skills of the organization's members. There are no definite formulae for achieving this kind of capability, but here are some suggestions that might be helpful.

Fostering Healthy Skepticism about Data. Those involved in evaluating promotion effectiveness should have an understanding of both the usefulness and the limitations of the data and measures they use. Valid conclusions from the data should not be ignored, but a healthy skepticism sets the stage for refinements to the evaluation process and sharpens analytic skill. Relatedly, it is important that no single department be solely responsible for generation and analysis of promotion data. This encourages a feeling of "ownership" of the data and may set up defensiveness both in those who produce the data and analysis and in those who are supposed to use the data (and who sometimes feel that the data is being used against them). A mutual understanding between these groups is so crucial that the success of any promotion evaluation system depends upon it.

Regarding Decisions as Experiments. One way of avoiding polarity over promotion evaluation and encouraging creative thinking and development of intuition is to remove judgment and sanctions from the evaluation process by treating each promotion decision as a sort of experiment. After all, whether a decision is a success or a failure, the organization has gained in experience that will serve future decisions. To gain the most from this experimental view, it is essential that promotion decisions be recorded when they are made and that the results of the decisions be measured and recorded in some way that can be used later.

Establishing A Priori Criteria for Success. A technique borrowed from the methods of science is consistent with this experimental model. Much as hypotheses are developed before scientific experiments are performed, each individual promotion evaluation project should be carefully defined and criteria for a successful campaign carefully delineated *in advance*. Developing a priori criteria focuses attention on the questions for which answers are sought, which can be very helpful in planning the "experimental" promotional campaign. It also tends to damp down later excuses for failure and after-the-fact justifications based on alleged spillover results or anticipated subsequent enrollments. Finally, it allows the organization's decision makers to establish their own standards for accountability and helps the organization develop a sense of what it means to be successful in promotion.

Summary

Intuition, the seat-of-the-pants "feel" that guides so many decisions in CE promotion, can be aided by the use of the quantitative techniques examined in this chapter. CE organization managers can help the development of intuition in their staff by working to establish an experimental attitude in organization members, requiring that *a priori* success criteria be established and that promotion campaigns be defined in advance but at the same time allowing experimenters to guess wrong without fear of sanction. They can require that results of promotion campaigns be compared to the preestablished criteria and fed back to the decision makers and that reports of the evaluations of campaigns be made in standardized formats and filed so that others can use them later.

Most important of all, managers should understand how difficult it is to promote effectively, how important effective promotion is to the CE organization, how difficult it is to measure effectiveness, and how valuable are those individuals whose experience and analytic skills have informed their promotion intuition. Proper recognition of these factors is the real key to effective promotion.

Bibliography

Farlow, H. *Publicizing and Promoting Programs.* New York: McGraw-Hill, 1979.

Levitt, T. "Marketing Myopia." *Harvard Business Review,* 1960, *38,* 45–56.

Rados, D. L. *Marketing for Nonprofit Organizations.* Boston: Auburn House, 1981.

Strother, G. B., and Klus, J. P. *Administration of Continuing Education.* Belmont, Calif.: Wadsworth, 1982.

9

Determining
and Allocating
Indirect Costs

We have already discussed indirect costs in several parts of this book, but this subject is so important to the life of a CE organization that it deserves its own chapter. This chapter will help you understand the ways in which the indirect (overhead) costs of a CE organization can be allocated to operating units or cost objects. It will also spell out the effects different allocation methods are likely to have on the behavior of members of the organization. Although I will be talking about indirect cost allocations *within* the CE organization, what I say should also help you understand the theory, practice, and implications of indirect cost allocations *to* the CE organization from a parent institution.

Another set of indirect cost rates, which should not be confused with the rest of this discussion, sometimes also applies. Colleges and universities often develop institutional indirect cost rates for use in connection with government (and private) contracts and grants. These rates are developed from institution-wide overhead cost pools and are usually negotiated with government and subject to audit. They may be imposed on top of the internal overhead rates of the CE organization. This sometimes means that the CE organization gets to keep all or a part of the overhead generated, or, more commonly, must list these costs as direct costs in grant and contract proposal budgets in order to recover them.

Indirect costs, as we have often stated, are costs that cannot be directly or easily associated with a particular cost object, such as a course or responsibility center. In Chapters Two and Three, we examined indirect cost allocations from the programmer's point of view. One "level of financial success" for courses was defined as that point at which all direct and indirect costs are covered. I also listed some common bases for allocating indirect costs to courses and pointed out that distorted behavior can be caused by an indirect cost allocation system that is misunderstood or poorly applied.

Chapters Four and Five looked at indirect cost allocations from the CE manager's point of view. Well-conceived allocation schemes were shown to be powerful tools for motivating and channeling behavior toward institutional objectives and for creating a sense of the whole organization in all its members. Determining the allocation method was described as an early and basic decision in the budgeting process. We showed how to estimate the costs of service departments and how to test this estimate of indirect costs through successive steps of the budgeting process.

In this chapter we will describe further a number of allocation options, detailing more explicitly potential outcomes and trade-offs and raising other issues related to indirect cost treatment.

Why Indirect Costs Should Be Allocated

What Are Indirect Costs? Organizations differ widely in what they decide to classify as indirect costs. One, for example, might treat all telephone expense as an indirect cost to be allocated to courses, perhaps proportional to the total direct expense of the course, while another might require that long distance charges be assigned to courses as a direct cost. It is possible, however, to list some categories of indirect costs and cite some common examples.

An indirect cost *pool,* you may remember, is a group of naturally associated indirect costs that will all be allocated on the same basis. For instance, the indirect portion of telephone costs in the example just cited might be naturally associated with other kinds of office costs, such as supplies, office machine maintenance, reproduction charges, receptionist salary, office rent, subscriptions, and office janitorial service.

One common and obvious category of indirect cost pools is service or overhead departments, as described in Chapter Four. All costs associated with a given department are often allocated as one pool or total. Of course, it is possible to add these pools together to form even larger pools, and it might be appropriate to do so where several departments are to be allocated on the same basis. For instance, registration, student records, and the cashier's office might be combined and allocated on the basis of number of enrollments.

Other cost pools may be more difficult to identify. For example, programming departments have indirect costs of their own. They sometimes count programmers' salaries among indirect costs.

A third category of indirect cost pools is line item pools— costs that generally show up as line items on a budget. For example, administrative rent or classroom rent, where the rent charge is fixed over a specified period, may have to be spread over a number of cost objects. Colleges and universities also tend to treat fringe benefits as a separate line item overhead charge. Many line item pools present special difficulties because they require sequential allocation. For instance, since the service departments all take administrative space, they incur administrative rental costs. Rather than allocating administrative rent directly to courses, it may make sense to allocate rent first to all departments, including the service departments, adding rent costs to the departmental costs, and then allocate total departmental costs, including rent, to the final cost objects. We will discuss this sequential allocation procedure later.

Why Should Indirect Costs Be Allocated? All this complexity may evoke the question: Why bother? Why do indirect costs have to be allocated at all? One option discussed later in this chapter is that of not making allocations. Indeed, in traditionally funded CE organizations—those more or less subsidized or those with fixed resources—indirect cost allocations are not required and would not be as useful as they are in self-supporting CE units. But it is worth the trouble to allocate indirect costs, even when it is not required, because such allocations allow an organization to carry out the "full cost" concept discussed in Chapter Four. Full costing in CE has the advantage (or, sometimes, the disadvantage) of displaying to all levels of the decision-making hierarchy, including, most importantly, the programmers, the total costs of courses and the relationship of the parts of the organization to the whole. Making the comprehensive financial structure of the organization concrete can have a positive effect on morale and the quality of communication.

Used wisely and with care, indirect allocation can also be an effective management tool. If indirect costs are built into the financial planning of every course, it is less likely that the organization will come up short at year's end. In financially self-conscious organizations, furthermore, the manipulation of indirect cost allocation algorithms can be an effective way of directing decisions. For instance, the elimination of the assessment of indirect costs to courses presented in rural areas may encourage more extensive programming in those areas.

Criteria for Successful Allocation

Problems of Allocation. Discussions, even arguments, about overhead allocations are so common that the term *overhead* has gained a negative connotation. Almost by definition, overhead costs, since they are not *directly* associated with the production process, are "unproductive." In organizations large enough to be segmented into departments, it is natural that rivalries and resentment will sometimes develop along departmental lines and that these rivalries may deepen when an income-generating department is "charged" for the costs of a service department. Resentment may increase further because, as we have noted, allocations always carry with them a certain arbitrariness and are always, in some sense, unfair. Negotiations concerning overhead can be protracted, hard fought, and divisive, which makes them expensive to the organization.

Allocations can also be expensive in a more direct way. They require records, calculations, paperwork, clerical operations, and system design and operation. The more fair and equitable the allocation system is, the more complex and costly it is likely to be.

But by far the most important problem facing managers trying to design an indirect cost allocation system is that of avoiding distorted behavior caused by the system. An appropriate allocation method should reinforce behaviors that advance the goals of the organization and discourage those that do not. Allocation methods can become symbolic and frequently troublesome beyond their proper function. They can be misread and misunderstood, leading to unintended effects. The method and the rationale behind it should therefore be clearly articulated, and management should continually monitor its effects on decision making. When they make sense, exceptions should be made to the allocation rules. Courses that show a substantial margin before being burdened with overhead, or courses important for other than financial reasons, are possible candidates for such exceptions.

Criteria for Allocation Methods. A good allocation method avoids most of these problems by meeting the following criteria:

- It is consistent with the goals and objectives of the organization and leads to budgeting, financial, and programming decisions that are also in line with the aims of CE management.
- It is viewed as fair and legitimate by those who must follow it.
- It is rational and easily understood.
- It is easy to calculate and inexpensive to operate.
- It is integrated with the budget and financial control system.

Methods of Allocation

Three main categories of indirect cost allocation methods are available to CE managers: transfer pricing, cost allocations, and non- or "hidden" allocations. Within each of these general categories there are a number of options. We will examine each category in turn.

Transfer Pricing

Strictly speaking, transfer pricing is not an allocation method at all; rather, it involves turning an indirect cost into a direct cost. A transfer price is the price of a good or service used in recording the passing of that good or service from one part of the organization to another. Thus, a service department using transfer pricing resembles an outside vendor, although there can be some significant differences. A common one is that the internal department is often given a monopoly within the organization; other departments are not allowed to go to outside suppliers, as is possible in the open market. Another difference from the open market is that management can set the transfer price.

Transfer pricing can be used effectively where there is a clearly defined good or service provided, where a rate sheet or a pricing schedule can be developed, and where the using department can be easily determined. A reprographics department, a promotion department, a computer services department, and a classroom facility all are potential candidates for the transfer pricing method because their products can be identified. The director's office is not a good candidate, because the "product" called management or administration is hard to define and its consumption is hard to attribute to operating units. (I was tempted to end that last sentence with "because no one knows what the director does.")

The most significant advantage of transfer prices is their flexibility and the immediacy and directness of their effect. They can be set high to encourage efficiency, low to encourage use, or anywhere in between, and they can be changed frequently, often simply by publishing a new rate sheet. Transfer prices can be calculated in many ways; here are some of the most common.

Full Cost Plus Markup. This method requires that all costs of operating a service department plus an amount in excess of cost of operation be allocated to the products of the department. This method has the advantage of being similar to the method employed by outside vendors in arriving at prices, so that *under some circumstances,* especially where outside vendors offer comparable services, the relative efficiency of the internal operation can be judged by comparing its prices with those of outsiders. This should be done with care, however, since outsiders' cost structure may be significantly different from that of the internal department. For instance, internal departments may not have financing, promotion, or tax expenses, and they may be subsidized in other ways. Also, this method provides no incentive to service department management to keep costs low and remain efficient.

Budgeted Cost. Under this method, transfer prices are based on budgeted costs, with the goal of "breaking even" at the year's end. This method has the advantages of being well integrated with the budget system and of having a clearly defined standard of success. Large deficits or surpluses indicate clearly that budgetary adjustments must be made. Transfer pricing based on budgeted costs is most appropriate where operations are relatively stable from year to year and there is no basis for external comparison. However, where budgeted costs are subject to debate and negotiation, they may not be a good basis for transfer prices. In cases where significant changes in the volume of activity may result in volume variances, prices based on budgeted costs may be off the mark. In most situations, budget-based transfer prices do not provide incentives for savings and efficiency.

Budgeted Cost Plus Markup. This variation of the budgeted cost method attempts to introduce the profit incentive. It has the advantage of providing a cushion (the markup) against a deficit, with the possible accompanying disadvantage of being unfair to the buyer (user). Performance can be judged by the size of the surplus (if any) at year's end.

Market Prices. Where service department products (including services) are similar to those offered by outside vendors and where there are easily determined market prices for the products, market prices can be used as transfer prices. Pegging transfer prices to the market has some clear advantages. First, it can reduce price-related user complaints, since prices are established by external forces. Second, it will bring quality issues to the surface. If a better product is available for the same price on the outside, management will hear about it. Third, it provides clear information on inefficient operations—if a service department loses money at market prices, something is wrong. The disadvantage of market-based transfer prices is that market prices, which must build in a profit and provision for costs not normally incurred by internal units, may not be a good measure. A relatively inefficient operation, allowed to charge market prices but not subject to market cost structures, might continue undetected for a long period. Another difficulty is that true market prices are sometimes hard to determine. Outside vendors may "lowball" prices charged to a large organization in the hopes of securing business, raising prices after a relationship has been established. Furthermore, when market prices are used, there is a temptation to make overly simple comparisons between outsiders and the internal department that may not recognize the hidden costs of dealing with outside vendors, such as the lack of control over quality and scheduling of work and the paperwork and administration that may be required. There may also be less incentive for internal units to show loyalty to the internal department.

Negotiated Prices. Transfer prices arrived at through negotiation have the advantage, theoretically, of having the approval of the parties involved. Their disadvantages are that negotiations can be time-consuming and divisive and the prices arrived at may not provide management with a good standard for judging the operating efficiency of the service department. Since prices may or may not reflect the cost structure of the department and may or may not be set in a consistent manner from period to period, operating results will not tell a clear story.

Combination of Transfer Price and Pro Rata Allocation. It is sometimes desirable that service department costs be allocated through both a transfer price mechanism and an allocation scheme. This combination is common where, for the good of an organization, a service department must be subsidized or run at a loss or where a transfer price reflecting the full cost of operations would price the department out of the market. For instance, with advances in printing technology, small-scale printing or reprographics operations are becoming less and less economical because the cost of new equipment is growing, requiring higher volumes of work to justify the investment. However, in order to assure a dependable and timely source of promotion and course material reproduction services, the CE management may want to maintain a printing operation. Under these circumstances it may be appropriate to make the transfer price equal to prices set by outside suppliers, placing any deficit resulting from the use of this price "on the overhead" for allocation on another basis. Similarly, to encourage the use of a new classroom facility, management may set classroom rental rates artificially low, absorbing the excess of costs over (internal) income in some other way. It may also be appropriate in some cases to separate service department fixed costs from variable costs, using transfer prices to cover variable costs and allocations to cover fixed costs. Thus the user department is charged directly for its use of the service, but "ready to serve" costs are distributed through overhead allocations.

From this listing of transfer pricing methods it should be clear that transfer pricing can be an effective management tool. It is often used to make a service department more accountable. For instance, a large university recently placed its computer operations on a recharge (or transfer price) basis, removing the appropriation to support the computer center from its own, separate budget while at the same time increasing the operating budgets of the computer user departments. Theoretically, this change made the computer center more responsive to user needs, since it then had to view users as customers rather than supplicants.

A counterbalancing disadvantage of transfer prices is the frequent difficulty of calculating them. This is especially true where there is a large "mix" of products or services. For instance, it may be fairly simple to compute an average "per impression" charge for a printing operation by dividing the total costs of the operation by the estimated total impressions produced. However, this average may not be a fair price because small jobs are more expensive per impression than large jobs due to setup and preparation time. Setting a price on this basis may encourage users to go outside with the very sort of large jobs that the service department needs to keep its cost per impression down. Further, the printing operation may do other things—binding, cutting, folding—that are part of some jobs and not others, and to burden all jobs with the cost of these special services may not be fair. However, the process of computing fair transfer prices, despite its difficulty, can force service department management to examine operations for inefficient and costly processes that otherwise might go unnoticed. For many service operations, transfer pricing is an obvious and very useful option.

Cost Allocations

Once indirect costs have been determined and cost objects defined, a basis for allocation should be chosen. As we noted earlier, the allocation basis determines how indirect costs are going to be grouped or pooled. Let us examine a number of bases for indirect cost allocation.

Fixed Cost Bases. Indirect costs can be made to behave either as fixed costs or as variable costs, and the choice can have profound effects. Fixed cost allocations usually specify a dollar amount per cost object or are tied in some way to existing fixed costs. For instance, we might allocate director's office costs to programs by dividing the total costs of the office by the total number of programs offered. We would then charge each course, say, $300. Alternatively, we might take an existing direct fixed cost, say, personnel costs, and allocate some indirect costs (telephone, office supplies, or whatever) to cost centers in the ratio that personnel costs of the cost center bear to total personnel costs. The advantages of fixed cost allocation methods are that they are usually easy to compute and apply and the rationale for their application is easily understood.

Another characteristic of fixed cost allocations is that their influence on decisions is either absent or subdued; they tend to "drop out" of calculations. If every course were charged $300 for director's office indirect costs, such an allocation would play no part in deciding which course is more promising financially. This can be either an advantage or a disadvantage. It is often helpful that indirect costs *not* play a part in decisions about courses or about the efficiency of departments, since programmers and department managers rarely have any control over these costs. On the other hand, when programmers and department managers ignore the effects of their decisions on indirect costs, the organization as a whole and the operations of particular service departments can be adversely affected. For instance, an allocation method that charges every course $200 for the services of a registration office might encourage programmers to program high-enrollment, low-fee courses because they are not required to recognize that the costs of registration are tied to the number of students who will be registering.

Variable Cost Bases. Variable indirect cost allocation bases mean that the amount of overhead allocated to a cost object varies with the volume of activity, which becomes the basis for allocation. Let us examine a few of the more common bases of variable cost allocation and the possible effects of employing them.

• *Number of students (enrollments).* Some indirect cost pools are naturally associated with the number of students or enrollments. Registration costs and cashiering costs are obvious cases. Generally a "per student" cost is calculated and charged to each responsibility center or course. The more students are enrolled, the higher will be the indirect cost charged. This has the advantage of making programmers aware of the real costs involved in registering the students. It is easy to compute, apply, and understand, and it has an air of fairness about it. Heavier users are charged more. However, it tends to discourage the presentation of high-enrollment courses because high per student charges force fees higher, thereby tending to reduce enrollments where there is elasticity of demand and, at the same time, decreasing the reward to the programmer for a very successful program. Also, where registration services are underutilized and cannot be varied to meet changes in work loads, per student charges may act against the interests of the organization. A per student rate, furthermore, may hide some inequities. For instance, credit enrollments may cost more to process than noncredit enrollments, since more care, more record keeping, and more counseling may be necessary. In such a case, student record-keeping costs might be segregated in their own cost pool and allocated to credit enrollments alone; or two rates, one for credit and one for noncredit courses, might be calculated.

• *Number of courses.* Some costs, such as program processing costs, classroom use costs, and perhaps administrative costs and certain types of indirect promotion costs, might be assigned to responsibility centers on the basis of the number of courses offered (or attempted). This method is "variable" only for cost objects involving a grouping of courses; by the time such costs are allocated to individual courses, they behave like the fixed allocations previously described. Like the per student allocation basis, the per course basis can be adjusted for a variable mix of course type. Here, too, the credit or noncredit categorization may be most appropriate, or other categories, such as course format, geographical location, number of credit hours, or subject matter may lead to a more equitable distribution of indirect costs. Per course allocations, like per student allocations, are easy to compute and understand and can result in fair division of costs. However, especially when they are assessed against *attempted* courses, such allocations may encourage a reduction in course offerings and discourage valuable risk taking by programming staff.

•   *Percentage of income.* Dividing the total (actual or anticipated) indirect costs in a particular pool by the total (actual or anticipated) income yields a percentage by which indirect costs can be allocated on the basis of income received. This simple, widely used method is especially useful where large-scale allocations must be made. Income is usually a readily obtainable figure, and in some systems it is known more accurately and earlier than any other factor, including number of enrollments. It can often be projected more accurately for the overall operation than other elements. In most instances it can be used as a surrogate for the number of enrollments, because it tends to vary proportionately with the number of enrollments.

However, there are some decided weaknesses in this allocation method. First, it appears to penalize behavior that would normally be encouraged, that is, the generation of income; second, it can result in some significant inequities. Course fees are often artificially raised either to cover abnormally high costs or for the convenience of the student. For instance, a travel course fee may include a provision for student travel and accommodations. As explained in Chapter Four, the full fee will be recorded as income in such a case but will include an element of cost that "passes through" the organization to the supplier of the services. Under the percentage of income method, this kind of course would have to bear an artificially high overhead burden, or else the income of the course would have to be scrubbed of the "pass-through" element, a task that can be cumbersome and subject to error. Furthermore, the amount of income is directly associated with few, if any, elements of indirect cost. For example, it costs just as much to process a $35 enrollment as it does a $1,000 enrollment; low-fee courses therefore enjoy an unearned advantage under this allocation system, while high-income courses that have the potential of generating a significant excess of income over expense may be penalized (see the example given in Chapter Three).

• *Percentage of direct expense.* This is calculated in the same way as percentage of income, substituting total direct expense for total income. Certain indirect cost pools, such as the business office, which processes invoices and other items associated with expense, and perhaps the director's office, are naturally associated with total direct expense. When indirect costs are applied on top of direct costs, there is an incentive to keep direct costs down, so desired behavior is rewarded. However, total direct costs have the disadvantage of being difficult to forecast, and actual direct expenses are usually determinable only late in the game when all the costs of a course are in. Furthermore, this method shares some of the inequities of the total income method: The cost of dealing with expense-related operations is more a function of the number of transactions than of total dollar volume. Again, a high-cost program that nevertheless brings in a healthy margin before overhead is applied can be completely smothered by this method.

• *Specific items of expense.* It is sometimes possible to apply overhead costs on the basis of specific items of expense. For instance, indirect promotion costs might be applied on the basis of direct promotion costs on the theory that the higher the direct costs, the more the indirect services were utilized. The cost of the personnel office might be applied on the basis of total direct salary expense or total number of full-time equivalent (FTE) employees. Direct labor cost or number of FTEs is a common basis for allocations, since both can be associated with a variety of indirect costs, from whole service departments (director's office, personnel office) to line items (telephone expense, office supplies). Where there is a direct relationship between a direct and an indirect cost that is viewed as legitimate, this method can be effective. When it is used, however, programmers and managers generally try to keep direct cost as low as possible. This may be a positive influence, but it may also discourage the proper mix of program expenditures, say, in the promotion area, thus hurting some programs.

- *Program days, contact hours, or hours of use.* Sometimes indirect costs are allocated on the basis of the period of instruction. This basis is usually appropriate for allocating overhead costs associated with the use of a classroom facility or a computer lab. Actual hours of use is usually the best basis to apply, but other measures that are surrogate for hours of use, such as number of credit hours (contact hours for noncredit programs) or number of days the course will meet, may also be appropriate. This allocation basis is fair in the sense that heavier users are charged more, and it is easily understood and calculated. However, where certain facilities are underutilized or management wishes to encourage the use of facilities, this allocation basis may not be the best. This method also requires that the hours of use be recorded in a manner that may be difficult or expensive, since their measurement is not part of the normal financial recording system in the way enrollment or income figures are.

There are many more bases of allocation besides these common ones. In an effort to arrive at fair allocations, some organizations have developed elaborate formulae, often combining two or more bases in some weighted average. But as I have often explained, the more elaborate and complex the allocation method, the more expensive it is to calculate and understand. As with most management decisions, the choice of an indirect cost allocation method involves careful weighing of alternatives.

Non- or "Hidden" Allocations

In a large CE organization it is often unfair to charge all courses or responsibility centers on the same basis. We might reasonably expect some centers, say the business and management and the engineering departments, to contribute a larger proportion of their income to the covering of overhead costs, than, say, the community service and adult literacy departments. Trying to reflect this difference in the allocation scheme itself can raise a number of problems, including organizational jealousies, excessively complex allocation formulae, and creation of "second-class citizen" departments. To avoid some of these problems, management might set "available for overhead" targets for each department based on a realistic expectation about what that department might be able to produce rather than on a predetermined formula. In this approach, management would calculate the total amount needed for overhead (including a cushion or contingency) and then apportion that amount among the responsibility centers. This closely resembles the fixed cost allocation method we examined at the beginning of this discussion. It places most of the burden for fairness on the subjective judgments of management, and its effectiveness will be related to the accuracy of those judgments.

In a few fixed resource organizations, especially those receiving full or partial support or subsidy, formal indirect cost allocations may not be required or necessary. However, in order to test the accuracy of management's assessment and to reveal the true contribution (and cost) of each center, some allocation method or methods should be employed. Allocations can be made in memo form or in special financial statements. The disadvantage of the latter procedure is that it tends to shroud overhead costs in mystery and to make it unnecessary for responsibility centers to understand or help pay for indirect costs.

This discussion of indirect cost allocation methods reveals that the subject can be complex and is certainly worthy of thought and care. We must now add still another complexity to the picture: the timing and order of allocations.

Timing and Sequence of Allocations

Transfer prices and allocations may be computed in advance, on the basis of estimates (usually budgetary estimates or the experience of the immediately prior fiscal period), or in arrears, on the basis of actual figures. The advantage of computing allocations in advance is that the transfer price or allocated charge is known at the beginning of the period and can be used throughout the period, guiding decisions and facilitating accounting and financial reporting. The disadvantage is that an adjustment will probably be necessary at the end of the period to correct the estimates to the actual figures. The advantage of setting prices or allocations at the end of the period is that no such adjustment is necessary. However, using the arrears method means that during the budget period, information on the effect of indirect cost allocations is not known.

Determining the sequence of indirect cost allocations is especially important where several allocation methods are used. Until now we have assumed that indirect costs are allocated immediately to the final cost object, either the programming department or the course. In reality, however, most indirect cost pools are added to other indirect costs. For instance, where administrative rent is assessed, all departments, including the service departments, should be assessed for the space they use. Similarly, the costs of the director's office should be borne by all the departments subject to the director's administration. This suggests that allocations follow a certain sequence. First, the most universal indirect cost, rent, should be allocated to all departments on its allocation basis (perhaps square feet occupied). Then the director's office costs, which now include the cost of rent, are allocated on their basis (perhaps number of FTEs), and so on until all indirect costs have finally been allocated to the programming departments (or the courses). If all of the rent were directly allocated to the programming departments, some of the intermediate allocation schemes and their carefully constructed purposes would be bypassed.

The advantage of a sequential allocation is that the full integrity, continuity, and rationale of the allocation process can be maintained. The disadvantage is that such a method can be complex and hard to calculate. It also assumes that there are no reciprocal relationships between service departments. For instance, the director's office may use the services of the personnel office, and of course the personnel office is administered by the director's office. Which department should be allocated to the other? Fortunately, in a CE organization such reciprocal relationships are usually few and relatively unimportant, so no large inequity will result from ignoring them.

Allocating the Cost and Value of Programmer Time

As a conclusion to this discussion, let us turn to the allocation of programmer time. In Chapter One we explored the two components of programmer time, cost and value. As you may recall, the cost of the time was the amount of resources that the organization expended for the employees involved (salary, fringe benefits), and the value of the time was the amount of net resources the programmer (and related clerical support staff) could generate for the organization. The value of the time was thus an assessment of its opportunity cost.

Theoretically, the best way to handle both the cost and the value of programmer time is to charge them directly to the cost object, the course. This is what was done in the example course budget shown in Figure 2.8. An accurate direct system for charging payroll and opportunity costs to courses can be valuable to programmers, helping them allocate their time and decide which courses to develop. It is also an important factor in determining the ultimate profitability of a course. In practice, however, such direct charging is rarely done, because it requires so much recordkeeping and timekeeping or is so subject to estimation that it is not useful. Further, since it depends to such a great extent on the conscientiousness and honesty of the programmer, it is rarely useful at administrative levels above the programmer. Therefore, programmer time, despite its proximity to the course, is most often treated as an indirect cost.

The most common method of allocating programmer time as an indirect cost is the use of a per course basis. The total payroll cost of the programmer and related clerical staff is divided by the number of courses to be offered. This at least allows financial assessment of an average of programmer time spent per course, a measure that can be easily understood and to which a realistic assessment of the actual time spent can be compared. For instance, a programmer planning a new course in a new subject area that can be offered only once would expect to spend more time in developing the course than the average and would therefore look for a higher potential return on that course. A variation on the overall average per course allocation is to divide courses into different categories and allocate different amounts per course to the different categories. For instance, previously offered courses might be charged less than new courses on the theory that new courses will take more time and effort. This might discourage new course development, but the method could still be a useful aid to planning.

Because people work in different ways and think about their work differently, and because programmer productivity is related to so many factors, the treatment of programmer time is a touchy subject. For some workers, time is not really a good measurement of productivity or effort or value; rather, it is their creativity and their ability to respond to the world around them that are of value to the organization, and these abilities can never be quantified. Still, all of us have an interest in managing our time more effectively, and the system that can achieve this will pay good dividends.

Summary

This discussion has described a number of common methods for applying indirect costs to programming departments. More important, it has suggested ways to relate the use of a particular method to certain effects on behavior and decision making.

As conditions change, as goals and objectives change, so should allocation methods. Methods should be chosen to minimize resentment. One measure of the managerial maturity of a continuing education professional is the demonstration of an understanding and responsible attitude toward overhead and its allocation. This chapter should help the maturation process.

Bibliography

Louderback, J. G., III, and Dominiak, G. F. *Managerial Accounting.* (3rd ed.) Boston: Kent, 1982.

Titard, P. L. *Managerial Accounting: An Introduction.* Hinsdale, Ill.: Dryden Press, 1983.

=10=

Dealing with Special Continuing Education Functions

This chapter deals with the budgeting and administration of a number of CE functions not directly related to presentation of classroom instruction. In many institutions, the CE organization is responsible for activities such as independent study (correspondence) instruction, media centers, film libraries, television and instructional aid offices, publication production and sales units, conference centers, and "public service" programs of many kinds. We will cover budgeting aspects of these functions and will also treat the special considerations involved in inventory budgeting, cash budgeting, and capital budgeting.

Inventory Budgeting

An inventory, like any other asset, is of potential value to an organization. We normally think of inventories as being tangible goods, but it can also be useful to think of a program planned for future terms as an "inventory" of courses. In most CE organizations, inventories of actual goods such as office supplies and course materials are simply "expensed" when they are purchased, but in some CE activities, inventories are large and are likely to exist for some time. An independent study operation may stock texts, audio and video cassettes, and other course materials for anticipated enrollees, and a publications operation is likely to print quantities of material that remain "in inventory" until they are sent out to customers. Film/video rental libraries will have an inventory of films and video tapes to distribute, media centers and television offices will have inventories of equipment, and a printing operation may have an inventory of paper and other supplies. There are many more examples. One CE organization reports an inventory of solar heating equipment used in a statewide program to promote solar water heating in private homes!

Inventories are sometimes made rather than purchased. For instance, an independent study organization might purchase texts from an outside publisher but also prepare in-house course syllabi and notes. When inventories are created in house, the inventory account becomes the cost object, and all costs associated with the creation of that inventory are accumulated and identified with it. Inventories are usually valued at cost—that is, at what it cost the organization to acquire them—but sometimes, for the sake of convenience, they are valued at what the organization will sell them for, using a mark-down formula to calculate inventory cost as required by generally accepted accounting principles.

Flow of Resources. It is important to understand the flow of resources associated with inventories. Items in inventory begin their lives as assets of the organization, and usually the organization acquires them by trading other assets (such as cash) for them (although they may be bought on credit, in which case the organization has incurred a debt). They end up as costs or expenses; as they are sold, their cost becomes a "cost of goods sold" (to use an accounting term), which passes into expense in the same period as the sale is recorded. Usually a physical inventory is taken at the end of every period—that is, the items are counted and the cost determined. A record of the cost of additions to the inventory is also maintained throughout the period. The cost of goods sold can then be derived by using the following equation:

Beginning inventory (or ending inventory of previous period)
    + Additions during period
    – Cost of goods sold
    = Ending inventory

This equation may help to explain why inventories operate like sponges, soaking up other assets (primarily cash) and then releasing them into the income stream of the organization as goods are sold. A significant difference between beginning and ending inventories means that inflows and outflows of inventory are not matched within the period. This can be a significant problem for organizations that must follow fund accounting rules or that do not use or have access to balance sheet accounts. For instance, suppose that just before year end, the independent study division of a CE organization has the chance to purchase a large amount of material at a significant discount. Under normal fund accounting rules, that purchase would have to come from current year funds, even though the inventory will benefit from it in future periods. If that purchase has to be treated as a current operating expense, operating results for the current year will be worse and results for the next year will be better than they would be if the purchase had not occurred or if standard, nonfund rules had been followed. To correct this distortion of operations, some fund accounting organizations create an inventory fund (and a corresponding inventory asset account) outside of operating fund groups, recording transfers between it and the operating fund either as inventory is added to through purchases or relieved through sales, or, more likely, once per year (or period) as a period-end adjustment for the difference between beginning and ending inventory.

Inventory Problems. A number of problems are associated with building and maintaining an inventory. First, it can be costly. The money needed to build an inventory has an opportunity cost; that is, it could have been spent on something else. Investment in inventory can also have a real money cost if interest is to be paid on cash used for its acquisition. Significant cost can be involved in ordering inventory, receiving it, inspecting it, and paying for it. It costs money to keep track of inventory, too: Physical inventories must be taken, costs calculated, locations tracked, reorder quantities determined. Storage costs are significant as well. Rent or opportunity costs for storage space, shelving, heating or cooling, lighting, and salaries and wages associated with putting material in and taking it out can add up to significant sums.

Second, there is always the risk of loss or obsolescence. The larger the inventory, the greater the risk. The monetary risk of loss can sometimes be reduced through insurance (at a further cost), but it usually cannot be eliminated entirely: Not being able to fill an order, even if it is because the warehouse burned down, can be costly to reputation. Further, more insurance will cover the cost of the inventory but not the replacement cost and not the cost of the loss of the margin that the organization could have realized through sale of the inventory. The risk of obsolescence is usually not covered by insurance at all. This is a particular problem with educational materials, which can go out of date very quickly in some fields, and with independent study operations. Suppliers often offer large volume discounts, enticing the unwary into building inventories that cannot be sold. New editions of textbooks are released with alarming frequency, making supporting materials based on the old editions out of date. The cost of obsolete inventory must be written off, that is, expensed, in the period that it is determined to be obsolete. Thus a mistake in a prior period can burden the future.

Against these costs must be weighed the cost of running out of inventory (a "stockout" condition), thereby losing sales and disappointing customers. There is nothing more frustrating or wasteful than being unable to serve a ready, willing, and able customer. If there is no product to be sold, all the effort that contributed to obtaining a sale is wasted.

Careful inventory management helps in solving these problems. After assuring that physical measures are taken to safeguard the inventory, such management is directed primarily at determining how big the inventory should be. The manager has three important tools to help in this determination: economic order quantity (EOQ) calculation, safety stock and reorder point determination, and careful budgeting.

Economic Order Quantity. The economic order quantity (*EOQ*) is the amount of inventory the organization should order each time to minimize order and carrying costs. The formula for determining the *EOQ* is

$$EOQ = \sqrt{\frac{2\,OU}{C}}$$

where O = order cost per order
$\quad\quad U$ = number of units used annually
$\quad\quad C$ = carrying cost per unit

The hardest part of this formula is determining O and C. *Order cost* is the cost of placing an order for more inventory, receiving and inspecting the goods, placing them in stock, and processing and paying the invoice. Calculation of this cost is usually made by rough and ready estimates supported, perhaps, by calculating total cost of these functions divided by the number of transactions per year. *Carrying costs* are all the costs of maintaining an inventory, including space, insurance, utilities, and so on. These costs are divided by an average number of "units" in inventory at any one time. In an inventory of textbooks, for instance, unless there is a significant variation in the size of the texts, the total average number of texts can be used, and smaller items such as course syllabi can be expressed in terms of the text unit—say, 0.5 texts.

Let us illustrate the calculation of EOQ with an example. Suppose an independent study operation has 500 enrollments per year in an accounting course, each of which requires a text. The operation's total inventory for texts for all courses is 10,000 units, and it costs \$7,000 per year to maintain the inventory, including the salary of a half-time storekeeper. It costs \$65 per order to order anything. The EOQ would then be determined as follows:

$$O = \$65$$

$$U = 500$$

$$C = \frac{\$7,000}{\$10,000} = \$.70$$

$$EOQ = \sqrt{\frac{2(\$65 \times 500)}{\$.70}}$$

$$EOQ = \sqrt{\frac{65,000}{.70}}$$

$$EOQ = \sqrt{92,857}$$

$$EOQ = 304.72$$

This calculation tells us that this organization ought to order 304 or 305 texts at a time. We can round this off to 300. This calculation can also be done in tabular form, as shown in Figure 10.1.

An important limitation of the *EOQ* calculation is that it does not incorporate an obsolescence factor. It would obviously be unwise to order a six-month supply of a text if a new edition of it was coming out in two months.

Safety Stocks. Determining safety stocks and reorder points is a very important aspect of inventory management. A *safety stock* is an extra amount of inventory that the organization wants to have on hand to cover longer than expected delivery times of goods—an emergency supply, in other words. Where delivery times are long and supplies uncertain, it makes sense to have a relatively large safety stock. The cost of a "stockout" should also be considered: What will the organization lose if it runs out of inventory? When safety stocks are set, the variation in lead times and the average daily use should be considered as well. The *lead time* is the time between the placing of an order and the delivery of the goods. Suppose, in the example just cited, that the normal lead time for receiving an order of textbooks is thirty days and the average daily use of books is 1.4 (500 annual enrollments/365 days per year). Suppose also that the organization has experienced delivery delays of up to two weeks beyond the usual four weeks and occasionally experiences an average use of four books a day. We might calculate the safety stock

Figure 10.1. Table Determination of EOQ.

(a) Number Orders per Year	(b) Number Units Ordered (500/a)	(c) Average Inventory (b/2)	(d) Annual Ordering Costs ($65 x a)	(e) Annual Carrying Costs ($.70 x c)	(f) Total Annual Costs (d + e)
1.00	500	250	$ 65	$175	$240
1.67	300	150	109	105	214
2.00	250	125	130	88	218
3.00	167	84	195	59	254
4.00	125	63	260	44	304
5.00	100	50	325	35	360

to be fourteen days (the two-week extra delay) times four books (the highest average use), or fifty-six books.

   With these calculations we can determine the *reorder point,* the level the organization should allow the stock to reach before ordering more inventory. The formula is:

Reorder point (RP) = Safety stock + (Lead time × Daily use)

In our case:

$$EOQ = 300 \text{ books}$$
$$\text{Daily use} = 1.4 \text{ books}$$
$$\text{Lead time} = 30 \text{ days}$$
$$\text{Safety stock} = 56 \text{ books}$$
$$RP = 56 + (30 \times 1.4)$$
$$RP = 56 \times 42 = 98$$

Thus, when the stock in inventory reaches the level of 98 units, our example organization should order 300 more texts. By the time it receives the order, its inventory would be down to the safety stock level of 56 books given average use, or lower if it had higher than average use and had to go into the safety stock. It is usually a good idea to check the level of the safety stock at the time the new order is received to see if safety stock ought to be adjusted. Note that the safety stock is not used in the calculation of average inventory for the EOQ calculation because it is constant for all order sizes.

   Inventory Budgets. A final element of inventory control is careful budgeting. The two calculations just discussed are for individual items of inventory and should be supported by a review of the total picture. Along with income and expense, the ending level of the inventory, additions to the inventory during the year, and the cost of sales should also be budgeted at the beginning of the period. Wide fluctuations in the inventory and significant deviations from the budget might call into question either the method of budgeting or the efficacy of the calculations of EOQ, safety stock, and reorder points. If these changes are not correlated with budget variances in income, something is wrong.

So far we have been dealing with the kind of inventories that are ultimately sold and pass into the possession of the customer. However, there are inventories, such as film rental libraries and audiovisual equipment, in which the items pass out of and back into the organization. This kind of inventory has elements in common with both regular inventory and capital items. Here the emphasis is on custody control and on the maintenance of the quality of the inventory. Therefore, to all the costs we have already discussed must be added the costs of booking, maintenance, and repair. The acquisition of such inventory follows rules different from those we have been discussing. We will talk about this kind of "capital" inventory in this chapter's section on capital budgeting.

CE managers who have to deal with inventories should know about inventory accounting and inventory control methods and should be able to trace the effect of inventory fluctuations on the operating results of the organization. This is sometimes difficult because inventories are not common in, and are not well handled by, the fund accounting methods characteristic of most educational and service institutions.

Cash Budgeting

Cash budgeting refers to the projecting and controlling of the cash or liquid resources of an organization. Again, most CE organizations, being part of a larger parent, are not likely to be directly involved in the management or budgeting of cash. But as parent organizations become more and more sophisticated in cash handling, and as more and more CE organizations become important net cash generators, CE administration needs increasingly to be aware of the elements of cash budgeting and the effects of the flow of CE-related cash on the CE organization as well as on the parent. Also a few CE organizations must do formal cash budgeting, and, indeed, may earn interest on positive cash balances or have to pay interest on negative cash balances.

Sources of Cash. Cash budgeting and cash projecting require careful and sometimes quite detailed estimation of each source and use of cash. The format of the master cash budget usually shows first the sources of cash (cash receipts) and then the uses of cash

(cash disbursements), coming down to a cash surplus or a cash requirement. A standard cash budget format, adapted slightly for several items typical of CE organizations, is shown in Figure 10.2.

Forecasting sources of cash is closely tied to the forecasting of income—in our case, student fee income. In the cash budget in Figure 10.2, which covers six months, it is assumed that the CE organization is on the trimester system, with terms beginning in late January and mid-June. Cash, therefore, is received mostly around the term beginning dates. It is also assumed that the CE organization offers a deferred payment plan to its students that allows them to spread fee payments over as long as two months. To figure out the cash implications of this plan, we have to determine when the students will enroll and when they will pay. An example of this computation is shown in Figure 10.3.

In this example we assume that experience has shown that half of the deferred fees are collected within the first month, that 30 percent is collected in the next month, and that the remaining 20 percent is collected two months after enrollment. The total collections per month computed on this schedule are posted to the cash budget (Figure 10.2) and labeled "Collection on fees receivable." Our example of sources of cash also assumes that the CE organization does in-house training programs, bills the customers of this service on the first day of each course, and receives payment within thirty days. A calculation of the timing of these collections is shown on the next line, "Collections of billed contracts." CE organizations also often have "other" sources of cash, such as rental of facilities, sale of books or notes, counseling and processing fees, and so on.

Uses of Cash. Uses of cash (cash disbursements) fall into three categories. The first and most difficult to forecast is variable use. In our sample cash budget we have used teacher compensation and course supplies and expense as examples of variable uses. In this CE organization, teachers are paid at the end of the course when they turn in their grades. Thus, most of the cash outflow comes at the end of the term. Most course supplies and related expenses are ordered and incurred at the beginning of the course and are payable shortly afterward.

Figure 10.2. CE Organization Cash Budget.

	Jan.	Feb.	Mar.	Apr.	May	June	Total
Sources of cash							
Beginning balance	$ 5,000	$ 5,000	$ 5,000	$ 5,000	$ 5,000	$ 5,000	$ 5,000
Student fee inc. - cash	70,000	55,000	30,000	42,000	63,000	60,000	$320,000
Col. on fees receivable	14,400	15,600	13,000	10,100	7,400	13,800	74,300
Col. of billed contracts	16,000	4,500	22,000	7,000	15,000	3,000	67,500
Other	2,000			2,000			4,000
Total sources	$107,400	$80,100	$70,000	$66,100	$90,400	$81,800	$495,800
Uses of cash							
Variable uses							
Teach. comp.	$ 3,000	$2,000	$30,000	$30,000	$10,000	$27,000	$102,000
Course supplies & expense	12,000	4,000	9,000	10,000	7,000	4,000	46,000
Total variable	$15,000	$6,000	$39,000	$40,000	$17,000	$31,000	$148,000
Uniform uses							
Payroll	$30,000	$30,000	$30,000	$30,000	$30,000	$30,000	$180,000
Fringe benefits	7,000	7,000	7,000	7,000	7,000	7,000	42,000
Office expense	8,000	8,000	8,000	8,000	8,000	8,000	48,000
Total uniform	$45,000	$45,000	$45,000	$45,000	$45,000	$45,000	$270,000
Minimum cash require	5,000	5,000	5,000	5,000	5,000	5,000	5,000
Total uses	$65,000	$56,000	$89,000	$90,000	$67,000	$81,000	$448,000
Cash to (from) parent	$42,400	$24,100	($19,000)	($23,900)	$23,400	$800	$47,800

Figure 10.3. Projected Collection of Deferred Fees Receivable.

```
                                  Nov.      Dec.       Jan.
Fees received on deferment plan  $5,000    $3,000    $25,000

Collections:
  Second prior month (20%)                           $ 1,000
  First prior month (30%)                                 900
  Current month (50%)                                  12,500
        Total collections                             $14,400
```

Uniform uses fall into two classifications, those that truly are uniform from period to period and those that are treated as uniform because their occurrence cannot be accurately predicted. Payroll costs and fringe benefits usually belong to the first group. Although there may be some variation, those variations can usually be calculated in advance. Some components of office expense may be in the latter classification. For instance, there may be an item for machine repair. Computing equipment especially requires periodic repair. We can usually calculate this amount fairly accurately over a year's time, but we cannot predict when the machines will break down. So, for want of some better basis, we spread it over the whole year uniformly, thinking that, on average, we will be right.

The minimum cash requirement is also a use of cash, but it is offset by a source of cash called beginning cash balance, at least in this example. Minimum balances are more usually associated with stand-alone organizations and are maintained to assure that the checking account of the organization does not become overdrawn. Minimum balances in the parent-subsidiary situation serve as a contingency reserve.

Cash Budgets. The bottom line on the cash projection is the amount of cash the parent will be able to draw from, or have to provide to, the CE organization. During the months of March and April in our example, cash sources will be less than cash uses, so the CE organization will have to "borrow" from the parent. For many CE organizations this "borrowing" is invisible because it is automatic, analogous to a line of credit at a bank but without the formality or cost attached to that comparison. The role of the CE organization in generating positive cash flows can also be hidden,

Feb. $15,000	Mar. $7,000	Apr. $10,000	May $6,000	June $20,000	Total $91,000
$ 600	$ 5,000	$ 3,000	$1,400	$ 2,000	$13,000
7,500	4,500	2,100	3,000	1,800	19,800
7,500	3,500	5,000	3,000	10,000	41,500
$15,600	$13,000	$10,100	$7,400	$13,800	$74,300

even from relatively sophisticated administrators (although not the really canny financial officer!) in the parent organization. The CE administrator should be aware of both effects.

As with any budget, the cash budget should be compared with actual results, and significant variances should be analyzed. It is often useful to compare both the latest period and the cumulative year-to-date figures. This kind of comparison is shown in Figure 10.4.

Figure 10.4. Cash Budget Compared to Actual.

	Mar. Actual	Mar. Budget	Better (Worse)	Y-T-D Actual	Y-T-D Budget	Better (Worse)
rces of cash						
eginning balance	$ 5,000	$ 5,000		$ 5,000	$ 5,000	
tudent fee inc. - cash	32,000	30,000	$2,000	172,000	155,000	$17,000
ol. on fees receivable	11,000	13,000	(2,000)	37,000	43,000	(6,000)
ol. of billed contracts	14,000	22,000	(8,000)	36,500	42,500	(6,000)
ther	2,100			2,100	5,600	2,000	3,600
Total sources	$64,100	$70,000	($5,900)	$256,100	$247,500	$ 8,600
s of cash						
ariable uses						
Teach. comp.	$32,000	$30,000	($2,000)	$40,500	$35,000	($5,500)
Course supplies & expense	11,000	9,000	(2,000)	18,000	25,000	7,000
Total variable	$43,000	$39,000	($4,000)	$58,500	$60,000	$1,500
niform uses						
Payroll	$29,500	$30,000	$ 500	$ 87,000	$90,000	$3,000
Fringe benefits	6,500	7,000	500	19,600	21,000	1,400
Office expense	4,000	8,000	4,000	27,000	24,000	(3,000)
Total uniform	$40,000	$45,000	$5,000	$133,600	$135,000	$1,400
Minimum cash require	5,000	5,000		5,000	5,000	
Total uses	$88,000	$89,000	$1,000	$197,100	$200,000	$2,900
n to (from) parent	($23,900)	($19,000)	($4,900)	$59,000	$47,500	$11,500

From this analysis we can see that our example organization is comfortably ahead of its cash forecast for the year to date but that March was not as good as expected, posting an actual "worse than budget" of $4,900. The problem appears to be mainly in the collection of billed contracts, which was $8,000 worse than the original estimation for March. Cash needed for teacher compensation is also more than expected. Although more was spent than predicted on course supplies and expenses in March, for the year the organization was well ahead of budget, and the same is true for payroll and fringe benefits. We might examine each of these items to determine the cause of the variance and what effect it will have on operations.

Like most other kinds of budgeting we have examined, cash budgeting requires close attention to details and some guessing. It deals with an important issue, the management of an organization's liquid resources. No matter how insulated a CE organization may be from the world of finance, how protected it is by the parent from negative cash balances, it cannot escape altogether the underlying economics that drive every organization: All bills must be paid, eventually, in cash.

Capital Budgeting

Capital budgeting means planning the expenditure of funds for items that will be of benefit to the organization for longer than the budget period. It may involve large expenditures for tangible property such as buildings, classroom facilities, or equipment, or for intangible property such as computer programs, the rights to media materials, or long-range program development. The methods of analysis I will describe in this section may also be used for smaller long-term expenditures, such as items of audiovisual equipment, films and videotapes, and small reproduction equipment.

Capital budgeting differs from the sort of budgeting examined so far in this book in several respects. First, in many ways it is more important because it can commit the organization to a future plan of action involving a great deal of money and several years. Capital budgeting thus involves risk taking. Whereas adjustments can be made in day-to-day budgeting operations as conditions change, such quick adjustments often cannot be made with capital items. For instance, the decision to establish an instructional computer laboratory is fraught with risk: The technology might change, the market might diminish, competition might increase, software might change—and once the equipment is delivered, we are stuck with it. But to balance these risks there is the possibility of rewards, and this balancing is the purpose of capital budgeting.

Second, capital budgeting is not so much a target against which actual results may be judged as an aid to deciding between one alternative and another. As with much of decision making, capital expenditure alternatives rarely present themselves in an orderly fashion. Should we spend $60,000 on a new computer lab, or not? Would some other project be more useful than the lab? Capital budgeting is an attempt to put alternatives in some order and clarify the real choices.

Finally, capital budgeting deals with issues of finance, the outflow of present value for the inflow of future value. Present and future value as formal concepts are not widely addressed in continuing education, although we discussed them briefly in the context of cost/benefit ratios and return on investment in Chapter One. Fund accounting principles do not provide any convenient mechanism for allocating acquisition costs to operations. There is no fund accounting counterpart to depreciation expense, used in for-profit businesses to charge future periods with a portion of the cost of capital expenditures. This creates a number of problems for CE management.

Problems in Capital Budgeting

Fund accounting treatment of capital items makes financial measures of effectiveness difficult. For instance, suppose a CE organization has acquired a computer for its registration system. Usually this acquisition is made not from current year operating funds but from some special fund set up specifically for such purchases (often called a reserve fund), or else it is acquired as a gift. In either case it is "free" to the operation; no part of the acquisition cost will ever be charged against the registration operation, which has, in effect, received an unrecorded subsidy that, hopefully, will reduce the cost of operations for some time to come. Registration operations will thus appear artificially cost effective, and comparisons with other operations will be virtually impossible.

Further, and perhaps more seriously, the failure to record and "write off" assets often obscures responsibility for the stewardship of the assets and the value contained in them. For instance, higher education institutions for years have been building a "physical plant capital deficit," which amounts to billions of dollars. During hard times these institutions tried to balance their budgets by delaying periodic maintenance to buildings and equipment. Ignoring this need was easier because there was no requirement that the effect of long-term assets on current operations be recognized in any way, and certainly not through depreciation. As these assets began falling apart, however, the institutions were caught in a bind: They were forced to replace or repair the assets on an emergency basis at current, inflated prices. This situation has created crises on many college and university campuses (Jenny, 1980).

Ignoring the effect of the cost of long-term assets can be particularly damaging to self-support organizations, where it is possible to adjust prices. The registration system in our earlier example will eventually have to be replaced. What if there is no reserve fund or willing donor at the time? If the cost of the system had been recognized over the term of its use and reflected in the fee structure—or, even better, if the replacement cost had been so reflected—the organization might have been able to build up a reserve, or at least, through the showing of deficits, a warning would have been sounded.

Capital budgeting looks past these accounting problems and attempts to estimate the full effect of the proposed acquisition on the organization. To do this it concentrates first on cash flows and the quantitative financial aspects of decisions. How much will the organization have to spend, and how much monetary return will it receive? Once these factors have been derived, the qualitative factors can be considered—better service to students, more accurate and quicker information, a more polished and professional organizational image.

Crucial to the understanding of capital budgeting are the concepts of incremental cash flow and internal rate of return. An *incremental cash flow* is the difference between the inflow and the outflow of cash associated with the investment. For instance, in acquiring a new registration system for $60,000, an organization may be able to sell some of the old cash registers it has been using for, say, $3,000. The incremental cash flow (in this case, an outflow) is then $57,000. This incremental flow is associated with the *acquisition* of the capital asset. Other flows are associated with subsequent *operations* related to the asset. For instance, the new registration system will have new operating costs associated with it—operator salary, systems support, paper costs, machine maintenance, utility costs, and so on. But the new system may also save some money by eliminating salaries or allowing present personnel to do other things. The difference between these two flows is the operating incremental cash flow.

The *internal rate of return* is the opportunity cost of any investment—the rate of return that an organization would receive by investing funds differently. It is used primarily as a benchmark against which to judge capital investment proposals. For instance, if our organization could earn a 9 percent annual return on its $57,000, then, all factors other than finance aside, the new registration system should return at least 9 percent per year to the organization. Arriving at an internal rate of return can be difficult where issues of finance are far removed from the CE organization, and they may not be relevant where the organization does not earn money on accumulated reserves. But even so, CE management should have some idea of an opportunity cost—a return goal for each investment.

Methods of Capital Acquisition Analysis

With this background we can now examine several commonly used methods of capital budgeting and capital acquisition analysis.

Payback Method. The payback method is the simplest and, therefore, the most widely used method for analyzing acquisitions. The payback period is the length of time it takes for an organization to recover its original investment through incremental cash inflows. Under the assumption of even incremental cash inflows, the formula for the payback period is:

$$P = \frac{I}{CI}$$

where P = payback period
I = incremental investment
CI = incremental cash inflow from the investment.

Suppose we are considering the purchase of a new portable overhead projector. The projector costs $500, but we will be able to get a $50 trade-in on an old piece of equipment. We will be able to rent the projector to programming and other departments at $18 per day, and we figure that the cost of booking the equipment, inspecting it when it returns, and maintaining it will be $4 per booking. The payback period is then calculated this way:

$$P = \frac{\$500 - \$50}{\$18 - \$4} = \frac{\$450}{\$14} = 32 \text{ days}$$

This tells us that the investment will be "paid back" when the projector has been rented for thirty-two days. By itself, that may be interesting information, but it is more useful if it is compared with other alternatives. For example, overhauling the old machine, say at a cost of $200, might be an alternative to purchasing a new one. We will be able to rent the overhauled machine, because it is an older model, at only $15 per day, and we expect that, because of higher maintenance, the cost of fulfillment will be $6 per booking. In this case the payback period is calculated at twenty-two days:

$$P = \frac{\$200}{\$15 - \$6} = 22 \text{ days}$$

Thus, if other things are equal, we will choose to overhaul the old machine, since that investment will be paid back in a shorter period. Of course there may be other, nonmonetary factors to consider: The new machine might be easier to use, create a better impression of our organization, aid in generating good will with our instructors, and provide images of better quality. Also, even after being overhauled, the old machine may not have much survival value and may soon break down.

Dealing with uneven cash flows is slightly more difficult than dealing with the situation just described; it usually requires a tabular analysis. Suppose we are considering the purchase of a sixty-minute film for our film rental library for $900. We will rent the film for $60 per showing. Because of the current popularity of the film, we expect to be able to rent it four times in the first month, three times the second and third months, and two times per month for the next six months. We have calculated our booking, inspecting, shipping, and overhead costs to be $15 per rental. The payback period could then be calculated as follows:

Month	Rental Income	Fulfillment Costs	Net Cash Inflow	Cumulative Inflow
1	$240	$60	$180	$180
2	180	45	135	315
3	180	45	135	450
4	120	30	90	540
5	120	30	90	630
6	120	30	90	720
7	120	30	90	810
8	120	30	90	900

It should take us eight months to recover our investment.

Note that in the equipment rental example given earlier, the payback period was given in *rental* days, not actual calendar days, whereas in this example we are using the calendar month as the payback period. This is because we assumed that we had a captive market for the projector and that, whether old or new, it would be used at the same rate over the payback period. We could convert the rental day measure into a calendar day figure simply by computing how many times per month the overhead projector would be rented. Since we cannot assume this equality with films—one film may be booked much more often than another—booking frequency becomes an important element in the film calculation.

The payback method has a number of disadvantages, which these examples illustrate. First, it does not take into account the useful life of the investment or its residual value at the end of that life. We would expect the new machine in the first example to last a lot longer after the payback period than the older machine and to have a higher trade-in (or scrap, or salvage) value. Second, it does not provide an indication of the profitability of the investment. For instance, at the end of the payback period for the older machine (twenty-two rental days) the organization would have received $198 in surplus ([$15 - $6] × 22). After twenty-two rental days the new machine would have provided $308 ([$18 - $4] × 22) and at the end of the payback period $448 ([$18 - $4] × 32). Of course, the older machine required an initial outlay of only $200 versus the $450 for the new machine, freeing $250 for additional investment. Further, the payback method does not consider the "time value of money," which we will examine shortly.

Despite these disadvantages, the payback method can be very useful as a screening device and for comparing parallel alternatives. It has the advantage of incorporating some measure of risk where the holding period of an asset is an important element of risk. A payback period of more than two years on microcomputer equipment, for instance, may indicate a poor investment because of rapidly changing technology.

Unadjusted Rate of Return. The unadjusted rate of return method incorporates a measure of profitability and is, perhaps, easier to interpret than the payback method. It is called "unadjusted" because it does not use the time-adjusted value of money. The formula for computing this measure is:

$$R = \frac{CI - D}{I}$$

where R = the unadjusted annual rate of return
$\quad CI$ = the annual incremental cash flow
$\quad D$ = the incremental depreciation on the investment
$\quad I$ = the incremental investment.

In continuing education, where depreciation is not used, we use a substitute that is calculated by subtracting any residual value from the cost of the investment and dividing by the number of years of useful life. Although this formula is expressed in terms of years and annual rates, any period of time can be used as long as it is finally expressed as an annual measure.

Let's use a more complex example to illustrate this calculation. Suppose we are considering the renovation of a computer lab, changing it from eight-bit machines to sixteen-bit machines. We determine that we could offer thirty-two more courses per year, each of which would net us $1,000, if we do this—but we would have to pay an additional $3,000 per year in maintenance costs, and we could not offer four courses we presently offer that have been netting us $700 each (for a total of $2,800). The new machines would cost $70,000, and we could sell our old machines for $5,000. We estimate that the new machines would be used for four years. From this information we can calculate each of the values for the formula:

$$CI = \$32,000 - \$3,000 - \$2,800 = \$26,200$$
$$I = \$70,000 - \$5,000 = \$65,000$$
$$D = \$65,000/4 = \$16,250$$

and from this we can calculate the unadjusted rate of return:

$$R = \frac{\$26,200 - \$16,250}{\$65,000} = 15.3\%$$

This rate of return can be compared with other rates similarly calculated to arrive at the best investment decision from presented alternatives. Again, nonfinancial factors are not considered here but would have to be introduced to the decision-making process before a wise decision could be made.

The disadvantage of this method, as with the payback method, is that it ignores the time value of money. For example, our $65,000 could be invested in the current year at today's prevailing interest rate. It would have interest added to the principal every year, and that sum would earn interest for the next year (that is, that sum would compound). Furthermore, the positive cash flows generated by such an initial investment could also be invested at prevailing interest rates each year and could thus earn interest. The next two methods we will examine assume that you understand or can obtain (through introductory finance or managerial accounting textbooks) an understanding of the time value of money and of discounted cash flow techniques.

Net Present Value Method. This method determines the present value of all cash inflows and outflows, then adds them together. A positive net present value indicates a worthwhile investment, while a negative net present value indicates that the investment should not be made. The specified interest rate may be the internal rate of return, or it may be a target rate of return (a time-adjusted annual rate of return). Using our computer lab renovation as an example, and specifying that our internal rate of return should be 14 percent (that is, that we know other alternatives that can assure a return on our investment of at least 14 percent), we can compute the net present value of the proposal:

	Years	Amount	Present Value Factor (at 14%)	Present Value
Net cash inflows	4	$26,200	2.914	$76,347
Initial investment	0	65,000	1	(65,000)
Net present value				11,347

The present value factor was obtained from a table, usually called "the present value of an annuity of one." It helps us calculate what we would have to invest now in order to receive an annual amount of $26,200 (principal and interest) each year for the next four years if we could invest at 14 percent interest. Since our initial investment is in the present, it has a factor of one. The fact that there is a positive net present value means that this investment is better than the alternative of investing at 14 percent.

This investment can be compared to other proposals by using the *present value index*. This is simply the present value of the cash inflows from the investment divided by the amount of the investment. From our example:

$$PVI = \frac{\$76,347}{\$65,000} = 1.175$$

This index is useful because the investment with the highest net present value may not be the most profitable if it requires a disproportionally high initial outflow.

The net present value method is theoretically sound and has no disadvantage except that it is a bit more difficult to use than the previously described methods and does not give the real rate of return of a specific investment. It has the advantage of comparing alternatives to a predetermined investment target. It is also quite flexible; in our example we assumed an even cash inflow, but the method can be used with uneven cash inflows and outflows. Each flow need only be reduced to a present value.

Time-Adjusted Rate of Return. The last method we will examine is a computation of the rate of return on an investment that incorporates the time value of money. The question it answers is simple. Using our example, what return, expressed as an annual percentage, would we get if we were to invest $65,000 today and get back $26,200 each year for four years? The formula for this calculation is:

$$PV = F \times A$$

where *PV* is the present value of the investment, *F* is a factor on the "present value of an annuity" table, and *A* is the annual annuity. In our example we know the *PV* and the *A* and so can compute the *F*:

$$F = \frac{PV}{A} = \frac{\$65,000}{\$26,200} = 2.481$$

By extrapolating from the "present value of an annuity" table for four periods, we can determine that the rate of return is about 22.3 percent. That is, when $65,000 is invested at 22.3 percent per year, the investor can get back $26,200 (principal and interest) per year for four years. This calculation finally reduces the capital budgeting decision to a single, understandable, theoretically sound number that can be compared to similar calculations for other investment opportunities both inside and outside the organization. Its disadvantage is that it is sometimes hard to calculate, especially where there are uneven cash flows. In such a situation, using tables requires a trial-and-error method of extrapolation. But, as with many complex calculations these days, it is possible to sidestep such problems by using computer programs designed to do discounted cash flow calculations.

Once a capital investment decision has been made, capital budgeting proceeds much like other budgeting. The assumptions that led up to the decisions are tested against reality: Was the initial investment estimated correctly? Are the cash flows what were projected? This feedback aids in subsequent capital investment decisions.

Although rarely encountered formally in continuing education, capital budgeting can play an important part in CE management. As with any other organization, the CE organization must continually look ahead; it must invest now to obtain future rewards. In fact, this forward-looking expenditure is often the most important that an organization can make. It need not come in large bites, either. The building of a film rental library and the development of courses and materials in independent study operations are examples of situations in which individual decisions involving relatively small amounts of money can add up quickly to determine the success of an organization. The capital budgeting methods explained here can help in that decision process, but even more importantly, they can focus management attention where a good part of it ought to be—on the long-term future.

Budgeting for Independent Study Operations

Many CE organizations include an independent study component. It may be a full-fledged operating department or just a few courses that use the independent (correspondence) study form of delivery. Budgeting for independent study courses and departments differs significantly from the kind of budgeting that is the subject of most of this book, although many of the same basic principles apply. Except for the maintenance of an extended relationship with students, independent study operations are closer to publishing operations than they are to CE organizations, so much of what is contained in this section applies to CE-related publications units as well.

Characteristics of Independent Study Operations. Budgeting differences between independent study and other CE organizations arise from certain underlying operating and philosophical differences between the two types of organizations:

- *Reliance on inventories.* A large part of the "product" of an independent study operation is included in its inventory of course materials, so the principles discussed in the inventory section earlier in this chapter are much more important for independent study than for other types of continuing education.

- *Longer lead times.* Independent study courses generally require longer to develop, dependent as they are on the writing and production of course materials. Once these materials are "on the shelf," they do not produce students all at once as "live" courses do but rather do so over a period of months or even years. Thus, the return on the initial investment in each course is spread out into the future. This means that analysis of those returns must often take the form of capital investment analysis, discussed in the previous section of this chapter. Also, unlike normal CE courses, independent study courses have no luxury of a "go, no-go" decision based on enrollments: Virtually all the costs of a course are sunk before the first student is enrolled, which is another way of saying that the "go" decision must be made before any significant development has occurred.

- *Risk of obsolescence.* Because of this long return period, the risk is much higher that an independent study course will become obsolete through developments in subject matter or, more likely, through the revision or unavailability of the text upon which the course is based.

- *Different organizational division.* The internal operations of an independent study organization usually divide themselves cleanly, sometimes rather sharply, between the development of new courses and the fulfillment of student enrollments, and budgeting should reflect this division. The fulfillment function is heavily clerical in nature. It demands responsiveness to students, accuracy, student advising, and, of course, evaluation of students by the instructor. The development process, on the other hand, requires foresight and academic sensibility of a high order. Bringing these two very different kinds of skills together in the same organization often means that the organization's management and budgeting systems tend to exhibit a kind of schizophrenia.

- *Retention rates.* The rate at which independent study students complete a full course of study can have some significant implications for budgeting and financial projections, but often these implications are not clear. On the one hand, students who complete only, say, the first two of ten lessons are usually much less costly to serve than the ones who do the full course, take the final, and have grades recorded. A low retention rate thus means that the organization can save money in processing costs, which puts the financial aspect of the organization at odds with its educational goals in a way that does not arise in other CE enterprises. On the other hand, since a student who does not complete one course is unlikely to enroll in another, a low retention rate may indicate a low repeat rate and thus fewer students in the future. Financial budgeting for independent study operations must be based in part on a realistically estimated retention rate, but it also should involve setting targets for retention rates with the long-term interests of the organization clearly in view.

Budgeting Needs of Independent Study Operations. These characteristics have clear implications for budgetary, administrative, and managerial action. First, the inventory should be carefully "managed" in accordance with the suggestions made earlier. It should be neither so large that it wastes space and carrying costs (including the risk of loss) nor so small that enrollments have to be turned away because of "stockout" conditions. Independent study inventory management requires estimates of enrollments, rate of enrollment, and retention rates. Estimates of enrollments and the rate of enrollment are involved in the computation of the *EOQ* and the reorder point. The estimate of retention rates is particularly important where the cost of course materials is high relative to the handling costs for sending out materials. Management can avoid sending later lessons out to students who are not making progress, thus saving some cost. However, for most independent study units, the cost of handling is so much greater than the cost of materials that holding back materials will not save anything.

Course development and revision costs should also be carefully budgeted and monitored. Here our earlier discussion of capital budgeting can be of help. For any proposed course development, the costs of development should be estimated (budgeted) and a return on investment of some kind, perhaps the payback method or one of the time-adjusted rates of return, should be calculated. In addition, when comparisons between two or more proposed courses are being made, break-even enrollments should be calculated. This break-even calculation has a number of elements also found in the rate of return calculations and is only slightly more complex than what we have dealt with so far, because fulfillment as well as retention rates must be estimated. Suppose we are considering developing a course that will cost $5,000, carry a fee of $150, and have ten lessons. We will send out all ten lessons at the start of the course and will pay an instructor $5 per lesson to review students' work. We know, from careful cost accounting estimates, that the cost of sending out the lessons plus the cost of enrolling a student is $30 and that the lessons cost a total of $20 to produce. Assuming that every student who enrolled completes the course, the break-even enrollment would be calculated as follows:

Income per enrollment		$150
Less variable costs:		
Initial enrollment	$30	
Fulfillment costs (10 × $5)	50	
Production cost of lessons	20	(100)
Contribution margin		$50

Break-even:
$5,000/$50 = 100 students

Now let us assume that for every student who completes the course of ten lessons there is one who does not get past the fourth lesson. This is another way of saying that the average number of lessons completed by enrollees in this course is seven ([10 + 4] / 2). Now we calculate break-even again, taking this into account:

Income per enrollment		$150
Less variable costs:		
Initial enrollment	$30	
Instructor compensation		
(7 × $5)	35	
Production costs	20	(85)
Contribution margin		$ 65

Break-even:
$5,000/$65 = 77 students

Note, first, that these calculations, in addition to requiring estimation of retention rates, also require a knowledge of the costs of instruction and materials. This knowledge should arise from careful budgeting of these functional areas.

Good independent study management also involves minimizing costs. Costs in this kind of operation usually involve the following elements:

• the cost of the materials sent out
• the cost of handling the distribution of lessons
• the cost of postage or conveyance
• the cost of instructor compensation
• the cost effect of the retention or completion rate

The most important relationship here is between the cost of the materials sent out in each lesson and the cost of handling the distribution of lessons. As noted previously, if the cost of the materials is high, we have an opportunity to reduce costs by doling out materials to students as they complete individual lessons, counting on the fact that some students will not complete the course and therefore will not cause us to incur the material costs of the later lessons. Each time we send something to a student, there is a handling charge, and this can be very expensive. Finding the pattern of fulfillment that produces the minimum cost can be difficult, especially where the cost of lessons within a course varies and where material costs vary from one course to another, as they are likely to do. However, dividing the total material cost of a course by the cost of each fulfillment action can give us a rough estimate of the number of times lessons should be sent out. For instance, suppose the materials for a radiology course cost $53 and the cost of handling distribution of each lesson is $15 (exclusive of postage, which we will assume is a constant, varying directly with weight). It would probably not make sense to send lessons out more than three times over the life of the course, since the cost of sending four packages is $60 (4 × $15), a value greater than the value of the materials.

How lessons should be packaged for distribution—every two lessons, every three, or perhaps in a pattern that varies from course to course depending on the cost of materials and the retention rate expectation of the course—depends on so many variables that it is not possible to create a general rule. However, a careful review of all factors can often result in cost savings. For example, postage costs can be minimized by reducing the number of times a particular piece is sent through the mails, reducing the weight of materials sent, using appropriate mail classifications, and designing assignments carefully.

The best way to treat independent study instructor compensation is usually to establish a rate per lesson. This makes instructor compensation a variable cost and allows the organization to benefit from dropouts. In rare instances, it may be economical to structure courses so that earlier lessons are less expensive to correct or evaluate than later lessons and then build this into instructor compensation schemes, accentuating the dropout savings.

A final aspect of independent study management has to do with the accounting treatment of inventories and development costs. As noted earlier in this chapter, the fund accounting system often does not reflect changes in asset values and thus has a tendency to distort operating results and, in some cases, managerial behavior. This problem is particularly important in independent study operations because inventories and development costs play so great a role in them. For example, because the organization was not allowed to reflect fluctuating inventory values in its operating statements, one independent study director kept the inventory low by ordering no more than twenty lessons at a time, even though substantial volume discounts could have been obtained by ordering fifty or more at a time. This practice placed additional burdens on staff and led to a number of cases where students could not be served because of stockouts.

It makes more sense to try to work out adjustments and accommodations with the accounting and financial system, whether by maintaining records in certain ways or by arranging for appropriate deferrals and accruals at year end. For instance, development costs expended during the year for courses not yet bringing in income might be deferred until the next fiscal year. Changes in inventory carrying value can also sometimes be handled by deferring increases in value and by adjusting future deferrals to reflect decreases in value. However these issues are treated on the books of the organization, their effects must be understood by independent study management.

Managing an independent study enterprise presents a set of challenges different from those involved in managing other kinds of CE organizations and requires some specialized knowledge and skills. In a sense, because of the longer time span of the planning process, managers of independent study operations find careful budgeting even more important than do their counterparts in other CE fields. Budgeting and planning functions in independent study are more complex because they must be integrated with inventory control and capital budgeting techniques.

Other Functions

Two other functions typically housed within the CE organization deserve some attention here: publications and media-based services.

Publications Operations. Many CE organizations contain departments that produce or distribute publications (aside from bookstore operations). Such publication operations often have their origin in the need to produce specialized material for a CE course. Publication departments can range all the way from full-blown press operations to very small-scale "hip pocket" operations engaged mainly in the fulfillment process for a limited number of titles. Sometimes the main task of these operations is the distribution of proceedings from conferences sponsored by the CE organization, which often builds the cost of producing the proceedings into the course budget.

Publication operations face many of the same problems that independent study operations do. The size of the potential market must be measured against the size of the initial inventory and the cost of reprinting. The rate of return and the break-even point must be calculated in order to judge the worthiness of any proposed publication project. The issue of fulfillment costs, especially in less well-established operations, is also important. Whereas it is relatively simple to budget the cost of producing a publication, budgeting for the cost of fulfilling orders can be difficult. Often fulfillment costs become invisible because they are included as part of the duty of someone who is hired primarily for other purposes— and these costs can be considerable, often costing well over $5 per copy for even the smallest volume.

CE publication operations also face other problems. Publication decisions are sometimes made on the basis of political rather than financial grounds. A faculty member may insist that his course notes be published for purchase by students, or a conference coordinator may require that conference proceedings be produced and distributed in spite of a poor prospect for financial return. Facilities for storing inventories and procedures for dealing with bookstores and other wholesale subdistributors may not be worked out. Volume discounts, consignment sale arrangements, and billing arrangements are required of most publication operations. Dealing with returns and with aging inventories (remaindering) are also likely to be unfamiliar activities for the CE organization unless the publication operation is of such a size that mechanisms are already in place. For these reasons, if publication departments become large enough, they present significant problems for the organization and, to be financially viable, probably will require some form of subsidy.

Media-Based Services. CE organizations often operate service centers that provide audiovisual equipment services, film and video media selection purchase and rental (and even sales) services, instruction in the use of audiovisual equipment and media in the classroom, and media libraries of all kinds. These services can be grouped into two general categories, people-based and inventory-based. People-based services depend upon skills developed by individuals. For instance, a media center might provide the services of someone who helps faculty members find appropriate audiovisual material or instructs them in the use of equipment. Inventory-based services depend on the maintenance of some form of inventory, such as an equipment inventory or a film or videotape library, that circulates to users and then back to a central depository or even, in some cases, is sold to users.

Budgeting and financial control systems should recognize the difference in the goals and objectives of each type of service. People-based services aim to increase the level of skill of the individuals providing services and to retain them within the organization. Thus budgeting will concentrate on payroll matters and on actions designed to make the individuals more productive. Control will concentrate on measures of productivity such as number of users served or cost per service unit. Inventory-based budget systems will concentrate more on inventory control features and on investment decisions of the kind discussed under capital budgeting. For instance, the acquisition of a new film can be analyzed either through the break-even method or by one of the methods used to calculate return on investment. Control is then exercised by comparing the actual results with the calculations that led to the decision to acquire the film.

Another category of CE media-based services involves the production of videotaped courses or the use of telecommunications technology for long-distance instruction. Most such operations require budgetary subsidies and thus face budget and financial control problems of the kind described for fixed resource organizations. Because of the initial investment in equipment that is usually required, many of the considerations described in the capital budgeting section of this chapter also apply. Just as with conventional CE and independent study courses, they will require break-even analysis and careful budgeting. The wide range of the technology involved, its rapidly changing nature, and the almost infinite variety of financial arrangements that support such operations make detailed discussions difficult. It is easy to "lose your shirt" in such enterprises, which are typically an area of blue-sky promotions.

Summary

Effective budgeting for a CE organization often involves elements not typically associated with the day-to-day process of developing and presenting "live" education courses. Independent study, media-based, and publications operations involve an understanding of relationships and special circumstances that we have not previously covered.

Perhaps the most important of these special functions is the role that inventories play in the financial life of some organizations. If inventory fluctuations are not taken into account in budgeting and financial reporting, significant distortions can occur in financial reporting and in managerial decisions based on those reports. Once this reporting problem is solved, managerial attention can be devoted to establishing the proper size of the inventory through established techniques for determining appropriate economic order quantities, safety stocks, and inventory budgets.

CE organizations are also sometimes involved in cash budgeting and cash management, for themselves or in conjunction with their parent organization. Cash budgeting requires the careful estimation of future cash inflows and outflows and the net cash requirements or surplus calculated for specified future periods. Understanding the implications of cash flows and being able to predict them is important to CE directors in institutions where cash is carefully managed and controlled.

All CE organizations face capital budgeting decisions of some kind. Capital budgeting involves planning for expenditures that will result in a return of value to the organization over future periods. The acquisition of major pieces of equipment or real property (classrooms and offices) are examples of typical capital items. This kind of decision is often quite important to an organization because it commits the organization to a course of action over a long period of time. Capital budgeting differs from other kinds of budgeting in that it is usually used more to decide between alternatives than to set a standard for future performance. A number of techniques are used in capital budgeting. The payback method and the unadjusted rate of return method are relatively easy to compute but do not include the important concept of the time value of money, whereas the net present value method and the time-adjusted rate of return method, although more difficult to compute and understand, result in a theoretically sound analysis.

Both capital budgeting and inventory control are relatively more important in independent study operations than in other CE operations. Independent study operations differ from other CE operations in other ways as well. For one thing, the operating cycle of independent study units is longer—course enrollments are usually counted by year rather than by term. Also, because of the long lead times between course development and the first course enrollment, budgeting for course development must be more methodical and comprehensive. Independent study arms are usually divided into the development and the fulfillment functions, and these two functions are separately budgeted. Media-based and publications operations run by CE organizations also require careful budgeting, with special attention given to capital budgeting.

The CE director may be called on to manage a wide variety of educationally related functions and therefore must be aware of the special characteristics of each of these functions and the specialized techniques managers use to budget and control them.

Bibliography

Jenny, H. H. *Hang-Gliding, or Looking for an Updraft.* Wooster, Ohio, and Boulder, Colo.: The College of Wooster and John Minter Associates, 1980.

Louderback, J. G., III, and Dominiak, G. F. *Managerial Accounting* (3rd ed.) Boston: Kent, 1982.

Montgomery, A. T. *Managerial Accounting Information.* Reading, Mass.: Addison-Wesley, 1979.

Titard, P. L. *Managerial Accounting: An Introduction.* Hinsdale, Ill.: Dryden Press, 1983.

══11══

Using Computers
for Improved
Budgeting and Reporting

This chapter seeks to help you design and implement a computerized budget and financial control system. It is not a detailed explanation based upon specific hardware or software configurations; rather, it raises issues and makes suggestions that should be relevant to most computer environments. We will take a "systems approach" that tries to view computer applications for budget and financial control in their broadest context. The earlier parts of this book have already defined the objectives we want to achieve, and much of what usually constitutes preliminary systems development has therefore been done. Output (report) formats have been specified in the many figures. File attributes have also been listed, and file structures have been described, although this last will require some further discussion. This chapter will attempt to show you how to use this earlier material in designing a computerized budget system. I will try to confine my discussion to computerization of the budgetary and financial control functions of the CE organization, though we realize that most organizations want such a system integrated with those that serve the day-to-day operations of enrolling students, taking in money, recording grades, and promoting courses. Such integration is possible with some software that runs on large microcomputers or minicomputers, but it is an ideal rarely achieved.

The distinction between operations systems and information centers is important to keep in mind. The latter, used in most budget and financial control systems, provide a number of users with the information they need to make decisions, primarily by manipulating, summarizing, correlating, and displaying data. Operations systems, on the other hand, serve the organization with day-to-day processing. In CE organizations, enrollment processing, cashiering, mailing list maintenance and operation, hiring and paying instructors, and ordering goods and services and paying for them are operations functions. Naturally, since the purposes of operations systems and information centers are so different, the computer environment for each is also often different. Operations systems generally require larger computers and must be able to handle a large volume of transactions. They are usually centralized and tightly controlled. Information centers call for a wide distribution of computer service, with many users having independent access to information contained in the computer and independent ability to manipulate it.

There are three general categories of computers: mainframe, mini, and micro. Mainframes are large machines, generally requiring large-scale system development and able to handle large volumes of activity. They are usually expensive to buy and to operate and are relatively inflexible and difficult to change. Minicomputers are smaller than mainframes but are still able to handle a large amount of data; they are big enough to handle, for instance, most of the data processing needs of even the largest CE organization. They are more flexible than mainframes but still require significant systems development effort. A mini system now costs somewhere between $50,000 and $300,000. Microcomputers are much smaller and less expensive than minis ($1,000–$10,000). They may be too small for operations systems of really large CE organizations, but they are well suited to information processing and to the wide distribution needed in budgeting and financial control. "Top end" micros with expanded memory can now do as much as some minis. Micros are often used in conjunction with minis and mainframes in "distributed" (spread out) computer systems, too. A knowledgeable consultant can help you decide on the size of computer you need.

CE organizations obtain computer services in a variety of ways. Perhaps most common is the situation in which the CE organization is provided with computers and systems support from a parent organization, often at a level that the CE organization by itself would not be able to afford. Such a situation may have disadvantages as well as advantages. First, the hardware, software, and systems support services may not quite fit the needs of the CE organization, which operates differently from the rest of the parent. Second, when the parent changes its system (and change it will), the change may be made without full regard for the consequences to the CE organization and may ignore some of the auxiliary systems developed by that organization. Third, because parent computer systems are usually recharged to the CE organization on some allocation basis, the latter organization has little control over computer costs and can find itself dependent upon a system that overnight, through a change in allocation policy, may become very expensive. Finally, in some cases the CE organization may be considered to be a low-priority user of the computer and may have to wait in line for crucial information or processing services.

CE organizations not tied into a parent computer will usually fit into one of several categories. First, they may be supplied with computer services by a service bureau. Unless there are several possible suppliers and unless the system in use can be easily transported to other suppliers, many of the dangers of the parent computer situation are present here too. Additionally, when an organization uses a service bureau, there is little or no opportunity to develop in-house expertise.

Second, the CE organization may have been able to purchase (or obtain through donation) a computer of its own and to develop its own operations and information systems. Even if the computer and the systems are presently operating well, this situation has its own dangers. All hardware and all systems are potential victims of obsolescence, which can overtake a system with startling suddenness. Parts and repair service expertise on older equipment (especially from smaller manufacturers) can vanish, and so can the programming expertise needed to continuously maintain and modify the system. Older equipment also often lacks capabilities currently considered necessary (justifiably or otherwise) for the conduct of business.

Another situation that is increasingly common might be called the patchwork microcomputer situation. As various parts of an organization perceive needs that can be filled inexpensively by microcomputers, individual microcomputer work stations spring up, serving a hodgepodge of functions from word processing to electronic mail. This can be dangerous to an organization because it discourages cooperation and communication and can result in a systems nightmare of feuding camps. Micros, whether separate or linked, can do a good deal for an organization, but some kind of system coordination is essential.

Whatever the computer environment, CE management eventually will be faced with decisions about computers. The first step in making such decisions is to assess the present situation, resources available, and environment (including the stage of computerization of the parent institution). The next step is to come to a realistic and well-defined understanding of what needs to be done. Managers must balance dependence on outsiders against the responsibility, headaches, and rewards of an internally developed and maintained system. They also need to make intelligent guesses about how their needs and the technology will change in the future.

Beginning Computerization

Before examining the details of a computer system designed for budgeting, let us briefly discuss some of the general skills and knowledge required of the planners of such a system and some kinds of software likely to be involved in it.

Systems Analysis. Managers will have to be aware of the techniques of systems analysis. I will not describe these in detail, but I will note that the basic steps are as follows:

1. Define and identify the requirements and objectives of the system.
2. Describe the existing system and the important changes that are needed in it.
3. Define criteria (requirements) for the new system.

4. Prepare a feasibility study and a cost-benefit analysis of the main alternatives.
5. Select the most promising alternative.
6. Design the new system, first an overall design and then detailed designs, including human interfaces.
7. Implement the new system.
8. Evaluate the new system.

Each of these steps can be further broken down. To begin with, some specialized means of describing systems and their many interrelationships is required. Graphic representations such as flow charts or structure charts are indispensable, and some standardized descriptive method should be agreed upon early on in any system development. Systems often are segmented into key modules so that the details of each process can be studied in depth; yet at the same time, the whole must also be kept clearly in view. This approach is sometimes known as "top-down" analysis: System design begins with the overall goal and proceeds down to the details.

Step 6, the design of the new system, is the most important step in the process, so we will concentrate on this step, with specific reference to the human factor. One of the most common mistakes in system design is concentration on mechanical objectives and neglect of the way the system will interface with the human systems surrounding it. Taking time to design the new system properly pays dividends later. A "walk through," during which each process in the new system is carefully modeled and examined, is essential. It can take a great deal of time, but it is usually time well spent.

Three mistakes are common in systems analysis and design. The first is to design a computer system based on a formal (written) system that, in fact, is *not* being used. For instance, we might design a system in which course budgets are added together to obtain responsibility center budgets. This is a sensible enough choice, but if programmers and others in the organization have some other method of formulating a budget, based perhaps on estimates of gross income, or "average" courses, then our system will not be used and the effort spent in developing it will be wasted. The second mistake, which the same example might also serve to illustrate, is to ignore the importance of user involvement in the design process.

Users can provide information essential to design, and their involvement here can encourage their subsequent involvement in the implementation stage, when their cooperation is crucial to success.

A third common mistake is to underestimate the amount of time and effort that the system design process will take. Discovering the real system in use, determining present needs, and involving all users can be time-consuming and exhausting. Converting from a manual system to a computer system is especially complicated. Usually there are so many changes, for operating procedures on up to, sometimes, institutional policy, that few design projects can be accomplished quickly. There are also bureaucratic delays and the time required to bid on equipment, software, and programming help.

Project Management. Since there are so many steps in the system design process and so many people involved, it is clear that the whole computerization project should be managed consciously and according to a definite plan. Coordination is crucial. Like systems analysis, project management has been the subject of many books and courses. It is not itself a technique but rather requires a managerial attitude combined with certain techniques to achieve results. The principles of project management are worth brief recitation here because they are so important to the success of any system development project.

1. Set simple and discrete goals. Most projects seem so large at first that they intimidate those responsible for carrying them out. The trick is to break the task down into more manageable parts with intermediate goals. For instance, the first task in designing a budget system might be the design of the course budget format, followed by the design of other reports, one or a few at a time.
2. Communicate and document decisions and findings. The free exchange of ideas, especially in the early stages of a project, is highly desirable. At the same time, it should be recognized that projects are team efforts and that the team should be productive and focused on goals. One technique to achieve team productivity is to separate analysis and data gathering from

solutions and to attempt early in the process to identify issues that are unrelated to the established goals. It is a good idea to disseminate minutes of meetings.

3. Assign specific tasks and responsibilities. Everyone involved in the project should be aware of what is expected of him or her. The assignment of tasks should be documented and their fulfillment monitored.

4. Set deadlines. The propensity for projects to drift along without meaningful results can be corrected by establishing deadlines at the same time responsibilities are assigned. This is especially important when tasks are interrelated and where there is external time pressure.

5. Follow up in a nonthreatening way. Follow-through is particularly important in project management because it conveys the message that assignments are taken seriously. The manner of the follow-through, however, is just as important. Since project assignments are often given in addition to regular day-to-day duties, it may happen that a member of the project is not able to meet a deadline. Deadlines should be set and checked with day-to-day responsibilities in mind in order to preserve the good will of the members toward the project.

Data Bases. Understanding what a data base is and some of the theories that apply to data base management is important in systems development. A data base system differs from the traditional file environment. In the latter, each user defines a particular application and has a program written and a file built with the data elements needed by the application. Figure 11.1 is a representation of such an environment, with each user, described on the left, "owning" a particular file.

In order to schedule rooms for the next term, the room scheduler might want a report listing each course's name and number, budgeted enrollment, and subject matter. A file for this application would have to be built. The budget analyst might want some of the same information (course number and budgeted enrollment) and some additional information. A separate program would be written and another file would be built for this use. The same would happen for each additional user of the computer

Figure 11.1. The File Environment.

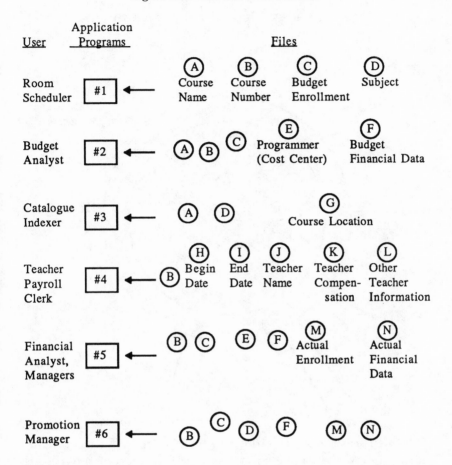

system. This system closely parallels normal procedures in a noncomputerized environment, with its waste in the form of duplicated effort and data.

The data base environment tries to eliminate repetitious processes by placing all data in one pool and devising a generalized program—a *data base management system*—for extracting data in different forms and combinations to serve multiple users. Figure 11.2 depicts a data base environment with a number of users pulling data from a central reservoir through the data base management system.

Figure 11.2. The Data Base Environment.

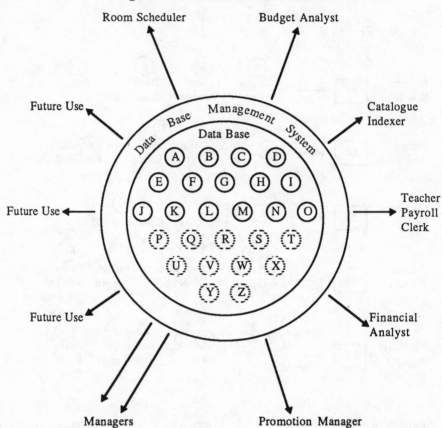

It is easy to see that the data base environment has several advantages over the file environment. First, it can serve additional users with relative ease by adding new elements to the data base (shown in the figure as dotted circles). The larger the data base, the more easily it can incorporate unforeseen uses. With a file environment, on the other hand, even though the data needed may be in the computer somewhere, each new use must go through the same laborious process of new application programming and file building. Furthermore, a change in one program may set off a chain reaction requiring changes in other programs. This usually does not happen in a data base environment, where a report generation program can be changed without disturbing other report programs.

The data base environment is intended to make the data independent of the programs that use the data. This approach makes control over data and data quality easier to maintain, since the data are all in one place and can be placed under the control of centralized authority.

However, there are some disadvantages to a data base environment. First, data bases must be constructed with care, including guesses about future uses of the data. This means that the initial development of the system may be more expensive. Second, development of a data base requires a high order of cooperation among users: The independence that users experience in the file environment (an independence that is itself dependent on expert programmers) is sacrificed to greater overall efficiency and flexibility, although even relatively untrained users can learn to "program" the system for customized results. Third, generally speaking, the larger the data base, the more slowly it responds to individual users. However, this can often be counteracted by careful data base structuring, proper indexing, and extraction of parts for further manipulation.

The real key in designing data bases is to see them from each user's point of view. Everyone looks at data differently, assigning different priorities to data elements and desiring different levels of detail and analytic sophistication. In our case, the main users are likely to be CE programmers and administrators, although administrators from the parent institution must also be considered. Programmers presumably will concentrate on course budgets and on their own term and annual budgets and financial reports, whereas administrators will be interested in the larger picture. A data base that does not serve the majority of users well is bound to disintegrate into something approaching a file environment as each user strikes out independently to get better information. User involvement is probably more important in data base system development than anywhere else.

Of course there is a great deal more to data base theory than is mentioned here. The development of most data bases require the advice of a data base or systems expert, and this advice can be worth its cost.

Spreadsheets. The three most common kinds of packaged software (programs) available for microcomputers are word processing programs, data base management systems, and spreadsheets. Sometimes these are combined in "integrated software" packages. Of the three, financial control systems will make most extensive use of data base management systems and spreadsheets.

At least two features of spreadsheet packages are particularly useful in budgeting and financial control. The first is the ability to create and save templates—spreadsheet formats containing no data. Such templates allow one to use a particular format again and again without having to enter its specifications each time. It also serves the purpose (especially important in a budget system) of arranging data in the same way for each user, much like a manual worksheet.

This feature makes easier the second important use of spreadsheets in budgeting—the ability for data from spreadsheets to be used in conjunction with a data base management system. This allows data from a number of worksheets (course budgets, for instance) to be combined to create new worksheets (the term budget for one programmer, for instance). Although this ability may exist internally in some packaged spreadsheet programs, the combinatory flexibility needed for most budgeting tasks requires spreadsheet data to be transmitted into (or from) a data base program.

For most readers of this book, taking the time to learn how to use one of the spreadsheet programs currently available will pay significant dividends. The generalized knowledge gained will enable spreadsheet analysis to be used for a wide variety of purposes. The bibliography at the end of this chapter contains several references on the use of computer spreadsheets.

Elements of a Computer System

The design of a new computer system requires specification of the following elements:

- outputs (reports)
- inputs
- file structure

- controls
- interfaces
- volumes, frequencies, and response requirements

Let us now examine each of these elements in detail.

Outputs. In designing a system it is usually wise to begin with the desired end product—in our case a report of some kind—firmly in mind. This helps define the scope and objectives of the project. The more detailed and specific the description of the output is, the more useful and comprehensive the design of the system will be. It is important that each element of output be identified with a clearly defined use, contributing information needed to make a certain kind of decision. Many of the figures in this book are outputs logically associated with a budgeting and financial control system. Perhaps the most important output for a CE budgeting system is the course budget (Figure 2.8). Every programmer will use this report in the development of virtually every course. Further, this output will often be used as input for other reports. For instance, course budgets for a particular programmer might be added together to produce the Programmer Course Summary Worksheet (Figure 5.12), which in turn could be combined with worksheets from other terms to produce the Programmer Term Summary Worksheet (Figure 5.11).

Once the reporting scheme illustrated in Parts One and Two has been adapted to your own organizational setting, much of the work of specifying outputs is completed. However, it is natural during early stages of the system development process for potential applications (and thus reports) to proliferate beyond the original conception of the project. In these early stages it is often a good idea to let imaginations soar, so long as expectations are kept to a realistic level. Users should keep in mind that each added report has the potential of adding geometrically to the complexity and cost of the application. However, it is also true that once a system is in place, users will find many new possible applications, so this early exploration can provide valuable information regarding future needs.

After all possible outputs have been specified, it is a good idea to list them in order of importance and subject them to the following questions:

- Why do we need this information? How will it help us? What decisions will be based on it?
- How often will it be used?
- What will we have to do if we do not have this report?
- How much will this report cost? How much would it cost if it were not computerized?
- What impact will it have on our work force? Will we have to hire people with new skills or retrain our present personnel?

As we have noted before, not all "interesting" information is useful, and some useful information is less important than other useful information. This questioning process will help to pare the project back to a manageable level and may also indicate what future enhancements should be taken into account in the initial design.

Although we have been talking about outputs as though they were the same as printed reports, outputs in fact often are not printed or are both printed and stored on the computer. For instance, it is desirable that the course budget (Figure 2.8) output be available to programmers "on screen" so that alternative ("what if") budgets can be calculated. It is more efficient to play with alternatives without printing them, printing only the final version. Each version is an output, even if it is not actually printed. Outputs may also be stored on magnetic tape, floppy disks, or other machine-readable media.

Inputs. Specifying inputs involves identifying and describing needed data elements and determining the manner of the input process. Identifying data elements is relatively simple once the outputs have been designed. They can usually be summarized in an input-output table like the one shown in Figure 11.3.

Figure 11.3 shows a partial table for the three outputs we used as examples before. The outputs are listed in the columns, and the inputs listed down the rows. An "X" indicates that the output incorporates the listed input, a "C" indicates that the output uses

Figure 11.3. Input-Output Table.

Data Element	# of Digits	Output 1 Course Budget (Fig. 3.8)	Output 2 Prog. Course Sum. Wksht. (Fig. 5.12)	Output 3 Prog. Term Sum. Wksht. (Fig. 5.11)
·ogram name	25	X	X	
·ogram i.d. number	6	X	X	
·edit (yes, no)	1	X		
·rm	1		X	X
·ogrammer name	15		X	X
·ticipated enroll.-Fee 1	3	X		
·ticipated enroll.-Fee 2	3	X		
·nimum enrollment	3	X		
·te begins	6	X		
·te ends	6	X		
·, no go decision date	6	X		
·acation	10	X		
·e 1	9	X		
·e 2	9	X		
·ss-through, per person	9	X		
·tal course income	9	C	D (1)	
·tal course pass-through	9	C	D (1)	
·djusted course income	9	C	D (1)	
·mber of programs per term	4		C	D (2)
·mber of enrollments per term	6		C	D (2)
·mber of programs per year	3			C
·mber of enrollments per year	6			C
·tal income per term	9		C	D (2)
·tal pass-through per term	9		C	D (2)
·djusted income per term	9		C	D (2)
·djusted income per year	9			C
·rinting expense-catalogue	7	X		
·rinting expense-brochure	7	X		
·ailing expense-catalogue	7	X		
·ailing expense-brochure	7	X		
·dvertising expense	7	X		
·tal promotion expense	7	C	D (1)	
·tal promotion expense/term	9		C	D (2)
·tal promotion expense/year	9			C

·egend:
  X = data element included in output
  C = data element computed from other data elements in output
  D = data elements derived from other data elements in data base
  (x)= output from which D element obtained

a value calculated from inputs, and a "D" indicates that the output uses a value derived from another output (the number of the output is in parentheses). Thus outputs 1 and 2 but not 3 use the course name; total course income is calculated for output 1 (by multiplying the anticipated enrollments at each fee by the fee and adding them together), and this calculated value is also used in output 2. Also listed for each input is the number of characters that will be required. This will help later when we try to estimate the amount of computer memory we will need and when the systems designer begins to format the reports.

This kind of tabulation illustrates the level of detail necessary in thinking through a system. It also has the advantage of indicating the relationship of one report to another and begins the process of defining the data base or file structure. Further, it will help determine the relative and incremental cost of outputs. Generally, a report that requires no new input data will be less expensive to produce than one requiring additional data. Thus, a report listing total adjusted program income by programmer by term would be relatively simple to produce, since all the necessary data are already being used in other reports, but a report listing total adjusted income by subject designation would require the addition of a subject matter coding scheme, which would add to the cost and complexity of the system.

Another thing to keep in mind when specifying input is the kind of labels that will be used. *Virtual* labels are usually easily understood words or numbers, while *coded* labels are arbitrarily assigned representations. Take the label for "location" in the course budget, for instance. We can leave a blank field of ten spaces as indicated in the input-output table, allowing almost anything to be entered in the field, or we can assign, say, three spaces to the field and require that the input specify a location code of three numbers. Virtual labels have the advantage of being more easily understood, but they have a significant disadvantage in that usually the computer cannot group data unless *exactly* the same label is used for each case. "Downtown Center" thus becomes a separate category from "Downtown," and "Tolman Hall" is different from "Tolman." On the other hand, a coding scheme that designates "010" as "Downtown Center" or "tol" as Tolman Hall forces the inputter to remember the meaning of the label and conform to a categorization scheme.

Once the data elements have been identified, the source and nature of each input item should be carefully described in writing. How will the computer get the data? What will the data entry operator have to do, and to what will he or she have to refer? Often there will be some sort of "input document" containing information to be entered through a keyboard into the computer. For example, invoices may be coded with the program i.d. number by the programmer at the time each invoice is approved for payment. The operator could then enter the i.d. number, the amount of the invoice, the type of expense, and perhaps the name of the vendor. Often input screens can be designed to standardize input and help to make sure that the information is complete and free of error. For the example just cited, an input screen might look like this:

Program I.D. number: _____

Amount: $ _____

Vendor name: _____

Category of expense:

Printing catalogue	——
Printing brochure	——
Mailing catalogue	——
Mailing brochure	——
Advertising	——
Teacher compensation	——
Audiovisual equipment	——
Instructional material	——
Coffee/meals	——
Staff travel	——
Facilities rental	——
Other	——

An input screen should be uncluttered and easy to use, follow an order corresponding to the order that the operator will be following, focus the eye at a specific point of the action, offer easily understood options, and have the ability to jump the cursor forward and

394 Effective Budgeting in Continuing Education

backward. By prompting the operator and narrowing choice to a set number of categories we control the quality of the input. The design of input screens and controls is an important task of the systems designer. A full treatment of this subject is beyond the scope of this discussion; however, most systems design texts provide useful guides to screen design (see particularly Martin, *Design of Man-Computer Dialogues*, 1973). Many modern data base management systems provide tools that make it easy to design screens and validate data.

Sometimes there is no input document at all and the operator must begin with either just the screen or a spreadsheet template, which is the spreadsheet version of an input screen. The course budget is a likely example of this kind of input. Figure 11.4 shows the same course budget presented in Figure 2.8 produced from such a spreadsheet template.

For example, a programmer might sit down at the computer and, without referring to any document, begin entering values for estimated income and expenses for a proposed course. The final version of the course budget could be printed out and also entered directly into a data base for subsequent inclusion in other reports.

One of the trickiest parts of designing input systems for budget and financial control is the development of a coding process to identify income and expenses in a meaningful way. Coding schemes generally have two elements, a responsibility center element and a natural classification element. The responsibility center code in our case is usually either a course i.d. number or a service department code. The course i.d. number ties the course in some way to successively larger responsibility centers, such as programmers or departments. It does so either by information embedded in the number or through association tables in the file or data base. The natural classification coding relates to expense line items. (A listing of typical expense line items relating to courses was shown in Figure 4.3, and line items commonly used for service department financial analysis were shown in Figures 5.2 and 5.3.) For most items of expense, the coding can be done on an input document such as an invoice, a purchase order, or an authorization to pay an instructor. In a typical situation, an invoice for room rental, say, would be routed to the programmer who ordered the room.

The programmer would approve the invoice and code it with the appropriate course i.d. number. The invoice would then be sent to the accounting office, where the natural classification code, "facilities rental," would be entered on the document.

A final thing to keep in mind about inputs is editing requirements. Editing, in computer terms, is the ability to change, add to, or delete from a record. It is often needed to correct input errors or change a record after entry. An invoice entered in the amount of $400 might subsequently be changed to $380 because a discount was missed or because of an adjustment made later by the vendor, for example. Unless the record can be retrieved easily and quickly changed, the integrity and accuracy of the input system is jeopardized. Unfortunately, many packaged software systems presently on the market have cumbersome editing functions.

Specifying inputs and outputs is best done by the end users of the system. Much of this book can serve as a model and guide for input/output design for a budget-related system. The remaining system specifications require a more thorough knowledge of systems design and/or the details of specific software packages than this book can cover, but some important elements of each step will be discussed here briefly.

File and Data Base Structure. The structure of data storage in a computer system is important because, in large measure, it will determine the nature of the use of the information. We have already talked about the difference between a file structure and a data base structure. The file structure will be a direct result of the output specifications, whereas a data base structure will require more thought and effort.

Data base structures can be divided into two general categories: applications and subject. Applications data bases are quite similar to files in that they are developed with a particular application in mind. They are capable of behaving like true data bases but, being designed for a specific purpose, fail to incorporate features that could make them more generally useful. A subject data base, by contrast, is designed to incorporate as many attributes of a given subject as are likely ever to be used in reports. For instance, in preparing Figure 11.3 we began with the course budget (output 1) and simply listed all the information on the header of that report:

Figure 11.4. Course Budget.

Description

```
Course name   : Exploring the Sierra Nevada  Credit/non-cred.: Credit
Course I. D.  : EDP232                        Semester units  : 5
Programmer    : Joe Jones                     CEU's           : 0
Assistant     : Bill Smith                    Contact hours   : 75
Term          : Summer, 85                    Minimum enroll. : 19
Date begins   : June 1, 1985                  Maximum enroll. : 40
Date ends     : August 31, 1985               Go, no-go       : May 1, 1985
Location      : Sierra Nevada                 Budget preparer : Joe Jones
Department    : Biology                       Budget approved :_____
Teacher name  : Muir
```

Financial Summary

Item	Total	Variable	Fixed	Sunk
Expected enrollments	35			
Income	$14,000			
Expense				
Promotion	$900	$0	$900	$900
Instructional costs	2,700	1050	1650	0
Other expenses	3,561	2240	1321	800
Cost of programmer time	1,000	0	1000	500
Indirect costs	3,150	350	2800	0
Total costs	$11,311	$3,640	$7,671	$2,200
Margin	$2,689			

```
Computations:
  Average fee                     400
  Enrollments needed to cover:
    Direct costs                12.65
    Dir. costs + prog.          15.92
    Cost to proceed-sunk        18.48
    All costs                   25.92
Reward/risk ratio                1.22
```

Income

Type Fee	Fee	Enrolls	Gross	Pass Through	Total
Type 1	$450	20	$9,000	$1,000	$8,000
Type 2	400	15	6,000		6,000
Type 3			0		0
Type 4			0		0
Totals		35	$15,000	$1,000	$14,000

Figure 11.4. Course Budget, Cont'd.

Item	Variable Costs Per Person	Total	Fixed Costs	Total Costs	Sunk Costs
...motion					
...atalogue (per cost guide)		0	250	250	250
...rochure printing		0	150	150	150
...rochure mailing		0	200	200	200
...aid advertising		0	300	300	300
...ther		0			0
Subtotal promotion	$0	$0	$900	$900	$900
...tructional costs					
...nstructor compensation					
Muir		$0	$1,000	$1,000	
Guest lecturer		0	500	500	
Guide/lecturer	25	875		875	
Subtotal	$25	$875	$1,500	$2,375	$0
...nstructor travel		0	150	150	
...eader fee	5	175		175	
Subtotal instr. costs	$30	$1,050	$1,650	$2,700	$0
...er expenses					
...oom rental		$0		$0	
...udiovisual		0		0	
...ourse materials	18	630	300	930	300
...eals, coffee, etc.	46	1,610		1,610	500
...taff expenses		0	96	96	
...ther:				0	
Pack train			750	750	
Insurance			75	75	
Shuttle bus			100	100	
Subtotal other	$64	$2,240	$1,321	$3,561	$800
...al direct costs	$94	$3,290	$3,871	$7,161	$1,700
...t of programmer time			1,000	1,000	500
Subtotal direct + prog.	$94	$3,290	$4,871	$8,161	$2,200
...irect costs					
...egistration fee	$10	$350		$350	
			2,800	2,800	
Subtotal indirect	$10	$350	$2,800	$3,150	$0
...al costs	$104	$3,640	$7,671	$11,311	$2,200

course name, course i.d. number, and so on. The fifth data element, "term," was not included in the course budget but is absolutely necessary for the generation of outputs 2 and 3; not including this attribute would make these reports impossible to extract from the data base. The omission of a single attribute (or data element) can thus materially decrease the value of the data base to us. This argues for the subject approach. For instance, if the course is the subject of the data base, we might think of other attributes of a course that are not listed on the beginning of our input-output table, such as teacher name, course format, time, day of week, subject matter, and so on. This would make possible listings of courses by all (or any combination of) these attributes as well as financial summaries based on these categories. Furthermore, this "course" subject data base, which contains only one element about a teacher, "teacher name," might be supplemented with another data base that has "teacher" as a subject and contains not only each teacher's name but also his or her address, telephone number, social security number, subjects and courses taught, and so on. This might be a natural separation, since only a small proportion of the data elements contained in the course data base would ever be used with any of the data elements contained in the teacher data base.

A systems analyst (and the CE administrator) should look for such natural groupings of data elements. Since large data bases tend to be more complex and harder to change after their initial establishment than small data bases, the objective is to achieve a balance between comprehensiveness and size. Again, an input-output table like that shown in Figure 11.3 can help by displaying "groupings" and the relationship between the outputs.

Controls. Computers cannot (so far) protect themselves: One must therefore protect them and the information inside them. This is done by controlling access to the system, controlling the accuracy of input and output, and taking steps to prevent loss of data. Again, the actual design of the controls is usually up to the systems analyst, but the nature and importance of controls should be specified by the organizational user.

Control over access to the computer and its contents can take several forms. *Query* controls determine who may ask the system for information and what information will be available to questioners.

For instance, we may want some budget information—say, payroll information—not to be available to everyone who will use the system. In this case a control would have to be designed to allow only those who need to know and use payroll information to have access to it. *Data entry* controls are sometimes desirable to control who can add what to the data base. For instance, in collecting course budget information, we may want to have permission to add course budgets restricted to the budget officer to assure that all budgets added to the system have been properly reviewed and authorized. Similarly, we may want to institute control over changes to the data. For instance, it is often desirable that all changes to existing records be approved in advance to avoid the possibility of fraud, sabotage, or other improper tampering. Finally, we may want to impose *manipulation controls* to restrict the way in which the data within the system can be manipulated. For instance, we may not want those outside the budget office to be able to produce financial reports or analyses unrelated to their own areas. Thus we may want certain reports (outputs) to be unavailable except upon approval.

The accuracy of data is another important subject for control. Most such controls have to do with the accuracy of input, which can be "edited" in a number of ways. For instance, simple edit functions (often built into software) might prohibit the use of an alphabetic character in a field reserved for numeric data, prohibit the entry of a set of characters longer than the field length provided, or recognize an invalid code for a specified field. Another typical input control is the use of the check sum digit precedure, whereby numeric codes (say, course i.d. numbers) are assigned so that, for instance, the last digit of the number will always be a function (say, the sum) of the first five digits.

Controls may also be placed on the accuracy of the output. This is especially desirable when using packaged spreadsheet programs. Because it is so easy to create incorrect formulae that carry through an entire worksheet, it is a good idea to create check cells that have formulae independent of other cells. For instance, footing and cross-footing columns and rows can be checked by establishing a cell outside the worksheet that contains the sum of all the columns. This total can usually be compared automatically (by establishing an equality condition) with the sum of the rows.

There are also spreadsheet auditing systems available for use with some of the more popular spreadsheet software programs. This can provide documentation of the formulas used. Finally, it is a good idea to develop one's own report-reviewing routines. It is surprising how many errors can creep into computer-generated reports. Fortunately, a common-sense review of the data can catch most of these errors.

Controls must also be established to prevent multiple entry of data and to make sure that data entry is complete. Assigning a number series to inputs (say, course budgets) is a simple procedure, as are routines to account for numerical sequence (either within or outside the computer) and to calculate batch totals and combine them with comparison routines. It is also often a good idea to maintain activity logs noting what was entered when, what programs were run and when, and what reports were issued and to whom. Such logs make tracing errors and correcting bad reports much easier.

One further kind of control is control over the loss of data. The establishment of comprehensive backup procedures is essential for any computer system. Microcomputer systems are especially vulnerable because they lack the built-in procedures present in mini and mainframe systems and thus must depend to some extent on human intervention and manual systems outside the computer. The systems designer must assume that data will sooner or later be lost through sudden power failure, operator error, sabotage, or some other event. The cost of losing the data and restoring it must therefore be measured against the cost of maintaining a backup system. For most CE organizations, the loss of budget and fiscal data will not cause the organization to come to a complete halt, the way the loss of data about current student enrollments or accounts receivable would. However, maintaining a continuity of reporting statistics does have significant value to an organization, and it is worth careful backup procedures. A simple backup method is to save all data input documentation for a particular accounting period. This may be in the form of "hard copy"—that is, paper documents—which would have to be reentered into the computer in the event of loss; or it might be in machine-readable form—say, a set of floppy disks—which could be entered more easily and cheaply. Whatever the mechanics of the backup process, it should be carefully devised, set down in writing, and established before the first use of the system.

Interfaces. An interface is a connection between one system and another. Although this term is often used to designate the connection between one computer system and another, the integration of a computer system with manual systems is just as important. In setting up an interface, the first task is to identify the other systems that now or later will be connected with the system we are designing. The budget and financial control system is likely to interface with the following other systems within the CE organization:

- Parent institution accounting and budgeting systems
- CE or parent enrollment, cashiering, and registration systems
- CE or parent order entry, cash disbursement, and payroll systems
- CE mailing and promotion systems
- Collateral management information systems of the parent or of units existing within the CE organization.

Another interface that has to be examined carefully in some applications, particularly those that use microcomputers, is the interface between a spreadsheet program and the data base program. Although these two kinds of programs are now often combined in "integrated" software, larger or more complex applications may require the use of two or more different programs that have to interface. Often this interface will have to be designed by a professional.

Wherever possible, it is desirable to develop automatic interfaces that reduce to a minimum the necessity for human intervention. This decreases the operating cost of the system and the possibility for error. For instance, the cash disbursement system, designed to produce checks and financial statement information for the parent institution, might be made to feed directly (without further key entry) into the CE organization budget and financial control system simply by adding one or two more fields. Where automatic interfaces cannot be arranged, written manual procedures, including internal controls to assure timely and accurate processing, should be established.

Volumes, Frequencies, and Response Requirements. Throughout the system design process it is a good idea to keep track of volumes and frequencies of use because ultimately these factors will determine the size and shape of the system, the method of access to it, and the means of using it to make reports. Toward the end of the design process these volumes and frequencies should be summarized so that hardware and software parameters can be determined.

This quantification step begins with some simple mathematical calculations. Usually we will know how many characters each record requires and will be able to make a rough estimate of the number of records that we will ultimately have, within some broad ranges. We will also have to estimate how many records can be originated in a given time span (say, a day) and therefore how many input devices we will need and whether these will have to be operating simultaneously, separately, interactively, or in some kind of batch mode. We should also estimate the number and frequency of additions, changes, queries, and errors, on the current file as well as on the noncurrent or backup files. This calculation will help determine the structure and importance of the edit function and perhaps the number of work stations. Another important estimate has to do with the number, size, and frequency of reports that the system will generate. This is especially important in microcomputer-based systems because report generation often requires real machine time, tying up the computer so that other processes cannot take place. This measure will also determine the number, size, speed, and quality of printers required and whether or not print buffers (arrangements that allow the machine to hold text to be printed in a buffer so that the computer can print reports at the same time it does other operations) will be required. As a rule of thumb, most systems designers, after making careful estimates of volumes and frequencies, double their estimates to provide an adequate cushion for error and for future needs.

So far we have been talking about volumes and frequencies of machine operations—inputs, outputs, file sizes, and so on. But another category of volume is also important, especially in microcomputers: the size of the software necessary to perform the operations. "Size" here refers to the amount of the computer's random access memory (RAM) that the program needs. The available memory in most micros is limited, but it may be increased in 64K or 256K increments through the addition of RAM chips. Packaged software will specify the minimum memory necessary to efficiently run the program. Most spreadsheet programs, because of their complexity, require at least 192K of RAM, and the prudent person will usually add memory capacity well beyond the minimum. Some programs can take advantage of memory that exceeds the minimum required, so that they run faster or can handle more data as memory expands.

Finally, in addition to those specific calculations, we should make some estimate of total machine utilization and its impact on response time, that is, the amount of time it takes the computer system to respond to a command. Peak as well as normal operating utilization should be considered.

Unfortunately, there is no easy or accurate way to make these estimates because, unless a prototype system is available for experimentation, we will have to make many guesses about how long, say, data entry, searches, or sorts will take. However, usually preliminary estimates can be made and can help in the selection process.

Selecting a System

Because of rapidly changing technology and the lack of reputable and objective expertise, the CE administrator charged with selection of hardware and software for any computer application faces a decision process that can be very frustrating and usually puts the organization (and the administrator's own career) at some risk. Since selection must deal very directly with the particular situation, needs, and skills available, a comprehensive treatment of this process is beyond the scope of this (or perhaps any) book. The following general guidelines may be of help, however.

Features of Administrative Systems. First, keep in mind that administrative uses of computers are significantly different from instructional and research uses. Combining administrative functions with other computer functions normally present in an academic environment is likely to present many problems. For one thing, administrative systems rarely become obsolete. Newer, faster, and more efficient technology may come along, but as long as the system is doing the job for which it was designed, it is still meeting the organization's need. In instruction and research the impetus is always to be "state of the art," operating on the leading edge of the technology. With administrative systems, in contrast, the goals are stability, dependability, and ease of use—qualities rarely present in new technology. An administrative system that changes with each innovation will be in constant turmoil and will place unnecessary stress on the personnel who must implement the changes. This means that in selecting both hardware and software the supplier's reputation, staying power, and ability to service the product (and to continue that service into the future) are important factors. It is also desirable that hardware and software have the capability of being easily changed and upgraded, say for additional memory. Computer applications never grow smaller, so it is a good idea to provide for future expansion in some way in the initial purchase, either by selecting a system that is bigger than presently required, or by selecting a manufacturer who offers increasingly powerful options on favorable terms.

Software Selection. A current axiom of computer system selection is to choose software before hardware. As things settle down in the computer industry so that hardware becomes more standardized and software becomes more generalized and capable of being run on a variety of hardware, this link between software and hardware selection will begin to weaken. Right now, most packaged software comes in versions that run on most major brands of computers. This trend is expected to continue, so that hardware decisions, especially with regard to the way hardware will have to change in the future, are becoming more important. For limited applications, however, including some budgeting and financial reporting applications, some packaged programs will do a much better job than others, so selection of software first can help to narrow the hardware options.

Know what you want the software to do before you go into the marketplace. If you follow the systems design steps listed earlier in this chapter, even for relatively simple applications, you will have the knowledge you need to take charge of the selection process rather than relinquishing the initiative to a salesperson trained only to tout the positive features of some particular product. You will be able to present clearly defined specifications and insist that recommended software meet them, thus shifting part of the burden to the other side.

As noted earlier, the CE administrator will often be faced with a "make or buy" decision for budget and financial control systems. There are many packaged financial programs on the market, some of them relatively inexpensive, and they can be an attractive option. However, there are trade-offs. It is unlikely that any packaged program will do exactly what you want, especially because the CE field has elements of both the for-profit business world and the traditional nonprofit world. On the other hand, a custom-designed system is likely to be quite costly. A compromise position is to purchase a packaged program and then alter or tailor it to meet your more specific needs. Some data base systems, for example, include powerful programming facilities for advanced uses. With clearly articulated specifications, the trade-offs can be explored in more detail and with more concrete cost information. It is often possible to get a demonstration of software fulfilling specifications similar to those you desire before you actually commit to its acquisition. This is more likely with packaged software than with customized software and is one of the major advantages of the packaged variety: At least if you are acquiring something less than you want, you can get a clear idea of how much less it is and the costs of either getting or doing without those features that it does not incorporate.

Costs. We have not yet dealt directly with perhaps the most important selection criterion, cost. This was intentional because cost considerations, at least detailed cost considerations, should come relatively late in the systems design and selection process. System costs can be divided into two categories: acquisition and operating. *Acquisition costs* are all the costs associated with obtaining the system. They generally occur only once, during a short period of time at the beginning. Although good accounting practice dictates that these acquisition costs be spread over the useful life of the system, in the CE environment this is rarely done. *Operating costs* are the costs required to maintain and operate the system once it is fully implemented. Both categories of costs should be understood in their broadest context. For instance, acquisition cost calculations should include the following:

• *Cost of hardware.* This is the most obvious acquisition cost. It should include the cost of all needed peripherals and supporting equipment: terminals, printers, cables, electrical fixtures and devices, operating manuals, facility alterations such as air conditioning equipment, memory and adapter boards, disks, and furniture, including desks, storage cabinets, bookshelves, and chairs. In addition to these "out-of-pocket" costs, there are the less tangible costs of obsolescence and incompatibility. You should make some estimation of how long the system will be useful and how easy it will be to upgrade or adapt to future needs. It may also be important that the new hardware be compatible with other hardware already in place. Thus, the cheapest system may not be the best when the broader picture is considered.

• *Cost of software.* This is another obvious acquisition cost, but it sometimes has hidden features. Estimating the cost of customized software is often very difficult because no programmer or systems designer is able fully to predict how much time it will take to design and program a system or what problems will arise. The purchase of packaged software usually carries with it the obligation to comply with the terms of a license agreement restricting the use of the software, sometimes to only one machine. It may be necessary to negotiate with the supplier for a more extensive license if you contemplate using the software in several places. Certainly multiple copies of user manuals should be easily available, and backup copies of the machine-readable software should be maintained and included in the cost of the initial acquisition. Further, the cost of modifying or adapting the software to the specific application should be considered.

• *Training costs.* Another acquisition cost, less obvious than the preceding two, is the cost of training personnel. This includes not only direct tuition fees for employees taking instruction in the new system but also the cost of the employees' time while they are in training.

• *In-house development costs and parallel system costs.* Any new system will require present operating personnel to be involved in the development and implementation of the system. It is also sometimes necessary to run parallel systems—the new alongside the old—in order to test the new system properly before depending upon it. These tasks will often be performed by employees in addition to their normal duties, and this will cost the organization something in the form of overtime pay, lost efficiency, lost opportunities, or greater chance of serious error. Although difficult to calculate, these costs can be much greater than the more obvious acquisition costs listed earlier.

The calculation of operating costs should include the following:

• *Day-to-day operating costs.* These include the maintenance contract (or maintenance costs), electrical costs, machine operator salaries, paper costs, floppy disk costs, and space and facility rental costs.

• *System support costs.* Change is characteristic of most computer systems. New reports and new capabilities are always needed, unforeseen errors and breakdowns occur, requirements change. The cost of retaining the services of someone who understands the system (hardware and software) and is capable of handling changes and crises can often be significant, but it is absolutely necessary to the organization.

The out-of-pocket acquisition costs of hardware and software often prove to be a relatively minor proportion of the total cost of a computer system. Sometimes a system more expensive to install initially will be less expensive and more dependable to operate later on. Thus, concentration on the most easily calculated costs— hardware and software acquisition costs—can result in a poor decision. You should also keep in mind that the main purpose of a computer system is not to save you money or allow you to eliminate employees but rather to provide increased amounts of useful information, thus resulting in better administrative decisions, or to increase the productivity of present employees. These elements are hard to quantify, making a purely objective decision about computer systems almost impossible. In the end the selection process must be based on a good deal of blind faith.

References. Fortunately, others have struggled with the selection problem, and guides and references are available for many phases of the selection and design of computer systems. The bibliography for this chapter has been organized under headings related to different aspects of the process. I have tried to list books directed at reasonably well-informed managers rather than more generalized computer books that attempt to overcome supposed distaste for computers by adopting a "cute," humorous, or excessively colloquial tone. Some of our references contain brief guides to the selection process that are part of a more general discussion of computers.

Summary

Implementing computerization in any form, including those related to budgeting and financial reporting, calls on all the managerial skill of the CE director. Computerization is organizational change at its most profound, and it usually calls into examination not only the operating procedures of an organization but also its institutional policies, its structure, and the people within it. Computer decisions can place the organization at considerable risk and therefore weigh heavily on CE management.

Under these circumstances, an understanding of basic facts about computers and systems design is essential. A broad understanding of the organization and its people is also needed— the kind of understanding that no outside computer expert can gain within the scope of the usual systems design process. CE management should know enough to guide the systems design process firmly through all its steps and should provide the resources, both time and money, to give the process a good chance of success. Although many CE budgeting and financial control systems can be implemented relatively inexpensively today on microcomputers with packaged software, the implications of the computerization of even a small part of an organization are never clear. It can open a Pandora's box of expectations that are impossible to fulfill without a major computer system. CE management needs to be aware of this in order to avoid complications. With computers, as with so much else, success is attributed broadly throughout the organization, while failure is always the fault of management.

Bibliography

Systems Design

Alter, S. L. "How Effective Managers Use Information." *Harvard Business Review*, Nov.–Dec. 1976, pp. 97–104.

Arte, S. *Data Base: Structured Techniques for Design, Performance, and Management.* New York: Wiley, 1980.

Davis, W. S. *Systems Analysis and Design, a Structured Approach.* Reading, Mass.: Addison-Wesley, 1983.

FitzGerald, J., FitzGerald, A. F., and Stallings, W. D., Jr. *Fundamentals of System Analysis.* (2nd ed.) New York: Wiley, 1981.

Gane, C., and Sarson, T. *Structured Systems Analysis: Tools and Techniques.* Englewood Cliffs, N. J.: Prentice-Hall, 1979.

Kroenke, D. M. *Business Computer Systems.* (2nd ed.) Santa Cruz, Calif.: Mitchell, 1984.

Martin, J. *Principles of Data Base Management.* Englewood Cliffs, N.J.: Prentice-Hall, 1976.

Martin, J. *Computer Data Base Organization.* (2nd ed.) Englewood Cliffs, N.J.: Prentice-Hall, 1977.

Martin, J. *Strategic Data-Planning Methodologies.* Englewood Cliffs, N.J.: Prentice-Hall, 1982.

Martin, J. *Managing the Data Base Environment.* Englewood Cliffs, N.J.: Prentice-Hall, 1983.

Martin, J. *An Information System Manifesto.* Englewood Cliffs, N.J.: Prentice-Hall, 1984.

Senn, J. A. *Analysis and Design of Information Systems.* New York: McGraw-Hill, 1984.

The Selection Process

Bear, J. *Computer Wimp.* Berkeley: Ten Speed Press, 1982.

Canning, R. G., and Leeper, N. C. *So You Are Thinking About a Small Business Computer.* (1982–1983 ed.) Englewood Cliffs, N.J.: Prentice-Hall, 1982.

Donohue, B. C. *How to Buy an Office Computer or Word Processor.* Englewood Cliffs, N.J.: Prentice-Hall, 1983.

Frankenhuis, J. P. "How to Get a Good Mini." *Harvard Business Review,* May–June 1982.

Gagliardi, G. *How to Make Your Small Computer Pay Off.* Belmont, Calif.: Wadsworth, 1983.

Glossbrenner, A. *How to Buy Software.* New York: St. Martin's, 1984.

Haueisen, W. D., and Camp, J. L. *Business Systems for Microcomputers.* Englewood Cliffs, N.J.: Prentice-Hall, 1982.

Isshiki, K. R. *Small Business Computers: A Guide to Evaluation and Selection.* Englewood Cliffs, N.J.: Prentice-Hall, 1982.

Kelly, F., and Poggi, P. *Strategy of Computer Selection: A Step-by-Step Approach.* Reston, Va.: Reston, 1984.

Kenny, D. P. *Personal Computers in Business.* New York: AMACOM, 1985.

Press, L. *The IBM PC and Its Applications.* New York: Wiley, 1984.

Rinder, R. M. *A Practical Guide to Small Computers for Business and Professional Use.* New York: Monarch, 1983.

Werner, D. M., and Warrner, T. W. *Micros, Minis, and Mainframes: Computing Options for the Business Manager.* Radnor, Pa.: Chilton, 1984.

Spreadsheets

Cohen, N., and Graff, L. *Financial Analysis with Lotus 1-2-3.* Bowie, Md.: Brady Communications, 1984.

Miller, H. "Introduction to Spreadsheets." *PC World,* Aug. 1984, pp. 67–75.

Williams, A. *What If? A User's Guide to Spreadsheets on the IBM PC.* New York: Wiley, 1984.

Williams, A. *Lotus 1-2-3 from A to Z.* New York: Wiley, 1985.

General

Frank, W. L. "The Evolution of Microcomputer Software." *Computerworld,* Apr. 26, 1982, p. 41.

Gibson, C. F., and Nolan, R. L. "Managing the Four Stages of EDP Growth." *Harvard Business Review,* Jan.–Feb., 1974, pp. 78–88.

Lechner, H. D. *The Computer Chronicles.* Belmont, Calif.: Wadsworth, 1984.

Martin, J. *Design of Man-Computer Dialogues.* Englewood Cliffs, N.J.: Prentice-Hall, 1973.

Glossary

Absorption costing. See full costing.

Accrual accounting. An accounting method requiring that costs be associated or matched with the income that the incurring of those costs helped to produce and that both be reported in the same accounting period. Often contrasted with cash accounting, which see.

Alternative level budgeting. A budgeting practice that requires budgets to be prepared according to universal assumptions, for several levels of activity, or for certain increases above or decreases below the "base" or the previous budget.

Analysis of variance. A form of budget analysis designed to determine the underlying causes of variances of actual results from figures predicted by the budget.

Applications data base. A data base developed with a particular application in mind. Contrasted with subject data base, which see.

413

Autocratic organizations. Organizations led in a manner that discourages the exercise of initiative by those not in the top leadership.

Available for overhead. Income minus direct expenses; that is, the amount left after all direct expenses have been covered. Also known as margin, surplus, or profit.

Backup. A copy of a computer program or data file made for safekeeping in case the original is lost or damaged.

Balance sheet. A financial statement that lists the assets, liabilities, and ownership or fund balances of an accounting entity.

Balance sheet budgets. Budgets that project and control the values of assets, liabilities, and capital accounts or fund balances of organizations. Not frequently encountered in continuing education.

Base. Funding for the normal and continuing activity of an organization or program. Such funding can usually be considered secure from one budget period to the next. Sometimes base is contrasted with incremental budgeting, which see. See also zero-based budgeting.

Batch mode. Accumulating data in advance and processing them into or within a computer as a group.

BEP. Break-even point. See break-even analysis.

Break-even analysis. The determination of the level of activity (volume of sales) at which total income will equal total expense. This level is called the break-even point (BEP).

Budget object. That which is being budgeted. In this book, the budget object is usually the course (Part One) or the CE organization or a segment of that organization (Parts Two and Three).

Capital budgeting. The process of selecting and planning for the financing of the acquisition of capital items.

Capital item. An asset or a proposed expenditure for something that will be of value to an organization for a period longer than one year.

Carrying cost. The cost of maintaining and servicing an inventory.

Cash accounting. A method of accounting for operations that focuses on the effect of the transactions on the cash balance. Contrasted with accrual accounting, which see.

Cash budgeting. The process of forecasting or planning the flow of cash into and out of an organization. Sometimes contrasted with accrual accounting, which see.

Centralized organizations. Organizations in which most important operating decisions are made by the highest management level. In the CE context, "centralized" means that the jurisdiction and control over continuing education is concentrated in a single operating entity or organizational segment. Contrasted with decentralized organizations, which see.

Coded label. A label, used in a data base or the like, that uses a code (letters or numbers in combination) to indicate elements of a category. Contrast with virtual label.

Collegial organizations. Organizations in which management decisions are arrived at through a process of discussion, participation, and negotiation involving a broad spectrum of the membership of the organization, including members of several levels of managerial hierarchy. Also called participative organizations.

Commitment. A planned and definite outlay of funds that will occur before the end of the budget period. Unlike an encumbrance (which see), it is not legally binding.

Common fixed indirect costs. Fixed indirect costs that cannot be identified with the incremental volume brought by any one responsibility center. Also called "ready-to-serve" costs. Contrasted with separable fixed indirect costs, which see.

Consumer surplus. The positive difference between what a consumer is willing to pay for a good or service and the actual price of the good or service.

Continuous budgets. Budgets prepared continuously throughout the year, say, every month, rather than only once. Usually this means that each month a new budget for the twelfth month is prepared and all other monthly budgets are updated. Also called rolling budgets.

Contribution margin. The amount over direct, variable cost produced by one additional unit sale—in continuing education, usually one enrollment.

Control structure. The sum of the methods by which management exercises control of the behavior of the members of an organization.

Controls. Checks built into a computer system designed to catch errors, protect data, control access to data, and prevent loss of data.

Conversion ratio. The ratio of the number of people who buy a good or service (in continuing education, the number of people who enroll in a course or program) to the number of people who express interest in it.

Cosponsorship. A situation in which more than one organization is involved in presenting a course of instruction, so that costs, income, and responsibilities must be divided.

Cost-benefit analysis. An analysis designed to compare the resources given up through a course of action with the benefits received from that course of action.

Cost center. A responsibility center (which see) in which the manager is assigned responsibility for controlling costs but not for generating income.

Cost mix. The mixture within one cost object of different categories of costs, such as fixed and variable, direct and indirect, or sunk and unsunk.

Cost object. That for which an organization wishes to accumulate costs. In this book, the cost object is usually either the course (Part One) or the CE organization (Part Two).

Cost of goods sold. The amount of value, at cost, that an organization gives up in a sale, usually involving inventory.

Cost of programmer time. The total resources of the organization that must be given up to secure the services of a programmer. See also value of programmer time.

Cost per unit. See unit cost.

Cost pool. See indirect cost pools.

Cost workup method. A method of determining the price of a good or service by first determining the total cost of it and then basing the price on the cost.

Critical path method. A method for organizing the course-planning process whereby each element of the development of the course is plotted on a chart and its cause-and-effect relationship to each other element is shown.

Data base. A large collection of organized data accessible for use in more than one application.

Data base management system. A software system facilitating the creation, maintenance, and use of a data base.

Decentralized organizations. Organizations in which operating decisions are made by relatively low levels of management and responsibility is broadly delegated. In the continuing education context, "decentralized" means that continuing education is offered separately by a number of segments of the parent organization.

Decision/process model. A conceptual framework for analyzing the potential financial return of a course throughout its development and implementation; defined in detail in this book.

Depreciation. The amount of the cost of a capital item that is charged to the operating costs of a particular period, or the process by which the purchase price of an item whose useful life will extend over several operation periods is allocated to those periods.

Direct costs. Costs that can be directly and easily associated with (attributed to) a particular cost object.

Director. In this book, the person who is responsible for administering all or part of an organization that presents continuing education courses, regardless of actual title (dean, chair, chancellor, or whatever).

Discretionary funds. Funds remaining in the budget that are uncommitted and therefore may be expended at the discretion of management.

Distorted behavior. Behavior that runs counter to the overall welfare and objectives of the organization; may be caused by poor management or poor design of the budgetary and financial control system.

Downside risk. The risk of loss that would arise from the complete failure of a project or course.

Economic order quantity (EOQ). The amount of inventory that should be ordered to minimize carrying and ordering costs.

Elasticity of demand. The effect of price on the number or amount of the sales of a good or service (such as enrollments in a course). When a decrease or increase in the price of a good or service markedly affects sales, demand is said to be elastic; when changes in the price have little or no effect on the number of sales, demand is said to be inelastic.

Encumbrance. A legally executed, fully completed transaction requiring the future outlay of funds. Compare expenditure and commitment.

EOQ. See economic order quantity.

Expenditure. In accounting, a fully completed actual outlay of funds. Compare encumbrance and commitment.

Expenditure budgets. Budgets that concentrate on where and how resources will be spent, ignoring where the funds came from and not explicitly calculating the effect on cash balances. Contrasted with financial budgets, which see.

Field. A specified area in a data base record used for a particular category of data.

File. A collection of related data records treated as a unit; may be part of a data base or may exist separately.

Financial budgets. Budgets concerned with the financing of activities or with the disposition of and investment return on financial assets. Contrasted with expenditure budgets, which see.

Fixed costs. Costs that do not vary with the level or volume of activity. Contrasted with variable costs, which see.

Fixed resource organization. An organization for which the amount of resources available in any period is fixed and known at the beginning of the period. Most subsidized CE organizations are fixed resource organizations. Contrasted with variable resource organization, which see.

Flexible budget. Same as variable budget, which see.

Floppy disk. A flexible, flat, circular plate with a magnetic coating that can store computer programs or data.

FTE. See full-time equivalent.

Full costing. The practice by which the "full cost"—that is, both direct and indirect costs—is assigned to cost objects.

Full-time equivalent (FTE). A measure of full-time work load against which work loads of part-time employees or students can be compared.

Fund accounting. A set of accounting rules and practices, followed by most nonprofit organizations, that segregates and accounts for expenditures according to the source of the funding of those expenditures.

Fund budgeting. Budgeting used in fund accounting to assure that funds or groups of resources are used for the purpose for which the funds were established and that the funding limits are not exceeded.

Future value. The value of the receipt of cash in the future as opposed to the present at a specified rate of interest.

Gantt chart. A chart that shows the timing of activities and expenditures involved in a project, such as the planning of a course.

Go, no-go decision. The crucial decision about whether to go or not go ahead with the presentation of a course.

Hard money. A funding source that is relatively stable and can therefore be depended upon to fund line items, including salaries, from one budget period to the next. Contrasted with soft money, which see.

Hidden subsidies. Sources of funding for an activity that are not budgeted or disclosed in financial reports. In this book, hidden subsidies are resources (clerical time, office supplies, and so on) devoted to continuing education but paid from sources not formally associated with continuing education activity.

Incremental budgeting or funding. Budgeting or funding that concentrates on new activities as opposed to "base" activities or that deals primarily with increases or decreases in funding from one budget period to the next. See also base; zero-based budgeting.

Incremental cash flow. The difference between cash inflow and outflow related to a capital expenditure.

Incremental costing. A cost accounting method under which only the additional or incremental costs, rather than the full costs, associated with a cost object are attributed to it. See also full costing.

Indirect cost pools. Groupings of individual elements of indirect costs that are allocated by the same basis or method.

Indirect costs. Costs that cannot be directly or conveniently associated with (attributed to) any particular cost object. Often called overhead. Contrasted with direct costs, which see.

Inelastic demand. See elasticity of demand.

Information center. Provides a number of users with the information they need to make decisions. Similar to data base. Contrasted with operations system, which see.

Information overload. A situation in which the quantity of available information is so large that it clouds rather than clarifies issues about which decisions must be made.

Inputs. Data to be put into a computer.

Interface. The connection or linkage between two systems.

Internal rate of return. The rate of return on an investment, expressed as an annual percentage, that an organization sets as a standard against which to judge potential investment opportunities. Sometimes same as target rate of return, which see.

Inventory. Usually the quantity of goods on hand to be sold, such as textbooks and course materials; but courses themselves may also be regarded as a kind of inventory.

Investment center. An organizational responsibility center whose object is to measure and, presumably, maximize the return on investment of a defined group of assets.

K. Abbreviation for kilobyte, a unit of computer memory.

Lapsing funds. Funds that, if not spent, lapse or are returned to the funding source at the end of the budget period.

Lead time. The period of time between placing an order for a good or service and the time of its delivery.

Levels of financial success. Course financial break-even points, computed by calculating course costs at several levels.

Line item budget. A budget concerned mainly with the projection and control of "line items" or "natural classifications" of expense, without regard to the underlying purposes or objectives of the expenses. Often contrasted with a program budget, which see. Examples of line items are instructional compensation, room rent, office supplies, and promotion expense. Line item budgets are used in traditional budgeting.

Mainframe. A large computer, usually requiring large-scale system development and able to handle large volumes of activity.

Management by exception. A practice whereby management of an organization concentrates its time, effort, and attention on exceptional (usually problem) situations, segments, or processes.

Management by objectives (MBO). A strategy in which management clearly describes its objectives and assigns responsibility for meeting those objectives, then evaluates performance in terms of achievement of the objectives.

Management information system (MIS). The process and/or system by which information is provided to management for the purpose of making decisions.

Margin. The positive difference between the income and expense of an activity where the level of expense is carefully defined; used in this book instead of "profit." Also called available for overhead, which see.

Marginal cost. The cost of producing one more item or, in our case, enrolling one more student.

Margin of safety. The "cushion" or contingency between projected revenues and projected expenditures.

Master budget. The largest, most inclusive budget in an organization.

MBO. See management by objectives.

Microcomputer. The smallest and least expensive of the three main sizes of computers. May not be large enough for operations systems of large CE organizations but is usually well suited to the needs of budgeting and financial control. Compare mainframe, minicomputer.

Minicomputer. A computer intermediate in size and price between a mainframe and a microcomputer (which see). Minis are able to handle most of the data processing needs of even the largest CE organization.

MIS. See management information system.

Montage funding. Funding of a particular project, organization, or entity from more than one source.

Multiple-source funding. See montage funding.

Natural classification. Classifying or naming expenses according to the general reason for the expenditure, such as rent, instructor compensation, utilities, promotion, and so on. See also line item budget. Often contrasted with expense classification schemes used in program budgets, which see.

Net present value. The difference between present and future cash inflows and outflows, expressed as a present value at a specified annual interest rate.

Open-ended budgeting. A budget preparation policy that places no restrictions on the amount of money that can be requested for the next budget period.

Operating budget. The budget that projects and controls the day-to-day operations of an organization.

Operations system. A computerized system that serves the day-to-day processing needs of an organization, such as enrollment processing, cashiering, and mailing list maintenance. Contrasted with information center, which see.

Opportunity cost. The benefit foregone when one alternative is chosen over another.

Order cost. The cost of placing an order for more inventory, receiving and inspecting the goods, placing them in stock, and processing and paying the invoice.

Organization segmentation. The process by which a large organization is divided into smaller, more manageable parts, for purposes of financial control (including budgeting) and assignment of managerial responsibility. These parts are sometimes known as cost centers or responsibility centers, which see.

Outputs. Reports or other products generated by computers.

Overhead. See indirect costs.

Parent. The larger institution of which a CE organization is a part.

Partial services. Services, such as registration or logistical services, that CE organizations may be called upon to provide for conferences sponsored by others.

Participative organizations. See collegial organizations.

Partly variable costs. See semivariable costs.

Pass-through costs. Amounts included in the fee for a course that are for cost items unrelated to instruction. They may be said to "pass through" the organization to vendors and thus cannot logically be included in income for the course. Student travel and accommodations in travel programs are examples.

Payback method. A method of capital budgeting that determines how quickly an organization will recover its investment in a capital item.

Pools, indirect cost. See indirect cost pools.

PPBS. See program planning and budgeting system.

Present value. The value of having cash now as opposed to later, given a specified interest rate.

Present value index. An index used to determine the relative profitability of alternative investments, obtained by dividing the present value of cash inflows by the acquisition cost.

Present value of an annuity. The present value of the right to receive a specified future pattern of cash inflows, given a rate of interest.

Print buffer. Temporary storage for data being passed from a computer to a printer. A buffer may be needed where the computer and the printer operate at different speeds or times.

Profit center. A responsibility center (which see) in which the manager is concerned with generating income as well as controlling costs. Compare cost center, investment center.

Program budget. A budget that summarizes income and expense associated with a particular endeavor or responsibility center. Usually contrasted with line item budget, which see.

Programmer. In continuing education, an employee responsible for planning or programming CE courses.

Programming department. A CE organization segment dedicated primarily to programming. Contrasted with service department, which see.

Program Planning and Budgeting System (PPBS). A budgeting system in which each budget submission requires justification of each "program" for which it seeks funding.

Project budget. A program budget covering the carrying out of a defined task. Usually project budgets span one or more operating cycles of the organization.

Promotion. The specific steps taken to get people to buy a good or service—in continuing education, usually a course of study.

Quota budget methods. Budget preparation practices that establish limits on the amount of money that can be requested in the next budget period beyond the "base" (which see).

RAM. See random access memory.

Random access memory (RAM). The part of a computer's memory used as temporary storage for programs and data. Some programs require large amounts of RAM in order to run effectively.

Ready-to-serve costs. See common indirect fixed costs.

Relative contribution. The contribution toward the success of a project (say, the presentation of a course) as compared with the contributions of other elements.

Relevant range. The range of activity over which fixed costs remain fixed.

Reorder point. The level of inventory at which more inventory should be ordered.

Repeater rate. The rate at which new enrollees enroll in subsequent courses given by the same CE organization.

Residual value. The estimated value of a capital item at the end of its use or at its expected disposition.

Response ratio. The number of responses (inquiries or enrollments) produced by a promotion campaign, divided by the number of people (or households) estimated to have been reached by the campaign. The resulting percentage is a measure of promotion effectiveness.

Response time. The time it takes for a computer to respond to a command.

Responsibility center. A segment of an organization that is assigned responsibility for carrying out a particular task and for which an individual is assigned managerial responsibility.

Responsibility structure. The formal system of assigning and monitoring responsibility in an organization.

Retention rate. The number of students completing a course of study divided by the total number of students who initially enroll.

Return on investment (ROI). The amount gained from an investment; technically, the percent of an investment returned per year.

Reward/risk ratio. The potential reward of a project divided by the potential risk (of loss) of the project. In this book, a common reward/risk ratio is the potential available for overhead divided by the sunk costs.

ROI. See return on investment.

Rolling budgets. See continuous budgets.

Safety stock. The amount of inventory that an organization keeps on hand in order to serve customers in the event that an order to replenish the inventory is delayed; an emergency supply.

Segmentation. See organization segmentation.

Semivariable costs. Costs that contain both fixed and variable elements. Sometimes called semifixed costs.

Separable fixed indirect costs. Fixed indirect costs that can be assigned to a particular responsibility center. Contrasted with common fixed indirect costs, which see.

Service department. A CE organization segment dedicated primarily to serving the programming departments (which see). The registration office, director's office, and cashier's office are examples.

Soft money. A funding source available only for a stated period of time or one that is uncertain from one period to the next. Often arises from contracts and grants.

Software. Computer programs. Often sold in "prepackaged" forms designed to do specific kinds of tasks.

Spillover effect. The effect by which a promotion campaign causes customers to buy a good or service (produced by the same organization) other than the one at which the campaign was aimed. Institutional advertising, for example, is not designed to cause students to enroll in a particular course but, by making students aware of the CE organization's name, may prompt a later enrollment.

Spreadsheet. A way of arraying data in columns and rows. One of the main kinds of packaged software available for microcomputers that is useful in budgeting.

Step function. The behavior of fixed costs that respond to large increases in volume or activity by moving upward in sharply defined "steps" rather than in smooth, continuous curves.

Stockout condition. A condition in which an organization cannot serve a customer because it does not have enough inventory on hand.

Subject data base. A data base that focuses on one subject and incorporates as many attributes as are likely ever to be used in reports. Contrasted with applications data base, which see.

Sunk costs. Past or previously incurred costs, especially direct course costs that must be expended before the decision about whether to actually present the course is made. Sometimes called up-front costs.

Surplus. See available for overhead.

Systems analysis. The process of analyzing or designing a system with the goal of arriving at the most efficient operation.

Target rate of return. The rate of return on capital investments that the organization sets as a standard against which to judge investment alternatives.

Time-adjusted rate of return. A capital budgeting technique that determines the true rate of return on a proposed capital investment, considering the time value of money.

Time value of money. The idea that the value of a cash flow depends upon when it is received; the opportunity cost of not investing cash.

Top-down analysis. A way of approaching the design of a system that starts with the broadest objectives and proceeds "downward" through successive levels of greater detail.

Tracking system. A system for discovering the promotion campaign that produced each enrollment; used to determine the effectiveness of promotion.

Traditional budgeting. See line item budget.

Transfer pricing. A method of assigning costs within an organization in which one segment of the organization charges other segments for goods or services according to preset, often published, prices.

Unadjusted rate of return. A capital budgeting method used to estimate the return on a capital project without considering the time value of money.

Unit cost. The cost of producing one "unit." In this book, the unit cost is usually the cost per enrollment, which is derived by dividing a particular element of cost by the number of enrollments associated with it.

Up-front costs. See sunk costs.

Upside potential. The potential gain from a project if it is successful.

Value of programmer time. The net amount of resources that a programmer can generate for an organization within a specified period; often seen as an opportunity cost. See also cost of programmer time.

Variable budget. A budget or series of budgets prepared for different levels of activity. Also called flexible budget.

Variable costs. Costs that vary with the level of activity. Often contrasted with fixed costs, which see.

Variable resource organization. An organization in which the amount of resources available in any period is, at least to some extent, unknown at the beginning of the period and is usually dependent on the performance of the organization. Most self-supporting CE organizations are variable resource organizations. Contrasted with fixed resource organization, which see.

Variance. Positive or negative difference between figures projected in a budget and actual performance. See also analysis of variance.

Virtual label. A label, used in a data base or the like, that consists of letters or numbers that can be easily understood. Contrasted to coded label.

Volume variance. That part of the difference between budget and actual results caused by a difference between the budgeted volume of activity (for example, number of enrollments) and the actual volume of activity.

Walk-away position. The limit beyond which one will not go in a negotiation. Programmers should calculate a walk-away position before discussing compensation with instructors, for example.

Zero-based budgeting (ZBB). A budget method in which there is no "base"; every expenditure in the budget submission must be fully justified regardless of past practice or activity. See also base; incremental budgeting.

Index

433